Concise Information and Communication Technologies (ICT) Fundamentals Volume II

Volume 2: First Edition

Bright Siaw Afriyie

This Book is recommended by Ghana Education Service

Author's Contact Information:

Bright Siaw Afriyie
1129 Beechwood Lane,
Cedar Hill, Texas 75104
U.S.A.

bsiawa@aol.com,

Nana Taaka II
P.O. Box 1
Adanse-Atobise,
Ghana

bsiawa@atobiase.org

Concise Information and Communication Technologies (ICT) Fundamentals – Volume Two

By Bright Siaw Afriyie
(Nana Taaka II, Adanse-Atobiase Chief)

Editor: Bright Siaw Afriyie, Sr. Information Technology Analyst
City of Dallas, Texas, USA.

Order this book online at www.trafford.com
or email orders@trafford.com

Most Trafford titles are also available at major online book retailers.

Printed in the United States of America.

ISBN: 978-1-4669-6785-4 (sc)
ISBN: 978-1-4669-6784-7 (e)

Trafford rev. 11/20/2012

 www.trafford.com

North America & International
toll-free: 1 888 232 4444 (USA & Canada)
phone: 250 383 6864 ♦ fax: 812 355 4082

Preface

As the title suggests, this book is intended for students who want to learn about computers. It's a useful tool for both continuation of volume one of Concise ICT Fundamentals and students in introductory class of computer technology in colleges and universities.

The main reason behind the publishing of this book is to offer a little contribution to a concise learning material to boost computer literacy among the mass population that have some difficulties in coping up with the fast pace of the endless computer evolution. To some, it may sound weird, but the undeniable fact is that even if you're an expert in the field you would still have to be on your toes to be able to catch up with the fast growing pace of today's computer technologies. It will therefore make sense to gain a prior exposure to some of the vital fundamental concepts covered in this book. The reader may occasionally make references to both my first and second books entitled "Introduction to Computer Fundamentals, second edition" and Concise ICT Fundamentals volume one for further studies.

An unavoidable question is, "Why would anyone want to use a computer". The answer is simple: to enhance any business activity. The world is now believed to be in information technology era. Almost no efficient work could be done without the computer power. There is a greater need for any user, being an individual or a business, to know which computers to use for a particular job, which software, what are the specifications for internet, which implies that appropriate specifications must be considered before even deciding to purchase.

This book contains useful information that readers need to know to lay a solid foundation in computing - embracing Spreadsheet (Microsoft. Excel), PowerPoint presentation, Data processing (Ms. Access), and Object-Oriented Programming (OOP) using Visual Basic.Net. This book provides a concise learning material for ICT with the objective of guiding readers to understand the full concepts of the software mentioned above. The main goal here is to acquaint the reader with the main professional software components, and the fundamental concepts of modern ICT programming methodology – enough so you would be able to continue your passion in computer education on your own.

This book is straightforward and concise to the subject matter. From chapter one of basic concepts of Excel Spreadsheet through chapter ten of Visual basic .Net object oriented programming language, the reader would have a lot to discover from the 418 pages in the present edition. The book contains four sections which are sub-divided into ten chapters, 165 assignments and 129 multiple choice questions, 293 illustrations and a glossary at the end.

The Book's Audience

As an introduction to Information and Communication Technologies this book is primarily addressed to two groups of readers:

- Beginners in general computer technology and,
- First year college students and Second and Upper years Senior High School Students

Beginners group: The beginners group includes first time computer users, students reading computer science and information technology, computer sales representatives and new marketing agents. It's also useful for anyone who wants to know more about the in-and-outs of computing. Though, no previous experience is required to use this book, however it will make more sense to readers who have read or have had prior knowledge of the volume one of these series.

First year college users and Second and Upper years Senior High School Students: The first year college users and second and upper year senior high school student users include general computer users, computer technicians, students reading computer science and engineering. System engineers, developers and computer professionals may also find this book very interesting for the full blown concepts in Spreadsheet, PowerPoint presentation, Data processing, and Object-Oriented Programming (OOP) and general computing concepts they may have long forgotten. New programmers may also fall into this category of this book audience. Computer experts can also take full advantage of this book by using it as a reference manual and a companion handbook.

Organization of this Book

Concise ICT Fundamentals Volume 2 covers the second and third years Senior High School ICT curriculum and beyond, with extra details that will certainly prepare students for their final exams. The organization of this book follows the principles of modern designing methodology commencing with simple abstraction, and gradually walking readers through more advanced stuffs without feeling the pinch.

Each chapter ends with two sets of questions, project assignments and multiple choice questions. The questions begin with student 165 assignments which are followed by 129 multiple-choice exercises spread across the chapters.

The book has four sections and ten chapters. The chapters are numbered from one to ten and each subdivided under various topics. For instance 1.3.5 means: Chapter 1, Topic 3, and Sub-Topic 5. The tables and diagrams are also labeled in similar fashion. For example Table 1-5 means the fifth table of chapter 1. Similarly, Figure 1-5 means the fifth diagram of chapter 1.

The symbols commonly used in the book include < >,+, >>, >. For example **<Ctrl>+<O>** means press on the **control key** and the letter "**O**" simultaneously. Also **File >> Open** or **File > Open** means Click on File and then Click Open.

SECTION I: (From Chapter 1 to 7)
1. Introduction to Spreadsheet Applications
2. Editing Spreadsheet Applications
3. Formatting Worksheets in Excel Spreadsheet
4. More Functions, Formulas and Macros
5. Managing Worksheets
6. Conditional Formatting and Data Analysis
7. Working with Excel Tables, Charts, Page Layout and Printing

Chapter 1. Introduction to Spreadsheet Applications

This chapter begins with the basic concepts and introduction to spreadsheet applications and their Importance. Students will learn about the general concepts of spreadsheet and the meaning of spreadsheet terminologies. The reader will be introduced to the overview of Microsoft Excel Spreadsheets and learn the basics. In this chapter we discuss the workbook features of Microsoft Excel and the basic facts about Microsoft Excel Spreadsheet application.

The student will be able to identify spreadsheet packages and their uses, explain the importance of Spreadsheet application in data management in Spreadsheet. The reader will finally be introduced to formulas, functions, cells, ranges, etc.
The spreadsheet basics discussed in this chapter will comprise creating a new workbook, opening a workbook, navigating a worksheet, entering labels, and values. Students will be able to create and save Workbook. This chapter will explain the application of selected formulas and functions by constructing and inserting simple formulas and functions; selecting a cell range, overview of Formulas and using AutoSum. The chapter will teach students how to enter formulas, and use AutoFill and understanding Absolute and Relative cell references, using Undo and Redo commands. For the purpose self-evaluation we have provided the project assignments and multiple choice questions in the end of this chapter.

Chapter 2. Editing Spreadsheet Applications

Chapter 2 covers the editing of an Excel Worksheet using editing tools, moving, copy/cut and paste facilities, etc. The student will learn how to modify data in excel spreadsheets. In this chapter we will discuss inserting cells, rows, and columns. We will fully discuss the methods of deleting cells, rows, and columns. We also discuss how to use the search tool in Excel such as Find and Replace. The spell check functions are also discussed with illustrated examples. Students will learn how to insert and modify cell comments, and also students will learn about tracking changes in excel spreadsheet. For the purpose self-evaluation we have provided the project assignments and multiple choice questions in the end of this chapter.

Chapter 3. Formatting Worksheets in Excel Spreadsheet

As the continuation of the previous chapter we now lay emphasis on formatting labels and values. The process of adjusting row height and column width will be discussed in this chapter. The readers will learn how to perform cell alignments; and we will also expand their formatting knowledge in adding cell borders, background colors and patterns in excel spreadsheet. Students will acquire hands-on experience in using format painter, cell styles, and document themes. We will also lay emphasis on the methods involved in applying conditional formatting in excel spreadsheet. The student will learn how to define data ranges on a spreadsheet. The chapter ends with project assignments and multiple choice questions for the purpose self-evaluation.

Chapter 4. More Functions, Formulas and Macros

Chapter four generally deals with functions, formulas and macros. It begins by discussing the definitions of formulas, functions and cell ranges. The chapter explores the concept of defining relative and absolute cell addresses and explains their importance. Formulas using multiple operators are thoroughly discussed along with emphasis on inserting and editing formulas and functions. The students will learn about auto-calculate and manual calculation in excel spreadsheet. We will also discuss defining names, using and managing defined names. In this chapter the reader will plunge into a little advanced stuff like creating macros in excel.

Chapter 5. Managing Worksheets

This chapter covers managing worksheets. The chapter further discusses how to modify the width and height of columns, and how to insert row or column. It also further explores the inserts or deletes of cells in worksheet or moving data in worksheet or workbook and organizing worksheets in a workbook. The chapter will walk readers through how to change the color of gridlines, default fonts and themes in a worksheet. It covers freeze or lock rows and columns; Hide or show worksheets or workbooks.

Chapter 6. Conditional Formatting and Data Analysis

This chapter begins with the introduction to Conditional Formatting and Data Analysis. It covers conditional formatting using the range of values and also explores the application of CountIF and SUMIF functions in Microsoft Excel 2007 to 2010. The chapter discusses Data Tables, Scenarios and Goal Seek in Microsoft Excel spreadsheet application.

Chapter 7. Working with Excel Tables, Charts, Page Layout and Printing

In chapter seven we introduce the reader to Tables in Excel Spreadsheet. We cover the whole concept of creating a Table, and working with Table size, Total Row, and Table Data. The reader will learn about the process of summarizing a Table into creating a PivotTable. The chapter covers the concept of Inserting Slicer In Pivot Tables, and Creating Charts. Readers will be able to identify the types of charts in Excel spreadsheet.

SECTION II
Chapter 8. PowerPoint Presentation Application

This is a one-chapter section that covers several sub-chapters describing the use of Microsoft PowerPoint Application. The student will learn the fundamental concepts of PowerPoint presentation. The student will be able to identify what is a good PowerPoint presentation and learn how to create a presentation from the scratch or from a template. This section discusses the inserting of slide master, normal slides, and how to navigate from a slide to another. To customize slides, student will learn how to change slide background, themes, colors, fonts and theme effects. Students will be able to edit and save a presentation. This chapter will explain how to produce PowerPoint handouts, insert hyperlink, tables and images. To crown it all, the section teaches final embellishment of a presentation that includes adding sound and animations to PowerPoint presentation.

SECTION III
Chapter 9. Data Processing

In this lesson, we will discuss how raw data is converted into useful information. We will explain the importance of computers in carrying out the various data processing activities. Discussion about hierarchy of data is also included in this lesson. The reader will be able to identify the data, datum, and information. Student will learn about Data processing, facts and figures. Students will be able to differentiate between Data and Information. Thorough discussion of the Concept of Data Processing is covered in this chapter. The chapter will cover a series of actions or operations that converts data into useful information. In data processing system, we will discuss the resources that are used to accomplish the processing of data. We will discuss the involvement of the arrangement of data items in a desired sequence.

Students will be able to explain various data processing activities: Sorting, Comparison, Data Processing Life Cycle and Data Organization. This lesson explains data elements, records, files and databases and creation of Tables. We will discuss data entry processes generating Data Entry forms from a defined table. We will discuss Structured Query Language (SQL). This chapter will provide a brief introduction of Microsoft Access which is a relational database management system.

SECTION IV
Chapter 10. Basic Concept of Programming using VB.Net

This is a one-chapter section that covers several sub-chapters teaching the basic concepts of programming. The student will learn the fundamental concepts and the elements of programming. The student will learn basic computer systems analysis leading to creation of computer algorithms, data flow charts for a computer project. The student will be able to create simple programs. This section discusses the fundamental concepts of object oriented programming (oop). Students will be able to identify various types of classes, objects, and methods. The chapter discusses data types, variables, constants, arrays, functions, procedures, and constructors and their applications in loops, and conditional decisions in programs. The student will acquire knowledge on dot net platform particularly in Microsoft Visual Basic dot Net programming environment while working with classes, data and how to store information.

Why I should buy this book?

Knowing that this world is now moving towards a global village – we are in information era where practically nothing can be done without the power of computers in most industries. A solid knowledge about fundamentals of computing has become indispensable in everyday life. This book has been prepared for you to uncover several confusing concepts that pose a big challenge to computer learners and users. I am coming from both educational and professional standpoint to better alienate the hinges that serve as obstacles to high-tech solutions to everyone. It is the togetherness of a great practical experience, educational and teaching skills, technical know-how and continuous customer value-added service research that has always been the source of creation of this book and three other computer science books entitled Concise ICT Fundamentals volume one, Introduction to computer fundamentals and Introduction to object oriented programming using java. The feedbacks so far received from few professors in Information technology in Dallas, Texas area strongly suggests the use of these books as a great fundamental and companion material for computer science students. In Ghana, the Education Service and Curriculum Research and Development Department, CRDD has approved the Concise ICT Fundamentals textbook as the recommended supplementary material for the teaching and learning of ICT in Senior High Schools, Technical Schools, and Colleges of Education and for general usage.

The organization of the core material in this book both provides support training unconditionally to everyone who wants to be computer literate, and also extends its learning curve to high quality ICT systems engineering to individuals or companies already operational in the high-tech industry. This book provides a solid foundation for information technology. This book is essentially prepared for Senior High School and First year college students. You don't want to miss this good news.

About the Author

Bright Siaw Afriyie is a professional Information Technology Analyst. He is also the founder of Sab Softech USA, and in Ghana. Bright Siaw Afriyie, completed High School in Opoku Ware School in Kumasi, had a baccalaureate degree (BSc.) in Computer Science and an advanced degree in Telecommunications in University of Quebec in Canada. Bright also holds an MBA obtained from Graduate School of Management (GSM) at University of Dallas, Texas.

Bright Siaw Afriyie worked as a programmer/statistics for the World Health Organization (WHO) Onchocerciaisis Control Program in West Africa for seven years while stationed in Ouagadougou in Burkina Faso.

Bright still maintaining his great passion for Information Technology, served as Professor Assistant teaching Computer Data Communications in University of Quebec in Montreal for two years. Bright Siaw Afriyie's Information Technology professionalism has extended to the United States where he has been teaching Visual Basic Programming in Brookhaven College and Object Oriented Java programming in Mountain View College. Bright's innovation continues in the United States where he's presently serving as Senior Information Technology professional in the City of Dallas, Texas in designing and maintaining several automated systems for Dallas 9-1-1 emergency dispatch. He has created several cross-platform systems that are currently functional supporting 24/7 emergency operations.

On the other side of the aisle Bright Siaw Afriyie is a traditional ruler having been enthroned as the chief of Adanse-Atobiase in May 5, 2005. His stool name is Nana Taaka II.

DEDICATION

This book is dedicated to:

1. My Son, Samuel Kofi Siaw Afriyie Jr.
2. My Dearest Wife, Lucy Siaw Afriyie for her love and support.
3. My parents: my Mother Nana Adufah, and Late Father, Samuel Kwasi Siaw

GHANA EDUCATION SERVICE

In case of reply the
Number and date of this
Letter should be quoted

Our Ref. No.CRDD/047/SF.2/VOL. XII/165

Republic of Ghana

HEADQUARTERS
Ministry Branch Post Office
P. O. Box M. 45
Accra

14ᵗʰ December, 2010

NANA TAAKA II
P. O. BOX 1
ADANSE- ATOBISE
GHANA

Dear Sir,

BOOK ASSESSMENT
CONCISE ICT FUNDAMENTALS BY BRIGHT SIAW AFRIYIE

The above-named book which was submitted to the Textbook and Educational Equipment Committee (TEEC) through the Curriculum Research and Development Division (CRDD) of the Ghana Education Service (GES) has been assessed.

Decision: The book is recommended as a supplementary material for the teaching and learning of ICT in Senior High Schools, Technical Schools, Colleges of Education and for general usage.

Thank you.

Yours faithfully

SARAH AGYEMAN-DUAH (MRS)
DIRECTOR, CRDD
for: TEXTBOOKS AND EDUCATIONAL
EQUIPMENT COMMITTEE

ACKNOWLEDGEMENT

I am most thankful to My Heavenly Father for His amazing grace and guidance in designing, teaching and research work. I thank my family for their unchanging support for consistent long hours of research work and editing. A special thanks to my dear wife for her enduring support, and even sitting by me in late night long hours of each day that passed.

My sincere thanks go to the editor Lauren Hunt Wilson of University of Dallas for her constant collaborations and her special commitment for fast-track editing.

I wish to use this occasion to express my great appreciation to my own younger brother Eric Owusu Siaw and his wife for their word of encouragement and their moral support.

Finally, I will not end this acknowledgement, without mentioning the guidance and the support I received from Apostle John Adjormo Gama, and Reverend E. Dadebo. I sincerely thank the Curriculum Research and Development Division (CRDD) of Ghana Education Service, for their efficient book assessment and evaluation.

BRIGHT SIAW AFRIYIE
SAB-SOFTECH

Table of Contents

Preface..*iii*

Organization of this Book .... *iv*

Why I should buy this book? .... *ix*

About The Author .... *x*

Dedication .... *x*

Ghana Education Services Approval Letter.................. *xi*

Acknowledgement ....*xii*

Table of Contents ....*xiii-xxvii*

SECTION I   SPREADSHEET APPLICATIONS **1-36**

CHAPTER 1 ....**5**

Introduction to Spreadsheet Applications 5

1.1. Introduction to Spreadsheet Applications and Importance 5

11.1.1 VisiCalc 5

1.1.2 Lotus 1-2-3 and other MS-DOS spreadsheets 6

1.1.3 Microsoft Excel.. 7

1.1.4 OpenOffice.org Calc...................................... 8

1.1.5 Quattro Pro... 9

1.1.6 IBM Lotus Symphony 9

1.2 The General Concepts of Spreadsheet......................... 9

1.2.1 The Cells of Spreadsheet................................. 10

1.2.2 The Sheets of Spreadsheet............................... 11

1.2.3 The Cells and Values of Spreadsheet..................... 12

1.2.4 Data Format 13

1.2.5 Formulas in Spreadsheet 14

1.2.6 Functions in Spreadsheet................................ 15

1.2.7 Charts in Spreadsheet................................... 16

1.3 Overview of Microsoft Excel in Spreadsheet and Basics.......... 16

1.3.1 The Microsoft Excel File Format........................... 17

1.4 The Workbook Features of Microsoft Excel.. 20

1.4.1 The Home Tab Ribbon of Microsoft Excel.. 20

1.4.2 The Insert Tab Ribbon of Microsoft Excel 22

1.4.3 The Page Layout Tab Ribbon of Microsoft Excel 23

1.4.4 The Formulas Tab Ribbon of Microsoft Excel... 24

1.4.5 The Data Tab Ribbon of Microsoft Excel 25

1.4.6 The Review Tab Ribbon of Microsoft Excel.. 25

1.4.7 The View Tab Ribbon of Microsoft Excel.. 26

1.4.8 The Add-Ins Tab Ribbon of Microsoft Excel 27

1.4.9 The Team Tab Ribbon of Microsoft Excel 27

1.5 The Basic Facts about Microsoft Excel 28

1.5.1 Displaying filename extensions within Excel 29

1.5.2 Common Facts about Microsoft Excel... 29

1.6 Assignment Questions 33

1.7 Multiple Choice Questions 25-45.. 34

CHAPTER 2 .... **37-68**

Editing Spreadsheet Applications **37**

2. Editing Cell Contents.. 37

2.1 Edit cell contents 38

2.2 Replace cell contents 38

2.3 Clear cell contents... 38

2.4 Cutting, Copying, and Pasting Cells 39

2.4.1 Copy cells... 39

2.4.2 Cut Cells... 39

2.4.3 Paste Cells 40

2.5 Moving and Copying Cells Using the Mouse 40

2.6 Using the Office Clipboard 41

2.7 Using the Paste Special Command.. 42

2.8 Checking Your Spelling 43

2.9 Inserting Cells, Rows, and Columns 45

2.9.1 Insert cells 45

2.9.2 Insert rows or columns 46

2.10 Deleting Cells, Rows, and Columns 46

2.10.1 Delete Cells 46

2.10.2 Delete rows or columns 47

2.11 Using Find and Replace 47

2.11.1 Find 48

2.11.2 Replace 48

2.11.3 Search Options 49

2.12 Using Cell Comments 50

2.12.1 Insert a comment 50

2.12.2 View a comment 50

2.12.3 Edit a comment 51

2.12.4 Delete comment 51

2.13 Tracking Changes 51

2.13.1 Track changes 51

2.13.2 Accept/reject changes 52

2.14 Cancel or undo edits 52

2.14.1 Wrap text in a cell 53

2.14.2 Exit Edit mode 53

2.14.3 Enter data in multiple worksheets at the same time 54

2.14.4 Fill data automatically in worksheet cells 55

2.14.5 Enter data manually in worksheet cells 55

2.14.6 Enter text or a number in a cell 55

2.14.7 Enter a number that has a fixed decimal point 55

2.14.8 Enter a date or a time in a cell 56

2.14.9 Enter the same data into several cells at the same time 56

2.14.10 Enter the same data on several worksheets at the same time 57

2.15 Adjust worksheet settings and cell formats 58

2.15.1 Change the direction for the ENTER key 58

2.16 Change the format of a number.. 58

2.16.1 Format a number as text 58

2.16.2 Automatically repeat values that already exist in the column 59

2.16.3 Turn off automatic completion of cell values 59

2.16.4 Find or replace text and numbers on a worksheet....................................... 59

2.16.5 For each cell in column A, have three rows in column B 61

2.17 Assignments & Exercises... 62

2.18 Multiple choice exercises 11- 45 63-68

CHAPTER 3 .... **69-134**

Formatting Worksheets in Excel Spreadsheet...................................**69**

3. Highlight Cells 69

3.1 Create a cell style to highlight cells 69

3.2 Use Format Painter to apply a highlight to other cells 71

3.3 Display specific data in a different font color or format.................................. 71

3.4 Insert ASCII or Unicode Latin-based symbols and characters 71

3.4.1 Inserting ASCII characters 72

3.4.2 Inserting Unicode characters.. 72

3.4.3 Using the Character Map 73

3.5.1 Mimic a watermark in Excel.. 77

3.5.2 Use a picture in a header or footer to mimic a watermark 77

3.6 Preview font formatting in Excel 78

3.6.1 Applying Number Formatting 79

3.6.2 Improving readability by formatting numbers.. 79

3.6.3 Using automatic number formatting.. 80

3.6.4 Formatting numbers by using the Ribbon.. 80

3.6.5 Using shortcut keys to format numbers 81

3.6.6 Formatting numbers using the Format Cells dialog box 81

3.7 When Numbers Appear to Add Up Incorrectly 82

3.7.1 Change the character used to separate thousands or decimals.................... 84

3.7.2 Change the decimal places displayed for numbers 84

3.7.3 Increase or decrease the decimal places on a worksheet............................84

3.7.4 Specify the decimal places for a built-in number format..............................85

3.7.5 Specify a fixed decimal point for numbers...85

3.7.6 Change the way negative numbers are displayed......................................86

3.8 Convert dates stored as text to dates..87

3.8.1 Convert text dates with two-digit years by using Error Checking................88

3.8.2 Convert text dates by using the DATEVALUE function.............................88

3.8.3 Convert numbers stored as text to numbers...89

3.8.4 Use error checking to convert numbers that are stored as text to
numbers 90

3.8.5 Apply a number format to numbers that are stored as text.......................91

3.8.6 Convert numbers in multiple nonadjacent cells or ranges of cells..............91

3.8.7 Create or delete a custom number format...92

3.9 Review guidelines for customizing a number format.....................................92

3.9.1 Guidelines for including text and adding spacing 93

3.9.2 Guidelines for using decimal places, spaces, colors, and conditions..........94

3.9.3 Guidelines for currency, percentages, and scientific notation format.........96

3.9.4 Guidelines for date and time formats...97

3.10 Create a custom number format...99

3.10.1 Delete a custom number format 100

3.10.2 Display numbers as credit card numbers 100

3.10.3 Display credit card numbers in full..100

3.10.4 Display only the last few digits of credit card numbers..........................101

3.10.5 Display numbers as currency 102

3.11 Create a workbook template with specific currency formatting settings 105

3.12 Display numbers as dates or times 106

3.13 Display numbers as fractions 108

3.13 Display numbers as percentages 109

3.14 Display numbers as percentages 109

3.15 Display numbers as postal codes...111

3.15.1 Apply a predefined postal code format to numbers 111

3.15.2 Create a custom postal code format.. 112

3.15.3 Include leading characters in postal codes..................................... 112

3.15.4 Display numbers as Social Security numbers 112

3.16 Hide or display cell values.. 114

3.16 How Excel Handles Dates and Times 114

3.16.1 Understanding date serial numbers.. 115

3.16.2 Choose Your Date System: 1900 or 1904 115

3.16.3 Entering dates 116

3.16.4 Searching for Dates.. 117

3.16.5 Understanding time serial numbers.. 118

3.16.6 Entering times 119

3.16.7 Formatting dates and times.. 120

3.16.8 Problems with dates 120

3.16.9 Excel's leap year bug 121

3.16.10 Pre-1900 dates... 121

3.16.11 Inconsistent date entries 122

3.17 How to handle leading zeros and precision in number codes 122

3.17.1 The number format removes leading zeros by default 122

3.17.2 Use a custom or special format to keep the leading zeros 123

3.18 Understanding Floating Point Precision 124

3.18.1 Overview of Floating Point Precision 126

3.18.2 Various Methods of Rounding Numbers.. 130

3.19 Assignment s... 133

CHAPTER 4 .... **135-162**

More Functions, Formulas and Macros............................... **135**

4.1 Introduction to Formulas in Spreadsheet.. 135

4.2 Relative and Absolute References 136

4.3 Cell Ranges... 137

4.4 Functions in Spreadsheet.. 138

4.5 The Formulas Tab Ribbon of Microsoft Excel 138

4.6 Performing Calculations with Formulas in Microsoft Excel 139

4.6.1 Basic Formula Requirements 140

4.7 Creating a Formula for a Single Worksheet 140

4.8 Writing Formula for Multiple Worksheet 145

4.8.1 Using Special Characters 145

4.8.2 Creating a Link to a Single Worksheet in the Same Workbook 145

4.8.3 Analysis of Formulas in Multiple Worksheets 147

4.8.4 Creating a Link to More than One Worksheet in the Same Workbook 148

4.8.5 Writing Formulas for Other Workbook Files - From Same Directory 149

4.8.6 Writing Formulas for Other Workbook Files- From Different Directory 150

4.9 Using Range Names in Formulas 150

4.10 Calculating Your Workbook 151

4.10.1 Changing to Manual Calculation 152

4.11 Using More Relative Addressing 152

4.12 Visual Basic for Applications (VBA) 153

4.13 Assignment Questions 157

4.14 Multiple Choice Questions.. 158-162

CHAPTER 5 .... **163-188**

Managing Worksheets...**163**

5.0 Introduction 163

5.1 Change the color of gridlines in a worksheet....................165

5.2 Change the default Font in Excel 167

5.2.1 Change the default Theme...167

5.3 Change the Font or Font size in Excel 169

5.3.1 Change the font or font size in a worksheet 170

5.3.2 Change the default font or font size for new workbooks................170

5.3.3 Change the number of worksheets in a new workbook 170

5.3.4 Change the width of all columns with one command...................171

5.3.5 Freeze or lock rows and columns................................171

5.4 Hide or show worksheets or workbooks 173

5.4.2 Hide a worksheet 173

5.4.3 Display a hidden worksheet 173

5.4.4 Hide a workbook window 174

5.4.5 Display a hidden workbook window 174

5.4.6 Hide or display workbook windows on the Windows taskbar 174

5.5 Insert or delete a worksheet 174

5.5.1 Insert a new worksheet 175

5.5.2 Insert multiple worksheets at the same time 175

5.5.3 Change the number of worksheets in a new workbook 175

5.5.4 Insert a new sheet that is based on a custom template 176

5.5.5 Rename a worksheet 176

5.5.6 Delete one or more worksheets 176

5.6 Move or copy a worksheet 176

5.6.1 Move or copy worksheets to another location in a workbook 177

5.6.2 Move or copy worksheets to another workbook 178

5.6.3 Move or copy data to another worksheet or workbook 179

5.6.4 Drag data between open workbook windows in Excel 180

5.6.5 Drag data to another workbook of Excel 180

5.7 Show or hide columns and rows 181

5.7.1 Hide one or more rows or columns 181

5.7.2 Display one or more hidden rows or columns 181

5.7.3 Display all hidden rows and columns at once 182

5.7.4 Unhide the first row or column of the worksheet 182

5.8 Switch to full or normal screen view 183

5.8.1 View two or more worksheets at the same time 183

5.8.2 View two worksheets in the same workbook side by side 183

5.8.3 View two worksheets of different workbooks side by side 183

5.8.4 View multiple worksheets at the same time 184

5.9 Where are my worksheet tabs? 185

5.10 Assignment Questions (1- 22) 187

CHAPTER 6 ....**189-214**

Conditional Formatting and Data Analysis **189**

6.0 Introduction 189

6.1 Conditional Formatting by Range of Values 189

6.2 CountIF in Microsoft Excel 2007 to 2010........................... 194

6.3 SUMIF in Microsoft Excel 2007 to 2010 196

6.4 Data Tables in Microsoft Excel 2007 to 2010 198

6.5 Scenario - A Second Data Table in Microsoft Excel 2007 to 2010 200

6.6 Scenarios in Microsoft Excel 2007 to 2010 202

6.7 Goal Seek in Microsoft Excel 2007 to 2010....................... 207

6.7.1 More Goal Seek in Microsoft Excel 2007 to 2010 208

6.8 Assignment Questions 210

6.9 Multiple Choice Questions.. 211

CHAPTER 7 ....**215-248**

Working with Excel Tables, Charts, Page Layout and Printing ..**215**

7.0 Introduction: Working with Tables in Excel 2010 215

7.1 Creating a Table in Excel 2010 215

7.2 Create Data Form and Add Records to an Excel 2010 Table 218

7.3 Add or remove table rows and columns in an Excel table 220

7.4 Resize a table 220

7.5 Using Data Form to Find Records in an Excel 2010 Table.......................... 221

    a. How to find records in a table manually.................................... 221

    b. How to use search criteria to find table records 222

7.6 Edit Records in an Excel 2010 Table 223

7.7 Apply a Table Style to an Excel 2010 Table........................ 224

7.8 Filter Records in an Excel 2010 Table with AutoFilter 224

7.9 Filter Numbers in an Excel 2010 Table 226

    Filtering for top or bottom values.. 226

    Filtering for above- or below-average values 227

7.10 Excel 2010 - Pivot Tables.. 231

7.10.1 How To Create A Pivot Table In Excel 2010 232

7.10.2 Insert Slicer In Pivot Tables & Charts – Excel 2010 234

7.11 Print a worksheet in landscape or portrait orientation............................ 240

7.12 Define or clear a print area on a worksheet... 241

7.13 Assignment Questions 242

7.14 Multiple Choice Questions... 244

SECTION II   POWERPOINT APPLICATIONS **249**

CHAPTER 8 .... **253-306**

Working With Presentation in PowerPoint... 253

8.0 Presentation Basics... 253

8.1 What Makes A Good PowerPoint Presentation.. 253

8.1.1 Creating a New Presentation.. 255

8.1.1a Creating a New Blank Presentation... 255

8.1.1b Creating a New Presentation from a Template................................... 256

8.1.2 Inserting Slides and Selecting a Layout 257

8.1.2.1 Creating a PowerPoint Template.. 258

The PowerPoint Slide Master 259

Changing The Background... 259

8.1.2.2 Applying A Theme 261

8.1.3 Slide Master Layouts.. 261

8.1.4 Create A PowerPoint Theme 262

8.1.4.1 Theme Colors.. 263

8.1.4.2 Theme Fonts 264

8.1.4.3 Theme Effects 264

8.1.4.4 Saving Your PowerPoint Theme 264

8.1.5 Opening a presentation 265

8.1.6 Navigation of Presentation 266

Navigation keystrokes 266

Slide tab 267

8.1.7 Using Undo, Redo and Report 267

    1.Undo a single action...267

    2.Undo multiple actions 267

    3.Redo an action 268

    4.Repeat an action 268

8.1.8 Saving a Presentation 268

8.1.9 Using Print Preview 271

8.1.10 Printing a Presentation 273

8.1.10.1 PowerPoint Handouts...273

8.1.11 Closing a Presentation 275

8.2. Insert PowerPoint Hyperlink 275

8.2.1 Insert A Table In PowerPoint 2010..276

8.2.2 Insert Images In Microsoft PowerPoint 2010.......................................277

8.3 Creating A Quiz In PowerPoint...278

8.3.1 Creating A Multiple Choice PowerPoint Quiz 278

8.3.1.1 The Question Slide...279

8.3.1.2 The Right Answer Slide...281

8.4 Creating Multimedia Presentations 282

8.4.1 Animating Slides 283

    Types of Animation...283

    Built-in Animation Effects 283

    Custom Animation Effects 283

    Adding Transition Effects 284

    About Transitions 284

8.4.2 Animation Painter 284

8.4.3 PowerPoint Animations 286

8.4.4 Applying A PowerPoint Animation 287

8.4.5 Previewing an Animation 287

8.5 Assigning A Sound File To An Object 288

8.5.1 Add Sound To PowerPoint 289

8.6 Working with Tables, Charts, and Diagrams 290

8.6.1 Inserting and Formatting a Table.. 290

8.6.1.1 Creating Tables 291

8.6.1.2 Formatting Tables 291

8.6.1.3 Importing Excel Worksheets 291

8.6.1.4 Inserting a Link in A Slide 292

8.6.2 Inserting and Formatting a Chart.. 293

8.6.2.0 Inserting and Formatting an Organization Chart................................ 295

8.6.2.1 Creating Organization Charts 295

8.6.2.2 Formatting Organization Charts 296

8.6.2.3 Create an organization chart with pictures 297

8.6.2.4 Add or delete boxes in your organization chart 297

8.6.2.5 Delete boxes in your organization chart 298

8.6.2.6 Change a solid line to a dotted line 299

8.6.3 Change the hanging layout of your organization chart 299

8.6.4 Change the colors of your organization chart.. 300

8.6.4.1 Change the background color of a box in your organization chart.......... 301

8.7 Assignment and Exercises 301

8.8 Exercises And Multiple Choice Questions.. 303

SECTION III - DATA PROCESSING **307**

CHAPTER 9 .... **309-334**

Data Processing - Using Microsoft Access Database 309

9.0 Define Data Processing, Data and Information 309

9.1 Concepts of Data Processing... 310

9.1.1 Collection 311

9.1.2 Conversion 312

9.1.3 Manipulation 312

9.1.4 Managing the Output Results 314

9.1.5 Communication 314

9.2 The Data Processing Cycle 315

9.2.1 Input 315

9.2.2 Processing 316

9.2.3 Output 316

9.2.4 Storage 316

9.3 The Data Organization 316

9.3.1 Data Item 316

9.3.2 Field 317

9.3.3 Record 317

9.3.4 File 318

9.3.5 Database 318

9.4 Variable and Fixed Length Records 318

9.4.1 Fixed Length Records 318

9.4.2 Variable Length Records 319

9.5 Logical Versus Physical Record 319

9.6 Lesson Summary 319

9.7 Creating Tables For Data Entry 320

9.7.1 Creating Database in MS. Access 320

9.7.2 Creating Table under a Database in MS. Access 322

9.8 Creating Data Entry Form 324

9.9 Structured Query Language 326

9.9.1 Types of Queries 326

9.9.2 Sorting On FirstName Field 327

9.9.3 Filtering Data On Credit Field 328

9.10 Assignment Questions 329

9.11 Multiple Choice Questions 331

SECTION IV - BASIC CONCEPT OF PROGRAMMING 335

CHAPTER 10 .... **339-385**

Basic Concept of Programming 339

10.0 Overview of Basic elements of Programming 339

10.1 What is Computer Programming? 339

10.1.1 Computer Algorithms 341

10.1.2 Expressing Algorithms 342

10.1.3 Variables 342

10.2 Programming languages 343

10.2.1 Creating a Simple Program 344

10.2.2 Analysis 344

10.2.3 Designing 344

10.2.4 Coding 345

10.2.5 Testing 345

10.3 Application of Programming Methodology 346

   1. Analysis 347

   2. Design 347

   3. Coding The Add Machine Program 349

10.4 Basic Object Oriented Concepts 350

   1. An Object 350

   2. Messages 350

   3. Class 350

   4. Abstract Class 350

   5. Base Class 350

   6. Sub Class 351

   7. Super Class 351

   8. Inheritance 351

   9. Encapsulation 351

   10.Instance 351

   11.Extends 351

   12.Method 351

13. Class Method 351

14. Instance Method 352

15. Class Variable 352

16. Instance Variable 352

17. Interface 352

18. Package 352

10.4.1 Abstract Classes and Methods in Visual Basic.Net 352

10.4.2 Object: 3 Key characteristics of Object 355

10.5 Programming Concept in Visual Basic.Net 356

10.5.1 Visual Basic.Net – Object-Oriented Language Concepts 357

10.6 Visual Studio Integrated Development Environment (IDE) 358

10.6.1 Visual Studio (IDE) Menu Bar 362

10.7 How to Store Information 363

10.7.1 Object Access Concept 364

10.7.2 Review on the Code of Calculator Program 366

10.8 General Visual Basic (VB) Language Reference 366

10.8.1 Data type 366

10.8.2 Data Type Summary 367

10.8.3 Constant 367

10.9 Arrays 368

10.9.1 How an array is defined in Visual Basic.Net 369

10.9.2 Navigating Through Array Elements 371

10.9.3 Navigating Through Multi-Dimension Array 373

10.10 Instantiating Classes 374

10.11 Storing Data in Text File 376

10.12 User- Defined Types 378

10.12.1 Data Types Conversion 381

10.13 Assignments and Exercises 382

Common Term Glossary **387-408**

Book Index **409-417**

Bibliography & References **418**

The Beginning of the textbook

CONCISE

ICT FUNDAMENTALS

VOLUME TWO

COVERS

SPREADSHEET   *POWERPOINT*   *DATA PROCESSING*   *PROGRAMMING*

SECTION I

SPREADSHEET

APPLICATIONS

SUMMARIZED OBJECTIVES:

This section comprises seven chapters that cover spreadsheet applications with the main focus on Microsoft Excel. The student will be able to identify spreadsheet packages and their uses, explain the importance of Spreadsheet application in data management and related concepts and terminologies in Spreadsheet. Identify features in Spreadsheet application window. Identify types of data and state their uses. The fundamentals, starting excel 2007 and 2010, understanding the excel program screen. Worksheet basics: creating a new workbook, opening a workbook, navigating a worksheet, entering labels, values are discussed. Students will be able to create and save Workbook. This chapter will explain the application of selected formula and functions by constructing and inserting simple formulae and functions; Selecting a Cell Range, Overview of Formulas and Using AutoSum. The chapter will teach students how to enter formulas, and using AutoFill and understanding Absolute and Relative Cell References, using Undo, Redo and Repeat. Previewing and Printing a Worksheet. Students will familiarize themselves with Formatting Worksheet Using Formatting Tools changing column width row height, inserting rows, columns, cells, etc.

The Objectives

➢ **Chapter 1: Introduction to Spreadsheet Applications**
  - ○ Introduction to Spreadsheet Applications and Importance
  - ○ The General Concepts of Spreadsheet and Terminologies
  - ○ Overview of Microsoft Excel Spreadsheets and Basics
  - ○ The Workbook Features of Microsoft Excel
  - ○ Basic Facts about Microsoft Excel
  - ○ Assignment and Multiple Choice Questions

➢ **Chapter 2: Editing Spreadsheets**
  - ○ Editing an Excel Worksheet Using Editing Tools
  - ○ Moving, Copy/Cut and Paste Facilities, Etc.
  - ○ Inserting Cells, Rows, and Columns
  - ○ Deleting Cells, Rows, and Columns
  - ○ Using Find and Replace
  - ○ Spell Check Functions.
  - ○ Using Cell Comments, Tracking Changes

➢ **Chapter 3: Formatting Excel Spreadsheets**
  - ○ Formatting Labels and Values
  - ○ Adjusting Row Height and Column Width
  - ○ Working with Cell Alignments.
  - ○ Adding Cell Borders, Background Colors and Patterns
  - ○ Using Format Painter, Cell Styles, Document Themes
  - ○ Applying Conditional Formatting
  - ○ Working with Data Ranges

➢ **Chapter 4: More Functions, Formulas and Macros**
  - ○ Formulas with Multiple Operators
  - ○ Inserting and Editing a Functions
  - ○ AutoCalculate and Manual Calculation
  - ○ Defining Names, Using and Managing Defined Names
  - ○ Displaying and Tracing Formulas, Understanding Formula Errors

➢ **Chapter 5: Managing Worksheets**
  - ○ Introduction: Modify width and height of columns; Insert row or column
  - ○ Insert or delete cells in worksheet or Worksheets
  - ○ Move data in worksheet or workbook
  - ○ Change the color of gridlines, default fonts and Themes in a worksheet
  - ○ Freeze or lock rows and columns; Hide or show worksheets or workbooks
  - ○ Move or copy a worksheet
  - ○ Switch to full or normal screen view

➢ **Chapter 6: Conditional Formatting and Data Analysis**
  o Introduction
  o Conditional Formatting by Range of Values
  o CountIF in Microsoft Excel 2007 to 2010
  o SUMIF in Microsoft Excel 2007 to 2010
  o Data Tables in Microsoft Excel 2007 to 2010
  o Scenarios in Microsoft Excel 2007 to 2010
  o Goal Seek in Microsoft Excel 2007 to 2010

➢ **Chapter 7: Working with Tables, Charts, Page Layout and Printing**
  o Introduction
  o Creating a Table, and Working with Table Size
  o Working with the Total Row, and Working with Table Data
  o Summarizing a Table with a PivotTable
  o How To Create A Pivot Table In Excel 2010
  o Insert Slicer In Pivot Tables & Create Charts – Excel 2010
  o Types of Charts in Excel 2010
  o Setting Print Area and Printing worksheets in Excel 2010

CHAPTER 1

Introduction to Spreadsheet Applications

Objectives:

- o *Introduction to Spreadsheet Applications and Importance*
- o *The General Concepts of Spreadsheet and Terminologies*
- o *Overview of Microsoft Excel Spreadsheets and Basics*
- o *The Workbook Features of Microsoft Excel*
- o *The Basic Facts about Microsoft Excel(Formulas, Ranges, Cells, etc.)*

1.1. Introduction to Spreadsheet Applications and Importance

An application that simulates a paper or accounting worksheet, which displays multiple cells that together make up a grid consisting of rows and columns, each cell containing either alphanumeric text or numeric values. It is used to analyze financial information, calculations, create forecasting models, etc. Common examples of spreadsheet applications are **Lotus 1-2-3,** which was the leading spreadsheet when DOS was the dominant operating system, the **Microsoft Excel** which now has the largest market share on the Windows and Macintosh platforms, **VisiCalc** which is usually considered the first electronic spreadsheet on Apple II computer, and Multiplan which was Microsoft's predecessor to Excel using the R1C1 cell addressing which is still available as an option in Excel. Lotus 1-2-3 dominated the market on its release on 1982.

Below is the list of the most popular spreadsheet packages:

- VisiCalc
- Lotus 1-2-3 and other MS-DOS spreadsheets
- Microsoft Excel
- OpenOffice.org Calc
- Quattro Pro
- Other spreadsheets e.g. IBM Symphony

11.1.1 VisiCalc

The first spreadsheet application was introduced in the late 1970's. The idea behind VisiCalc was developed by Dan Bricklin, and the actual programming was performed by a friend named Bob Frankston. Bricklin needed a computer tool to complete repetitive calculations associated with case studies at the Harvard

Business School. VisiCalc was the first spreadsheet that combined all essential features of modern spreadsheet applications, such as WYSIWYG interactive user interface, automatic recalculation, status and formula lines, range copying with relative and absolute references, formula building by selecting referenced cells.

Figure 1.1
Calc running in an MSDOS window

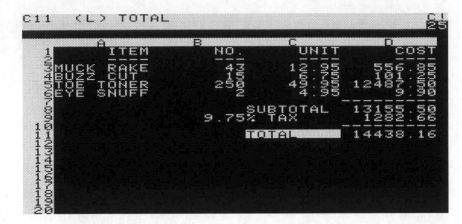

PC World magazine has called VisiCalc the first electronic spreadsheet. Bricklin idea became VisiCalc, the first application that turned the personal computer from a hobby for computer enthusiasts into a business tool. VisiCalc remains best known as "an Apple II program. After gaining popularity as an Apple application, the product was sold to Lotus Development Corporation, and led to the development of the Lotus 1-2-3 spreadsheet for the PC in 1983.

1.1.2 Lotus 1-2-3 and other MS-DOS spreadsheets

A spreadsheet program designed for IBM-compatible personal computers by Lotus Corporation in 1982. Lotus 1-2-3 spreadsheet was the first MS-DOS based spreadsheet package which was released on January 26, 1983. It was designed especially for the IBM PC and compatibles with the improvements in speed and graphics compared to VisiCalc on the Apple II. Lotus 1-2-3, along with its competitor Borland Quattro, soon displaced VisiCalc and became the leading spreadsheet package for DOS in 1983. The release of Lotus 1-2-3 package also boosted the sales for IBM PCs and compatibles. Lotus 1-2-3 was the first publicly available program to combine graphics, spreadsheet functions and data management (three functions, hence the name). Its relative ease of use and flexibility made it an enormous success and contributed to the acceptance of personal computers in business.

Lotus 1-2-3 is a spreadsheet program from Lotus Software now part of IBM. The Lotus Development Corporation was founded by Mitchell Kapor, a friend of the developers of VisiCalc. The 1-2-3 version was originally written by Jonathan Sachs, who had written two spreadsheet programs previously while working at Concentric Data Systems, Inc. Lotus 1-2-3 has been improved to 65,536 rows by 256 columns. Lotus 1-2-3 also offers native HTML support with XML support.

1.1.3 Microsoft Excel

Microsoft Excel is a commercial spreadsheet application written and distributed by Microsoft for Microsoft Windows and Mac OS X. Among its features includes calculation, graphing tools, pivot tables and a macro programming language called Visual Basic for Applications. It has been a very widely applied spreadsheet for these platforms, especially since version 5 in 1993. The more robust Windows 3.x platforms of the early 1990s made it possible for Excel to take market share from Lotus. By the time Lotus responded with usable Windows products, Microsoft had started compiling their Office suite.

Figure 1.2
MS Excel
Spreadsheet
running in
MS Windows

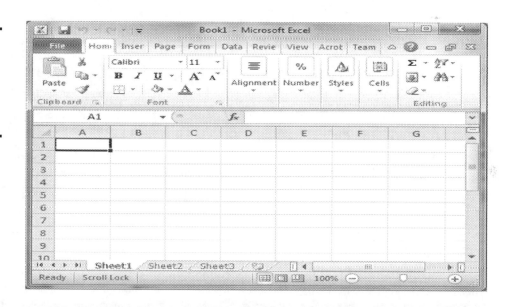

Starting in the mid 1990's continuing through the present time, Microsoft Excel has dominated the commercial electronic spreadsheet market till now. Excel forms part of Microsoft Office. The current versions are 2010 for Windows and 2011 for Mac.

1.1.4 OpenOffice.org Calc

OpenOffice.org Calc is a free, open-source program modeled after Microsoft

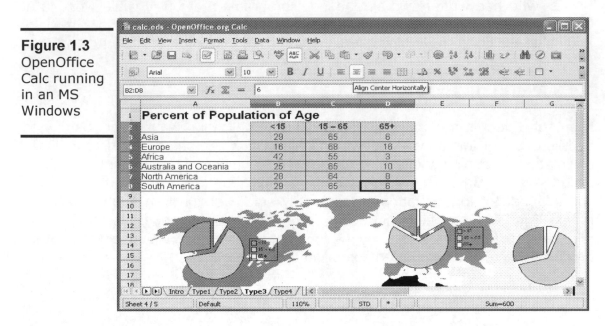

Figure 1.3
OpenOffice
Calc running
in an MS
Windows

Excel. Calc can both open and save in the Excel (XLS) file format. You can save your spreadsheets in OpenDocument format, the new international standard for office documents. This XML based format makes Calc platform independent which means you are not tied in to CALC. You can access your spreadsheets from any OpenDocument compliant software.   Calc can be acquired as both an installation file and a portable program, capable of being run from a device such as a USB memory drive. It can be downloaded from the OpenOffice.org website.

It is intuitive and easy to learn about the comprehensive range of advanced functions such as Advanced DataPilot technology which makes it easy to pull in raw data from corporate databases; cross-tabulate, summarize, and convert it into meaningful information.

Natural language formulas let you create formulas using words. The Intelligent Sum Button inserts a sum function or a subtotal automatically, depending on context. CALC's solver component allows solving optimization problems where the optimum value of a particular spreadsheet cell has to be calculated based on constraints provided in other cells. Scenario Manager allows "what if ..." analysis at the touch of a button - e.g. compare profitability for high / medium / low sales forecasts. Since version 3.0, CALC has been able to read .xlsx files created with Microsoft Office 2007 or Microsoft Office 2008 for Mac OS X.

1.1.5 Quattro Pro

Quattro Pro is a spreadsheet program developed by Borland and now sold by Corel, most often as part of Corel's WordPerfect Office. Historically, Quattro Pro used keyboard commands similar to Lotus 1-2-3. It is commonly said to have been the first program to use tabbed sheets. Actually, Boeing Calc, the first modern spreadsheet had tabbed sheets earlier. It currently runs under the Windows operating system. Quattro Pro avoided the 65,536 row by 256 column spreadsheet limitations inherent to pre-2007 versions of Microsoft Excel by allowing a maximum worksheet size of one million rows by 18,276 columns. Since about 1996 Quattro Pro has run a distant second to Excel's market domination. When version 1.0 was in development, it was codenamed "Buddha" since it was meant to "assume the Lotus position", #1 in the market. When the product was launched in 1988, its original name was Quattro (the Italian word for "four", a play on being one step ahead of "1-2-3"). Borland changed the name to Quattro Pro for its 1990 release.

The common file extension of Quattro Pro spreadsheet file is .qpw. Older versions of Quattro Pro used also the following file extensions: wb3, wb2, wb1.

1.1.6 IBM Lotus Symphony

IBM Lotus Symphony is a suite of applications for creating, editing, and sharing text, spreadsheet, presentations and other documents, and is currently distributed as freeware. First released in 2007, the suite has a name similar to the 1980s DOS suite Lotus Symphony, but the two programs are otherwise unrelated. The previous Lotus application suite, Lotus SmartSuite is also unrelated.

1.2 The General Concepts of Spreadsheet

All spreadsheets have common characteristics which are defined by a basic concept. The main concepts are those of a grid of cells, called worksheet, with either raw data, called values, or formulas in the cells. The grid has Columns run up and down (**vertical**) and Rows run side to side (**horizontal**) Formulas say how to mechanically compute new values from existing values. Values are generally numbers, but can be also pure text, dates, months, etc. Extensions of these concepts include logical spreadsheets. Various tools for programming sheets, visualizing data, remotely connecting sheets, displaying cells dependencies, etc. are commonly provided.

The general characteristics of spreadsheet packages may include the following:

- Cells
- Rows
- Columns
- Values
- Cell ranges
- Sheets
- Formulas
- Functions
- Charts
- Workbook

- Cell reference
- Data Format
- Named cells
- Cell formatting
- Automatic recalculation
- Real-time update
- Subroutines
- Remote spreadsheet
- Multi-dimensional
- Logical spreadsheets

The above list represents the basic and common terminologies in spreadsheet jargon. But this list is not exhaustive there are many more in advanced studies.

1.2.1 The Cells of Spreadsheet

A cell is a representation of box in a grid. A **cell** can be thought of as a box for holding a datum. Cells are grouped horizontally (rows of cells) and vertically (columns of cells). A cell address is given by the column letter label and a row number, e.g. A1, B3. A single cell is usually referenced by its column and row (A3 would represent the cell below containing the value 5). A cell may contain a value or a formula, or it may simply be left empty. By convention, formulas usually begin with **= sign**.

Usually rows are referenced in decimal notation starting from 1, while columns use 26-adic bijective numeration using the letters A-Z as numerals. Its physical size can usually be tailored for its content by dragging its height or width at box intersections (or for entire columns or rows by dragging the column or rows headers).

Figure 1.4
Spreadsheet

	A	B	C	D	E
1					
2	value1	value2	added	multiplied	B3/A3
3	5	15	20	75	3
4					
5					

The cell addresses contain the following values: A3=5, B3=15, C3=20, D3=75 and E3=3. At the same time E2 contains the label B3/A3 which equals to the value in cell E3 or 3.

a. **Row** is a group of cells that are arranged horizontally in contiguous fashion (rows of cells). In the figure 1.4 above the rows are numbered from 1 to 5. The standard size of rows has been 65,536 rows, all numbered. That makes 16,777,216 cells. That was the case up to Excel 2003. Row number 3, are cells that contain the values 5, 15, 20, 75 and 3. In Excel 2007 or 2010 the maximum number of rows per worksheet was increased to 1,048,576

b. **Column** is a group of cells that are arranged vertically in contiguous fashion (columns of cells). In the figure 1.4 above the columns are lettered from A to E. Column labeled A, are cells that contain the values value1, and 5. The columns are labeled by letters starting from A to Z and beyond. After Z you get AA, AB, AC etc. until you get to AZ. Then it is BA, BB, BC and so on. The number of columns depends on the version of spreadsheet package. However the standard amount of columns has been 256. In Excel 2007 or 2010 the number of columns increased to 16,384 which is column XFD.

1.2.2 The Sheets of Spreadsheet

An array of cells is called a "**sheet**" or "**worksheet**". A worksheet can be described as contiguous cells analogous to an array of variables in a conventional computer program. In most implementations, many worksheets may be located within a single spreadsheet. A worksheet is simply a subset of the spreadsheet or workbook divided for the sake of clarity. Functionally, the spreadsheet operates as a whole book and all cells operate as global variables within the spreadsheet. Spreadsheet has several worksheets or sheets organized into a workbook or book.

Figure 1.5
Spreadsheet
Showing a
Workbook
containing
three Sheets

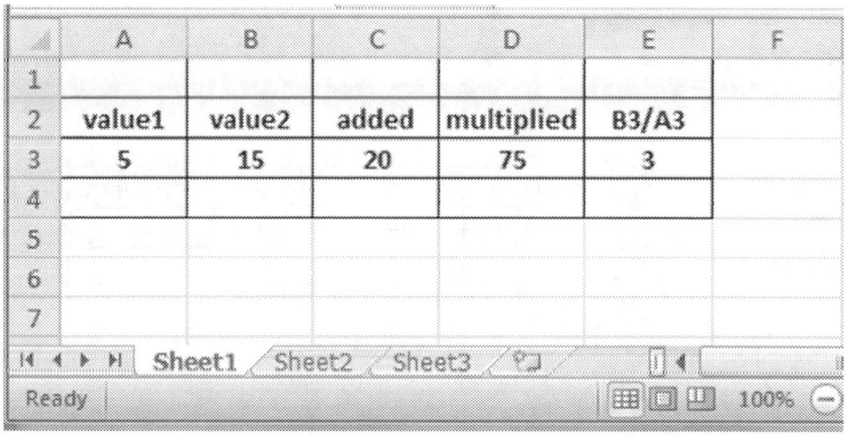

	A	B	C	D	E	F
1						
2	value1	value2	added	multiplied	B3/A3	
3	5	15	20	75	3	
4						
5						
6						
7						

Sheet1 / Sheet2 / Sheet3

Ready   100%

The figure 1.5 is a workbook that contains three sheets or worksheets labeled by default as sheet1, sheet2, and sheet3. To add more sheets just click on the envelop symbol to the right of the last sheet (in this case Sheet3). To rename a sheet double click on a sheet's tab or right-click on it and select Rename from the list of options, and retype the new sheet's name.

Many spreadsheet applications permit charts, graphs or histograms to be generated from specified groups of cells which are dynamically re-built as cell contents change. The generated graphic component can either be embedded within the current sheet or added as a separate object.

In Excel 2007 or 2010 the maximum number of rows per worksheet increased to 1,048,576 and the number of columns increased to 16,384 which is column XFD. That makes 17,179,869,184 cells in a single worksheet. Excel 2010 has the same amount or rows and columns. Excel 2007 or Version 12.0 can handle 1M (2^{20}=1048576) rows, and 16384, (2^{14}) as labels.

1.2.3 The Cells and Values of Spreadsheet

A value can be entered from the computer keyboard by directly typing into a cell itself or copied from one cell to another. Alternatively, a value can be based on a formula (see below), which might perform calculations, display the current date or time, or retrieve external data such as a text file or a database value. A cell's value relies solely on the formula the user has typed into the cell. The formula may rely on the value of other cells, but those cells are likewise restricted to user-entered data or formulas. The only output is to display the calculated result inside its occupying cell. There is no natural mechanism for permanently modifying the contents of a cell unless the user manually modifies the cell's contents.

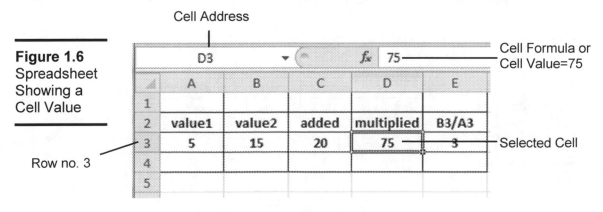

Figure 1.6
Spreadsheet
Showing a
Cell Value

What is your observation when you select or click on a cell? The answer is obvious as indicated in the diagram above. However, when you select the cell address or Name Box E3 the value is a formula in the formula box and the value or the result of this formula is shown in the cell address (E3) as the value of 3. Unlike figure 1.6 above the formula (*fx*) shows =B3/A3 and the cell address E3 shows the value of 3. Cell E3 holds two values, a formula and its calculated value.

Figure 1.7
Spreadsheet
Showing two
value in a
Cell: a
Formula
and a Value

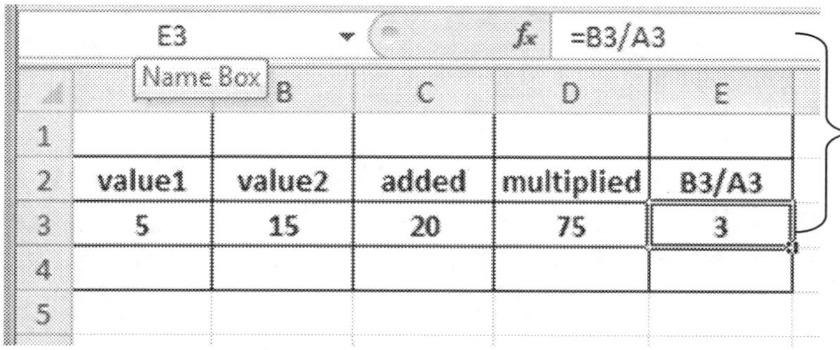

	E3	▼	*fx*	=B3/A3
	Name Box B	C	D	E
1				
2	value1	value2	added	multiplied	B3/A3
3	5	15	20	75	3
4				
5				

Cell **E3** has
two values a
formula
=B3/A3,
And a
Value=3

A value in a cell can be a number, currency, text, date, time, Boolean (true or false), a fraction, percentage or label. Any number entered into a cell is treated as numeric value, but to render it as label you must an apostrophe ['] in front.

1.2.4 Data Format

The data format represents how the values in cells are displayed. A cell or range of cells can optionally be defined to specify how the value is displayed. The default display format is usually set by its initial content if not specifically previously set, so that for example "31/12/2007" or "31 Jan 2007" would default to the cell format of "date". Similarly adding a % sign after a numeric value would tag the cell as a percentage cell format. The cell contents are not changed by this format, only the displayed value. Some cell formats such as "numeric" or "currency" can also specify the number of decimal places. This can allow invalid operations (such as doing multiplication on a cell containing a date), resulting in illogical results without an appropriate warning. Below are the possible data formats:

1. General
2. Currency
3. Number
4. Time
5. Date
6. Percentage
7. Text
8. Scientific
9. Fraction
10. Special
11. Accounting

Below are brief definitions of the data format in spreadsheets:

General	General format cells have no specific number format.
Number	Number is used for general display of numbers. Currency and Accounting offer specialized formatting for monetary value. It displays decimals, a comma before 1000, and negative or positive numbers
Currency	Currency formats are used for general monetary values. Use Accounting format to align the decimal points in a column. By default the Currency symbol is $.
Date	Format displays Date and Time serial numbers as date values.
Time	Format displays Date and Time serial numbers as date values.
Text	Text format cell is treated as text even when a number is in the cell. The text is displayed exactly as entered
Percentage	Format multiples the cell value by 100 and displays result with percent symbol.
Fraction	Express ion of fractions up to (1/4), up to two (21/25), up to 3 digits (321/375), halves(1/2), quarters(1/4), eights(3/8), etc.
Scientific	Scientific formats provide decimal places up to 30.
Accounting	Formats line up currency symbol and decimal points in a column
Special	This format is useful for tracking lists and database values. E.g. phone numbers, zip codes, and social security numbers.

1.2.5 Formulas in Spreadsheet

In spreadsheet a formula identifies the calculation needed to place the result in the cell it is contained within. A cell containing a formula therefore has two display components; the formula itself and the resulting value. The formula is normally only shown when the cell is selected by "clicking" the mouse over a particular cell; otherwise it contains the result of the calculation. A formula assigns values to a cell or range of cells, and typically has the format:

> **= expression (e.g. =B3/B2)**
>   where the expression consists of:
>   - values, such as 4, 9.15 or 5.69E-12;
>   - references to other cells, such as, e.g., A1 for a single cell or B1:B5 for a range of cells;
>   - arithmetic operators, such as **+, -, *, /,** and others;
>   - relational operators, such as **>=, <,** and others; and,
>   - functions such as **SUM(), AVERAGE(), TAN(),** and many others.

When a cell contains a formula, it often contains references to other cells. Such a cell reference is a type of variable (*a symbolic name associated with a value and whose associated value may be changed*). Its value is the value of the referenced cell or some derivation of it. If that cell in turn references other cells, the value depends on the values of those. References can be relative (e.g., A1, or B1:B6), absolute (e.g., $A$1, or $B$1:$B$6) or mixed row-wise or column-wise absolute/relative (e.g., $A1 is column-wise absolute and A$1 is row-wise absolute).

The availability or options for valid formulas depends on the particular spreadsheet implementation but, in general, most arithmetic operations and quite complex nested conditional operations can be performed by most of today's commercial spreadsheets. Modern implementations also offer functions to access custom-build functions, remote data, and applications.

A formula may contain a condition (or nested conditions) - with or without an actual calculation - and is sometimes used purely to identify and highlight errors. In the example below, it is assumed the sum of a column of percentages (B1 through B6) is tested for validity and an explicit message put into the adjacent right-hand cell.

=IF(SUM(B1:B6) > 100, "More than 100%", **SUM(B1:B6))**

What will happen when SUM (B1:B6) is 120?

A spreadsheet does not, in fact, have to contain any formulas at all, in which case it could be considered merely a collection of data arranged in rows and columns (a database) like a calendar, timetable or simple list. Because of its ease of use, formatting and hyperlinking capabilities, many spreadsheets are used solely for this purpose.

1.2.6 Functions in Spreadsheet

Spreadsheets usually contain a number of supplied functions, such as arithmetic operations (for example, summations, averages and so forth), trigonometric functions, statistical functions, and so forth. In addition there is often a provision for user-defined functions. In Microsoft Excel these functions are defined using Visual Basic for Applications in the supplied Visual Basic editor, and such functions are automatically accessible on the worksheet. In addition, programs can be written that pull information from the worksheet, perform some calculations, and report the results back to the worksheet. Functions themselves cannot write into the worksheet, but simply return their evaluation. However, in Microsoft Excel, subroutines can write values or text found within the subroutine directly to the spreadsheet. To insert macros press **ALT+F11**.

1.2.7 Charts in Spreadsheet

Many spreadsheet applications permit charts, graphs or histograms to be generated from specified groups of cells which are dynamically re-built as cell contents change. The generated graphic component can either be embedded within the current sheet or added as a separate object. In spreadsheet like Microsoft Excel many types of charts such as column, line, pie, bar, area, scatter, and others can be generated.

1.3 Overview of Microsoft Excel in Spreadsheet and Basics

Microsoft Excel would be the preferred spreadsheet for this learning curriculum. The focus would be on Excel 2007 and 2010. The figure 1.8 below shows the first page of excel 2010. It begins with the file menu under which contains file management commands of 12 sub-menu items including Save, Save As, Open, Close, Info, Recent, New, Print, Save & Send, Help, Options, and Exit.

Figure 1.8
Spreadsheet
Showing the
screen of File
Menu 2010
Workbook

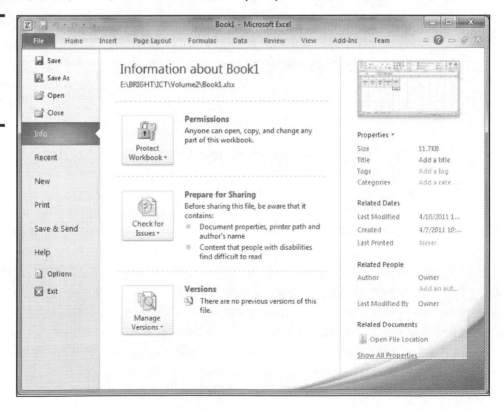

As illustrated above the "Info" sub-menu item was selected showing the properties of the workbook or Book1.xlsx. The toolbar basically comprises File tab, Home tab, Insert tab, Page Layout tab, Formulas tab, Data tab, Review tab, View tab, Add-Ins tab, Team tab, and Help tab. From the Home menu to Team displays the menu known as the **Ribbon** and it's shown in figure 1.9 far below located in page 20.

1.3.1 The Microsoft Excel File Format

One important thing to remember about excel is the file format. The file format for Excel 97 to Excel 2003 is **.xls**, and **.xlt** for the template, while the file format for Excel 2007 to 2010 is **.xls,** and **.xltx** for the template. There are however other file formats that are supported by excel as given in the table below:

File formats that are supported in Excel 2010

Extension	Name of file format	Description
.csv	CSV (Comma delimited)	Saves a workbook as a comma-delimited text file for use on another Windows operating system, and ensures that tab characters, line breaks, and other characters are interpreted correctly.
.csv	CSV (Macintosh)	Saves a workbook as a comma-delimited text file for use on the Macintosh operating system, and ensures that tab characters, line breaks, and other characters are interpreted correctly. Saves only the active sheet.
.csv	CSV (MS-DOS)	Saves a workbook as a comma-delimited text file for use on the MS-DOS operating system, and ensures that tab characters, line breaks, and other characters are interpreted correctly. Saves only the active sheet.
.dbf	DBF 3, DBF 4	dBase III and IV. Users can open these files formats in Excel. However, users cannot save an Excel file to dBase format.
.dif	DIF	Data Interchange Format. Saves only the active sheet.
.htm, .html	Web Page	A Web page that is saved as a folder that contains an .htm file and all supporting files, such as images, sound files, scripts, and more.
.mht, .mhtml	Single File Web Page	A Web page that is saved as a single file that includes an .htm file and all supporting files, such as images, sound files, scripts, and more.
.ods	OpenDocument Spreadsheet	A file format for saving Excel 2010 files so that they can be opened in spreadsheet applications that use OpenDocument Spreadsheet format, such as OpenOffice.org Calc. You can also open spreadsheets in .ods format in Excel 2010. Formatting might be lost when you save and opening .ods files.

Excel supported file format contd.

Extension	Name of file format	Description
.pdf	PDF	Portable Document Format, a format that preserves document formatting and enables file sharing. When the PDF format file is viewed online or printed, it keeps the format that you intended. Data in the file cannot be easily changed. The PDF format is also useful for documents that will be reproduced by using commercial printing methods.
.prn	Formatted Text (Space delimited)	Lotus space-delimited format. Saves only the active sheet.
.slk	SYLK (Symbolic Link Format)	Saves only the active sheet.
.txt	Text (Tab delimited)	Saves a workbook as a tab-delimited text file for use on another Windows operating system, and ensures that tab characters, line breaks, and other characters are interpreted correctly. Saves only the active sheet.
.txt	Text (Macintosh)	Saves a workbook as a tab-delimited text file for use on the Macintosh operating system, and ensures that tab characters, line breaks, and other characters are interpreted correctly. Saves only the active sheet.
.txt	Text (MS-DOS)	Saves a workbook as a tab-delimited text file for use on the MS-DOS operating system, and ensures that tab characters, line breaks, and other characters are interpreted correctly. Saves only the active sheet.
.txt	Unicode Text	Saves a workbook as Unicode text, a character encoding standard that was developed by the Unicode Consortium. Saves only the active sheet.
.xla	Excel 97–2003 Add-In	The Excel 97–2003 Add-In, a supplemental program that runs additional code and supports VBA projects.
.xlam	Excel Add-In	The XML-based and macro-enabled Add-In format for Excel 2010 and Office Excel 2007. An Add-In is a supplemental program that runs additional code. Supports VBA projects and Excel 4.0 macro sheets (.xlm).
.xls	Excel 97–Excel 2003 Workbook	The Excel 97–Excel 2003 Binary file format.
.xls	Microsoft Excel 5.0/95 Workbook	The Excel 5.0/95 Binary file format.

Excel supported file format contd.

Extension	Name of file format	Description
.xlsb	Excel Binary Workbook	The binary file format for Excel 2010 and Office Excel 2007. This is a fast load-and-save file format for users who need the fastest way possible to load a data file. Supports VBA projects, Excel 4.0 macro sheets, and all the new features that are used in Excel 2007 and Excel 2010. However, this is not an XML file format and is therefore not optimal for accessing and manipulating content without using Excel 2010 or Excel 2007 and the object model.
.xlsm	Excel Macro-Enabled Workbook	The XML-based and macro-enabled file format for Excel 2010 and Office Excel 2007. Stores VBA macro code or Excel 4.0 macro sheets (.xlm).
.xlsx	Excel Workbook	The default XML-based file format for Excel 2010 and Office Excel 2007. Cannot store VBA macro code or Microsoft Excel 4.0 macro sheets (.xlm).
.xlt	Excel 97 - Excel 2003 Template	The Excel 97 - Excel 2003 Binary file format for an Excel template.
.xltm	Excel Macro-Enabled Template	The macro-enabled file format for an Excel template for Excel 2010 and Office Excel 2007. Stores VBA macro code or Excel 4.0 macro sheets (.xlm).
.xltx	Excel Template	The default file format for an Excel template for Excel 2010 and Office Excel 2007. Cannot store VBA macro code or Excel 4.0 macro sheets (.xlm).
.xlw	Excel 4.0 Workbook	An Excel 4.0 file format that saves only worksheets, chart sheets, and macro sheets. You can open a workbook in this file format in Excel 2010. However, you cannot save an Excel file to this file format.
.xml	XML Spreadsheet 2003	XML Spreadsheet 2003 file format.
.xml	XML Data	XML Data format.
.xps	XPS Document	XML Paper Specification, a file format that preserves document formatting and enables file sharing. When the XPS file is viewed online or printed, it maintains exactly the format that you intended, and the data in the file cannot be easily changed.

Saving Workbook

Note all Worksheets are saved under the workbook with file extension **.xls** or **.xlsx**. Under the File Menu: Click on Save As **>>**Navigate to Folder**>>**Type Workbook Name or Press Enter (if you choose the default name given by Excel).

1.4 The Workbook Features of Microsoft Excel

The figure 1.9 is the illustration Excel workbook showing most basic features. By default the workbook displays three worksheets; Sheet1,Sheet2, and Sheets which can be extended to 255 or Sheet255.

Figure 1.9
Spreadsheet Showing the screen of 2010 Workbook

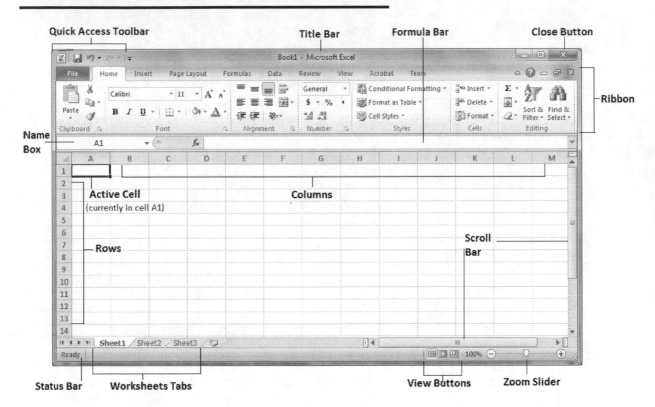

The most basic features to know about Excel spreadsheet includes the Quick Access Tool Bar, Title bar, Formula bar, Close button, Ribbon, Name box, Active cell, Columns, Rows, and Scroll Bar, Status bar, Worksheets, View buttons, and Zoom slider and so on.

1.4.1 The Home Tab Ribbon of Microsoft Excel

The ribbon tabs begin with the Home tab. The Home tab ribbon contains mostly seven editing tools including Clipboard group, Font group, Alignment group, Number group, Styles group, Cells group, and Editing group. Figure 1.10 below is an illustration of the Home tab ribbon.

Figure 1.10
Home tab showing the Editing tools

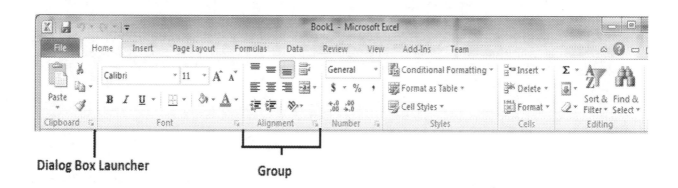

To Cut or Copy Text:

Select the text you want to cut or copy and click the ![] Cut or ![] Copy button in the Clipboard group on the Home tab.

To Paste Text:

Place the insertion point where you want to paste and click the ![] Paste button in the Clipboard group on the Home tab.

To Format Selected Text:
Use the commands in the Font group on the Home tab, or click the **Dialog Box Launcher** in the Font group to open the Font dialog box.

To Copy Formatting with the Format Painter: Select the text with the formatting you want to copy and click the ![] **Format Painter button** in the Clipboard group on the Home tab. Then, select the text you want to apply the copied formatting to.

To Change Paragraph Alignment: Select the paragraph(s) and click the appropriate alignment button (![] Align Left, ![] Center, ![] Align Right, or ![] Justify) in the Paragraph group on the Home tab.

To Indent a Paragraph: Click the ![] **Increase Indent button** in the Paragraph group on the Home tab.

To Decrease an Indent: Click the ![] Decrease Indent button in the Paragraph group on the Home tab.

To Find Text: Click the ![] Find button in the Editing group on the Home tab.

1.4.2 The Insert Tab Ribbon of Microsoft Excel

Figure 1.11
Insert tab showing group of items that can be inserted

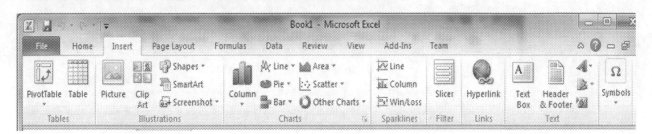

The Insert tab ribbon contains mostly eight groups of items that can be inserted into a worksheet. These group objects include Tables, Illustrations, Charts, Sparklines, Filter, Links, Text, and Symbols. Figure 1.1 above is an illustration of the Insert tab ribbon. When you desire to insert any of the objects you click on the group item and follow the instructions. For example I wanted to insert a Chart by following the following steps:

1. Select the range of cells containing the values
   EXAMPLE:
   =Expenses!$D$7:$E$11
   (Click on cement and drag the mouse to 415)

2. Click on the chart symbol, e.g. column

3. Press Enter

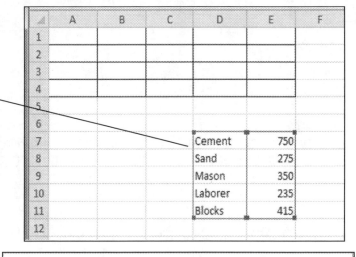

Figure 1.12
Specification of the range D7 thru E11

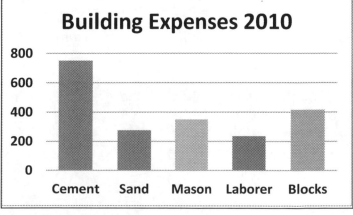

Figure 1.13
The Chart generated by the range of cell values.

1.4.3 The Page Layout Tab Ribbon of Microsoft Excel

The Page Layout tab ribbon contains five groups of items including Themes, Page Setup, Scale to Fit, Sheet Options, and Arrange.

Figure 1.14
Page Layout tab showing group of items

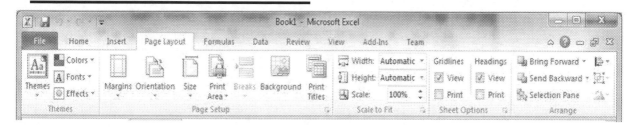

To Change a Document's Margins: Click the **Page Layout** tab on the Ribbon, click the **Margins** button in the Page Setup group, and select a setting.

To Change Page Orientation: Click the **Page Layout** tab on the Ribbon, click the **Orientation** button, and select an option from the list.

To Insert a Header or Footer: Click the **Insert** tab on the Ribbon and click the **Header** or **Footer** button in the Header & Footer group.

To Insert a Manual Page Break: Click the **Insert** tab on the Ribbon and click the **Page Break** button in the Page Setup group.

To Insert a Section Break: Click the **Page Layout** tab on the Ribbon, click the **Breaks** button in the Page Setup group, and select the type of break you want to insert.

To Move Text with the Mouse: Select the text you want to move, drag the text to a new location, and release the mouse button.

To Select a Print Area: Select the cell range you want to print, click the **Page Layout** tab on the Ribbon, click the **Print Area** button in the Page Setup group, and select **Set Print Area.**

To Adjust page Margins, Orientation, Size, and Breaks: Click the **Page Layout** tab on the Ribbon and use the commands in the Page Layout group, or click the **Dialog Box Launcher** in the Page Setup group to open the Page Setup dialog box.

1.4.4 The Formulas Tab Ribbon of Microsoft Excel

The Formulas tab ribbon contains four groups of items including Function Library, Defined Names, Formula Auditing, and Calculations.

Figure 1.15
Formulas tab showing group of items

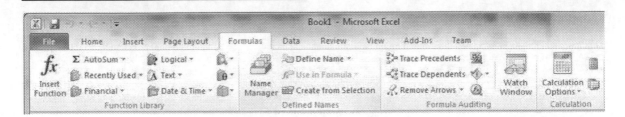

To Total a Cell Range: Click the cell where you want to insert the total and click the Sum ($\sum$) button in either Function Library group on Formulas tab or in the Editing group on the Home tab.

To Enter a Formula: Select the cell where you want to insert the formula, press [=], and enter the formula using values, cell references, operators, and functions. Press **Enter** when you're done.

To Insert a Function: Select the cell where you want to enter the function and click the Function fx button on the Formula Bar.

To Reference a Cell in a Formula: Type the cell reference (for example, B5) in the formula or click the cell you want to reference.

To Create an Absolute Cell Reference: Precede the cell references with a $ sign or press **[F4]** after selecting a cell range to make it absolute, e.g., $D$7:$E$11.

To Use Several Operators or Cell Ranges: Enclose the part of a formula you want to calculate first in parentheses.

1.4.5 The Data Tab Ribbon of Microsoft Excel

The Data tab ribbon contains five groups of items including Get External Data, Connections, Sort & Filter, Data Tools and Outline.

Figure 1.16
Data tab showing group of items

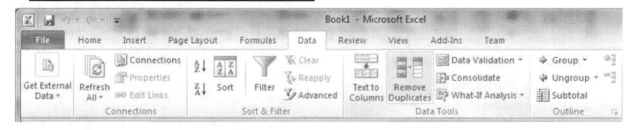

To Get External Data: Click on [Get External Data] to display five types of files as shown below:

The Excel spreadsheet can import the following data types:
1. Access table
2. SQL Server table
3. Web document or XML
4. Text delimited comma or tab

To Sort or Filter a Column: You have to select the range of cells in the column and click on the sort symbol [**A-Z**], or [**Z-A**] or Filter and press enter.

1.4.6 The Review Tab Ribbon of Microsoft Excel

The Review tab ribbon contains four groups of items including Proofing, Language, Comments and Changes.

Figure 1.17
Review tab showing group of items

Generally, you should not make the mistake of not checking your spelling and grammar when you are done the work on your document before you print or e-mail it. The Spelling & Grammar command is on the Review tab, because this is part of reviewing your work. Look toward the *far left*, in the Proofing group in the diagram above. This is similar to the review features in Word 2010 discussed in volume one of this book series.

Spelling checks and grammar commands are located under the Proofing group. In the same group, you will also find the commands for Research, Thesaurus, Translate and Translate ScreenTip, Set Language, and Word Count.

To Insert a Comment: Select the cell where you want to insert a comment and click the Review tab on the Ribbon. Click the New Comment button in Comments group. Type a comment, then click outside the comment text box and point to the cell to view the comment.

1.4.7 The View Tab Ribbon of Microsoft Excel

The View tab ribbon contains five groups of items including Workbook Views, Show, Zoom, Window and Macros.

Figure 1.18
View tab showing group of items

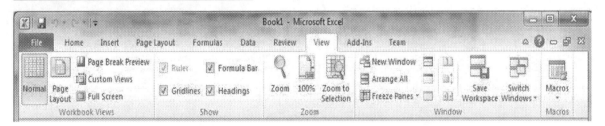

The View Tab is purposely for the Workbook or Worksheet management. For example:

To Freeze Panes: Place the cell pointer where you want to freeze the window, click the View tab on the Ribbon, click the Freeze Panes button in the Window group, and select an option from the list.

To Show Gridlines: By default the gridline does not show in Excel spreadsheet when you print. Select the cell range and click on Gridlines in Show group to check the check box.

1.4.8 The Add-Ins Tab Ribbon of Microsoft Excel

The Add-Ins tab ribbon contains in Custom Toolbars group, number of add-ins items how many add-ins you add to your Excel spreadsheet. In the example below the add-in is deskPDF

Figure 1.19
Add-Ins tab showing group of items

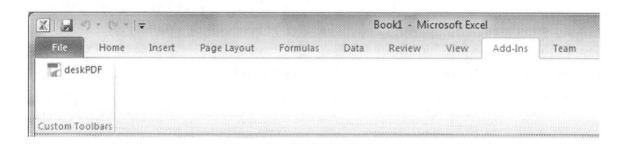

1.4.9 The Team Tab Ribbon of Microsoft Excel

The Team tab ribbon contains four groups of items including Work Items group, Tree groups, Reports group, and Help group.

Figure 1.20
Team tab showing group of items

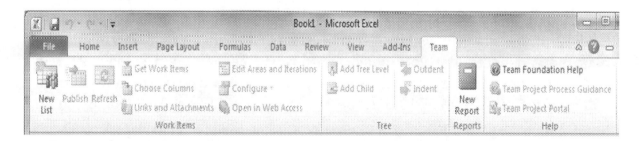

The New List tool allows user to connect to Team project collections and also allowing user to view the work of other members in the team.

1.5 The Basic Facts about Microsoft Excel

The Excel latest versions (versions 2007 and 2010) however do not support certain previous versions of certain types of spreadsheet files. Excel 2010 does not support the following:

- Excel Chart (Excel 2.0, 3.0, and 2.x file formats) (.xlc)
- Lotus 1-2-3 file formats (all versions) (.wk1, .wk2, .wk3, .wk4, .wks)
- Microsoft Works (all versions) (.wks)
- DBASE II- V file format (.dbf)
- Quattro Pro for MS-DOS file format (.wq1)
- Quattro Pro 5.0 and 7.0 for Windows (.wb1, .wb3)

Microsoft Excel 2010 supports the use of an XML-based file format called the Microsoft Office Open XML format. This file format as mentioned earlier carries the filename extension **.xlsx** for Excel workbooks and **.xlsm** for macro-enabled workbooks. The XML-based file format — introduced in Excel 2007 — is more efficient, resulting in smaller file sizes and offering superior integration with external data sources. Excel 2010 automatically saves any new workbook you create with the **.xlsx** extension unless you choose to save the file in a different format.

Fortunately, Excel 2010 has no trouble opening any workbook files saved in the **.xls** file format used by Excel versions 97 through 2003. More importantly, the program automatically saves all editing changes you make to these files in this original file format, and warns you if you add a new Excel 2010 or 2007 element to the existing workbook that is not supported by earlier versions.

Excel 2010 also supports a binary file format called Office Excel 2010 Binary, or **BIFF12**, that carries the **.xlsb** filename extension. Select this binary format for huge spreadsheets that you create that have to be backward compatible with earlier versions of Excel. If you are working in an office where all the workbooks you produce with Excel 2010 must be saved in the old Excel 97-2003 file format for compatibility, you can change the program's default **Save** setting so that the program always saves all new workbooks in the older file format. To do this, open the **Save** tab of the **Excel Options dialog box** (File>>Options>>Save) and then select Excel 97-2003 Workbook in the **Save Files in This Format** drop-down list box.

1.5.1 Displaying filename extensions within Excel

By default, filename extensions such as **.xlsx** and **.xls** do not appear as part of the filename in the Save As dialog box. However, you can change a setting in Windows to display these filename extensions by following these steps:

1. **Open Windows Explorer.**
   You can do this quickly by opening any folder on your desktop.
2. **Choose Tools>>Folder Options.**
   You may need to press the Alt key in order to see the menu bar. The Folder Options dialog box appears.
3. **Click the View tab.**
4. **Remove the check mark from the Hide Extensions for Known File Types option.**
5. **Click OK.**

1.5.2 Common Facts about Microsoft Excel

There are certain common facts the reader should remember about excel worksheets.

1. Cell Address is the combination of a column label and a row number.
2. Excel Format Anything as Text Upon Entry.
3. Excel Quick Math.
4. What does the # (number sign) mean when displayed in cells?
5. Entering Fractions in Excel spreadsheet begins with 0.
6. A message appears when attempting to add rows or columns.
7. More than 255 worksheets can be created in a workbook in Excel 2010.
8. That sheet is "History" – No worksheet can be named as "History".
9. Turn off the gridline display"- The gridlines can be turned off.
10. What happened to the Function Wizard?
11. Generate Random Numbers Between Two Stated Values
12. Excel: Quickly Clear All Spreadsheet Formatting
13. Excel: Shortcut to Insert Time/Date in Excel or Access
14. Excel: I want to print my worksheet but hide all of the values that are under certain limit is possible.
15. Excel: Concatenate Cells (Combine Cell Data)

1. Cell Address is a combination of a column label and a row number.

The cell name or address is always a combination of the label of a column and the row number. For example A1, A2, B1 and B2 where A and B are column labels, and 1 and 2 are row numbers. (show figure....)

2. Excel Formats Anything as Text Upon Entry

Excel automatically evaluates cell information when you press Enter. For instance, if you type a web address, pressing enter automatically turns this information into a hyperlink. Dates equivalents are also formatted upon entry automatically. For instance, when you enter 11/2, excel will format it as November 2, 2011 of the current year. If you want the information to be treated strictly as text and not be converted, just type an apostrophe as the first character in the cell.

3. Excel Quick Math

Excel has a built-in functionality to serve as a quick calculator - for more than just quick sums. Select cells that contain numbers only. For non-contiguous cells, press the Ctrl key and click to select. Look at the Status bar at the bottom of the window and you will see calculations. Alternate-click to change the type of calculation performed, alternate-click on the status bar and change the calculation to average, count, numerical count, minimum, maximum or sum. This was available in previous versions but not nearly as intuitive.

4. What does the # (number sign) mean when displayed in cells?

Most often, the reason for the # symbol displaying in a cell instead of the resulting value is that the column width is not large enough to display the contents. Resize the column and it should fix the problem. There is one other reason why the # symbol would show instead of numbers. If you have a formula that subtracts one time value from another and the result is a negative number, the number symbols will appear.

5. Entering Fractions in Excel

If you type a fraction into a cell that has not been preformatted for fractions, you will get a date value instead of what you typed. For instance, type 1/2 in cell A1, press Enter, and Excel translates this into January 2. To return a fraction value, type 0 1/2 and press Enter. This is the same for previous versions of Excel.

6. Excel 2007: A message appears when attempting to add rows or columns

Excel 2007 gives you a lot more real estate to work with. Typically you can insert rows and columns at will with one exception. If you are in the last available column (XFD) or row (1,048,576) you get a message box warning.

7. Excel 2007: More than 255 worksheets

You can have up to 255 worksheets in a new workbook. However, once the workbook is created, you **can add more worksheets up to what the amount of your computer's memory can handle.**

8. Excel 2007: That sheet is "History"

Can you insert a worksheet and name it history? You cannot, because this is a reserved name for a track changes or history feature in Excel. If you attempt to copy or add a worksheet with an existing sheet name, Excel will put a number next to the worksheet name.

9. Turn off the gridline display"

On the View tab, in the Show/Hide group, uncheck the option for Gridlines. This affects the active worksheet only.

10. What happened to the Function Wizard?

It actually still exists in Excel; it's now called **the Insert Function dialog box** now.

11. Generate Random Numbers Between Two Stated Values

There are websites that will generate random numbers for you; however, you can use an Excel function for the same purpose. Click in any cell and type **=RANDBETWEEN(1,50)** and press Enter to generate a random number between these two values. Use AutoFill to add random numbers to other cells on the worksheet. This example will generate random numbers between 1 and 50.

12. Quickly Clear All Spreadsheet Formatting

Press Ctrl+A to select all cells in the worksheet. From the Edit menu, choose Clear under Formats menu. Excel Insert a Return into an Excel Cell. To insert a hard return in a cell press ALT+Enter.

13. Excel: Shortcut to Insert Time/Date in Excel or Access

Use the following shortcut keys to insert the current time and date in a Microsoft Access table or Excel worksheet.

- Current date**: Press Ctrl+;** (semicolon)
- Current time**: Press Ctrl+Shift+;** (semicolon)
- Current date and time**: Press Ctrl+;** (semicolon), press the **Spacebar** and then **Ctrl+Shift+;** (semicolon)

Note: When you insert the date and time using this tip, the information remains static. To update this information automatically, you must use the **TODAY** and **NOW** functions.

14. Wanting to print my worksheet but hide all of the values that are under certain limit. This is possible

You can do this by applying conditional formatting. Select the entire worksheet (press **Ctrl+A**). From the Format menu, choose Conditional Formatting. Under **Condition 1**, set the following: *Cell Value Is - Less Than - 500*. Click the Format button. Click the drop-down arrow under Color and select **White**. Click OK twice to close the dialog boxes. All numerical values under **500** are formatted as white and will not show when printing unless your background is set to a darker color. In the event that you have color applied the worksheet, set the font color for the conditional the same as the background color.

15. Excel: Concatenate Cells (Combine Cell Data)

To join two or more cells, follow these steps:

i.   In cell A1, type your first name.
ii. Type your last name in cell A2.
iii. Click in Cell A3 and type **=A1&" "&A2**. Press Enter
iv. Or =CONCATENATE(A1, " ",A2)

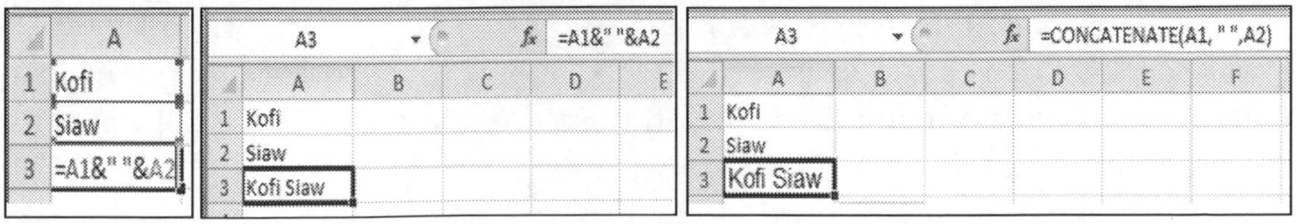

Figure 1.21 Concatenate two Cells Using Operator "**&**" and **Concatenate** Function

1.6 Assignment Questions

Answer the following project questions by showing all the appropriate steps that should be followed to arrive at the answer for each question.

1. What's a Spreadsheet? Briefly describe the basic concepts and elements of a spreadsheet.
   a. Differentiate the following terms: - workbook, worksheet, and cell.

2. Describe a Cell Address in a spreadsheet.

3. Filename extensions such as .xlsx, .xls .wk1, .wk2, .wk3, .wk4, .wks, and **wb3**, the default extensions for a spreadsheet. Name the type of spreadsheet and the year versions.

4. How will you insert a Comment in the cell of worksheet?

5. By default the workbook displays how many worksheets? How many maximum worksheets can be displayed in modern spreadsheet?

6. What is the effect of pressing ALT+F11 in excel 2007/2010?

7. What is a Row of cell? How many maximum rows can Excel 2010 handle?

8. What is a Column of cell? How many maximum rows can Excel 2010 handle?

9. Name the first electronic spreadsheet and which platform it ran. Briefly describe the features of this first electronic spreadsheet. .

10. How do you define a formula or equation in spreadsheet?
    a. Given the following formula: **=IF(SUM(B1:B6) > 100**
       What will happen when SUM (B1:B6) is 120?

    b. Given the following formula: **=RANDBETWEEN(1,50)**
       What will happen when you press enter?

11. How do you open Microsoft Excel?

12. How to insert formulas into Excel?

13. Describe how to use cell references in a formula.

14. How to use Autosum?

15. Describe how to merge cells in Excel , A1 and 1B.

16. Describe how to fill a cell with color.

17. Show the steps of how to add boarders in Excel worksheet.

18. Describe how to change the column width and row height.

19. How to change numbers into currency ($) format?

20. How to change font style and font size in Excel?

21. How to change font colors?

22. In a cell, what would you type in in order to add 25 and 75 together?

23. In a cell, what would you type to multiply 33 and 35?

24. In a cell, what would you type to divide 360 by 15?

1.7 Multiple Choice Questions 25-45

When you think that you are familiar with each of the buttons take the short quiz below from 25 to 31.

	A	B	C	D	
25					You have completed the worksheet and want to make certain that you have not made spelling or grammar errors. Which button do you select? A B C D
26	Σ				Text is highlighted and you want to remove the selection from the active document and place it on the clipboard. Which button do you select? A B C D
27					You have made a change to the active document and want to make certain that those changes are saved. Which button do you select? A B C D
28		Σ			You want to get a quick sum of a column of numbers. Which button do you select? A B C D
29					The worksheet had been checked for spelling errors, it has been saved, and now you are ready to print. Which button do you select? A B C D
30					A worksheet which has been saved into a folder on your computer is to be opened so changes can be made. Which button do you select? A B C D
31					The worksheet had been checked for spelling and has been saved. Before sending it to the printer you want to see how it will look. Which button do you select? A B C D

32. What is shortcut key to open cell format window?
    A. Ctrl+1
    B. Ctrl+F
    C. Ctrl+4
    D. Ctrl+Shift+Enter

33. Ctrl+B key makes the shortcut for making font in selected cell bold.
    A. True
    B. False

34.   **is icon on standard toolbar for following purpose.**

    A. Copy
    B. Paste
    C. Painter
    D. Format Painter

35.   **is icon on standard toolbar for following purpose.**

    A. Chart
    B. Formatting
    C. Conditional Formatting
    D. Editing Chart

36. This button Σ represents:
    A. The AutoCorrect button
    B. The AutoFormat button
    C. The AutoSum button
    D. The conditional format button
    E. None of the above

37. Labels are aligned at the _____ edge of the cell.
    A. left
    B. right
    C. top
    D. bottom

38. You can complete a cell entry by pressing.
    A. enter
    B. tab
    C. shift+tab
    D. an arrow key
    E. another cell

39. The default font keyed in a new work book Excel 2010 is.
    A. 12 pt. Times New Romans
    B. 10 pt. Arial
    C. 12 pt. Bradley Hand ITC
    D. 10 pt. Times New Roman
    E. 11 pt. Calibri

40. A_____ is a group of cells that form a rectangle on the screen.
    A. label
    B. workbook
    C. worksheet
    D. column
    E. range

41. On an Excel sheet the active cell is indicated by ____.
    a. a dark wide border
    b. a dotted border
    c. a blinking border
    d. none of the above

42. To select a column the easiest method is to _____.
    A. double-click any cell in the column
    B. drag from the top cell in the column to the last cell in the column
    C. click the column heading
    D. click the column label

43. If you press _____, the cell accepts your typing as its contents but the focus stays in the cell.
    A. ENTER
    B. CTRL + ENTER
    C. TAB
    D. INSERT

44. How do you know a range is active?
    A. It is highlighted on the screen.
    B. It has a marquee around it.
    C. The data changes to Bold to let me know it's active
    D. I'm psychic & I just Know!!

45. True or False. A range has an address called an range address?
    A. True
    B. False

CHAPTER 2

Editing Spreadsheet Applications

Objectives:

- o *Editing Cell Contents*
- o *Cutting, Copying, and Pasting Cells, and Moving Cells Using the Mouse*
- o *Using the Paste Special Command and Office Clipboard*
- o *Checking Your Spelling and Find and Replace*
- o *Inserting and Deleting Cells, Rows, and Columns*
- o *Using Cell Comments and Tracking Changes*

2. Editing Cell Contents

Once you have entered data into a cell, you can edit, clear, or replace those cell contents.

Exercise: (*Refer to figure 2.1 below for this exercise*)

Open Excel Worksheet and rename the Sheet1 as "**Expenses 2011**". Now edit Cell **D16** so it reads "**Expenses For 2011**" and Cell **D26** so it reads "Total Expenses." Then replace the contents of cell **D22** with "Lucy Siaw Afriyie". Clear cells **B18:B25**.

Figure 2.1 2010 Expenses Worksheet For Editing

	F27		f_x			
	B	C	D	E	F	G
16			**2010**			
17						
18	Item No	Date	Name	Amount	Rate	Equivalent GH¢
19	1	1/7/2010	Yaw Sego	360	1.41882	496.59
20	2	2/13/2010	George Oteng Mensah	510	1.41544	707.72
21	3	3/27/2010	George Oteng Mensah	260	1.4048	351.2
22	4	3/27/2010	Emilia Konadu Sarfo	370	1.4048	505.73
23	5	6/6/2010	Eric Owusu Siaw	159	1.4045	210.69
24	6	6/23/2010	Postage for 3 Books	79.63	1.4045	111.84
25	7	7/15/2010	Philomena Mensah	209	1.41135	282.27
26				1947.63		2666.04

2.1 Edit cell contents

1. Double-click the cell you want to edit.
   The cell is in edit mode
   Other Ways to Enter Edit Mode:
   Select the cell and press <F2>

2. Edit the contents of the cell in the cell.
   Use the arrow keys and the Delete and
   <Backspace> keys to help you with the cell
   Contents

3. Press <Enter>
   Other Ways to Edit Cell Contents
   Select the cell, then edit the cell's options
   In the Formula Bar and. Press <Enter> of
   Click the **Enter** button on the Formula bar

2.2 Replace cell contents

1. Select the cell
2. Type new text or data
3. Press <Enter>
   The newly typed information replaces the previous cell contents

2.3 Clear cell contents

1. Select the cell.
2. Press <Delete>

   Other Ways to Clear Cell Contents:
   Under the Home tab on
   the Ribbon, click the **Clear**
   button in the Editing
   group.

   Tip: Note that this clears the
   cell contents, not the

Figure 2.2 2010 Expenses Worksheet

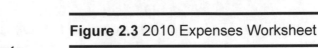
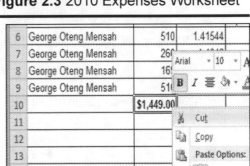

Figure 2.3 2010 Expenses Worksheet

Figure 2.4 Clear Contents in Contextual Menu

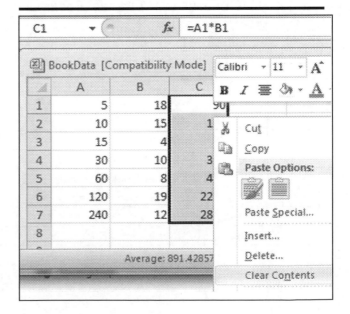

2.4 Cutting, Copying, and Pasting Cells

You can move information around in an Excel worksheet by cutting or copying and then pasting the cell data in a new place. You can work with one cell at a time or ranges of cells. You may cut, copy, and paste any item in a worksheet such as clip art or a picture, in addition to cell data.

2.4.1 Copy cells

When you copy a cell, the selected cell data remains in its original location and is added to the Clipboard.

1. Select the cell(s) you want to copy.

   Tip: If you want to cut or copy only selected parts of a cell's contents, double-click the cell to display a cursor and select the characters you want to cut.

2. Click the Home tab on the Ribbon and click the Copy button in the Clipboard group.
   Other Ways to Copy Cells:
   Press <**Ctrl**> + <**C**>. Or, right-click the selection and select **Copy** from the contextual menu.

Exercise: Copy cell B6 and paste it in Cell B9. Then cut cell A4 and paste it over the contents in cell B6.

Figure 2.5 Copying Cell Content

	A	B	C
4	30	10	300
5	60	8	480
6	120	19	2280
7	240	12	2880
8			
9		19	
10			(Ctrl) ▾
11			

A moving dashed border appears around a cell or cell range when you cut or copy it.

The Paste Options Smart Tag appears after pasting Click this button to specify how information is pasted into your worksheet

2.4.2 Cut Cells

When you *cut* a cell, it is removed from its original location and placed in a temporary storage area called the Clipboard.

1. Select the cell(s) you want to cut.
2. Click the **Home** tab on Ribbon and click the **Cut** button in the Clipboard group.
   A line of marching ants appears around the selected cells and the message "Select destination and press **ENTER** or choose Paste "appears on the status bar.

> **Other Ways to Cut Cells:**
> Press <**Ctrl**> + <**X**>. Or, right-click the selection and select **Cut** from the contextual menu.
> **Tip:** When you cut cells, you have a shortcut to pasting them: select the destination and press <**Enter**>

2.4.3 Paste Cells

After cutting or copying, select a new cell and paste the item that you last cut or copied into the worksheet.

1. Select the cell where you want to paste a range of cells you only have to designate the first cell where you want to paste the cell range.

2. Click the Home tab on the Ribbon and click the Paste button on the Clipboard group.
    The cut or copied cell that is pasted in the new location.

    Other Ways to Paste Cells

    Press <**Ctrl**>+<**V**>. Or, right-click where you want to paste and select paste from the contextual menu.

3. Press <**Enter**>

    The line of marching ants around the selected cell disappears.

Figure 2.6 Paste Options Smart Tag offers a list of pasting options

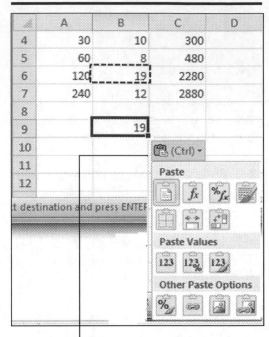

Paste Options Smart Tag

Tips: After pasting, a Paste Options Smart Tag may appear. Click this button to specify how information is pasted into your worksheet.

You may specify what you want to paste by using the Paste Special Command. Click the **Paste** button list arrow in the Clipboard group and select **Paste Special** from the list. Choose a paste option in the Paste Special dialog box.

To collect and paste multiple items, open the Office Clipboard.

2.5 Moving and Copying Cells Using the Mouse

Using the mouse to move and copy cells is even faster and more convenient than using the cut, copy and paste commands.

1. Select the cell(s) you want to move.
2. Point to the border of the cell or cell range.
3. Click and hold the mouse button.
4. Drag the pointer to where you want to move the selected cell(s) and then release the mouse button.

Tips: Press and hold the <Ctrl> key while clicking and dragging to copy the selection.

Exercise: Move the cell range A2:F9 down one row

The screen tip previews the address of the cell range as it is moved.

Figure 2.7
Moving a cell range using the mouse.

	A	B	C	D	E	F
1	Item No	Date	Name	Amount	Rate	Equivalent GH¢
2						
3	1	1/7/2010	Yaw Sego	360	1.41882	496.59
4	2	2/13/2010	George Ot	510	1.41544	707.72
5	3	3/27/2010	George Ot	260	1.4048	351.2
6	4	3/27/2010	Emilia Kon	370	1.4048	505.73
7	5	6/6/2010	Eric Owus	159	1.4045	210.69
8	6	6/23/2010	Postage fo	79.63	1.4045	111.84
9	7	7/15/2010	Philomena	209	1.41135	282.27
10	Total			1947.63		2666.04

2.6 Using the Office Clipboard

If you do a lot of cutting, copying, and pasting you will appreciate the Office Clipboard, which collects and pastes multiple items from Excel and other office programs.

1. Click the Home tab on the Ribbon and click the Dialog Box Launcher in the Clipboard group.
   The Clipboard task pane appears along the left side of the window.

2. Cut and copy items you normally would. The Clipboard can hold 4 items at a time. The icon next to each item indicates the program the item is from. Icons in the Clipboard Task Pane for examples of some common icons.

3. Click where you want to paste an item from the Clipboard.

4. Click the item in the Clipboard.

Tips: While the Clipboard is displayed, each cut or copied item is saved to the Clipboard. If the Clipboard is not displayed, the last cut or copied item is replaced.

Exercise: Display the Clipboard. Copy the cell range B3:F3, then copy the cell range A4:A12. In cell B14, paste the copied B3:F3 range from the Clipboard. Close the Clipboard. Clear the contents of cells B14:F14.

Table 2.1
Icons in the Clipboard Task Pane

	Content cut or copied from a Microsoft Excel Workbook.
	Content cut or copied from a Microsoft PowerPoint presentation.
	Content cut or copied from a Microsoft Word document.
	Cut or copied graphic object.
	Web page contents cut or copied from a Web browser.
	Content cut or copied from a program Microsoft Office.

- As long as the Clipboard is open, it collects items that are cut or copied from all Office programs.

- To remove an item from the Clipboard, click the item's list arrow and select Delete. Click the Clear All button in the task pane to remove all items from the Clipboard.

- Click the Options button near the bottom of the task pane to control how the Clipboard operates.

Figure 2.8
A worksheet with the Clipboard task pane displayed

Copied and out items appear in the Clipboard task pane.

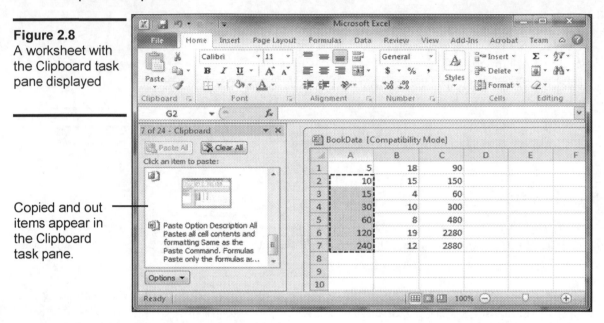

2.7 Using the Paste Special Command

Excel's Paste Special command lets you specify exactly what you want to copy and paste. For example, you can use the Paste Special command to replace the formula with its calculated value.

1. Copy or cut an item as you normally would.
2. Click the cell where you want to paste the item.
3. Click the Home tab and click the Paste button list arrow in the Clipboard group.

Use one of the paste special options that appear in the list, or open the Paste Special dialog box.

Exercise: Use the paste special command to replace the formula in cell range F4:F9 with their calculated values. Type "Home Exp." In cell A12 and enter the formula = C4-C10 in C12. Copy cell C12 and paste the formula to D12:G12

Figure 2.9 Paste Special Options

Table 2.2 Paste Special Options

Paste Option	Description
All	Pastes all cell contents and formatting. Same as the Paste Command.
Formulas	Paste only the formulas as entered in the formula bar
Values	Pastes only the values as displayed in the cells
Formats	Paste only cell formatting. Same as using the Format Paint button.
Comments	Pastes only comments attached to the cell.
Validation	Pastes data validation rules for the copied cells to the paste area.
All using Source theme	Pastes all cell contents and formatting, including the theme, if one was applied to the source data.
All except borders	Paste all cell contents and formatting applied to the copied cell except borders.
Column widths	Pastes only the width of the source cell's column to the destination cell's column.
Formulas and number formats	Pastes only the formulas and number formats.
Values and number	Pastes only the values and number formats.
Operation(several options)	Specifies which mathematical operation, if any, you want to apply to the copied data.
Skip blanks	Avoids replacing values in your paste area when blank cells occur in the copy area.
Transpose	Changes columns of copied data to rows, and vice versa.
Paste Link	Links the pasted data to the source data by pasting a formula reference to the source data

2.8 Checking Your Spelling

You can use Excel's spell checker to find and correct spelling errors in your worksheets. To check the spelling of a worksheet all at once, use the Spelling dialog box.

1. Click the **Review** tab on the Ribbon and click the **Spelling** button in Proofing group.

Excel begins checking spelling with the active cell.

Tips: Depending on which cell is active when you start the spell check, you may see a dialog box that asks you if you want to start your spell check from the beginning of the sheet. Select Yes.

Other Ways to check Spelling. Press **<F7>**

If Excel finds an error, the Spelling dialog box appears with the misspelling on the "Not in Dictionary" text box. You have several options to choose from when the Spelling dialog box opens:

- **Ignore Once:** Accepts the spelling and moves in to the next spelling error.

> **Exercise:** Run a spell check and correct spelling for entire worksheet.

- **Ignore All:** Accepts the spelling
- and ignores all future occurrences of the word in the worksheet.

Figure 2.10 The Special dialog

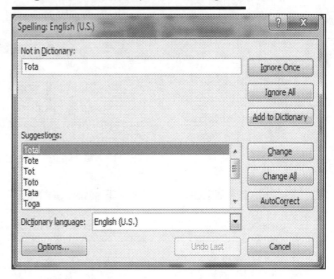

- **Add to Dictionary:** If a word is not recognized in the Microsoft Office Dictionary, it is marked as misspelled. This command adds the word to the dictionary so it is recognized in the future.

- **Change:** Changes the spelling of the word to the spelling that is selected in the Suggestions list.

- **Change All:** Change all occurrences of the word in the worksheet to the selected spelling.

Trap: Exercise caution when using this command – you might end up changing something you didn't want to change.

- **AutoCorrect:** Changes the spelling of the word to the spelling that is selected in the Suggestions list, and adds the misspelled word to the AutoCorrect list so that Excel will automatically fix it whenever you type it in the future.

2. If the word is spelled incorrectly, select the correct spelling from the Suggestions list. Then click **Change, Change All, or AutoCorrect**. If the word is spelled correctly, click **Ignore Once, Ignore All, Add to Dictionary.**

   Excel applies the command and moves on to the next misspelling. Once Excel has finished checking your worksheet for spelling errors, a dialog box appears, telling you the spelling check is complete.

3. Click OK
    The dialog box closes.

    Tips: Excel cannot catch spelling errors that occur because of misuse. For example, if you entered the word "through" when you meant to type "threw," Excel wouldn't catch it because "through" is a correctly spelled word.
    The AutoCorrect feature automatically corrects commonly misspelled words for you as typed.

2.9 Inserting Cells, Rows, and Columns

While working on a worksheet, you may need to insert new cells, columns, or rows. When you insert cells, the existing, cells shift to make room for the new cells.

2.9.1 Insert cells

1. Select the cell or cell range where you want to insert cells.

    The number of cells you select is the number of cells to be inserted.

2. Click the **Home** tab on the Ribbon and click the **Insert** list arrow in the Cells group. Select **Insert Cells**.

    The Insert dialog box appears. Here you can tell Excel how you want to move the existing cells to make room for the new ones by selecting "Shift cells right" or "Shift cells down."

    You can also select "Entire row" or "Entire column" in the Insert dialog box to insert an entire row or column and not just a cell or cells.

3. Select the insert option you want to use and click **OK.**

    The cell(s) are inserted and the existing cells shift.

Exercise: Select cell A7, insert a new cell and shift the existing cells to right. Insert a new row between rows 9 and 10.

Figure 2.11 Inserting a cell in a worksheet

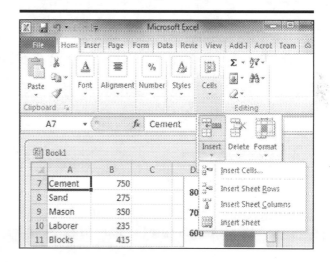

Other Ways to Insert Cells:
Right-click the selected cell(s) and select Insert from the contextual menu. Select an option and click OK.

2.9.2 Insert rows or columns

1. Select the row heading below or column heading to the right of where you want to insert the new row or column.

   The number of row or column headings you select is the number of row or columns that will be inserted.

2. Click the **Home** tab on the Ribbon and click the **Insert** list arrow in the Cells group. Select **Insert Rows** or **Insert Columns.**
   The row or column is inserted. Existing rows are shifted downward, while existing columns are shifted to the right.

   Other Ways Insert Rows or Columns:
   Right-click a row or column heading and select Insert from the contextual menu.

Figure 2.12 The Insert dialog box

2.10 Deleting Cells, Rows, and Columns

You can quickly delete existing cells, columns, or rows from a worksheet. When you delete cells the existing cells shift to fill the space left by the deletion.

2.10.1 Delete Cells

1. Select the cell(s) you want to delete.

2. Click the **Home** tab on the Ribbon and click the **Delete** list from the Cells group. Select **Delete Cells**.

   The Delete dialog box appears. Here you can tell Excel how you want to move the remaining cells to cover the hole left by the selected cell(s) by selecting "Shift cells left" or "Shift cells left up."

Exercise: Delete cell A1 and shift cells to the left. Delete row 10.

Figure 2.13 The Delete dialog box

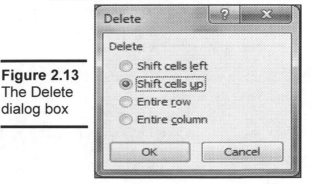

Tip: You can also select **Entire row** or Entire column in the Delete dialog box then delete an entire row or column.

3.   Select an option and click OK.
     The cell(s) are deleted and the remaining cells are shifted.
     Trap: Pressing the <Delete> key only clears a cell's contents, it doesn't delete the actual cell.

     Other Ways to Delete Cells:
     Right-click the selection and select **Delete** from the contextual menu. Select an option and click **OK**.

2.10.2 Delete rows or columns

1.   Select the row or column heading(s) you want to delete.

2.   Click the Home tab on the Ribbon and click the Delete button in the Cells group.

     The rows or columns are deleted. Remaining rows are shifted up, while remaining columns are shifted to the left.

     Other Ways to Delete Rows or Columns:
     Select the column or row heading(s) you want to delete, right-click any of them, and select Delete from the contextual menu. Or, click the Delete list arrow and select Delete Sheet Rows or Delete Sheet Columns. The row or column of the active cell is deleted.

2.11 Using Find and Replace

Don't waste time scanning your worksheet for labels and values that you want to replace with something new:
Excel's find and replace commands can do this for you with just a few clicks of your mouse.

Exercise: Use the Replace feature to find and replace all instances of "Expenses" with "Payment" in the worksheet.

2.11.1 Find

The Find feature makes it very easy to find specific words and values in a worksheet.

1. Click the Home tab on the Ribbon and click the Find & Select but in the Editing group. Select Find from the list.

   The Find tab of the Find and Replace dialog box appears.

   Other Ways to Find Text:
   Press <Ctrl>+<F>.

2. Type the text or value you want to find in the "Find what" text box.

3. Click the **Find Next** button.
   Excel jumps to the first occurrence of the word, phrase, or value that you entered.

4. Click the **Find Next** button again to move on to other occurrences. When you've finished, click **Close**.

Figure 2.14 Find tab of the Find and Replace dialog box

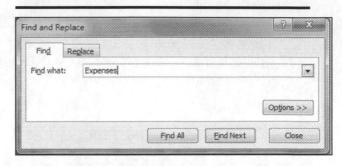

Figure 2.15 Replace tab of the Find and Replace dialog box

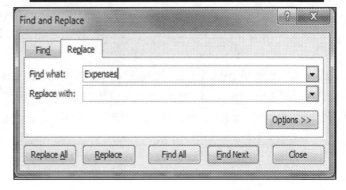

2.11.2 Replace

Replace finds specific words and values, and then replaces them with something else.

1. Click the Home tab on the Ribbon and click the Find & Select button in the Editing group. Select Replace from the list.

   The Replace tab of the Find and Replace dialog box appears.

   Other Ways to Replace Text:
   Press <Ctrl>+<H>.

2. Type the text or value you want replace in the "Find what" text box.
3. Type the replacement text or value in the "Replace with" text box.

4. Click the Find Next button.

Excel jumps to the first occurrence of the word, phrase, or value in the "Find what" box.

5. Choose how you want to replace the text:

- **Replace:** Click to replace the current item.
- **Replace All:** Click to replace each item found in the document. Use this command with caution: you might replace something you didn't want to replace.

6. Click Close, when done.

2.11.3 Search Options

Use Excel's search options to change how Excel searches in the document.

1. Click the More button in the Find and Replace dialog box to specify how to search for text.
Table 2-3: Find and Replace Search Options describes the Search Options available under the Find and Replace tabs.

Trap: If you specify Search Options make sure to turn them off when you have finished. Otherwise, subsequent find or replace commands will use the same search options.

Figure 2.16 The and Replace dialog box with search options displayed

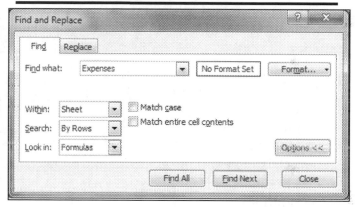

Table 2.3 Find and Replace Search Options

Within	Choose whether to search within just the current sheet or the entire workbook.
Search	Search by rows (left to right, the top to bottom) or columns (top to bottom, then left to right).
Look in	Specify which kinds of data you want to search in, such as formulas, values, or comments.
Match case	Searches exactly as text is typed in the text box.
Match entire cell contents	Searches only for cells that match the contents in the text box entirely. Parts of phrases or words are not included.
Format button	Specify formatting characteristics you want to find attached to the text in the Find what text box.

2.12 Using Cell Comments

Sometimes you may need to add notes to a workbook to document complicated formulas or questionable values, or to leave a comment for another user. Excel's cell comments command helps you document your worksheets and make them easier to understand. Think of cell comments as Post-It Notes that you can attach to any cell. Cell components appear whenever you point at the cell they're attached to.

2.12.1 Insert a comment

1. Click the cell you want to attach a comment to.
2. Click the Review tab on the Ribbon and click the New Comment button in the Comment group.
3. Type a comment.
4. Click outside the comment area when you have finished.

Other Ways to Insert a Comment:
Right-click the cell you want to attach a comment to and select New Comment from the contextual menu. Type a comment.

Figure 2.17 Entering a cell Comment

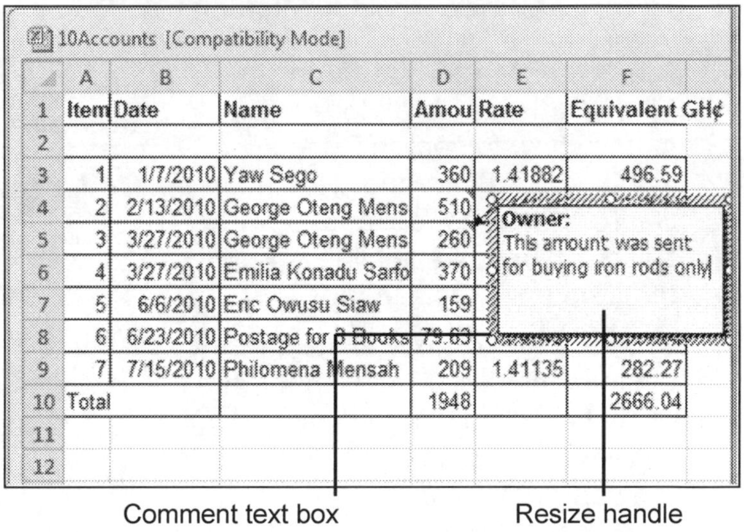

Comment text box   Resize handle

2.12.2 View a comment

1. Point to the red triangle-shaped comment marker that's located in the cell with the comment.

Tip: To display a comment all the time, click the cell with the comment, then click the Review tab on the Ribbon and click the Show/Hide Comments button in the Comments group. Or, click the Show All Comments button in the Comments group to display all the comments in a worksheet at once.

2.12.3 Edit a comment

1. Click the cell that contains the comment you want to edit.
2. Click the Review tab on the Ribbon and click the Edit Comment button in the Comments group.
3. Edit the comment.

You can change the size of a comment text box by clicking and dragging one of the eight sizing handles that surrounds the comment.

4. Click outside the comment area when you're finished.
   Other Ways to Edit a Comment:
   Right-click the cell with the comment you want to edit and select **Edit Comment** from the contextual menu. Edit the comment.

2.12.4 Delete comment

1. Click the cell that contains the comment you want to delete.
2. Click the Review tab on the Ribbon and click the Delete option of the Comments group.
   Other Ways to Delete Comment:
   Right-click the cell you want to delete and select Delete Comment from the contextual menu.

2.13 Tracking Changes

You can track changes made to a workbook, allowing easier collaboration with other users. When you choose to track changes, Excel also shares your workbook.

> Exercise: Turn on track changes while editing. Change cell A1 to "Revenue" and change B4 to "4000". Accept both of the changes.

2.13.1 Track changes

1. Click the **Review** tab on the Ribbon, click the Track Changes button in the Changes group, and select **Highlight Changes**.

   The Highlight Changes dialog box appears.

2. Click the **Track Changes** while editing check box.
3. Click the highlighting options you want to use and click **OK**.

Another dialog box appears, confirming that the workbook will be saved, and will now become a shared workbook.

4. Click **OK**
5. Make changes to the shared workbook.
   After you make a change, a cell comment appears in the affected cell, describing the change that was made and who made it.

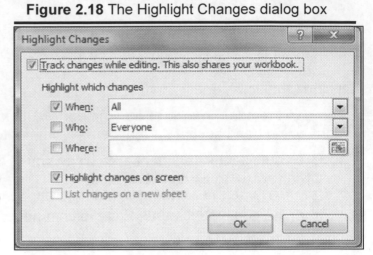

Figure 2.18 The Highlight Changes dialog box

2.13.2 Accept/reject changes

Once changes have been made and tracked in a workbook, you may decide whether to accept or reject those changes.

1. Click the **Review** tab on the Ribbon, click the **Track Changes** button in the Changes group, and select **Accept/Reject Changes**.

   A message appears, telling you that the workbook will be saved.

2. Click **OK**

   The Select Changes to Accept or Reject dialog box appears. Use the commands to tell Excel which changes you want to accept or reject.

3. Click **OK**

   The Accept or Reject Changes dialog box appears, displaying the changes that have been made to the document.

4. Click the **Accept** or **Reject** buttons as each change is highlighted.

2.14 Cancel or undo edits

Before you press **ENTER** or **TAB**, and before or after you press **F2**, you can press **ESC** to cancel any edits that you made to the cell contents.
After you press **ENTER** or **TAB**, you can undo your edits by pressing **CTRL+Z**, or by clicking **Undo** on the **Quick Access Toolbar**.

Adjust the way cell contents are displayed

After you edit cell contents, you may want to adjust the way they are displayed.
At times, a cell might display **#####.** This can occur when the cell contains a number or a date and the width of its column cannot display all the characters that its format requires. For example, suppose a cell with the Date format "**mm/dd/yyyy**" contains **12/31/2007.** However, the column is only wide enough to display six characters. The cell will display **#####.** To see the entire contents of the cell with its current format, you must increase the width of the column.

Change the width of a column

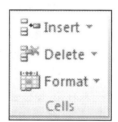

1. Click the cell for which you want to change the column width.
2. On the Home tab, in the Cells group, click Format.
3. Under Cell Size, do one of the following:
   - To fit all text in the cell, click **AutoFit Column Width.**
   - To specify a larger column width, click **Column Width**, and then type the width that you want in the **Column width** box.

NOTE: As an alternative to increasing the width of a column, you can change the format of that column or even an individual cell. For example, you could change the date format so that a date is displayed as only the month and day ("**mm/dd**" format), such as **12/31**, or represent a number in a Scientific (exponential) format, such as **4E+08**.
- If there are multiple lines of text in a cell, some of the text might not be displayed the way that you want. You can display multiple lines of text inside a cell by wrapping the text.

NOTE: When Excel is in **Edit mode**, you cannot change the way text wraps.

2.14.1 Wrap text in a cell

1. Click the cell in which you want to wrap the text.
2. On the Home tab, in the **Alignment** group, click **Wrap Text.**

NOTE: If the text is a single long word, the characters won't wrap; you can widen the column or decrease the font size to see all the text. If not all text is visible in the cell after you wrap the text, you may need to adjust the height of the row.
On the Home tab, in the **Cells** group, click **Format**, and then under **Cell Size** click **AutoFit Row.**

2.14.2 Exit Edit mode

To stop working in Edit mode, do one of the following:
- Press **ENTER.**

Excel exits the Edit mode and selects the cell directly below the current cell.
You can also specify that by pressing **ENTER** to select a different adjacent cell.

1. Click the **Microsoft Office Button** or click **File** in Excel 2010, click Excel Options, and then click the **Advanced** category.
2. Under **Editing options**, do one of the following:

   - To make the selection remain in the cell that you were editing, clear the **After pressing Enter**, **move selection** check box.
   - To control the direction of the selection, select the **After pressing Enter**, **move selection** check box, click the arrow next to **Direction**, and then select a direction from the list.

   - Press **TAB**.
     This stops Edit mode and selects the cell to the right of the current cell. Pressing SHIFT+TAB selects the cell to the left.

   - Click a different cell.
     Excel exits Edit mode and selects the cell that you clicked.
   - Press **F2**.
     Excel exits Edit mode and leaves the cursor where it is.

2.14.3 Enter data in multiple worksheets at the same time

In Excel 2007 and 2010, it's possible to enter the same data into several worksheets without retyping or copying and pasting the text into each one. As an example, let's say you want to put the same title text into different worksheets. One way to do this is to type the text in one worksheet, and then copy and paste the text into the other worksheets. If you have several worksheets, this can be very tedious.

An easier way to do this is to use the **CTRL** key to group worksheets. When worksheets are grouped, whatever you do to one worksheet affects all other worksheets.

1. Start Excel. A new, blank workbook appears.
2. Press and hold the CTRL key, and then click Sheet1, Sheet2, and Sheet3.
   This temporarily groups the worksheets. In the title bar, you should see the name of the workbook followed by the word [Group].
3. Click in cell A1 in Sheet1, and then type:
   This data will appear in each sheet.
4. Click Sheet2 and notice that the text you just typed in Sheet1 also appears in cell A1 of Sheet2. The text also appears in Sheet3.
   TIP: When you click another worksheet, Excel automatically ungroups the worksheets for you.

2.14.4 Fill data automatically in worksheet cells

Instead of entering data manually on a worksheet, you can use the Auto Fill feature to fill cells with data that follows a pattern or that is based on data in other cells. This section does not explain how to enter data manually or enter data simultaneously on multiple worksheets. For information about how to manually enter data, see the section Enter data manually below.

2.14.5 Enter data manually in worksheet cells

You have several options when you want to enter data manually in Excel. You can enter data in one cell, in several cells at the same time, or on more than one worksheets at once. Worksheet is the primary document that you use in Excel to store and work with data. It is also called a spreadsheet. A worksheet consists of cells that are organized into columns and rows; a worksheet is always stored in a workbook. The data that you enter can be numbers, text, dates, or times. You can format the data in a variety of ways. And, there are several settings that you can adjust to make data entry easier for you.

This topic does not explain how to use a data form to enter data in worksheet. For more information about working with data forms, see Add, edit, find, and delete rows by using a data form.

 Important: If you cannot enter or edit data in a worksheet, it might have been protected by you or someone else to prevent data from being changed accidentally. On a protected worksheet, you can select cells to view the data, but you won't be able to type information in cells that are locked. In most cases, you should not remove the protection from a worksheet unless you have permission to do so from the person who created it. To unprotect a worksheet, click **Unprotect Sheet** in the **Changes** group on the **Review** tab. If a password was set when the worksheet protection was applied, you must first type that password to unprotect the worksheet.

2.14.6 Enter text or a number in a cell

TIP: To enter data on a new line within a cell, enter a line break by pressing **ALT+ENTER**

2.14.7 Enter a number that has a fixed decimal point

1. Click the Microsoft Office Button, and then click Excel Options.
3. Click Advanced, and then under Editing options, select the Automatically insert a decimal point check box.
4. In the Places box, enter a positive number for digits to the right of the decimal point or a negative number for digits to the left of the decimal point.

For example, if you enter 3 in the Places box and then type 2834 in a cell, the value will appear as 2.834. If you enter -3 in the Places box and then type 283, the value will be 283000.

5. On the worksheet, click a cell, and then enter the number that you want.
   NOTE: Data that you typed in cells before selecting the Fixed decimal option is not affected.
   TIP: To temporarily override the Fixed decimal option, type a decimal point when you enter the number.

2.14.8 Enter a date or a time in a cell

1. On the worksheet, click a cell.
2. Type a date or time as follows:
   - To enter a date, use a slash mark or a hyphen to separate the parts of a date; for example, type 9/5/2002 or 5-Sep-2002.
   - To enter a time that is based on the 12-hour clock, enter the time followed by a space, and then type **a** or **p** after the time; for example, 9:00 p. Otherwise, Excel enters the time as AM.
     TIP: To enter the current date and time, press CTRL+SHIFT+; (semicolon).
      NOTES
   - To enter a date or time that stays current when you reopen a worksheet, you can use the TODAY and NOW functions.
   - When you enter a date or a time in a cell, it appears either in the default date or time format for your computer or in the format that was applied to the cell before you entered the date or time. The default date or time format is based on the date and time settings in the Regional and Language Options dialog box (Control Panel). If these settings on your computer have been changed, the dates and times in your workbooks that have not been formatted by using the Format Cells command are displayed according to those settings.
   - To apply the default date or time format, click the cell that contains the date or time value, and then press **CTRL+SHIFT+#** or **CTRL+SHIFT+@.**

2.14.9 Enter the same data into several cells at the same time

1. Select the cells into which you want to enter the same data. The cells do not have to be adjacent.
   TIP: To cancel a selection of cells, click any cell on the worksheet.

2. In the active cell, type the data, and then press **CTRL+ENTER**.

TIP: You can also enter the same data into several cells by using the fill handle  to automatically fill data in worksheet cells. For more information, see the article Fill data automatically in worksheet cells.

2.14.10 Enter the same data on several worksheets at the same time

By making multiple worksheets active at the same time, you can enter new data or change existing data on one of the worksheets, and the changes are applied to the same cells on all the selected worksheets.

1. Click the tab of the first worksheet that contains the data that you want to edit. Then hold down **CTRL** while you click the tabs of other worksheets in which you want to synchronize the data.

The tabs for worksheets

NOTE: If you don't see the tab of the worksheet that you want, click the tab scrolling buttons to find the worksheet and then click its tab. If you still can't find the worksheet tabs that you want, you might have to maximize the document window.

2. On the active worksheet, select the cell or range in which you want to edit existing or enter new data.
   TIP: To cancel a selection of cells, click any cell on the worksheet.

3. In the active cell, type new data or edit the existing data, and then press **ENTER** or **TAB** to move the selection to the next cell.

4. Repeat the previous step until you have completed entering or editing data.

NOTES
- To cancel a selection of multiple worksheets, click any unselected worksheet. If an unselected worksheet is not visible, you can right-click the tab of a selected worksheet, and then click Ungroup Sheets.

- When you enter or edit data, the changes affect all the selected worksheets and can inadvertently replace data that you didn't mean to change. To help avoid this, you can view all the worksheets at the same time to identify potential data conflicts.

1. On the **View** tab, in the **Window** group, click **New Window**.
2. Switch to the new window, and then click a worksheet that you want to view.
3. Repeat steps 1 and 2 for each worksheet that you want to view.
4. On the **View** tab, in the **Window** group, click **Arrange All**, and then click the option that you want.
   To view worksheets in the active workbook only, select the Windows of active workbook check box.

2.15 Adjust worksheet settings and cell formats

There are several settings in Excel that you can change to help make manual data entry easier. Some changes affect all workbooks, some affect the whole worksheet, and some affect only the cells that you specify.

2.15.1 Change the direction for the ENTER key

When you press **TAB** to enter data in several cells in a row and then press **ENTER** at the end of that row, by default, the selection moves to the beginning of the next row. Pressing **ENTER** moves the selection down one cell, and pressing **TAB** moves the selection one cell to the right. You cannot change the direction of the move for the **TAB** key, but you can specify a different direction for the **ENTER** key. Changing this setting affects the whole worksheet, any other open worksheets, any other open workbooks, and all new workbooks.

1. Click the Microsoft Office Button [icon], and then click Excel Options.
   In Excel 2010 click File, and then click Excel Options.
2. In the **Advanced** category, under **Edit**, select the **After pressing Enter**, **move selection** check box, and then click the direction that you want in the **Direction** box.

2.16 Change the format of a number

In Excel, the format of a cell is separate from the data that is stored in the cell. This display difference can have a significant effect when the data is numeric. For example, when a number that you enter is rounded, usually only the displayed number is rounded. Calculations use the actual number that is stored in the cell, not the formatted number that is displayed. Hence, calculations might appear inaccurate because of rounding in one or more cells.

After you type numbers in a cell, you can change the format in which they are displayed.

1. Click the cell that contains the numbers that you want to format.
2. On the Home tab, in the **Number** group, point to **General**, and then click the format that you want.

TIP: To select a number format from the list of available formats, click **More**, and then click the format that you want to use in the **Category** list.

2.16.1 Format a number as text

For numbers that should not be calculated in Excel, such as phone numbers, you can format them as text by applying the Text format to empty cells before typing the numbers.

1. Select an empty cell.
2. On the Home tab, in the Number group, point to General, and then click Text.

3. Type the numbers that you want in the formatted cell.
NOTE: Numbers that you entered before you applied the **Text** format to the cells need to be entered again in the formatted cells. To quickly reenter numbers as text, select each cell, press **F2**, and then press **ENTER.**

2.16.2 Automatically repeat values that already exist in the column

If the first few characters that you type in a cell match an existing entry in that column, Excel automatically enters the remaining characters for you. Excel automatically completes only those entries that contain text or a combination of text and numbers. Entries that contain only numbers, dates, or times are not automatically completed. After Excel completes what you started typing, do one of the following:

- To accept a proposed entry, press **ENTER.**
  The completed entry exactly matches the pattern of uppercase and lowercase letters of the existing entry.
- To replace the automatically entered characters, continue typing.
- To delete the automatically entered characters, press **BACKSPACE.**

NOTES
- Excel completes an entry only when the cursor is at the end of the current cell contents.
- Excel bases the list of potential AutoComplete entries on the column that contains the active cell. Entries that are repeated within a row are not automatically completed.

2.16.3 Turn off automatic completion of cell values

If you don't want Excel to automatically complete cell values, you can turn off this feature.

1. Click the **Microsoft Office Button** , and then click **Excel Options**.
   In Excel 2010 click **File**, and then click **Excel Options**.
2. Click **Advanced**, and then under **Editing options**, clear or select the Enable AutoComplete for cell values check box to turn automatic completion of cell values on or off.

2.16.4 Find or replace text and numbers on a worksheet

1. In a worksheet, click any cell.
2. On the Home tab, in the Editing group, click Find & Select.
3. Do the following:
    - To find text or numbers, click Find.
    - To find and replace text or numbers, click Replace.

4. In the ***Find what box***, type the text or numbers that you want to search for, or click the arrow in the Find what box, and then click a recent search in the list.
   You can use wildcard characters, such as an asterisk (*) or a question mark (**?**), in your search criteria:

   - Use the asterisk to find any string of characters. For example, **s*d** finds "**sad**" and "**started**".
   - Use the question mark to find any single character. For example, **s?t** finds "**sat**" and "**set**".

   TIP: You can find asterisks, question marks, and tilde characters (~) in worksheet data by preceding them with a tilde character in the Find what box. For example, to find data that contains "?", you would type ~? as your search criteria.

5. Click Options to further define your search, and then do any of the following:
   - To search for data in a worksheet or in an entire workbook, in the **Within** box, select **Sheet** or **Workbook.**
   - To search for data in specific rows or columns, in the **Search** box, click **By Rows** or **By Columns.**
   - To search for data with specific details, in the Look in box, click **Formulas**, **Values,** or **Comments.**
   - To search for case-sensitive data, select the **Match case** check box.
   - To search for cells that contain just the characters that you typed in the **Find what** box, select the **Match entire cell contents** check box.

6. If you want to search for text or numbers that also have specific formatting, click **Format**, and then make your selections in the **Find Format** dialog box.

   TIP: If you want to find cells that just match a specific format, you can delete any criteria in the Find what box, and then select a specific cell format as an example. Click the arrow next to **Format**, click **Choose Format From Cell**, and then click the cell that has the formatting that you want to search for.

7. Do one of the following:
   - To find text or numbers, click Find All or Find Next.

     TIP: When you click **Find All**, every occurrence of the criteria that you are searching for will be listed, and you can make a cell active by clicking a specific occurrence in the list. You can sort the results of a **Find All** search by clicking a column heading.

   - To replace text or numbers, type the replacement characters in the **Replace with** box (or leave this box blank to replace the characters with nothing), and then click **Find** or **Find All.**
     NOTE: If the **Replace with** box is not available, click the **Replace** tab.
     If needed, you can cancel a search in progress by pressing **ESC**.

8. To replace the highlighted occurrence or all occurrences of the found characters, click Replace or Replace All.

Tips:
- Microsoft Office Excel saves the formatting options that you define. If you search the worksheet for data again and cannot find characters that you know to be there, you may need to clear the formatting options from the previous search. On the **Find** tab, click **Options** to display the formatting options, click the arrow next to Format, and then click **Clear Find Format.**
- You can also use the **SEARCH** and **FIND** functions to find text or numbers on a worksheet.

2.16.5 For each cell in column A, have three rows in column B

Problem: For each cell in column A, I want to have three rows in columns B and C, as shown in Figures 2.19 & 2.20. I also want to be able to perform calculations with the values in column C.

You can't easily calculate using numbers in column C.

You can use the **Merge** commands in Excel 2007/2010 to achieve an effect that is similar to the following:

Figure 2.19 The Merged Cells

	A	B	C
1	Samuel	Books	500
2		Soccer	275
3		Tuition	1500
4	Lucy	Books	200
5		Soccer	300
6		Tuition	1100

Merging Cells

Strategy: You might be tempted to use the **Alt+Enter** trick to enter three lines of data in columns B and C. However, this will not work well in column C. Although the numbers are displayed fine, there is no way to have the numbers in C calculate automatically.

To merge cells select **Merge & Center** under Alignment group

Figure 2.20 The Merged Cells

	A	B	C
1	Samuel	Books	500
2		Soccer	275
3		Tuition	1500
4	Lucy	Books	200
5		Soccer	300
6		Tuition	1100
7	Ernest	Books	300
8		Soccer	200
9		Tuition	950

Figure 2.21 Alignment Group

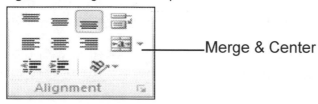

Merge & Center

A better option is to merge cells **A1:A3** into a single cell. You can then let the data in **B** fill **B1:B3**. Here's how:

1. Enter a value in **A1.** Leave cells **A2:A3** blank. Select cells **A1:A3**.

2. Select **Home** – 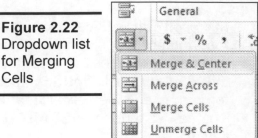 **Merge & Center dropdown**. Choose **Merge Cells**, as shown in Figure 2.21.

Figure 2.22 Dropdown list for Merging Cells

2.17 Assignments & Exercises

Answer the following project questions by showing all the appropriate steps that should be followed to arrive at the answer for each question.

1. When you Open Excel Workbook by you may see three Worksheets Sheet1, Sheet2 and Sheet3. Describe briefly how you will rename the Sheet1 as "Expenses 2011".

2. How will you edit the content of the cell? Briefly describe the process.

3. A cell contains the word "Bright" Describe the following processes:
   a. To replace this cell content with the number 1275.
   b. To clear this cell contents

4. Assuming the name "Bright" was typed in cell B5, describe how to Copy cell B5 and paste it in Cell B8.

5. What will you do in order to remove an item from the Clipboard?
   a. Show how you will remove all items from the Clipboard.

6. Describe how to insert new cells, columns, or rows in a worksheet.
   a. When you insert cells what may occur within the existing cells?
   b. Describe how to delete existing cells, columns, or rows from a worksheet.
   c. What happens to existing cells after the deleting cells?

7. Briefly describe the method to **insert comments** in the cell of worksheet.

8. You can track changes made to a workbook allow easier collaboration with other users. How will you track changes made in a workbook?

9. Describe the process to enter data in multiple worksheets at the same time without copying and pasting on each sheet.

10. Show how to enter the following data types a cell in worksheet:
    a. Enter text or a number in a cell in worksheet.
    b. Enter a number that has a fixed decimal point
    c. Enter a dates or a time in a cell
    d. Format a number as text

2.18 Multiple choice exercises 11- 45

When you think that you are familiar with each of the buttons take the short quiz below from 11 to 17.

	A	B	C	D	
11		B		%	You wish to call attention to a portion of your worksheet by making the text bold. Which button do you select? A B C D
12					You want to center the entries in selected cells. Which button do you select? A B C D
13					Cell A1 is to be stretched so it covers 6 cells Which button do you select? A B C D
14	I		12	$	To call attention to text, you want place a block of color behind the text to highlight it. Which button do you select? A B C D
15			12		Another way to call attention to a block of cells is to place a border around them. Which button do you select? A B C D
16		,		$	A column of numbers represents money and you want to apply currency style. Which button do you select? A B C D
17					A column of numbers has too many decimal places after the decimal point. Which button do you select? A B C D

18. Freeze Panes is option available in which of the following menu.
    A. Tools
    B. Data
    C. Windows
    D. Help

19. Which of following is the shortcut to select font option from Formatting toolbar?
    A. Ctrl+Shift+P
    B. Ctrl+K
    C. Ctrl+Shift+C
    D. Ctrl+Shift+F

20. Can I change the color of the worksheet tabs in my workbook? If yes, what is the shortcut key?
    A. No
    B. Yes, Alt+O+H+T
    C. Yes, Ctrl+O+H+T
    D. Yes, Shift+O+H+T
    E. Yes, Shift+O+H+M

21. True or False. If you choose a larger font size, the height of the row is automatically made taller.
    A. True
    B. False

22. Which button allows you to copy cell formats from one cell to another?
    A. enter
    B. autofit
    C. format painter
    D. esc

23. How do you know a range is active?
    A. It is highlighted on the screen.
    B. It has a marquee around it.
    C. The data changes to Bold to let me know it's active
    D. I'm psychic & I just Know!!

24. True or False. A range has an address called an range address.
    A.   True
    B.   False

25. An example of a range address.
   A. A1:B3
   B. A1;B3
   C. A1-B3
   D. A1=B3
   E. A1*B3

26. When you start to select a range of cells, you will see a thick white, cross shaped pointer called a _____.
   A. cell selector
   B. cell cross
   C. selection pointer
   D. range selector

27. On an Excel sheet the active cell is indicated by ____.
   A. a dark wide border
   B. a dotted border
   C. a blinking border
   D. none of the above

28. To select a column the easiest method is to _____.
   A. double-click any cell in the column
   B. drag from the top cell in the column to the last cell in the column
   C. click the column heading
   D. click the column label

29. If you press _____, the cell accepts your typing as its contents but the focus stays in the cell.
   A. ENTER
   B. CTRL + ENTER
   C. TAB
   D. INSERT

30. A_____ is a group of cells that form a rectangle on the screen.
   A. label
   B. workbook
   C. worksheet
   D. column
   E. range

31. True or False. If you choose a larger font size, the height of the row is automatically made taller.
   A. True
   B. False

32. **Which button allows you to copy cell formats from one cell to another?**
    A. enter
    B. autofit
    C. format painter
    D. esc

33. **When you start to select a range of cells, you will see a thick white, cross shaped pointer called a _____.**
    A. cell selector
    B. cell cross
    C. selection pointer
    D. range selector

34. **The cell reference for a range of cells that starts in cell B1 and goes over to column G and down to row 10 is _____.**
    A. B1-G10
    B. B1.G10
    C. B1;G10
    D. B1:G10

35. **The view that puts a blue line around each page that would be printed is the _____.**
    A. Print Preview
    B. Normal
    C. Page Break Preview
    D. Split View

36. **To select several cells or ranges that are not touching each other, you would _____ while selecting.**
    A. hold down the CTRL key
    B. hold down the SHIFT key
    C. hold down the ALT key
    D. hold down CTRL + SHIFT

37. **To create a chart with the Chart Wizard, you would use which button?**
    A.
    B.
    C.
    D.

38. Using the AutoSum button will place in the selected cell _____.
   A. the sum of values in the cell's column
   B. nothing until you select a range of cells
   C. the sum of the cell's row unless you change the range
   D. a formula which will add values in the range Excel guesses you want to add

39. AutoCalculate will quickly add selected cells if you _____ .
   A. right-click on the status bar and select SUM
   B. click the AutoCalculate button on the toolbar
   C. use the key combo CTRL + $
   D. double-click the selection

40. A certain spreadsheet shows in Page Break Preview that cells in Rows 1 - 25 have white background. The cells in Row 26 that contain data have a dark gray background. When you click the Print button, _____..
   A. nothing will print because some cells with data have been omitted
   B. only the cells with gray background will print
   C. the whole sheet will print
   D. only the cells with white background will print.

41. The default currency and the units used in measurement are set in _____.
   A. Regional Settings or Regional and Language Options
   B. Page Setup
   C. Options
   D. File | User Settings

42. To arrange rows in alphabetical order based on column A, you need to use the command _____.
   A. Tools | Sort
   B. Data | Sort
   C. Edit | Data | Sort
   D. none of the above

43. To edit existing data in a cell without having to retype it all, you should _____.
   A. double-click the cell
   B. click in the Formula bar
   C. hold SHIFT down while clicking the cell
   D. none of the above - you must retype.

44. If you select a cell with a date in it and drag the fill handle down across several cells, what happens is that _____.

A. the date is copied to each cell

B. the date is increased by 1 day into each cell

C. the date is increased by 1 week into each cell

D. nothing as AutoFill applies only to numbers

In the Table below, select which menu you would use to perform the stated action. Answer the questions from 45 to 54

	A	B	C	D	QUESTIONS
45.	File	Edit	View	None	You want to find where the entry "$235.54" appears in your worksheet. Which menu do you select?. Which button do you select? A B C D
46.	File	Edit	View	None	A document was saved to your disk and you want to open it. Which menu do you select? A B C D
47.	File	Edit	View	None	The Formatting toolbar has been removed and you want to add it back to your window. Which menu do you select? A B C D
48.	File	Edit	View	None	You have selected contents of a cell that you want to remove from the worksheet. Which menu do you select? A B C D
49.	File	Edit	View	None	Your spreadsheet is too wide, and you want to turn the page to landscape orientation for printing. Which menu do you select? A B C D
50.	File	Edit	View	None	You have placed comments in several cells and want to see all of them displayed at the same time. Which menu do you select? A B C D
51.	File	Edit	View	None	You have changed a worksheet and now want to save it with a different name. Which menu do you select? A B C D
52.	File	Edit	View	None	The number 234 was entered in a cell, but when you clicked into another cell the data you entered changed to 8/22/04. You want to change it back. Which menu do you select? A B C D
53.	File	Edit	View	None	You want to add a hidden note explaining something about the data in a cell. Which menu do you select? A B C D
54.	File	Edit	View	None	Before you show a worksheet to someone you want to hide one column of data. Which menu do you select? A B C D

CHAPTER 3

Formatting Worksheets in Excel Spreadsheet

Objectives:

- ○ *Create a cell style to highlight cells*
- ○ *Moving Cells Using the Mouse*
- ○ *Using the Paste Special Command and Office Clipboard*
- ○ *Checking Your Spelling and Find and Replace*
- ○ *Inserting and Deleting Cells, Rows, and Columns*
- ○ *Using Cell Comments and Tracking Changes*

3. Highlight Cells

Unlike other Microsoft Office programs, such as Word, Excel does not provide a button that you can use to highlight all or individual portions of data in a cell.

However, you can mimic highlights on a cell in a worksheet by filling the cells with a highlighting color. For a fast way to mimic a highlight, you can create a custom cell style that you can apply to fill cells with a highlighting color. Then, after you apply that cell style to highlight cells, you can quickly copy the highlighting to other cells by using Format Painter.

If you want to make specific data in a cell stand out, you can display that data in a different font color or format.

3.1 Create a cell style to highlight cells

1. On the Home tab, in the Styles group, click Cell Styles.

   TIP: If you do not see the Cell Styles button, in the Styles group, click the More button next to the cell styles box.
2. Click New Cell Style.(*See figure 3.2*)
3. In the Style name box, type an appropriate name for the new cell style.
   TIP: For example, type Highlight.
4. Click Format.

Figure 3.1 The Styles Group.

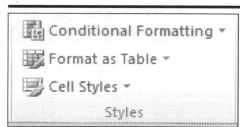

5. In the Format Cells dialog box, on the Fill tab, select the color that you want to use for the highlight, and then click OK.
6. Click OK to close the Style dialog box.
7. The new style will be added under Custom in the cell styles box.
8. On the worksheet, select the cells or ranges of cells that you want to highlight.
9. How to select a cell or a range
10. On the Home tab, in the Styles group, click Cell Styles.

TIP: If you do not see the Cell Styles button, in the Styles group, click the **More** button next to the cell styles box.

TIP: Custom cell styles are displayed at the top of the list of cell styles. If you see the cell styles box in the Styles group, and the new cell style is one of the first six cell styles on the list, you can click that cell style directly in the Styles group.

Figure 3.2 The Format Cells Dialog box (Created highlight Style)

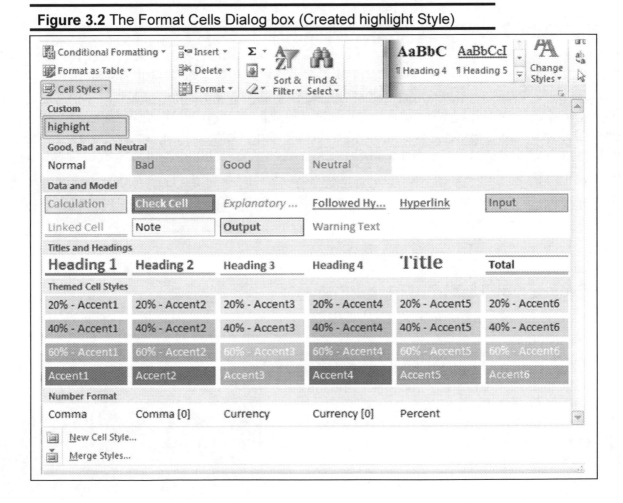

3.2 Use Format Painter to apply a highlight to other cells

1. Select a cell that is formatted with the highlight that you want to use.
2. On the Home tab, in the Clipboard group, double-click Format Painter ✐ and then drag the mouse pointer from E6 across as many cells or ranges of cells that you want to highlight.
3. When you're done, click Format Painter again or press ESC to turn it off.

Figure 3.3
Highlighting the cell range E6:E10 with highlight format style

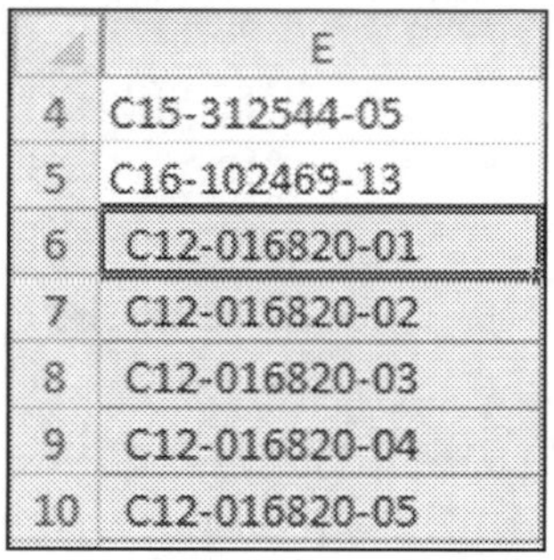

◢	E
4	C15-312544-05
5	C16-102469-13
6	C12-016820-01
7	C12-016820-02
8	C12-016820-03
9	C12-016820-04
10	C12-016820-05

3.3 Display specific data in a different font color or format

1. In a cell, select the data that you want to display in a different color or format.
2. On the Home tab, in the Font group, do one of the following:

- To change the text color, click the arrow next to Font Color 🄰 and then, under Theme Colors or Standard Colors, click the color that you want to use.
- To apply the most recently selected text color, click Font Color 🄰.
- To apply a color other than the available theme colors and standard colors, click More Colors, and then define the color that you want to use on the Standard tab or Custom tab of the Colors dialog box.
- To change the format, click Bold **B**, Italic *I*, or Underline U̲.

Figure 3.4
The Font Group

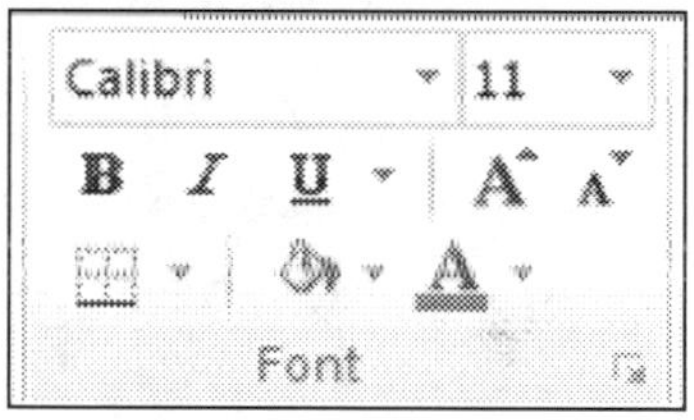

Keyboard shortcut:
You can also press **CTRL+B, CTRL+I,** or **CTRL+U**.

3.4 Insert ASCII or Unicode Latin-based symbols and characters

There are at times, you may be required to insert special characters into a spreadsheet. In this case the ASCII or Unicode Latin-based symbols and characters would play a very important role. ASCII and Unicode character encoding enables computers to store and exchange data with other computers and programs. Below are lists of frequently used ASCII and Unicode Latin-based characters. For Unicode characters for non-Latin-based scripts, see Unicode character code charts by script. The type of characters we can insert in our documents. Insert the type of an ASCII or Unicode character into a document.

- Common symbol character codes
- Common diacritical character codes
- Common ligature character codes
- ASCII nonprinting control characters

If you only have to enter a few special characters or symbols, you can use the Character Map or type keyboard shortcuts. See below, tables or Keyboard shortcuts for international characters for a list of ASCII characters.

Notes

Many languages contain symbols that could not be condensed into the 256-characters Extended ASCII set. As such, there are ASCII and Unicode variations to encompass regional characters and symbols, see Unicode character code charts by script. If you have trouble entering the characters codes for the characters that you want, try using the Character Map.

3.4.1 Inserting ASCII characters

To insert an ASCII character, press and hold down ALT while typing the character code. For example, to insert the degree (º) symbol, press and hold down **ALT** while typing **0176** on the numeric keypad.

Note: You must use the numeric keypad to type the numbers and not the keyboard. Make sure that the NUM LOCK key is on if your keyboard requires it to type numbers on the numeric keypad.

3.4.2 Inserting Unicode characters

To insert a Unicode character, type the character code, press **ALT**, and then press **X**. For example, to type a dollar symbol ($), type **0024**, press **ALT**, and then press **X**. For more Unicode character codes, see Unicode character code charts by script.

Important: Some of the Microsoft Office programs, such as PowerPoint and InfoPath, cannot convert Unicode codes to characters. If you need a Unicode character and are using one of the programs that doesn't support Unicode characters, use the Character Map to enter the character(s) that you need.

Notes: You must use the numeric keypad to type the numbers and not the keyboard. Make sure that the **NUM LOCK** key is on if your keyboard requires it to type numbers on the numeric keypad. If you have trouble getting the Unicode to convert to your character, type the code using the numeric keypad, select the code, and then click **ALT+X.**

If you are using Microsoft Windows XP or later, the universal font for Unicode is automatically installed. If you are using Microsoft Windows 2000, you need to install the Unicode font.

a. In Microsoft Windows 2000

1. Quit all programs.
2. In Control Panel, double-click the Add/Remove Programs icon. Do one of the following:
    i. If you installed your Microsoft Office program as part of an Office package, click Microsoft Office in the Currently installed programs box, and then click Change.
    ii. If you installed your Office program individually, click the name of your program in the Currently installed programs box, and then click Change.

b. In Microsoft Office 2003

1. Setup dialog box, click Add or Remove Features, and then click Next.
2. Select Choose advance customization of applications, and then click Next.
3. Expand the Office Shared Features list.
4. Expand the International Support list.
5. Click the icon next to Universal Font, and then select the installation option that you want.

3.4.3 Using the Character Map

Character Map is a program built into Microsoft Windows that enables you to view the characters that are available in a selected font. Using Character Map, you can copy individual characters or a group of characters to the Clipboard and paste them into any program that can display them.

For more information about the Character Map, see Using the Windows Vista Character Map to enter special characters FAQ.

1. Click Start, point to All Programs,
2. point to Accessories,
3. point to System Tools, and
4. Click Character Map.

To select a character in the Character Map.
1. click the character,
2. click Select,
3. click the right mouse button in your document where you want the character,
4. click Paste.

Common symbol character codes

For more character symbols, see the Character Map installed on your computer, ASCII character codes, or Unicode character code charts by script.

Table 3.1 Common symbol character codes

Glyph	Code	Glyph	Code
Currency symbols			
£	ALT+0163	¥	ALT+0165
¢	ALT+0162	$	0024+ALT+X
€	ALT+0128	¤	ALT+0164
Legal symbols			
©	ALT+0169	®	ALT+0174
§	ALT+0167	™	ALT+0153
Mathematical symbols			
°	ALT+0176	º	ALT+0186
√	221A+ALT+X	+	ALT+43
#	ALT+35	µ	ALT+0181
<	ALT+60	>	ALT+62
%	ALT+37	(	ALT+40
[	ALT+91	)	ALT+41
]	ALT+93	Δ	2206+ALT+X
Fractions			
¼	ALT+0188	½	ALT+0189
		¾	ALT+0190
Punctuation and dialectic symbols			
?	ALT+63	¿	ALT+0191

!	ALT+33	‼	203+ALT+X
-	ALT+45	'	ALT+39
"	ALT+34	,	ALT+44
.	ALT+46	|	ALT+124
/	ALT+47	\	ALT+92
`	ALT+96	^	ALT+94
«	ALT+0171	»	ALT+0187
«	ALT+174	»	ALT+175
~	ALT+126	&	ALT+38
:	ALT+58	{	ALT+123
;	ALT+59	}	ALT+125
Form symbols			
□	25A1+ALT+X	√	221A+ALT+X

Common diacritical character codes

For a complete list of the glyphs and their character codes for the common diacritical character codes, see the Character Map below.

Table 3.2 Common diacritical character codes

Glyph	Code	Glyph	Code
Ã	ALT+0195	å	ALT+0229
Å	ALT+143	å	ALT+134
Ä	ALT+142	ä	ALT+132
À	ALT+0192	à	ALT+133
Á	ALT+0193	á	ALT+160
Â	ALT+0194	â	ALT+131
Ç	ALT+128	ç	ALT+135
Č	010C+ALT+X	č	010D+ALT+X
É	ALT+144	é	ALT+130
È	ALT+0200	è	ALT+138
Ê	ALT+202	ê	ALT+136
Ë	ALT+203	ë	ALT+137
Ĕ	0114+ALT+X	ĕ	0115+ALT+X
Ğ	011E+ALT+X	ğ	011F+ALT+X
Ģ	0122+ALT+X	ģ	0123+ALT+X
Ï	ALT+0207	ï	ALT+139
Î	ALT+0206	î	ALT+140
Í	ALT+0205	í	ALT+161
Ì	ALT+0204	ì	ALT+141
Ñ	ALT+165	ñ	ALT+164
Ö	ALT+153	ö	ALT+148
Ô	ALT+212	ô	ALT+147

Table 3.2 *Continued*

Glyph	Code	Glyph	Code
Ō	014C+ALT+X	ō	014D+ALT+X
Ȍ	ALT+0210	ȍ	ALT+149
Ȏ	ALT+0211	ó	ALT+162
Ø	ALT+0216	ø	00F8+ALT+X
Ŝ	015C+ALT+X	ŝ	015D+ALT+X
Ş	015E+ALT+X	ş	015F+ALT+X
Ü	ALT+154	ü	ALT+129
Ū	ALT+016A	ū	016B+ALT+X
Ȕ	ALT+0219	û	ALT+150
Ȗ	ALT+0217	ù	ALT+151
Ú	00DA+ALT+X	ú	ALT+163
Ÿ	0159+ALT+X	ÿ	ALT+152

Character codes for ligature characters

For more information about typographic ligatures, see Typographic ligature. For a complete list of the ligatures and their character codes, see the Character Map.

Table 3.3 Character codes for ligature characters

Glyph	Code	Glyph	Code
Æ	ALT+0198	æ	ALT+0230
ß	ALT+0223	ß	ALT+225
Œ	ALT+0140	œ	ALT+0156
		ʩ	02A9+ALT+X
ʣ	02A3+ALT+X	ʥ	02A5+ALT+X
ʪ	02AA+ALT+X	ʫ	02AB+ALT+X
ʦ	0246+ALT+X	ʧ	02A7+ALT+X
Љ	0409+ALT+X	Ю	042E+ALT+X
Њ	040A+ALT+X	Ꙙ	047E+ALT+x
Ы	042B+ALT+X	Ꙩ	0468+ALT+X
Ҝ	049C+ALT+X	الله	FDF2+ALT+X

ASCII nonprinting control characters

ASCII table numbers 0–31 are assigned for control characters used to control some peripheral devices such as printers. For example, 12 represents the form feed/new page function. This command instructs a printer to go to the top of the next page.

Table 3.4
ASCII non-printing control characters

Decimal	Character	Decimal	Character
null	0	data link escape	16
start of heading	1	device control 1	17
start of text	2	device control 2	18
end of text	3	device control 3	19
end of transmission	4	device control 4	20
inquiry	5	negative acknowledge	21
acknowledge	6	synchronous idle	22
bell	7	end of transmission block	23
backspace	8	cancel	24
horizontal tab	9	end of medium	25
line feed/new line	10	substitute	26
vertical tab	11	escape	27
form feed/new page	12	file separator	28
carriage return	13	group separator	29
shift out	14	record separator	30
shift in	15	unit separator	31
space	32	DEL	127

3.5.1 Mimic a watermark in Excel

Watermark functionality is not available in Microsoft Office Excel. However, you can mimic a watermark in one of two ways.

You can display watermark information on every printed page — for example, to indicate that the worksheet data is confidential or a draft copy — by inserting a picture that contains the watermark information in a header or footer. That picture then appears behind the worksheet data, starting at the top or bottom of every page. You can also resize or scale the picture to fill the whole page. You can also use WordArt on top of the worksheet data to indicate that the data is confidential or a draft copy.

3.5.2 Use a picture in a header or footer to mimic a watermark

1. In a drawing program, such as Paintbrush, create a picture that you want to use as a watermark.
2. In Excel, click the worksheet that you want to display with the watermark.
   NOTE: Make sure that only one worksheet is selected.
3. On the Insert tab, in the Text group, click Header & Footer.
4. Under Header, click either the left, center, or right header selection box.

Figure 3.5 Character codes for ligature characters

5. On the Design tab of the Header & Footer Tools, in the Header & Footer elements group, click Picture 🖼 and then find the picture that you want to insert.

Figure 3.6 Character codes for ligature characters	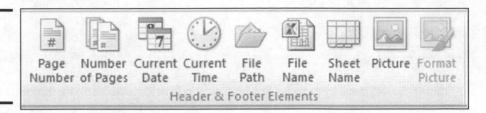

6. Double-click the picture to insert it in the header section box.

7. To resize or scale the picture, click Format Picture 🖼 in the Header & Footer elements group, and then, in the Format Picture dialog box, select the options that you want on the Size tab.

NOTES:
* Changes to the picture or picture format take effect immediately and cannot be undone.
* If you want to add blank space above or below a picture, in the header selection box that contains the picture, click before or after &[Picture], and then press ENTER to start a new line.
* To replace a picture, select & [Picture], click Picture 🖼 , and then click Replace.
* Before printing, make sure that the header or footer margin has sufficient space for the custom header or footer.
* To delete a picture, select & [Picture] and then press DELETE.
* To switch from Page Layout view to Normal view, select any cell, click the View tab, and then, in the Workbook Views group, click Normal.

3.6 Preview font formatting in Excel

1. Select the text that you want to format.
2. On the Home tab, in the Font group:
   * Click the Font box down-arrow, then move the pointer over the fonts.
   * Click the Font Size box down-arrow, then move the pointer over the font sizes.
   * Click the Fill Color button down-arrow, then move the pointer over the highlight or fill colors.
   * Click the Font Color button down-arrow, then move the pointer over the font colors.
   * To apply the previewed formatting, click the selected font name, font size, or color in the list.
   * To cancel live previewing without applying any changes, press **ESC.**

3.6.1 Applying Number Formatting

Number formatting refers to the process of changing the appearance of values contained in cells. Excel provides a wide variety of number formatting options. In the following sections, you will see how to use many of Excel's formatting options to quickly improve the appearance of your worksheets.

TIP: Remember that the formatting you apply works with the selected cell or cells. Therefore, you need to select the cell (or range of cells) before applying the formatting. Also remember that changing the number format does not affect the underlying value. Number formatting affects only the appearance.

3.6.2 Improving readability by formatting numbers

Values that you enter into cells normally are unformatted. In other words, they simply consist of a string of numerals. Typically, you want to format the numbers so that they're easier to read or are more consistent in terms of the number of decimal places shown.

Figure 3.7 shows a worksheet that has two columns of values. The first column consists of unformatted values. The cells in the second column are formatted to make the values easier to read. The third column describes the type of formatting applied.

Figure 3.7 Use numeric formatting to make it easier to understand what the values in the worksheet represent.

	A	B	C	D
1				
2	**Unformatted**	**Formatted**	**Type**	
3	15750	$15,750.00	Currency	
4	0.275	27.50%	Percentage	
5	5/12/2011	5/12/2011	Short Date	
6	5/12/2011	Thursday, May 12, 2011	Long Date	
7	125439872	125,439,872.00	Accounting	
8	5559784327	(555) 978-4327	Phone-Number	
9	453998792	453-99-8792	Social Securtiy Number	
10	0.653	3:40:19 PM	Time	
11	0.25	1/4	Fraction	
12	1532243121090	1.53224E+12	Scienctific	
13				

Sheet1 Sheet2 Sheet3

If you move the cell pointer to a cell that has a formatted value, the Formula bar displays the value in its unformatted state because the formatting affects only how the value appears in the cell — not the actual value contained in the cell.

3.6.3 Using automatic number formatting

Excel is smart enough to perform some formatting for you automatically. For example, if you enter 15.2% into a cell, Excel knows that you want to use a percentage format and applies it for you automatically. If you use commas to separate thousands (such as 125,436), Excel applies comma formatting for you. And if you precede your value with a dollar sign, the cell is formatted for currency (assuming that the dollar sign is your system currency symbol).

TIP: A handy default feature in Excel makes entering percentage values into cells easier. If a cell is formatted to display as a percent, you can simply enter a normal value (for example 12.5 for 12.5%). If this feature isn't working (or if you prefer to enter the actual value for percentages), access the Excel Options dialog box and click the Advanced tab. In the Editing Options section, locate the check box labeled Enable Automatic Percent Entry, and remove the check mark.

3.6.4 Formatting numbers by using the Ribbon

The Home ➔ Number group in the Ribbon contains controls that let you quickly apply common number formats (see Figure 3.8).

You can find number formatting commands in the Number group of the Home tab

Figure 3.8 Number formatting commands in the Number group

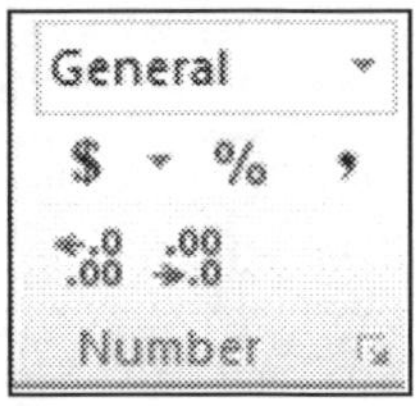

The Number Format drop-down list contains 11 common number formats. Additional options include an Accounting Number Format drop-down list (to select a currency format), plus a Percent Style and a Comma Style button. In addition, the group contains a button to increase the number of decimal places, and another to decrease the number of decimal places. When you select one of these controls, the active cell takes on the specified number format. You also can select a range of cells (or even an entire row or column) before clicking these buttons. If you select more than one cell, Excel applies the number format to all the selected cells.

3.6.5 Using shortcut keys to format numbers

Another way to apply number formatting is to use shortcut keys. Table 3.5 summarizes the shortcut-key combinations that you can use to apply common number formatting to the selected cells or range. Notice that these Ctrl+Shift characters are all located together, in the upper left part of your keyboard.

Table 3.5 Number-Formatting Keyboard Shortcuts

Key Combination	Formatting Applied
Ctrl+Shift+~	General number format (that is, unformatted values)
Ctrl+Shift+$	Currency format with two decimal places (negative numbers appear in parentheses)
Ctrl+Shift+%	Percentage format, with no decimal places
Ctrl+Shift+^	Scientific notation number format, with two decimal places
Ctrl+Shift+#	Date format with the day, month, and year
Ctrl+Shift+@	Time format with the hour, minute, and AM or PM
Ctrl+Shift+!	Two decimal places, thousands separator, and a hyphen for negative values

3.6.6 Formatting numbers using the Format Cells dialog box

In most cases, the number formats that are accessible from the Number group on the Home tab are just fine. Sometimes, however, you want more control over how your values appear. Excel offers a great deal of control over number formats through the use of the Format Cells dialog box, shown in Figure 3.9. For formatting numbers, you need to use the Number tab.

Figure 3.9 Number formatting commands in the Number group

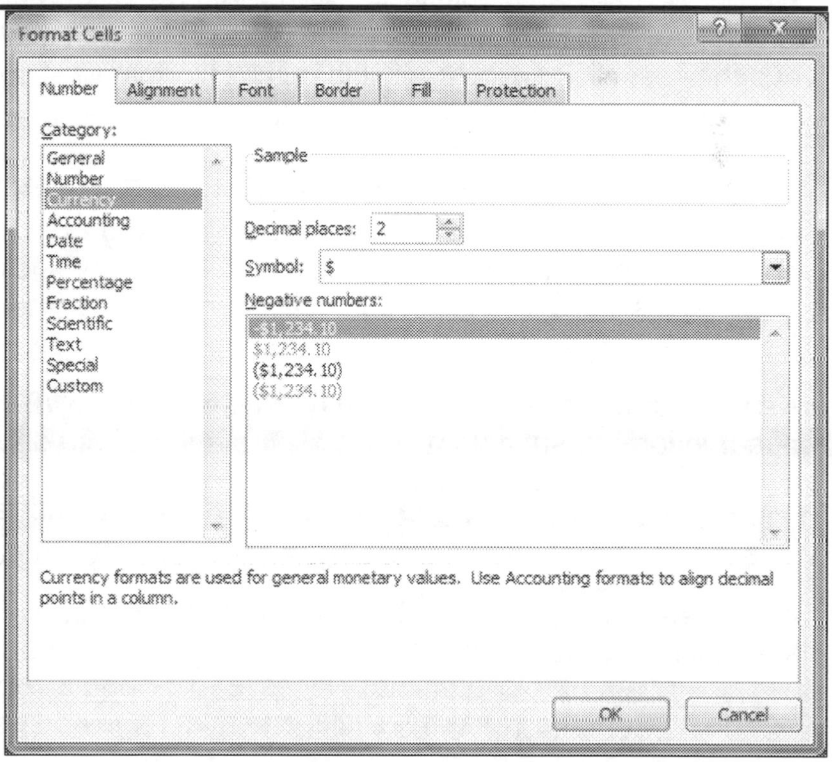

When you need more control over number formats, use the Number tab of the Format Cells dialog box. You can bring up the Format Cells dialog box in several ways. Start by selecting the cell or cells that you want to format and then do the following:

- Choose Home ➔ Number and click the small dialog launcher icon.
- Choose Home ➔ Number, click the Number Format drop-down list, and select More Number Formats from the drop-down list.
- Right-click and choose Format Cells from the shortcut menu.
- Press the Ctrl+1 shortcut key.

The Number tab of the Format Cells dialog box as shown in figure 3.9 above, displays 12 categories of number formats from which to choose. When you select a category from the list box, the right side of the tab changes to display the appropriate options. The Number category has three options that you can control:

1. the number of decimal places displayed,
2. whether to use a thousand separator, and
3. how you want negative numbers displayed.

Notice that the Negative Numbers list box has four choices (two of which display negative values in red), and the choices change depending on the number of decimal places and whether you choose to separate thousands.

The top of the tab displays a sample of how the active cell will appear with the selected number format (visible only if a cell with a value is selected). After you make your choices, click OK to apply the number format to all the selected cells.

3.7 When Numbers Appear to Add Up Incorrectly

Applying a number format to a cell doesn't change the value — only how the value appears in the worksheet. For example, if a cell contains 0.874543, you may format it to appear as 87%. If that cell is used in a formula, the formula uses the full value (0.874543), not the displayed value (87%).

In some situations, formatting may cause Excel to display calculation results that appear incorrect, such as when totaling numbers with decimal places. For example, if values are formatted to display two decimal places, you may not see the actual numbers used in the calculations. But because Excel uses the full precision of the values in its formula, the sum of the two values may appear to be incorrect.

Several solutions to this problem are available. You can format the cells to display more decimal places. You can use the ROUND function on individual numbers and specify the number of decimal places Excel should round to. Or you can instruct Excel to change the worksheet values to match their displayed format.

To do so, access the Excel Options dialog box and click the Advanced tab. Check the Set Precision As Displayed check box (which is located in the section named When Calculating This Workbook).

Caution: Selecting the Precision As Displayed option changes the numbers in your worksheets to permanently match their appearance onscreen. This setting applies to all sheets in the active workbook. Most of the time, this option is not what you want. Make sure that you understand the consequences of using the Set Precision As Displayed option.

The following are the number-format categories, along with some general comments:

Table 3.6 Number-Formatting Description

Format	Description
General	The default format; it displays numbers as integers, as decimals, or in scientific notation if the value is too wide to fit in the cell.
Number	Enables you to specify the number of decimal places, whether to use a comma to separate thousands, and how to display negative numbers (with a minus sign, in red, in parentheses, or in red and in parentheses).
Currency	Enables you to specify the number of decimal places, whether to use a currency symbol, and how to display negative numbers (with a minus sign, in red, in parentheses, or in red and in parentheses). This format always uses a comma to separate thousands.
Accounting	Differs from the Currency format in that the currency symbols always line up vertically
Date	Enables you to choose from several different date formats.
Time	Enables you to choose from several different time formats.
Percentage	Enables you to choose the number of decimal places and *always* displays a percent sign.
Fraction	Enables you to choose from among nine fraction formats
Scientific	Displays numbers in exponential notation (with an E): 2.00E+05 = 200,000; 2.05E+05 = 205,000. You can choose the number of decimal places to display to the left of E.
Text:	When applied to a value, causes Excel to treat the value as text (even if it looks like a number). This feature is useful for such items as part numbers.
Special	Contains four additional number formats (Zip Code, Zip Code +4, Phone Number, and Social Security Number).
Custom	Enables you to define custom number formats that aren't included in any other category.

TIP: If a cell displays a series of hash marks (such as **#########**), it usually means that the column isn't wide enough to display the value in the number format that you selected. Either make the column wider or change the number format.

3.7.1 Change the character used to separate thousands or decimals

By default, Microsoft Excel uses the system separators that are defined in the regional settings in Control Panel. If you sometimes need to display numbers with different separators for thousands or decimals, you can temporarily replace the system separators with custom separators.

1. Click the Microsoft Office Button , in Excel 2007 and then click Excel Options. In Excel 2010 click the File tab, and then click Excel Options.
2. On the Advanced tab, under Editing options, clear the Use system separators check box.
3. Type new separators in the Decimal separator and Thousands separator boxes.

TIP: When you want to use the system separators again, select the Use system separators check box.
NOTE: For a permanent solution, you must change the regional settings in Control Panel.

3.7.2 Change the decimal places displayed for numbers

For numbers that are already entered on a worksheet, you can increase or decrease the number of places that are displayed after the decimal point by using the **Increase Decimal** and **Decrease Decimal** buttons. By default, Excel displays 2 decimal places when you apply a built-in number format, such as a currency format or a percentage, to the cells or data. However, you can change the number of decimal places that you want to use when you apply a number format. To have Excel enter the decimal points for you, you can specify a fixed decimal point for numbers.

3.7.3 Increase or decrease the decimal places on a worksheet

1. Select the cell or range of cells that contains the numbers for which you want to change the decimal places.
2. On the Home tab, in the Number group, do one of the following:
   - Click Increase Decimal to display more digits after the decimal point.
   - Click Decrease Decimal to display fewer digits after the decimal point

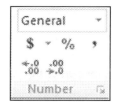

Figure 3.10 Number formatting commands in the Number group

3.7.4 Specify the decimal places for a built-in number format

Specify the decimal places for a built-in number format

1. On the Home tab, click the Dialog Box Launcher ☐ next to Number.
2. In the Category box, click **Number, Currency, Accounting, Percentage**, or **Scientific**.
3. In the Decimal places box, enter the number of decimal places that you want to display.

NOTE: You cannot change the default setting of 2 decimal places. To use more or less than 2 decimal places, you need to change the number of decimal places every time you apply a Number, Currency, Accounting, Percentage, or Scientific format. However, you can create a custom number format that displays the number of decimals that you want. For more information, see Create or delete a custom number format.

3.7.5 Specify a fixed decimal point for numbers

1. Click the Microsoft Office Button in Excel 2007, and then click Excel Options. In Excel 2010 click on File Menu, and then click Excel Options.
2. In the Advanced category, under Editing options, select the Automatically insert a decimal point check box.
3. In the Places box, enter a positive number for digits to the right of the decimal point or a negative number for digits to the left of the decimal point.
   For example, if you enter **3** in the Places box and then type **2834** in a cell, the value will be **2.834**. If you enter **-3** in the Places box and then type **283** in a cell, the value will be **283000.**
4. Click OK.

The Fixed decimal indicator appears in the status bar.
5. On the worksheet, click a cell, and then type the number that you want.
   NOTE: The data that you typed before you selected the Fixed decimal check box is not affected.

Tips:

- To temporarily override the fixed decimal option, type a decimal point when you type the number.
- To remove decimal points from numbers that you already entered with fixed decimals, do the following:
    1. Click the Microsoft Office Button 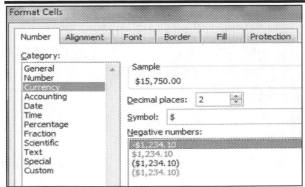 in Excel 2007, and then click Excel Options.
       In Excel 2010 click on File Menu, and then click Excel Options.
    2. In the Advanced category, under Editing options, clear the Automatically insert a decimal point check box.
    3. In an empty cell, type a number such as 10, 100, or 1,000, depending on the number of decimal places that you want to remove.
       - **TIP:** For example, type **100** in the cell if the numbers contain two decimal places and you want to convert them to whole numbers.

    4. On the Home tab, in the Clipboard group, click Copy .
       - Keyboard shortcut. You can also press **CTRL+C**.
    5. On the worksheet, select the cells that contain the numbers with decimal places that you want to change.
    6. On the Home tab, in the Clipboard group, click the arrow below Paste, and then click Paste Special.
    7. In the Paste Special dialog box, under Operation, click Multiply.

3.7.6 Change the way negative numbers are displayed

You can display negative numbers by using the minus sign, parentheses, or by applying a red color (with or without parentheses).

TIP: To cancel a selection of cells, click any cell on the worksheet.

1. Select the cell or range of cells that you want to format with a negative number style.
2. On the Home tab, click the **Dialog Box Launcher** ☐ next to **Number** as shown in figure 3.10 above.
3. In the Category box, click one of the following:

Figure 3.11 Number formatting Categories

- For simple numbers, click Number.
- For currency, click Currency.

4. In the Negative numbers box, select the display style for negative numbers.

TIP: You can also create your own number format for negative numbers. For more information, see Create or delete a custom number format.

3.8 Convert dates stored as text to dates

Occasionally, dates may become formatted and stored in cells as text. For example, you may have entered a date in a cell that was formatted as text, or the data might have been imported or pasted from an external data source as text.

Dates that are formatted as text are left-aligned instead of right-aligned in a cell. With Error Checking turned on, text dates with two-digit years might also be marked with an error indicator .

Because Error Checking in Microsoft Office Excel can identify text-formatted dates with two-digit years, you can use the automatic correction options to convert them to date-formatted dates. You can use the DATEVALUE function to convert most other types of text dates to dates.

Extracted Data from External Source

This Data contains 4 digits-year, 2 digits month and 2 digits day and hh:mm:ss.000.

When first copied into Excel spreadsheet it only displays the time without the dates. But when custom formatted like this:

"**yyyy-mm-dd hh:mm:ss.000**" we obtained the original format illustrated below:

Extracted Date Data
2011-05-21 00:18:00.001
2011-05-22 00:09:20.002
2011-05-23 00:10:01.000
2011-05-24 01:05:09.000
2011-05-25 00:12:10.000
2011-05-26 04:02:01.010

Figure 3.12
The worksheet Showing unformatted and formatted Date and Time data

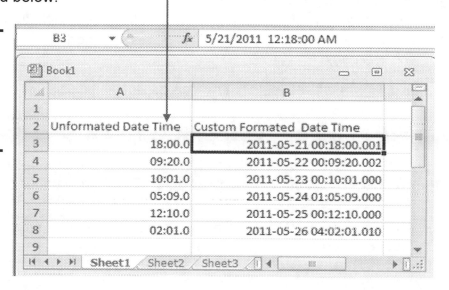

	A	B
1		
2	Unformated Date Time	Custom Formated Date Time
3	18:00.0	2011-05-21 00:18:00.001
4	09:20.0	2011-05-22 00:09:20.002
5	10:01.0	2011-05-23 00:10:01.000
6	05:09.0	2011-05-24 01:05:09.000
7	12:10.0	2011-05-25 00:12:10.000
8	02:01.0	2011-05-26 04:02:01.010
9		

B3   ƒx   5/21/2011 12:18:00 AM

Book1

Sheet1 Sheet2 Sheet3

Figure 3.13 Custom Format Category Showing Date and Time.

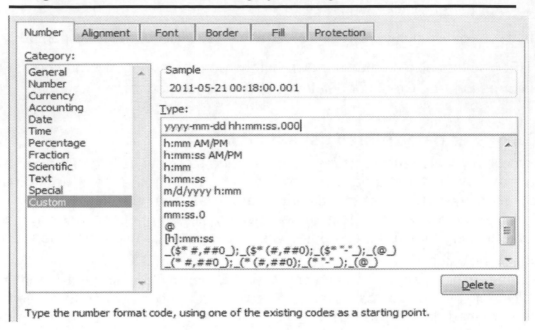

3.8.1 Convert text dates with two-digit years by using Error Checking

1. Click the Microsoft Office Button , and then click Excel Options.
   In Excel 2010 click on File Menu, and then click Excel Options.

2. Click Formulas, and then do all of the following:
   a. Under Error Checking, make sure that the Enable background error checking check box is selected.
   b. Under Error checking rules, make sure that the Cells containing years represented as 2 digits check box is selected.
   c. Click OK.

3. In the worksheet, select any cell or range of cells with an error indicator in the upper-left corner.
   NOTE: The selected cells must be adjacent.

4. Next to the selected cell or range of cells, click the error button that appears, and then click either Convert **XX** to **20XX** or Convert **XX** to **19XX**.

3.8.2 Convert text dates by using the DATEVALUE function

To convert a text date in a cell to a serial number, you use the **DATEVALUE** function. Then you copy the formula, select the cells that contain the text dates, and use Paste Special to apply a date format to them.

1. Select a blank cell and verify that its number format is General.
2. In the blank cell:

   a. Type **=DATEVALUE(**
   b. Click the cell that contains the text-formatted date that you want to convert.
   c. Type **)**
   d. Press **ENTER**.

The **DATEVALUE** function returns the serial number of the date that is represented by the text date.

3. To copy the conversion formula into a range of contiguous cells, select the cell in which you typed the formula, and then drag the fill handle 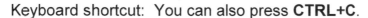 across a range of empty cells that matches in size the range of cells that contain text dates.
   After you drag the fill handle, you should have a range of cells with serial numbers that corresponds to the range of cells that contain text dates.

4. Select the cell or range of cells that contains the serial numbers, and then on the Home tab, in the Clipboard group, click Copy.

   Keyboard shortcut: You can also press **CTRL+C**.

5. Select the cell or range of cells that contains the text dates, and then on the **Home** tab, in the **Clipboard** group, click the arrow below **Paste**, and then click **Paste Special.**

6. In the **Paste Special** dialog box, under **Paste**, select **Values**, and then click **OK.**

7. On the **Home** tab, in the **Number** group, click the arrow next to the **Number Forma**t box, and then click **Short Date** or **Long Date.**

   TIP: For other date formats, click **More**. In the **Format Cells** dialog box, on the **Number** tab, click **Date** in the **Category** box, and then click the date format that you want in the **Type** box.

8. To delete the serial numbers after all of the dates are converted successfully, select the cells that contain them, and then press **DELETE.**

3.8.3 Convert numbers stored as text to numbers

Occasionally, numbers might be formatted and stored in cells as text, which later can cause problems with calculations or produce confusing sort orders.

For example, you might have typed a number in a cell that was formatted as text, or the data may have been imported or copied as text from an external data source. Numbers that are formatted as text are left-aligned instead of right-aligned in the cell. If numbers are entered in cells that are formatted as text, you can use error checking to convert the text to numbers. If numbers are imported as text or if they are formatted as text after they were entered in cells, you cannot use error checking to convert the text to numbers. However, you can apply a number format instead.

You can also quickly convert numbers that are formatted as text in multiple nonadjacent cells or ranges to numbers.

3.8.4 Use error checking to convert numbers that are stored as text to numbers

With Error Checking turned on, numbers that are entered in cells that are formatted as text are marked with an error indicator⬚ .

1. To turn on Error Checking, do the following:

    a. Click the Microsoft Office Button 🔘 , and then click Excel Options.
        In Excel 2010, click File, and then click Excel Options

    b. Click the Formulas category.

    c. Under Error Checking, make sure that the "**Enable background error checking**" check box is selected.

    d. Under Error checking rules, make sure that the Numbers formatted as text or preceded by an apostrophe check box is selected.

    e. Click OK.

2. On the worksheet, select any single cell or range of adjacent cells that has an error indicator in the upper-left corner ⬚ .
    NOTE: All cells in the selection must be adjacent.

3. Next to the selected cell or range of cells, click the error button that appears ◈ , and then click Convert to Number.

Figure 3.14 Worksheet Showing Error Number Entry

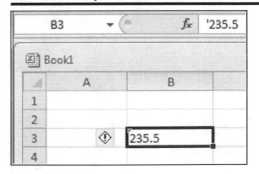

When you click on the button that appears. Excel will display six options to choose. These options are:

- Number Stored as Text
- Convert to Number
- Help on this error
- Ignore Error
- Edit in Formula Bar
- Error Checking Options

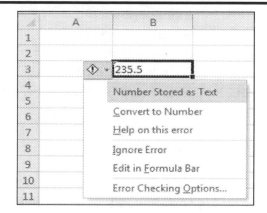

Figure 3.15 Display Menu Options After Clicking on Error Button.

3.8.5 Apply a number format to numbers that are stored as text

For this procedure to complete successfully, make sure that the numbers that are stored as text do not include extra spaces in or around the numbers.

To remove extra spaces from multiple numbers that are stored as text, you can use the TRIM function. For example **TRIM(A2: B14).**

1. Select the cells that contain the numbers that are stored as text.

2. On the Home tab, in the Number group, click the Dialog Box Launcher ☐ next to Number

3. In the Category box, click the number format that you want to use.

3.8.6 Convert numbers in multiple nonadjacent cells or ranges of cells

1. Select a blank cell and verify that its number format is **General.**

2. In the cell, type **1**, and then press **ENTER.**

3. Select the cell and then, on the **Home** tab, in the **Clipboard** group, click **Copy**.

4. Select the nonadjacent cells or ranges of cells that contain the numbers stored as text that you want to convert.

5. On the **Home** tab, in the **Clipboard** group, click the arrow below **Paste**, and then click **Paste Special**.

Figure 3.16 Paste Special Options List

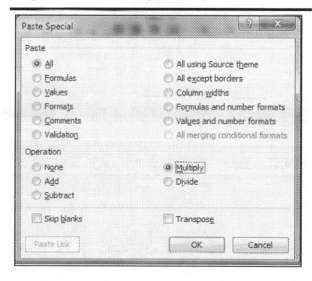

6. Under Operation, select **Multiply**, and then click **OK.**

7. To delete the content of the cell that you typed in step **2** after all numbers have been converted successfully, select that cell, and then press **DELETE**.

    NOTE: Some accounting programs display negative values as text, with the negative sign (–) to the right of the value. To convert the text string to a value, you must use a formula to return all the characters of the text string except the rightmost character (the negation sign), and then multiply the result by **–1**.

    For example, if the value in cell **A2** is "**175–**" the following formula converts the text to the value **–175.**

Figure 3.17 Data Formula To Convert to negative

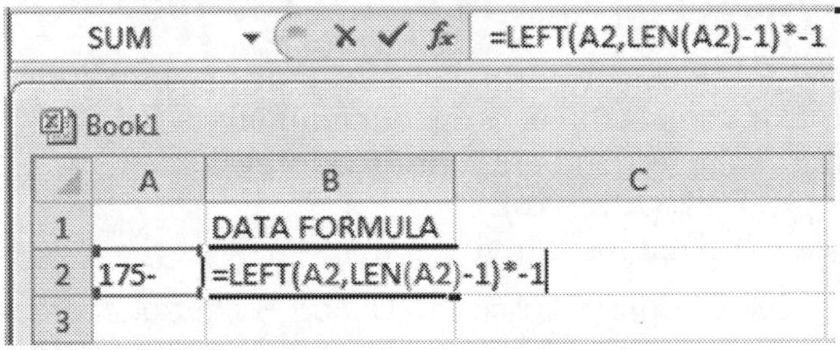

Figure 3.18 The Results of Data Formula (-175)

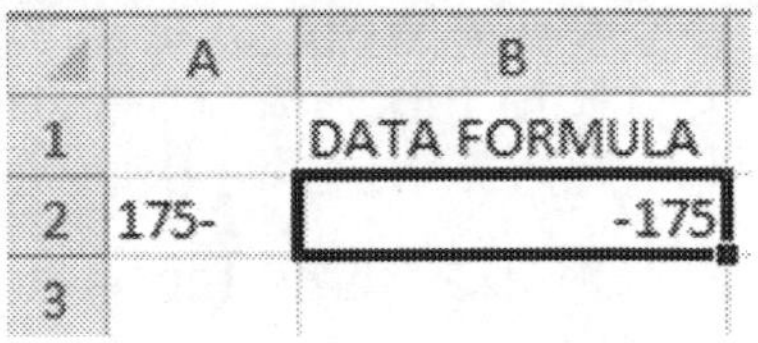

3.8.7 Create or delete a custom number format

Microsoft Office Excel provides many built-in number formats, but if these do not meet your needs, you can customize a built-in number format to create your own. To learn more about how to change number format codes, you may want to review the guidelines for customizing a number format before you get started.

You cannot delete a built-in number format, but you can delete a custom number format when you no longer need it.

3.9 Review guidelines for customizing a number format

To create a custom number format, you start by selecting one of the built-in number formats as a starting point. You can then change any one of the code sections of that format to create your own custom number format. A number format can have up to four sections of code, separated by semicolons. These code sections define the format for positive numbers, negative numbers, zero values, and text, in that order.
<POSITIVE>;<NEGATIVE>;<ZERO>;<TEXT>

For example, you can use these code sections to create the following custom format:

[Blue](#,##0.00_); [Red](#,##0.00); 0.00; "sales "@

You do not have to include all code sections in your custom number format. If you specify only two code sections for your custom number format, the first section is used for positive numbers and zeros, and the second section is used for negative numbers. If you specify only one code section, it is used for all numbers. If you want to skip a code section and include a code section that follows it, you must include the ending semicolon for the section that you skip.

The following guidelines should be helpful for customizing any of these number format code sections.

3.9.1 Guidelines for including text and adding spacing

- **Display both text and numbers**
  To display both text and numbers in a cell, enclose the text characters in double quotation marks **(" ")** or precede a single character with a backslash **(\)**. Include the characters in the appropriate section of the format codes. For example, type the format **$0.00" Surplus"**; **$-0.00" Shortage"** to display a positive amount as **"$115.75 Surplus"** and a negative amount as **"$-115.75 Shortage."** Note that there is one space character before both "Surplus" and "Shortage" in each code section.

  The following characters are displayed without the use of quotation marks.

- **Include a section for text entry:** If included, a text section is always the last section in the number format. Include an "at" character (@) in the section where you want to display any text that you type in the cell. If the @ character is omitted from the text section, text that you type will not be displayed. If you want to always display specific text characters with the typed text, enclose the additional text in double quotation marks **(" ")**. For example, "gross receipts for "@.
  If the format does not include a text section, any nonnumeric value that you type in a cell with that format applied is not affected by the format. In addition, the entire cell is converted to text.

- **Add spaces:** To create a space that is the width of a character in a number format, include an underscore character (_), followed by the character that you want to use. For example, when you follow an underscore with a right parenthesis, such as _), positive numbers line up correctly with negative numbers that are enclosed in parentheses.

Table 3.6 Characters and Descriptions

SYMBOL	DESCRIPTION		SYMBOL	DESCRIPTION
$	DOLLAR SIGN		-	Minus sign
+	Plus sign		/	Slash mark
(	Left parenthesis		)	Right parenthesis
:	Colon		!	Exclamation point
^	Circumflex accent (caret)		&	Ampersand
'	Apostrophe		~	Tilde
{	Left curly bracket		}	Right curly bracket
<	Less-than sign		>	Greater-than sign
=	Equal sign			Space character

- **Repeat characters:** To repeat the next character in the format to fill the column width, include an asterisk (*) in the number format. For example, type **0*-** to include enough dashes after a number to fill the cell, or type ***0** before any format to include leading zeros.

3.9.2 Guidelines for using decimal places, spaces, colors, and conditions

- **Include decimal places and significant digits**
  To format fractions or numbers that contain decimal points, include the following digit placeholders, decimal points, and thousand separators in a section.

- If a number has more digits to the right of the decimal point than there are placeholders in the format, the number rounds to as many decimal places as there are placeholders. If there are more digits to the left of the decimal point than there are placeholders, the extra digits are displayed. If the format contains only number signs (#) to the left of the decimal point, numbers less than **1** begin with a decimal point; for example, **.47.**

Table 3.7 Format Decimal Places

0 (zero)	This digit placeholder displays insignificant zeros if a number has fewer digits than there are zeros in the format. For example, if you type **8.9**, and you want it to be displayed as **8.90**, use the format **#.00**.
#	This digit placeholder follows the same rules as the 0 (zero). However, Excel does not display extra zeros when the number that you type has fewer digits on either side of the decimal than there are # symbols in the format. For example, if the custom format is **#.##**, and you type **8.9** in the cell, the number **8.9** is displayed.
?	This digit placeholder follows the same rules as the 0 (zero). However, Excel adds a space for insignificant zeros on either side of the decimal point so that decimal points are aligned in the column. For example, the custom format **0.0?** aligns the decimal points for the numbers **8.9** and **88.99** in a column.
. (period)	This digit placeholder displays the decimal point in a number.

Table 3.7 Decimal Number Display Format

TO DISPLAY	AS	USE THIS CODE
1234.59	1234.6	####.#
8.9	8.900	#.000
.631	0.6	0.#
12	12.0	#.0#
1234.568	1234.57	
44.398 102.65 2.8	44.398 102.65 2.8 (with aligned decimals)	???.???
5.25 5.3	5 1/4 5 3/10 (with aligned fractions)	# ???/???

- **Specify colors:**
  To specify the color for a section of the format, type the name of one of the following eight colors enclosed in square brackets in the section. The color code must be the first item in the section.

- **Specify conditions:** To specify number formats that will be applied only if a number meets a condition that you specify, enclose the condition in square brackets. The condition consists of a comparison operator and a value. For example, the following format displays

Table 3.8 Color Scheme

[BLACK]	
[Green]	
[White]	
[Blue]	
[Magenta]	
[Yellow]	
[Cyan]	
[Red]	

numbers that are less than or equal to 100 in a red font and numbers that are greater than 100 in a blue font.

[Red][<=100];[Blue][>100]

To apply conditional formats to cells (for example, color shading that depends on the value of a cell), on the Home tab, in the Styles group, click Conditional Formatting.

3.9.3 Guidelines for currency, percentages, and scientific notation format

- **Include currency symbols:** To type one of the following currency symbols in a number format, press **NUM LOCK** and use the numeric keypad to type the **ANSI** code for the symbol.

Table 3.9
ASCII Code Combination of ALT and Number

TO ENTER	PRESS THIS CODE
¢	ALT+0162
£	ALT+0163
¥	ALT+0165
	ALT+0128

- **NOTE:** Custom formats are saved with the workbook. To have Excel always use a specific currency symbol, you must change the currency symbol that is selected in the Regional Options in Control Panel before you start Excel.
- For information about how to change Regional Options, see Change the default date, time, number or measurement format..
- **Display percentages:** To display numbers as a percentage of 100 — for example, to display .08 as 8% or 2.8 as 280% — include the percent sign (%) in the number format.
- **Display scientific notations:** To display numbers in scientific (exponential) format, use the following exponent codes in a section.

(E-, E+, e-,e+)	Displays a number in scientific (exponential) format. Excel displays a number to the right of the "E" or "e" that corresponds to the number of places that the decimal point was moved. For example, if the format is **0.00E+00**, and you type **12,200,000** in the cell, the number **1.22E+07** is displayed. If you change the number format to **#0.0E+0**, the number **12.2E+6** is displayed.

3.9.4 Guidelines for date and time formats

- Display days, months, and years   To display numbers as date formats (such as days, months, and years), use the following codes in a section.

Table 3.10 List of Date Formats

M	DISPLAYS THE MONTH AS A NUMBER WITHOUT A LEADING ZERO.
mm	Displays the month as a number with a leading zero when appropriate.
mmm	Displays the month as an abbreviation (Jan to Dec).
mmmm	Displays the month as a full name (January to December).
mmmmm	Displays the month as a single letter (J to D).
d	Displays the day as a number without a leading zero.
dd	Displays the day as a number with a leading zero when appropriate.
ddd	Displays the day as an abbreviation (Sun to Sat).
dddd	Displays the day as a full name (Sunday to Saturday).
yy	Displays the year as a two-digit number.
yyyy	Displays the year as a four-digit number.

TO DISPLAY	AS	USE THIS CODE
Months	1–12	m
Months	01–12	mm
Months	Jan–Dec	mmm
Months	January–December	mmmm
Months	J–D	mmmmm
Days	1–31	d
Days	01–31	dd
Days	Sun–Sat	ddd
Days	Sunday–Saturday	dddd
Years	00–99	yy
Years	1900–9999	yyyy

- Display hours, minutes, and seconds   To display time formats (such as hours, minutes, and seconds), use the following codes in a section.

Table 3.11 List of Time Formats

H	DISPLAYS THE HOUR AS A NUMBER WITHOUT A LEADING ZERO.
[h]	Displays elapsed time in hours. If you are working with a formula that returns a time in which the number of hours exceeds 24, use a number format that resembles **[h]:mm:ss**.
hh	Displays the hour as a number with a leading zero when appropriate. If the format contains **AM** or **PM**, the hour is based on the 12-hour clock. Otherwise, the hour is based on the 24-hour clock.
m	Displays the minute as a number without a leading zero. **NOTE:** The **m** or **mm** code must appear immediately after the **h** or **hh** code or immediately before the **ss** code; otherwise, Excel displays the month instead of minutes.
[m]	Displays elapsed time in minutes. If you are working with a formula that returns a time in which the number of minutes exceeds 60, use a number format that resembles **[mm]:ss**.
mm	Displays the minute as a number with a leading zero when appropriate. **NOTE:** The **m** or **mm** code must appear immediately after the **h** or **hh** code or immediately before the **ss** code; otherwise, Excel displays the month instead of minutes.
s	Displays the second as a number without a leading zero.
[s]	Displays elapsed time in seconds. If you are working with a formula that returns a time in which the number of seconds exceeds 60, use a number format that resembles **[ss]**.
ss	Displays the second as a number with a leading zero when appropriate. If you want to display fractions of a second, use a number format that resembles **h:mm:ss.00**.
AM/PM, am/pm, A/P, a/p	Displays the hour using a 12-hour clock. Excel displays **AM**, **am**, **A**, or **a** for times from midnight until noon and **PM**, **pm**, **P**, or **p** for times from noon until midnight.

Table 3.12 List of Displayed Time Formats

TO DISPLAY	AS	USE THIS CODE
Hours	0–23	h
Hours	00–23	hh
Minutes	0–59	m
Minutes	00–59	mm
Seconds	0–59	s
Seconds	00–59	ss
Time	4 AM	h AM/PM
Time	4:36 PM	h:mm AM/PM
Time	4:36:03 P	h:mm:ss A/P
Time	4:36:03.75	h:mm:ss.00
Elapsed time (hours and minutes)	1:02	[h]:mm
Elapsed time (minutes and seconds)	62:16	[mm]:ss
Elapsed time (seconds and hundredths)	3735.80	[ss].00

3.10 Create a custom number format

1. Open the workbook in which you want to create and store a custom number format.
2. On the Home tab, click the Dialog Box Launcher ⬚ next to Number.
3. In the Category box, click Custom.
4. In the Type list, select the number format that you want to customize.

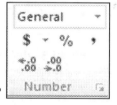

Figure 3.19 Number formatting commands in the Number group

The number format that you select appears in the Type box above the Type list.

NOTE: When you select a built-in number format in the Type list, Excel creates a copy of that number format that you can then customize. The original number format in the Type list cannot be changed or deleted.

5. In the Type box, make the necessary changes to the selected number format.

TIP: For more information about the changes that you can make, see Review guidelines for customizing a number format in this article.

NOTE: A custom number format is stored in the workbook in which it was created and will not be available in any other workbooks. To use a custom format in a new workbook, you can save the current workbook as an Excel template that you can use as the basis for the new workbook. For more information, see Create and use an Excel template.

3.10.1 Delete a custom number format

1. Open the workbook that contains the custom number format that you want to delete.
2. On the Home tab, click the Dialog Box Launcher ⬜ next to Number.
3. In the Category box, click Custom.
4. In the Type list, select the custom number format that you want to delete.
   NOTE: Built-in number formats in the Type list cannot be deleted.
5. Click Delete.
   NOTE: Any cells in the workbook that were formatted with the deleted custom format will be displayed in the default General format.

3.10.2 Display numbers as credit card numbers

When you type a number that contains more than 15 digits in a worksheet cell, Microsoft Office Excel changes any digits past the fifteenth place to zeros. In addition, Excel displays the number in exponential notation, replacing part of the number with **E+n**, where **E** (which signifies exponent) multiplies the preceding number by 10 to the nth power.

If you create a custom number format for a 16-digit credit card number (such as **################** or **####-####-####-####**), Excel still changes the last digit to a zero. To successfully display a 16-digit credit card number in full, you must format the number as text. For security purposes, you can obscure all except the last few digits of a credit card number by using a formula that includes the **CONCATENATE**, **RIGHT**, and **REPT** functions.

3.10.3 Display credit card numbers in full

1. Select the cell or range of cells that you want to format.
   TIP: You can also select empty cells, and then enter numbers after you format the cells as text. Those numbers will be formatted as text.
2. On the **Home** tab, click the Dialog Box Launcher ⬜ next to Number.
3. In the Category box, click Text.
   NOTE: If you don't see the Text option, use the scroll bar to scroll to the end of the list.
   TIP: To include other characters (such as dashes) in numbers that are stored as text, you can include them when you type the credit card numbers.

3.10.4 Display only the last few digits of credit card numbers

For common security measures, you may want to display only the last few digits of a credit card number and replace the rest of the digits with asterisks or other characters. You can do this by using a formula that includes the **CONCATENATE**, **REPT**, and **RIGHT** functions.

The following procedure uses sample data to show how you can display only the last four numbers of a credit card number. After you copy the formula to your worksheet, you can adjust it to display your own credit card numbers in a similar manner.

1. Create a blank workbook or worksheet.
2. In this Help article, select the following sample data without the row and column headers.

Type	Data
Credit Card Number	5555-5555-5555-5555
Formula	**Description (Result)**
=CONCATENATE(REPT("****-",3), RIGHT(B2,4))	Repeats the "****-" text string three times and combines the result with the last four digits of the credit card number (****-****-****-**5555**)

Figure 3.20 Concatenating Credit Card Number

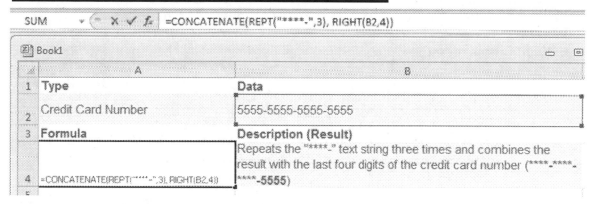

3. To copy the selected data, press **CTRL+C**.
4. In the worksheet, select cell **A1**.
5. To paste the copied data, press **CTRL+V**.
6. To switch between viewing the result and viewing the formula that returns the result, on the **Formulas** tab, in the **Formula Auditing** group, click **Show Formulas.**

   Keyboard shortcut : You can also press **CTRL+`** (grave accent).

NOTES:

- To prevent other people from viewing the entire credit card number, you can first hide the column that contains that number (column B in the example data), and then protect the worksheet so that unauthorized users cannot unhide the data. For more information, see Hide or display rows and columns and Protect worksheet or workbook elements.
- For more information about these functions, see **CONCATENATE, REPT,** and **RIGHT, RIGHTB.**

3.10.5 Display numbers as currency

If you want to display numbers as monetary values in Excel 2007 and 2010, you must format them as currency. To do this, you apply either the Currency or Accounting number format to the cells that you want to format. The number formatting options are available on the Home tab, in the Number group.

What's the difference between the Currency and Accounting formats?

Both the Currency and Accounting formats are used to display monetary values. The difference between the two formats is explained in the following table.

Table 3.13 Difference Between Currency and Accounting Formats

FORMAT	DESCRIPTION	EXAMPLE
Currency	When you apply the Currency format to a number, the currency symbol appears right next to the first digit in the cell. You can specify the number of decimal places that you want to use, whether you want to use a thousand separator, and how you want to display negative numbers. **TIP:** To quickly apply the Currency format, select the cell or range of cells you want to format, and then press **CTRL+SHIFT+$.**	**Currency Format** $5,365.00 $5,725.00 $167.00 $53,896.00 $0.00 -$45.00 -$4,568.00

FORMAT	DESCRIPTION	EXAMPLE

Accounting	Like the Currency format, the Accounting format is used for monetary values. However, this format aligns the currency symbols and decimal points of numbers in a column. In addition, the Accounting format displays zeros as dashes and negative numbers in parentheses. Like the Currency format, you can specify how many decimal places you want and whether to use a thousand separator. However, you cannot change the default display of negative numbers unless you create a custom number format. TIP To quickly apply the Accounting format, select the cell or range of cells you want to format. On the Home tab, in the Number group, click **Accounting Number Format** $. If you want to show a currency symbol other than the default, click the arrow next to the **Accounting Number Format** $ button and then select another currency symbol.	**Accounting Format**
		$ 5,365.00
		$ 5,725.00
		$ 167.00
		$ 53,896.00
		$ -
		$ (45.00)
		$ (4,568.00)

To change the default currency symbol for Microsoft Office Excel and other Microsoft Office programs, you can change the default regional currency settings in Control Panel. For more information, see Change the default country/region. Although the **Accounting Number Format button** $ image does not change when you do this, the currency symbol that you specified in Control Panel will be applied when you use either of the currency number formats.

Display numbers as currency

As mentioned earlier, you can quickly display a number with the default currency symbol by selecting the cell or range of cells, and then clicking **Accounting Number Format** in the Number group on the Home tab. (If you want to apply the Currency format instead, select the cells, and press **CTRL+SHIFT+$**.)

If you want more control over either format, or you want to change other aspects of formatting for your selection, you can use the following procedure.

1. Select the cells that you want to format.
2. On the Home tab, click the Dialog Box Launcher ⬜ next to Number.
3. In the Format Cells dialog box, in the **Category** list, click **Currency** or **Accounting**.
4. In the **Symbol** box, click the currency symbol that you want.

Figure 3.21 Number formatting commands in the Number group

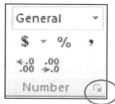

NOTE: If you want to display a monetary value without a currency symbol, you can click **None**.

5. In the **Decimal places** box, enter the number of decimal places that you want for the number. For example, to display **$1,750** instead of **$1,749.99** in the cell, enter **0** in the **Decimal places** box.

As you make changes, watch the number in the Sample box. It shows you how changing the amount of decimal places will affect the display of a number.

Figure 3.22 Currency Format

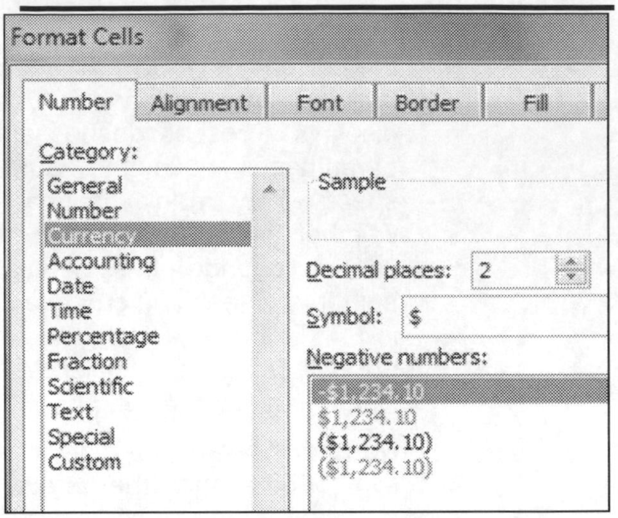

6. In the Negative numbers box, select the display style you want to use for negative numbers. If you don't like the existing options for displaying negative numbers, you can create your own number format. For more information about creating custom formats, see Create or delete a custom number format.

NOTE: The Negative numbers box is not available for the Accounting number format. That's because it is standard accounting practice to always show negative numbers in parentheses.

7. To close the Format Cells dialog box, click **OK**.

If Excel displays **#####** in a cell after you apply currency formatting to it, the cell probably isn't wide enough to display the data. To expand the column width, double-click the right boundary of the column containing the cells with the **#####** error. This automatically resizes the column to fit the number. You can also drag the right boundary until the columns are the size you want.

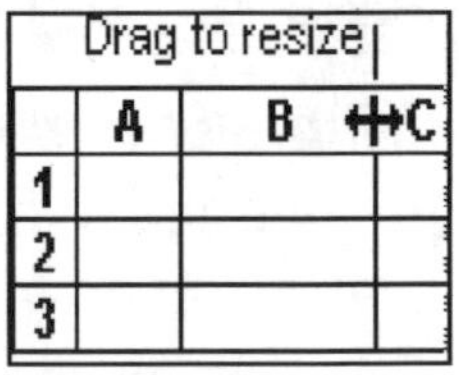

Remove Currency Formatting

If you want to remove the currency formatting, you can use the following procedure to reset the number format.

1. Select the cells that have currency formatting applied to them.
2. On the Home tab, in the Number group, click General.
3. Cells that are formatted with the General format do not have a specific number format.

3.11 Create a workbook template with specific currency formatting settings

If you often use currency formatting in your workbooks, you can save time by creating a workbook that includes specific currency formatting settings, and then saving that workbook as a template. You can then use this template to create other workbooks.

Create the template
1. Create a new workbook.
2. Select the worksheet or worksheets for which you want to change the default number formatting.

TO SELECT	DO THIS
A single sheet	Click the sheet tab. ⏮ ◀ ▶ ⏭ Sheet1 | Sheet2 / Sheet3 If you don't see the tab that you want, click the tab scrolling buttons to display the tab, and then click the tab. ⏮ ◀ ▶ ⏭ Sheet1 Sheet2 / Sheet3
Two or more adjacent sheets	Click the tab for the first sheet. Then hold down SHIFT while you click the tab for the last sheet that you want to select.
Two or more nonadjacent sheets	Click the tab for the first sheet. Then hold down CTRL while you click the tabs of the other sheets that you want to select.
All sheets in a workbook	Right-click a sheet tab, and then click **Select All Sheets** on the shortcut menu.

3. Select the specific cells or columns you want to format, and then apply currency formatting to them. Make any other customizations you like to the workbook.

4. Click the **Microsoft Office Button** , and then click **Save As.**
   In Excel 2010, click the File tab, and then click **Save As**
5. In the **File name** box, type the name that you want to use for the template.
6. In the **Save as type** box, click **Excel Template**, or click **Excel Macro-Enabled Template** if the workbook contains macros that you want to make available in the template.
7. Click **Save**.

The template is automatically placed in the Templates folder.

TIP: In Windows Vista, the Templates folder is usually **C:\Users\<your name>\AppData\Roaming\Microsoft\Templates.** In Microsoft Windows XP, the Templates folder is usually C:\Documents and Settings\<your name>\Application Data\Microsoft\Templates.

9. Close the template.
10. To use the template to create a new workbook, click the **Microsoft Office Button** , and then click **New**.
11. Under **Templates**, click **My Templates**.
12. In the **New** dialog box, double-click the template you just created.
Excel creates a new workbook that is based on your template.

3.12 Display numbers as dates or times

When a date or time is typed in a cell, it appears in a default date and time format. The default date and time format is based on the regional date and time settings that are specified in Control Panel, and changes when changes are made to those settings. You can display numbers in several other date and time formats, most of which are not affected by Control Panel settings.

1. Select the cells that you want to format.
2. On the Home tab, in the Number group, click the Dialog Box Launcher next to Number
3. In the Category list, click Date or Time.
4. In the Type list, click the date or time format that you want to use.

   NOTE: Date and time formats that begin with an asterisk (*) respond to changes in regional date and time settings that are specified in Control Panel. Formats without an asterisk are not affected by Control Panel settings.

   TIP: If you do not find the format that you are looking for in the Type list, you can create a custom number format by clicking Custom in the Category list, and then by using format codes for dates and times.

Table 3.14 Display Month and Time Formats

TO DISPLAY	USE THIS CODE
Months as 1–12	m
Months as 01–12	mm
Months as Jan–Dec	mmm
Months as January–December	mmmm
Months as the first letter of the month	mmmmm
Days as 1–31	d
Days as 01–31	dd
Days as Sun–Sat	ddd
Days as Sunday–Saturday	dddd
Years as 00–99	yy
Years as 1900–9999	yyyy

TO DISPLAY	USE THIS CODE
Hours as 0–23	h
Hours as 00–23	hh
Minutes as 0–59	m
Minutes as 00–59	mm
Seconds as 0–59	s
Seconds as 00–59	ss
Hours as 4 AM	h AM/PM
Time as 4:36 PM	h:mm AM/PM
Time as 4:36:03 P	h:mm:ss A/P
Elapsed time in hours; for example, 25.02	[h]:mm
Elapsed time in minutes; for example, 63:46	[mm]:ss
Elapsed time in seconds	[ss]
Fractions of a second	h:mm:ss.00

5. To display dates and times in the format of other languages, click the language setting that you want in the Locale (location) box.

    Dates or times that you enter in formatted cells will be displayed in the format that you selected.

Tips

- The number in the active cell of the selection on the worksheet appears in the Sample box, so that you can preview the number formatting options that you select.

- To quickly format a date or time, click the date or time format that you want in the Number Format box in the Number group on the Home tab.

- If you want to use the default date or time format, click the cell that contains the date or time, and then press CTRL+SHIFT+# or CTRL+SHIFT+@.

- A cell might display ##### when it contains data that has a number format that is wider than the column width. To see all text, you must increase the width of the column.

- When you try to undo a date or time format by selecting General in the Category list, Excel displays a number code. When you enter a date or time again, Excel displays the default date or time format. To enter a specific date or time format, such as January 2005, you can format it as text by selecting Text in the Category list.

3.13 Display numbers as fractions

Use the Fraction format to display or type numbers as actual fractions, rather than decimals.

1. Select the cells that you want to format.
2. On the Home tab, click the Dialog Box Launcher ☐ next to Number.
3. In the Category list, click Fraction in the Category list.
4. In the Type list, click the fraction format type that you want to use.

Table 3.15 Display Month and Time Formats

FRACTION FORMAT	THIS FORMAT DISPLAYS 125.456 AS
Single-digit fraction	125 1/2, rounding to the nearest single-digit fraction value
Double-digit fraction	125 26/57, rounding to the nearest double-digit fraction value
Triple-digit fraction	125 57/125, rounding to the nearest triple-digit fraction value
Fraction as halves	125 1/2
Fraction as quarters	125 2/4
Fraction as eighths	125 4/8
Fraction as sixteenths	125 7/16
Fraction as tenths	125 5/10
Fraction as hundredths	125 46/100

TIP: The number in the active cell of the selection on the worksheet appears in the Sample box, so that you can preview the number formatting options that you select.

NOTES:

- After you apply a fraction format to a cell, decimal numbers as well as actual fractions that you type in that cell will be displayed as a fraction. For example, typing .5 or 1/2 results in 1/2 when the cell has been formatted with a fraction type of Up to one digit.

- If no fraction format is applied to a cell, and you type a fraction such as 1/2, it will be formatted as a date. To display it as a fraction, apply a Fraction format, and then retype the fraction.

- If you don't need to perform calculations on fractions, you can format a cell as text before you type a fraction into it by clicking Text in the Category list. This way, the fractions that you type will not be reduced or converted to decimals. However, you cannot perform mathematical calculations on fractions that are displayed as text.

- To reset the number format, click General in the Category box (Format Cells dialog box) or in the Number Format box (Home tab, Number group). Cells that are formatted with the General format do not have a specific number format.

3.13 Display numbers as percentages

This section explains how to display numbers as percentages in Excel 2007/2010. However, it doesn't cover techniques for calculating percentages. To learn how to calculate values, such as sales tax for a certain amount or a percent change in sales between two fiscal quarters, see Calculate percentages.

How Excel 2007/2010 handles percentages

Although formatting numbers as percentages is straightforward, the results you get after applying the format may vary, depending on whether the numbers already exist in your workbook.

- **Formatting cells that contain numbers:** If you apply the Percentage format to existing numbers in a workbook, Excel multiplies those numbers by 100 to convert them to percentages. For example, if a cell contains the number 10, Excel multiplies that number by 100, which means that you will see 1000.00% after you apply the Percentage format. This may not be what you expected. To accurately display percentages, before you format the numbers as a percentage, make sure that they have been calculated as percentages, and that they are displayed in decimal format. Percentages are calculated by using the equation amount / total = percentage. For example, if a cell contains the formula =10/100, the result of that calculation is 0.1. If you then format 0.1 as a percentage, the number will be correctly displayed as 10%. To learn more about calculating percentages, see Calculate percentages.

- **Formatting empty cells:** Numbers that you type into cells after you apply the Percentage format to those cells are treated differently. Numbers equal to and larger than 1 are converted to percentages by default; and numbers smaller than 1 are multiplied by 100 to convert them to percentages. For example, typing 10 or 0.1 both result in 10.00%. (If you don't want to display the two zeros after the decimal point, it's easy to get rid of them, as explained in the following procedure.)

3.14 Display numbers as percentages

To quickly apply percentage formatting to selected cells, click Percent Style % in the Number group on the Home tab, or press CTRL+SHIFT+%.

If you want more control over the format, or you want to change other aspects of formatting for your selection, you can use the following procedure.

1. Select the cells that you want to format.
2. On the Home tab, click the Dialog Box Launcher ☐ next to Number.
3. In the Format Cells dialog box, in the Category list, click Percentage.

4. In the Decimal places box, enter the number of decimal places that you want to display. For example, if you want to see 10% instead of 10.00%, enter 0 in the Decimal places box.

Tips for displaying percentages

- To reset the number format of selected cells, click General in the Category list. Cells that are formatted with the General format have no specific number format.

- If you want negative percentages to stand out—for example, you want them to appear in red—you can create a custom number format (Format Cells dialog box, Number tab, Custom category). The format should resemble the following: 0.00%;[Red]-0.00%. When applied to cells, this format displays positive percentages in the default text color and negative percentages in red.

Figure 3.23 Format Cells dialog box, Showing the Category list - Percentage.

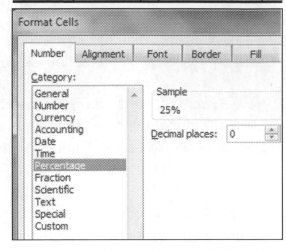

Figure 3.24 Custom number format.

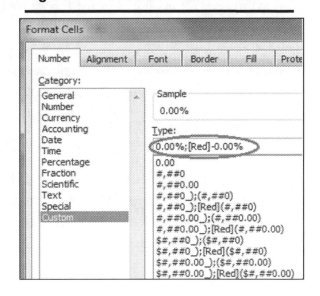

The portion that follows the semicolon represents the format that is applied to a negative value.

Similarly, you can display negative percentages in parentheses by creating a custom format that looks something like this: 0.00%_);(0.00%).

For more information on creating custom formats, see Create or delete a custom number format.

- You can also use conditional formatting (Home tab, Styles group, Conditional Formatting) to customize the way negative percentages appear in your workbook. The conditional formatting rule you create should be similar to the one shown in the following example. This particular rule instructs Excel to apply a format (red text) to a cell if the cell value is less than zero. For more information about conditional formatting, see Add, change, or clear conditional formats.

Figure 3.25 New Formatting Rule.

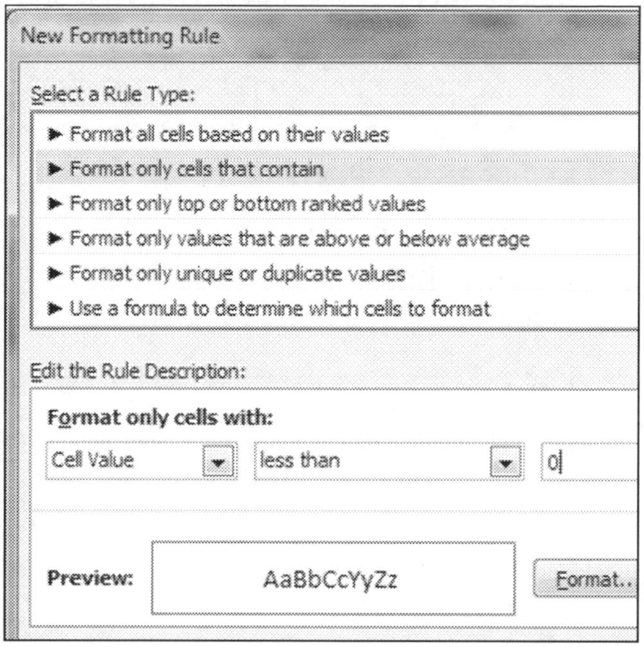

3.15 Display numbers as postal codes

Microsoft Office Excel provides two special number formats for postal codes, but you can also create a custom postal code format that displays the postal code correctly regardless of whether it has five or nine digits. In addition, you can create a custom format that displays the postal code preceded by leading characters to fill a cell's width.

3.15.1 Apply a predefined postal code format to numbers

1. Select the cell or range of cells that you want to format.
2. On the Home tab, click the Dialog Box Launcher ☐ next to Number.
3. In the Category box, click Special.
4. In the Type list, click Zip Code or Zip Code + 4.

NOTE: These codes are available in the Type list only if the Locale (location) is set to English (United States). Different locales provide different or no special codes in the Type list.

3.15.2 Create a custom postal code format

1. Select the cell or range of cells that you want to format.
2. On the Home tab, click the Dialog Box Launcher ⬛ next to Number.
3. In the Category box, click Custom.
4. In the Type list, select the number format that you want to customize.
   The number format that you select appears in the Type box above the Type list.

   NOTE: When you select a built-in number format in the Type list, Excel creates a copy of that number format that you can customize. The original number format in the Type list cannot be changed or deleted.

5. In the Type box, make the necessary changes to the selected number format.

   NOTE: If a range of cells contains both five-digit and nine-digit postal codes (ZIP Codes), you can apply a custom format that displays both types of ZIP Codes correctly. In the Type box, type [<=99999]00000;00000-0000
   For more information about how to create custom number formats, see Create or delete a custom number format.

3.15.3 Include leading characters in postal codes

You can format a cell or range of cells to display leading characters so that the postal code is preceded by enough characters to fill the cell's width. For example, you can use zeros or dashes to display a postal code as follows: 0000000 98052 or ------- 98052.

1. Select the cell or range of cells that you want to format.
2. On the Home tab, click the Dialog Box Launcher next to Number.
3. In the Category box, click Custom.
4. In the Type list, type *0 followed by the postal code format that you want to use. **TIP:** For example, for a 5-digit postal code, type ***0#####**

3.15.4 Display numbers as Social Security numbers

You can format a number as a Social Security number. For example, you can format a 9-digit number, such as 555501234, as 555-50-1234.

Display Social Security numbers in full
1. Select the cell or range of cells that you want to format.
2. On the Home tab, click the Dialog Box Launcher ⬛ next to Number.
3. In the Category box, click Special.
4. In the Type list, click Social Security Number.

Display only the last few digits of Social Security numbers

For common security measures, you may want to display only the last few digits of a Social Security number and replace the rest of the digits with zeros or other characters. You can do this by using a formula that includes the **CONCATENATE**, and **RIGHT** functions.

The following procedure uses example data to show how you can display only the last four numbers of a Social Security number. After you copy the formula to your worksheet, you can adjust it to display your own Social Security numbers in a similar manner.

1. Create a blank workbook or worksheet.
2. In this Help article, select the following example data without the row and column headers.

Figure 3.26 Worksheet Using A Formula To Format Social Security Number.

| SUM | ▾ | ✕ ✓ ƒx | =CONCATENATE("000-00-", RIGHT(B2,4)) |

🔲 Book1

	A	B
1	Type	Data
2	Social Security Number	555-50-1234
3	Formula	Description (Result)
4	=CONCATENATE("000-00-", RIGHT(B2,4))	Displays the "000-00-" text string instead of the first 5 digits of the Social Security number and combines it with the last four digits of the Social Security number (000-00-1234)

5. To copy the selected data, press CTRL+C.
6. In the worksheet, select cell A1.
7. To paste the copied data, press CTRL+V.
8. To switch between viewing the result and viewing the formula that returns the result, on the Formulas tab, in the Formula Auditing group, click Show Formulas.

    Keyboard shortcut : You can also press CTRL+` (grave accent).

NOTES

- To prevent other people from viewing the entire Social Security number, you can first hide the column that contains that number (column B in the example data), and then protect the worksheet so that unauthorized users cannot unhide the data.

For more information, see Hide or display rows and columns and Protect worksheet or workbook elements.

IMPORTANT: As a best practice, you may want to avoid storing complete Social Security numbers in your workbooks. Instead, store the full Social Security numbers in a location that meets stringent security standards (for example, a database program, such as Microsoft Office Access), and then use only the last four digits of the numbers in your workbooks.

* For more information about these functions, see **CONCATENATE** function, and **RIGHT, RIGHTB** functions.

3.16 Hide or display cell values

Suppose you have a worksheet that contains confidential information, such as employee salaries, that you do not want a co-worker who stops by your desk to see. Or perhaps you multiply the values in a range of cells by the value in another cell that you do not want to be visible on the worksheet. By applying a custom number format, you can hide the values of those cells on the worksheet.

Although cells with hidden values appear blank on the worksheet, their values remain displayed in the formula bar where you can work with them.

Hide cell values
1. Select the cell or range of cells that contains values that you want to hide.
2. On the Home tab, click the Dialog Box Launcher ⬜ next to Number.
3. In the Category box, click Custom.
4. In the Type box, select the existing codes.
5. Type ;;; (three semicolons).
6. Click OK.
   NOTE: The selected cells will appear blank on the worksheet, but a value appears in the formula bar when you click one of the cells.

Display hidden cell values
1. Select the cell or range of cells that contains values that are hidden.
2. On the Home tab, click the Dialog Box Launcher ⬜ next to Number.
3. Click unhide. (Or select custom – In the Type Box – select Erase)

3.16 How Excel Handles Dates and Times

In the Category box, click General to apply the default number format, or click the date, time, or number format that you want.

This section presents a quick overview of how Excel deals with dates and times. It includes coverage of the Excel program's date and time serial number system, and it offers tips for entering and formatting dates and times.

3.16.1 Understanding date serial numbers

1. To Excel, a date is simply a number. More precisely, a date is a ***serial number*** that represents the number of days since the fictitious date of January 0, 1900. A serial number of 1 corresponds to January 1, 1900; a serial number of 2 corresponds to January 2, 1900, and so on. This system makes it possible to deal with dates in formulas. For example, you can create a formula to calculate the number of days between two dates (just subtract one from the other).

2. Excel support dates from January 1, 1900, through December 31, 9999 (serial number = 2,958,465).

3. You may wonder about January 0, 1900. This *non-date* (which corresponds to date serial number 0) is actually used to represent times that aren't associated with a particular day. This non-date business becomes clear later in this chapter (see "Entering times").

4. To view a date serial number as a date, you must format the cell as a date. Choose Home >> Number >> Number Format. This drop-down control provides you with two date formats.

3.16.2 Choose Your Date System: 1900 or 1904

Excel actually supports two date systems: the 1900 date system and the 1904 date system. Which system you use in a workbook determines what date serves as the basis for dates. The **1900** date system uses **January 1, 1900**, as the day assigned to **date serial number 1**. The **1904** date system uses **January 1, 1904**, as the base date. By default, Excel for Windows uses the 1900 date system, and Excel for Macintosh uses the 1904 date system. Excel for Windows supports the 1904 date system for compatibility with Macintosh files. You can choose the date system for the active workbook in the Advanced section of the Excel Options dialog box. You can't change the date system if you use Excel for Macintosh.

Generally, you should use the default 1900 date system. And you should exercise caution if you use two different date systems in workbooks that are linked together. For example, assume that Book1 uses the 1904 date system and contains the date **1/15/1999** in cell **A1**. Assume that Book2 uses the 1900 date system and contains a link to cell A1 in Book1. Book2 displays the date as **1/14/1995**. Both workbooks use the same date serial number (**34713**), but they're interpreted differently.

One advantage to using the 1904 date system is that it enables you to display negative time values. With the 1900 date system, a calculation that results in a negative time (for example, 4:00 PM-5:30 PM) cannot be displayed. When using the 1904 date system, the negative time displays as -1:30 (that is, a difference of 1 hour and 30 minutes).

3.16.3 Entering dates

1. You can enter a date directly as a serial number (if you know it), but more often, you enter a date using any of several recognized date formats. Excel automatically converts your entry into the corresponding date serial number (which it uses for calculations), and it also applies the default date format to the cell so that it displays as an actual date rather than as a cryptic serial number.

2. For example, if you need to enter June 18, 2007, you can simply enter the date by typing June 18, 2007 (or any of several different date formats). Excel interprets your entry and stores the value 39251, the date serial number for that date. It also applies the default date format so that the cell contents may not appear exactly as you typed them.

    NOTE: Depending on your regional settings, entering a date in a format, such as June 18, 2007, may be interpreted as a text string. In such a case, you'd need to enter the date in a format that corresponds to your regional settings, such as 18 June, 2007.

3. When you activate a cell that contains a date, the Formula bar shows the cell contents formatted by using the default date format — which corresponds to your system's short date format. The Formula bar doesn't display the date's serial number. If you need to find out the serial number for a particular date, format the cell using a non-date number format.

    TIP: To change the default date format, you need to change a system-wide setting. Access the Windows Control Panel and select Regional and Language Options. Then click the Customize button to display the Customize Regional Options dialog box. Select the Date tab. The item selected in the Short Date Format drop-down list box determines the default date format used by Excel. These instructions apply to Windows XP and may vary with other versions of Windows.

    Table 3.16 shows a sampling of the date formats that Excel recognizes (using the U.S. settings). Results will vary if you use a different regional setting.

Table 3.16 Sampling of the date formats that Excel recognizes

Entry	Excel's Interpretation (U.S. Settings)
6-18-07	June 18, 2007
6-18-2007	June 18, 2007
6/18/07	June 18, 2007
6/18/2007	June 18, 2007
6-18/07	June 18, 2007
June 18, 2007	June 18, 2007
Jun 18	June 18 of the current year
June 18	June 18 of the current year
6/18	June 18 of the current year
6-18	June 18 of the current year
18-Jun-2007	June 18, 2007
2007/6/18	June 18, 2007

4. As you can see in Table 3.16, Excel is rather intelligent when it comes to recognizing dates entered into a cell. It's not perfect, however. For example, Excel does not recognize any of the following entries as dates:
   - June 18 2007
   - Jun-18 2007
   - Jun-18/2007

5. Rather, it interprets these entries as text. If you plan to use dates in formulas, make sure that Excel can recognize the date you enter as a date; otherwise, the formulas that refer to these dates will produce incorrect results.

6. If you attempt to enter a date that lies outside of the supported date range, Excel interprets it as text. If you attempt to format a serial number that lies outside of the supported range as a date, the value displays as a series of hash marks (#########).

3.16.4 Searching for Dates

If your worksheet uses many dates, you may need to search for a particular date by using the Find And Replace dialog box (which you can access by choosing **Home >> Editing >> Find & Select >> Find** or by pressing **Ctrl+F**). Excel is rather picky when it comes to finding dates. You must enter a full four-digit year into the Find What field in the Find dialog box. In addition, you must enter the date in the same format used to display dates in the Formula bar.

3.16.5 Understanding time serial numbers

When you need to work with time values, you simply extend the Excel date serial number system to include decimals. In other words, Excel works with times by using fractional days. For example, the date serial number for June 1, 2007, is **39234.** Noon (halfway through the day) is represented internally as **39234.5.**

The serial number equivalent of **one minute** is approximately **0.00069444.** The formula that follows calculates this number by multiplying 24 hours by 60 minutes, and dividing the result into 1. The denominator consists of the number of minutes in a day (**1,440**).   =1/(24*60)

Similarly, the serial number equivalent of **one second** is approximately **0.00001157,** obtained by the following formula: **1** divided by **24** hours times **60** minutes times **60** seconds. In this case, the denominator represents the number of seconds in a day (**86,400**). =1/(24*60*60)

In Excel, the smallest unit of time is **one one-thousandth** of a second. The time serial number shown here represents **23:59:59.999** (or one one-thousandth of a second before midnight):   **0.99999999**

Table 3.17 shows various times of day along with each associated time serial numbers.

Table 3.17 Times of Day and Their Corresponding Serial Numbers

Time of Day	Time Serial Number
12:00:00 AM (midnight)	0.00000000
1:30:00 AM	0.06250000
3:00:00 AM	0.12500000
4:30:00 AM	0.18750000
6:00:00 AM	0.25000000
7:30:00 AM	0.31250000
9:00:00 AM	0.37500000
10:30:00 AM	0.43750000
12:00:00 PM (noon)	0.50000000
1:30:00 PM	0.56250000
3:00:00 PM	0.62500000
4:30:00 PM	0.68750000
6:00:00 PM	0.75000000
7:30:00 PM	0.81250000
9:00:00 PM	0.87500000
10:30:00 PM	0.93750000

3.16.6 Entering times

As with entering dates, you normally don't have to worry about the actual time serial numbers. Just enter the time into a cell using a recognized format. Table 3.18 shows some examples of time formats that Excel recognizes.

Table 3.18 Time Entry Formats Recognized by Excel

Entry	Excel's Interpretation
11:30:00 am	11:30 AM
11:30:00 AM	11:30 AM
11:30 pm	11:30 PM
11:30	11:30 AM
13:30	1:30 PM

Because the preceding samples don't have a specific day associated with them, Excel (by default) uses a date serial number of 0, which corresponds to the non-day **January 0, 1900**. Often, you'll want to combine a date and time. Do so by using a recognized date-entry format, followed by a space, and then a recognized time-entry format. For example, if you enter **6/18/2007 11:30** in a cell, Excel interprets it as 11:30 a.m. on June 18, 2007. Its date/time serial number is **39251.4791666667**.

When you enter a time that exceeds 24 hours the associated date for the time increments accordingly. For example, if you enter **25:00:00** into a cell, it's interpreted as **1:00 AM** on **January 1, 1900**. The **day** part of the entry increments because the time exceeds 24 hours. Keep in mind that a time value without a date uses **January 0, 1900** as the date.

Similarly, if you enter a date and a time (and the time exceeds 24 hours), the date that you entered is adjusted. If you enter **9/18/2007 25:00:00**, for example, it's interpreted **as 9/19/2007 1:00:00 AM.**

If you enter a time only (without an associated date), into an unformatted cell, the maximum time that you can enter into a cell is **9999:59:59** (just under **10,000 hours**). Excel adds the appropriate number of days. In this case, **9999:59:59** is interpreted as **3:59:59 PM** on **02/19/1901**. If you enter a time that exceeds **10,000 hours**, the entry is interpreted as a text string rather than a time.

3.16.7 Formatting dates and times

You have a great deal of flexibility in formatting cells that contain dates and times. For example, you can format the cell to display the date part only, the time part only, or both the date and time parts.

You format dates and times by selecting the cells and then using the Number tab of the Format Cells dialog box, as shown in Figure 3.23. To display this dialog box, click the dialog box launcher icon in the Number group of the Home tab. Or, you can click the Number Format control and select More Number Formats from the list that appears.

The Date category shows built-in date formats, and the Time category shows built-in time formats. Some formats include both date and time displays. Just select the desired format from the Type list and click OK.

Use the Number tab in the Format Cells dialog box to change the appearance of dates and times.

Figure 3.27 Number tab in Format Cells dialog

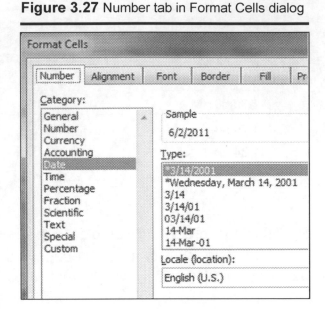

Figure 3.27 displays the Number tab in the Format Cells dialog box to change the appearance of dates and times.

When you create a formula that refers to a cell containing a date or a time, Excel automatically formats the formula cell as a date or a time. Sometimes, this automation is very helpful; other times, it's completely inappropriate and downright annoying. To return the number formatting to the default General format, choose Home >> Number >> Number Format, and select General from drop-down list Or, use this shortcut-key combination: **Ctrl+Shift+~.**

If none of the built-in formats meets your needs, you can create a custom number format. Select the Custom category and then type the custom format codes into the Type box.

3.16.8 Problems with dates

Excel has some problems when it comes to dates. Many of these problems stem from the fact that Excel was designed many years ago, before the acronym **Y2K** was even thought of. And, as I describe, the Excel designers basically emulated the Lotus

1-2-3 program's limited date and time features, which contain a nasty bug duplicated intentionally in Excel.

If Excel were being designed from scratch today, I'm sure it would be much more versatile in dealing with dates. Unfortunately, users are currently stuck with a product that .leaves much to be desired in the area of dates.

3.16.9 Excel's leap year bug

A leap year, which occurs every four years, contains an additional day (February 29). Although the year 1900 was not a leap year, Excel treats it as such. In other words, when you type **2/29/1900** into a cell, Excel interprets it as a valid date and assigns a serial number of **60.**

If you type 2/29/1901, however, Excel correctly interprets it as a mistake and doesn't convert it to a date. Rather, it simply makes the cell entry a text string.

How can a product used daily by millions of people contain such an obvious bug? The answer is historical. The original version of Lotus 1-2-3 contained a bug that caused it to consider 1900 as a leap year. When Excel was released some time later, the designers knew of this bug and chose to reproduce it in Excel to maintain compatibility with Lotus worksheet files.

Why does this bug still exist in later versions of Excel? Microsoft asserts that the disadvantages of correcting this bug outweigh the advantages. If the bug were eliminated, it would mess up millions of existing workbooks. In addition, correcting this problem would possibly affect compatibility between Excel and other programs that use dates. As it stands, this bug really causes very few problems because most users don't use dates before March 1, 1900.

3.16.10 Pre-1900 dates

The world, of course, didn't begin on January 1, 1900. People who use Excel to work with historical information often need to work with dates before January 1, 1900. Unfortunately, the only way to work with pre-1900 dates is to enter the date into a cell as text. For example, you can enter July 4, 1776 into a cell, and Excel won't complain.

You can't, however, perform any manipulation on dates entered as text. For example, you can't change its numeric formatting, you can't determine which day of the week this date occurred on, and you can't calculate the date that occurs seven days later.

To enable you work with any date in the years 0100 through 9999 you can download a trial version of Power Utility Pak from the following Web site (http://j-walk.com/ss).

3.16.11 Inconsistent date entries

You need to exercise caution when entering dates by using two digits for the year. When you do so, Excel has some rules that kick in to determine which century to use. And those rules vary, depending on the version of Excel that you use.

Two-digit years between **00** and **29** are interpreted as **21st century** dates, and two-digit years between **30** and **99** are interpreted as **20th-century** dates. For example, if you enter **12/15/28**, Excel interprets your entry as **December 15, 2028**. But if you enter **12/15/30**, Excel sees it as **December 15, 1930**, because Windows uses a default boundary year of 2029. You can keep the default as is or change it by using the Windows Control Panel. In Windows XP, display the Regional And Language Options dialog box. Then click the Customize button to display the Customize Regional Options dialog box. Select the Date tab and then specify a different year. This procedure may vary with different versions of Windows.

The best way to avoid any surprises is to simply enter all years using all four digits for the year.

3.17 How to handle leading zeros and precision in number codes

You may sometimes use social security, phone, and postal code numbers in your Office Excel data. What do these numbers have in common? Each of them is a number code that you don't use to count, but you may want to store them as numbers anyway. Unfortunately, Excel removes leading zeros that you may want to stay right where they are. Here's how to make Excel handle leading zeros in number codes the way that you want.

If you are using credit card numbers, or other number codes that contain 16 digits or more, you must use a text format because Excel has a maximum of 15 digits of precision and will round any numbers that follow the 15th digit down to zero.

3.17.1 The number format removes leading zeros by default

Number codes get into your Excel workbook in many ways. You might simply type them in, or copy and paste them from another program. Or, you might open a text file, or import data from a data source, such as an Access database. In many cases, Excel converts these number codes to a general or a number format. The default behavior of those formats is to remove any leading zeros and, depending on the length of the number, use scientific notation. You see, Excel treats a number code as just another number, but you know that it's a number code, and that the leading zeros need to stay put.

Table 3.19 Format for Social Security No., Phone Postal Code

NUMBER CODE	FICTITIOUS EXAMPLE	DEFAULT BEHAVIORS (VARIES WITH CELL WIDTH)
Social security	012345678	12345678 1.2E+07
Phone	0014255550177 0014255550177	14255550177 1.4E+10
Postal code	00123	123

You might not even see this happen if you are dealing with a long list of number codes. So it's important to be aware of the issue, especially when the data is used in other programs. Although you can convert the number format to a text format, you may not want to convert numbers to text, especially if you have a large list of long numbers, because this can increase the size of your workbook.

3.17.2 Use a custom or special format to keep the leading zeros

For number codes that contain fewer than 16 digits, if you want to resolve the issue just within the workbook because it's not used by other programs as a data source, you can use a custom or a special format to keep the leading zeros.

In addition, you can separate some of the digits in your number codes with dashes by adding these dashes to the custom format. For example, to make a phone number more readable, you can add a dash between the international code, the country/region code, the area code, the prefix, and the last few numbers.

Table 3.20 Customized Format for Social Security No., Phone

NUMBER CODE	FICTITIOUS EXAMPLE		NUMBER FORMAT AND NEW BEHAVIOR
Social security	012345678		000-00-0000 012-34-5678
Phone	0012345556789	0012345556789	00-0-000-000-0000 00-1-234-555-6789 00-1-234-555- 6789
Postal code	00123		00000 00123

Procedure

1. Select the cell or range of cells that you want to format.
   TIP: To cancel a selection of cells, click any cell on the worksheet.
2. On the Home tab, click the Dialog Box Launcher ⬜ next to Number.
3. In the Category box, click Custom and then, in the Type box, type the number format, such as **000-00-0000** for a social security number code, or **00000** for a postal code.

TIP: You can also click Special, and then select Zip Code, Zip Code + 4, Phone number, or Social Security Number.

Use a formula or calculated column

If you are using another program that opens the workbook as a data source, you should confirm to see how that program handles leading zeros. For example, you have a list of addresses in a workbook that you want to use as a data source to a Mail Merge operation, and one of the columns is a zip code with a custom format of **00000**. Office Access keeps the leading zeros, but Office Word removes the leading zeros. In the case of Word, you can specify a calculated column as the postal code field in the Mail Merge operation to ensure that the leading zeros are not removed.

Table 3.21 Formula for Calculated Column Format

	A	B	C	D
1	**NUMBER CODE**	**FICTITIOUS EXAMPLE**	**TEXT FUNCTION**	**NEW BEHAVIOR**
2	Social Security	012345678	=TEXT(B2,"000-00-0000")	012-34-5678
3	Phone	0012345556789	=TEXT(B3,"00-0-000-000-0000")	00-1-234-555-6789
4	Postal Code	0123	=TEXT(B4,"00000")	00123

To further complicate the matter, Excel has a maximum precision of 15 significant digits, which means that for any number containing 16 or more digits, such as a credit card number, the last digit is rounded down to zero.

Convert the number code to a text format

To convert a number code, such as a credit card number to text format, you can do the following:

Use the apostrophe character

For a small set of numbers, you can type an apostrophe character (') in front of the number code and then add back the leading zeros.

Convert the number to text when you import text data

In Step 3 of the Text Import Wizard (On the Data tab, in the Get External Data group, click From Text), you can select the column of data that contains the credit card number, and then explicitly choose a Text column data format.

3.18 Understanding Floating Point Precision

We sometimes users claim to have found a calculation error in Excel, when in fact the calculation is not wrong, but the side effects of binary floating point precision make it seem that way. The Excel team, discusses the way Excel performs calculations, explains why sometimes you see answers you may not expect, and provides some tips on how to avoid rounding issues. Take a look at the following table:

Table 3.22 Formatted to Four-Digits Decimal Places

	A	B	C
1	Expected	Measured	Absolute Difference
2	2.5094	2.5054	0.0040
3	2.5010	2.5070	0.0060
4	2.5029	2.5091	0.0062
5	2.5028	2.5109	0.0081
6	2.5058	2.5121	0.0063
7	2.5224	2.5184	0.0040

I want to be able to quickly identify the cases where the absolute difference is greater than or equal to **0.005**. So I apply a conditional formatting rule on the absolute difference column to format values greater than or equal to **0.005** to be red. As a scan down the table, I notice that the value of **0.005** is not highlighted. I check over my conditional formatting rule and the formula I used to calculate the absolute difference **(=ABS(A2-B2)),** they seem to be correct. I then increase the precision of the absolute difference column in order to get more precise results. I discover my results have changed. Why does **1.5240 - 1.5190 = 0.0049999999999999**?

Table 3.23 Formatted to 16-Digits Decimal Places

	A	B	C
1	Expected	Measured	Absolute Difference
2	2.5094000000000000	2.5054000000000000	0.0040000000000000
3	2.5010000000000000	2.5070000000000000	0.0060000000000002
4	2.5029000000000000	2.5091000000000000	0.0062000000000002
5	2.5028000000000000	2.5109000000000000	0.0080999999999998
6	2.5058000000000000	2.5121000000000000	0.0063000000000004
7	2.5224000000000000	2.5184000000000000	0.0040000000000000
8	2.5240000000000000	2.5190000000000000	0.0049999999999999

Have you ever encountered a similar situation where your spreadsheet does not give you the result you were expecting for a seemingly simple calculation?
You have checked over your calculations and still cannot figure out where it went wrong. Well the scenario you are facing may be due to floating point precision.

Table 3.24 Column D Formatted to 24-Digits Decimal Places

◢	A	B	C	D
	Expected	Measured	Absolute Difference 16 Decimal Places	Absolute Difference 24 Decimal Places
2	2.5094000000000000	2.5054000000000000	0.0040000000000000	0.004000000000000000000000
3	2.5010000000000000	2.5070000000000000	0.0060000000000002	0.006000000000000230000000
4	2.5029000000000000	2.5091000000000000	0.0062000000000002	0.006200000000000210000000
5	2.5028000000000000	2.5109000000000000	0.0080999999999998	0.008099999999999770000000
6	2.5058000000000000	2.5121000000000000	0.0063000000000004	0.006300000000000420000000
7	2.5224000000000000	2.5184000000000000	0.0040000000000000	0.004000000000000000000000
8	2.5240000000000000	2.5190000000000000	0.0049999999999999	0.004999999999999890000000

Note: We can see from this table that precision ends at the 15th significant digits in the decimal digit and after that all digits turned zeros. The column D illustrates this concept.

3.18.1 Overview of Floating Point Precision

Excel was designed in accordance to the IEEE Standard for Binary Floating-Point Arithmetic (IEEE 754). The standard defines how floating-point numbers are stored and calculated. The IEEE 754 standard is widely used because it allows-floating point numbers to be stored in a reasonable amount of space and calculations can occur relatively quickly.

The advantage of floating over fixed point representation is that it can support a wider range of values. For example, a fixed-point representation that has 5 decimal digits with the decimal point positioned after the third digit can represent the numbers 123.34, 12.23, 2.45, etc… whereas floating-point representation with 5 digit precision can represent 1.2345, 12345, 0.00012345, etc… Similarly, floating-point representation also allows calculations over a wide range of magnitudes while maintaining precision. For example,

Floating-point representation that has 4 digit precision:	$1.1 \times 10^{-1} \times 1.1 \times 10^{-1}$ $= 1.21 \times 10^{-2}$
Fixed-point representation that has 4 digit precision with the decimal point positioned after first digit:	$0.110 \times 0.110 = 0.012$

All numbers expressed in floating-point format are rational numbers. Irrational numbers such as π or $\sqrt{2}$, or non-terminating rational numbers must be approximated. The number of digits of precision also limits the accuracy of the numbers. Excel stores 15 significant digits of precision.

For example, the number 1234567890123456 cannot be exactly represented if 15 digits of precision are used. But in this case the 16th digit will turn 0.   The number 1234567890123456 in Excel will turn **1.23457E+15.** In decimals **0.1234567890123456,** the last digit will turn **0;** that is **0.1234567890123450.**

The IEEE 754 floating-point standard requires that numbers be stored in binary format. This means a conversion must occur before the numbers can be used in calculations. If the number can be represented exactly in floating-point format, then the conversion is exact. If not, then the conversion will result in a rounded value which will represent the original value. Numbers that appear exact in the decimal format may need to be approximated when converted to binary floating-point. For example, the fraction **1/10** can be represented in the decimal format as the rational number **0.1.** However, **0.1** cannot be represented precisely in binary floating-point of finite precision. **0.1** becomes the repeating binary decimal **0.0001100110011…,** where the sequence **1100** repeats infinitely. This number cannot be represented in a finite amount of space. So in Excel, it is rounded down by approximately **2.8E-17** when it is stored.

Structure of a Floating Point Number
A floating-point number is stored in binary in three parts within a 65-bit range:
the sign, the exponent, and the mantissa.

1 Sign Bit	11 Bit Exponent	1 Implied Bit	52 Bit Mantissa

The Sign Bit
The sign stores the sign of the number (positive or negative). **0** represents a positive number while **1** represents a negative number.

The Exponent
The exponent stores the power of **2** to which the number is raised or lowered. The exponent field needs to be able to represent both positive and negative exponents. To avoid having to store negative exponents, a bias value is added to the actual exponent. The bias for double-precision numbers is **1023.** For example, a stored value of 1000 indicates an exponent of 1000 - 1023, or -23.

The Mantissa
The mantissa stores the actual number. It is composed of an implied leading bit and the fraction bits. The storage size of the mantissa determines how close two adjacent floating point numbers can be. The mantissa and the exponent are stored in separate components. The precision of a number varies depending on the size of the mantissa. Excel can store numbers from **1.79769313486232E308** to **2.22507738585072E-308**; however, it can only do so within 15 digits of precision.

Common Examples of Error Due to Floating Point Calculation

Example 1: Loss of Precision When Using Very Large Numbers

The resulting value in **A3 is 1.2E+200**, the same value as **A1**. This is because Excel stores 15 digits of precision. At least **100** digits of precision would be required to calculate the formula above.

	A
1	1.20E+200
2	1.00E+100
3	=A1+A2

3	1.20E+200

Example 2: Loss of Precision When Using Very Small Numbers

	A
1	0.000123456789012345
2	1
3	=A1+A2

	A
1	0.000123456789012345
2	1
3	1.00012345678901

The resulting value in cell **A3** is 1.00012345678901 instead of **1.000123456789012345.** This is once again is because Excel stores 15 digits of precision. At least 19 digits of precision would be required to calculate the formula above.

Example 3: Repeating Binary Numbers

Many combinations of arithmetic operations on floating-point numbers may produce results that appear to be incorrect by very small amounts. For example, the equation **=1*(.5-.4-.1)** may be evaluated to the quantity (-2.78E-17), or -0.0000000000000000278 instead of 0. This is due to the fact that the IEEE 754 standard requires numbers to be stored in binary format. As I described earlier, not all decimal numbers can be converted exactly to binary, as in the case of 0.1. The conversion caused the loss of precision.

Correcting Precision Errors

Let us go back to my very first example where my conditional formatting seemingly did not work. I know now that was due to the fact that the numbers I was using to calculate the absolute difference did not have exact binary equivalents. This resulted in **1.3240 - 1.3190 = 0.0049999999999999**.

There are two basic ways in which you can compensate for some of the errors due to floating point calculation. The first method is to use the **ROUND()** function. The **ROUND()** function can be used to round the numbers to the number of decimal places that is required in your calculations. For my absolute difference column, I only require 4 decimals of precision. So I change the formula in the absolute difference column from: **=ABS(A2-B2).** The table below has values rounded to 4 digits.

To: =ROUND(ABS(A2-B2),4)

	A	B	C
1	**Expected**	**Measured**	**Absolute Difference**
2	2.5094	2.5054	0.0040
3	2.5010	2.5070	0.0060
4	2.5029	2.5091	0.0062
5	2.5028	2.5109	0.0081
6	2.5058	2.5121	0.0063
7	2.5224	2.5184	0.0040

Table 3.25 Column C carrying the Absolute Difference of columns A, and B

My conditional formatting rule works as expected now since 0.0049999999999999 has been rounded to 0.0050.

The second method to prevent rounding errors from affecting your work is by using the **Precision as displayed** option. This option forces the value of each number in the worksheet to be the displayed value. To turn on this option, follow these steps:

1. Click Microsoft Office Button **>>** Excel Options **>>** Advanced
   In Excel 2010 Click on File**>>**Excel Options **>>** Advanced
2. In the **When calculating this workbook** section, select the workbook you want, and then select the **Set precision as displayed** check box.

Figure 3.28 Excel Options

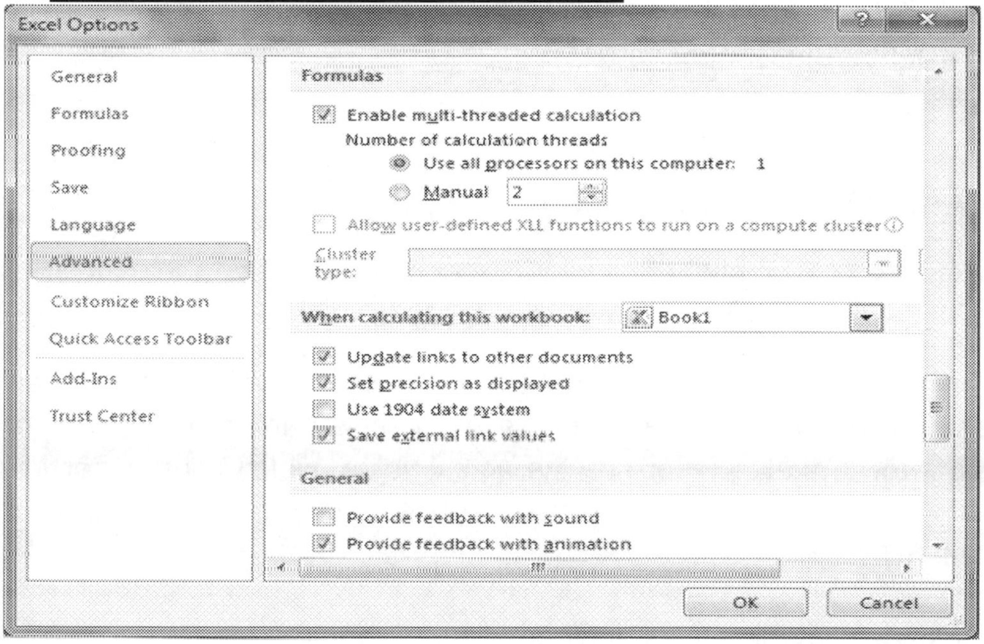

3. Click OK.

Going back to my absolute difference example, I set the number format to show four decimal places, and then I turned on Precision as displayed option. Since the display value is the actual value in the cell now, my conditional formatting works properly.

It is important to note that once the workbook is saved, all accuracy beyond four decimal places will be lost. This option affects the active workbook including all worksheets. You cannot undo this option and recover the lost data so save your workbook prior to enabling this option. This option is generally not recommended unless you are sure more precision will not ever be needed for your situation.

Show or hide the thousands separator

1. Select the cells that you want to format.
2. On the Home tab, click the Dialog Box Launcher ☐ next to Number.
4. On the Number tab, in the Category list, click Number.
5. To display or hide the thousands separator, select or clear the Use 1000 Separator (,) check box.

   Tip: To quickly display the thousands separator, you can click Comma Style ⟩ in the Number group on the Home tab.

   NOTE: By default, Microsoft Office Excel displays the system separator for thousands. You can specify a different system separator by changing the regional settings in Control Panel.

3.18.2 Various Methods of Rounding Numbers

Rounding numbers is a common task, and Excel provides quite a few functions that round values in various ways.

You must understand the difference between rounding a value and formatting a value. When you format a number to display a specific number of decimal places, formulas that refer to that number use the actual value, which might differ from the displayed value. When you round a number, formulas that refer to that value use the rounded number.

Table 3.26 below summarizes the Excel rounding functions.

Table 3.26 Excel Rounding Functions

Function	What It Does
CEILING	Rounds a number up (away from zero) to the nearest specified multiple
DOLLARDE	Converts a dollar price, expressed as a fraction, into a decimal number
DOLLARFR	Converts a dollar price, expressed as a decimal, into a fractional number
EVEN	Rounds up (away from zero) positive numbers to the nearest even integer; rounds down (away from zero) negative numbers to the nearest even integer
FLOOR	Rounds down (toward zero) a number to the nearest specified multiple
INT	Rounds down a number to make it an integer
MROUND	Rounds a number to a specified multiple
ODD	Rounds up (away from zero) numbers to the nearest odd integer; rounds down (away from zero) negative numbers to the nearest odd integer
ROUND	Rounds a number to a specified number of digits
ROUNDDOWN	Rounds down (toward zero) a number to a specified number of digits
ROUNDUP	Rounds up (away from zero) a number to a specified number of digits
TRUNC	Truncates a number to a specified number of significant digits

The following sections provide examples of formulas that use various types of rounding.

Rounding to the Nearest Multiple
The MROUND function is useful for rounding values to the nearest multiple. For example, you can use this function to round a number to the nearest 5. The following formula returns 135:   **=MROUND(133,5)**

Rounding Currency Values
Often, you need to round currency values. For example, a calculated price might be a number like $45.78923. In such a case, you want to round the calculated price to the nearest penny. This process might sound simple, but you can round this type of value in one of three ways:

• Round it up to the nearest penny.
• Round it down to the nearest penny.
• Round it to the nearest penny (the rounding can be up or down).

The following formula assumes that a dollar-and-cents value is in cell A1. The formula rounds the value to the nearest penny. For example, if cell A1 contains $12.421, the formula returns $12.42. **=ROUND(A1,2)**

If you need to round up the value to the nearest penny, use the **CEILING** function. The following formula rounds up the value in cell A1 to the nearest penny (if, for example, cell A1 contains $12.421, the formula returns $12.43): **=CEILING(A1,0.01)**

To round down a dollar value, use the **FLOOR** function. The following formula, for example, rounds down the dollar value in cell A1 to the nearest penny (if cell A1 contains $12.421, the formula returns $12.42): **=FLOOR(A1,0.01)**

To round up a dollar value to the nearest nickel, use this formula: **=CEILING(A1,0.05**)

Using the INT and TRUNC Functions

On the surface, the **INT** and **TRUNC** functions seem similar. Both convert a value to an integer. The **TRUNC** function simply removes the fractional part of a number. The **INT** function rounds down a number to the nearest integer, based on the value of the fractional part of the number.

In practice, **INT** and **TRUNC** return different results only when using negative numbers. For example, the following formula returns −14.0: **=TRUNC(-14.2)**

The next formula returns −15.0 because −14.2 is rounded down to the next lower integer: **=INT(-14.2)**

The **TRUNC** function takes an additional (optional) argument that's useful for truncating decimal values. For example, the following formula returns 54.33 (the value truncated to two decimal places): **=TRUNC(54.3333333,2)**

Rounding to n Significant Digits

In some situations, you might need to round a value to a particular number of significant digits. For example, you might want to express the value 1,432,187 in terms of two significant digits (that is, as 1,400,000). The value 84,356 expressed in terms of three significant digits is 84,300.

If the value is a positive number with no decimal places, the following formula does the job. This formula rounds the number in cell A1 to two significant digits. To round to a different number of significant digits, replace the 2 in this formula with a different number: **=ROUNDDOWN(A1,2-LEN(A1))**

For non-integers and negative numbers, the solution is a bit trickier. The following formula provides a more general solution that rounds the value in cell A1 to the number of significant digits specified in cell A2. This formula works for positive and negative integers and non-integers: **=ROUND(A1,A2-1-INT(LOG10(ABS(A1))))**

For example, if cell A1 contains 1.27845 and cell A2 contains 3, the formula returns 1.28000 (the value, rounded to three significant digits).

3.19 Assignment s

Answer the following project questions by showing all the appropriate steps that should be followed to arrive at the answer for each question.

1. Describe the steps required to create a new cell style.

2. Show how you will change the font color of cell contents in the range A1:B10 from black to blue color.

3. What will you achieve from the following Shortcut keys:
    (a) CTRL+B; (b) CTRL+I; (c) CTRL+U.

4. Describe the steps to obtain (√) symbol from the ASCII table.

5. Outline the general process of formatting the following:
    a. date and time in a cell.
    b. Font size of a cell content.
    c. A cell highlighted with orange color.
    d. A number in a cell as percentage.
    e. A number in a cell as currency.

6. Given $15,275.65 as the content of cell B1. Show how you will change the format to ¢15 275.65.

7. A date and time given as "5/21/11 0:18:00" we want to format this date so it will display the date as "2011-05-21 00:18:00.001".
    a. What format symbols are required to generate the date as indicated?
    b. Describe the steps required to achieve this objective.

8. With Error Checking turned on, a numbers was entered into cells that are formatted as text.
    a. Describe the resulting number in this cell.
    b. Which method will be appropriate to correct this error or change it to the appropriate number format.

9. Given the formula "**=LEFT(A3,LEN(A3)-1)*-1**", in cell A4; if the content of cell A3 is "**-155**", what is the result for the formula?

In the table below the second column shows the list of format codes and the third column contains the list of corresponding values to be formatted using the format codes. Use these two columns to answer the displayed values into the fourth column for questions 10 thru 21 by showing how the formatted values are presented.

Question No	USE THIS FORMAT CODE	USED THIS VALUES	DISPLAYED RESULTS
10.	####.#	1234.59	
11.	#.000	8.9	
12.	0.#	.631	
13.	#.0#	1234.568	
14.	#.0#	12	
15.	???.???	44.398	
16.	???.???	102.65	
17.	???.???	2.8	
18.	# ???/???	5.25	
19.	# ???/???	5.3	
20.	0.00E+00	15,200,000	
21.	#0.0E+0	15,200,000	

22. Derive the formula for displaying 20-digits credit card number displayed in the format as "**5555-5555-5555-5555**"

23. What will be returned by the formula "**=CONCATENATE("000-00-",R`IGHT(C2,4)**", when cell C2 contains 9-digits number.

24. Assuming cell A1 contains $15.421, what values will the following formula return:
    a. A2: =CEILING(A1,0.01)
    b. A3: =FLOOR(A1,0.01)
    c. A4: =ROUND(A1,2)

25. What values will be returned from running the following formula:
    a. =MROUND(143,5) ?
    b. =TRUNC(84.3333333,2) ?

CHAPTER 4

More Functions, Formulas and Macros

Objectives:

- o *Definitions Formulas, Functions and Cell Ranges*
- o *Define Relative and Absolute Cell Addresses*
- o *Formulas with Multiple Operators*
- o *Inserting and Editing Formulas and Functions*
- o *Auto Calculate and Manual Calculation*
- o *Defining Names, Using and Managing Defined Names*
- o *Creating Macros in Excel*

4.1 Introduction to Formulas in Spreadsheet

Formulas and functions were briefly discussed in chapter one. As had been described in chapter one under general spreadsheet overview a formula identifies the calculations needed, and places the result in the same cell which contains the formula. It is therefore important to remember that a cell containing a formula has two display components; the formula itself and the resulting value. The formula is normally only shown when the cell containing the results is selected by "clicking" the mouse over the particular cell; otherwise it contains the result of the calculations. A formula assigns values to a cell or range of cells, and typically has the format below:

All formulas begins with **Equal sign and Expression**

> **= expression** (e.g. **=B1/B2 or =A1+A2–A3*2, etc.)**

- The expression may consist of cell addresses and/or values, such as 4, 9.15 or 5.69E-12;
- References to other cells, such as, e.g., A1 for a single cell or B1:B5 for a range of cells;
- Arithmetic operators, such as **+, –, *, /,** exponents(^), ( ) and others;
- Relational operators, such as **=, >=, >, <, <>** and others; this returns Boolean value (true or false).
- Functions such as **SUM(), AVERAGE(), TAN(),** and many others.

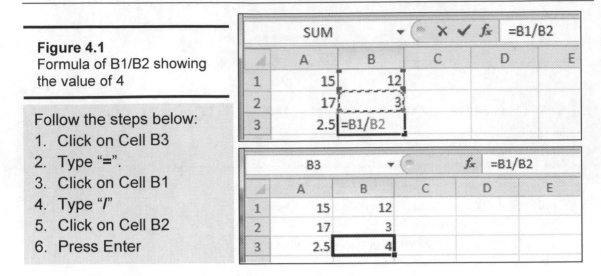

Figure 4.1
Formula of B1/B2 showing the value of 4

Follow the steps below:
1. Click on Cell B3
2. Type "=".
3. Click on Cell B1
4. Type "/"
5. Click on Cell B2
6. Press Enter

4.2 Relative and Absolute References

When a cell contains a formula, it often contains references to other cells. Such a cell reference is a type of variable (*a symbolic name associated with a value and whose associated value may be changed*). Its value is the value of the referenced cell or some derivation of it. If that cell in turn references other cells, the value depends on the values of those. When a cell address is used in a formula without a preceding dollar sign ($) like **A1** the reference cell is said to be *relative.* When the cell reference is preceded by dollar sign ($) such as **$A$1** this Cell reference is said to be *absolute*. The relative cell is reference is such that when you define a formula in this cell and you select this cell and drag it either through the rows or columns the defined formula will reflect the relative cell addresses; whereas the absolute will reference the original formula without changing the cell addresses. The illustration below demonstrates this phenomenon.

Figure 4.2
Formula of A1+B1 showing relative cell reference

Figure 4.3 Relative Reference
Formula of A1+B1 dragged down to reflect the relative cells:

=A1+B1	=> 27
=A2+B2	=> 20
=A3+B3	=> 6.5

Figure 4.4 Absolute Reference
Formula of $A$1+$B$1 dragged
down to reflect the relative cells:
=$A$1+$B$1 => 27
=$A$1+$B$1 => 27
=$A$1+$B$1 => 27

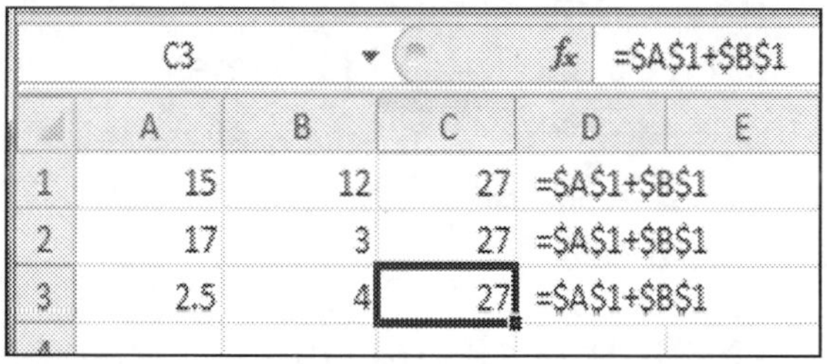

	C3			f_x	=$A$1+$B$1
	A	B	C	D	E
1	15	12	27	=$A$1+$B$1	
2	17	3	27	=$A$1+$B$1	
3	2.5	4	27	=$A$1+$B$1	

The above formula acts like a constant, both the cell address and value do not change. All formulae refer to the original defined formula.

4.3 Cell Ranges

References can be relative (e.g., A1, or B1:B6), absolute (e.g., $A$1, or $B$1:$B$6) or mixed row-wise or column-wise absolute/relative (e.g., $A1 is column-wise absolute and A$1 is row-wise absolute).

Note: **$A1** implies that column is *absolute* while the row is *relative*

   A$1 implies that row is *absolute* while the column is *relative*

The range is defined by:

   Starting cell address + colon (:) + end cell address. e.g. A1: B3

The start cell address can contain different columns or rows. The range is accomplished by clicking on the starting cell address and dragging the cursor to the end cell address. For example A1:A5

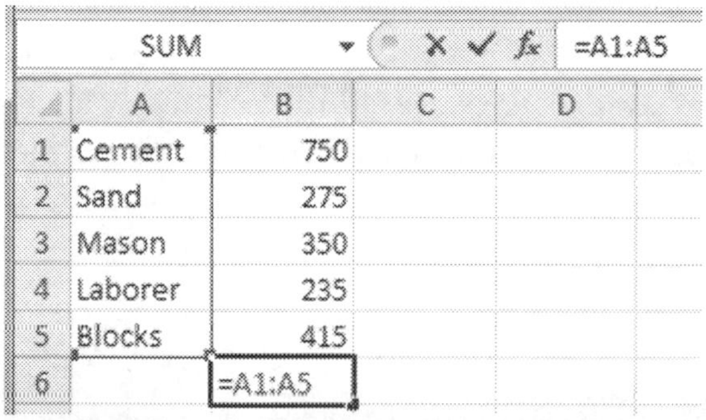

	SUM		f_x	=A1:A5
	A	B	C	D
1	Cement	750		
2	Sand	275		
3	Mason	350		
4	Laborer	235		
5	Blocks	415		
6		=A1:A5		

Figure 4.5. A1:A5

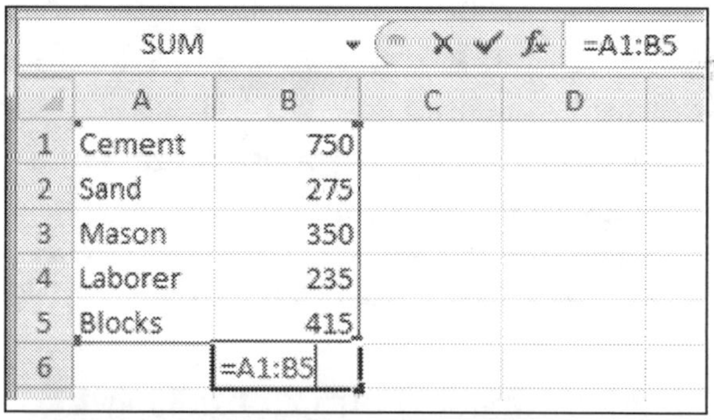

	SUM		f_x	=A1:B5
	A	B	C	D
1	Cement	750		
2	Sand	275		
3	Mason	350		
4	Laborer	235		
5	Blocks	415		
6		=A1:B5		

Figure 4.6 A1:B5

The availability or options for valid formulas will depend on the particular spreadsheet implementation but, in general, most arithmetic operations and quite complex nested conditional operations can be performed by most of today's commercial spreadsheets. Modern implementations also offer functions to access custom-build functions, remote data, and applications.

A formula may contain a condition (or nested conditions) - with or without an actual calculation - and is sometimes used purely to identify and highlight errors. In the example below, it is assumed the sum of a column of percentages (B1 through B6) is tested for validity and an explicit message put into the adjacent right-hand cell.

=IF(SUM (B1:B6) > 100, "More than 100%", **SUM (B1:B6))**

What will be the result of the above formula when SUM (B1:B6) is 120?

A spreadsheet does not, in fact, have to contain any formulas at all, in which case it could be considered merely a collection of data arranged in rows and columns (a database) like a calendar, timetable or simple list. Because of its ease of use, formatting and hyperlinking capabilities, many spreadsheets are used solely for this purpose.

4.4 Functions in Spreadsheet

Spreadsheets usually contain a number of supplied functions, such as arithmetic operations (for example, summations, averages and so forth), trigonometric functions, statistical functions, and so forth. In addition there is often a provision for user-defined functions. In Microsoft Excel these functions are defined using Visual Basic for Applications in the supplied Visual Basic editor, and such functions are automatically accessible on the worksheet. In addition, programs can be written that pull information from the worksheet, perform some calculations, and report the results back to the worksheet. Functions themselves cannot write into the worksheet, but simply return their evaluation. However, in Microsoft Excel, subroutines can write values or text found within the subroutine directly to the spreadsheet.

4.5 The Formulas Tab Ribbon of Microsoft Excel

The Formulas tab ribbon contains four groups of items including Function Library, Defined Names, Formula Auditing, and Calculations.

Figure 4.7 Formulas tab showing group of items

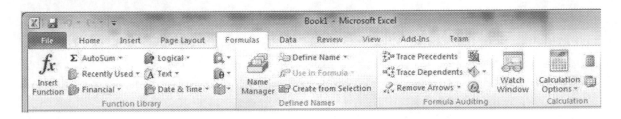

To Insert a Function: Select the cell where you want to enter the function and click the fx Insert Function button on the Formula Bar.

To Reference a Cell in a Formula: Type the cell reference (for example, B5) in the formula or click the cell you want to reference.

To Create an Absolute Cell Reference: Precede the cell references with a $ sign or press **[F4]** after selecting a cell range to make it absolute, e.g., $D$7:$E$11.

To Use Several Operators or Cell Ranges: Enclose the part of a formula you want to calculate first in parentheses.

4.6 Performing Calculations with Formulas in Microsoft Excel

All calculations in Excel are performed by using formulas and functions. A formula is a series of commands instructing Excel to perform calculations based on designated values, cell references, and commands. A function is a pre-written formula. A formula can be a single function or a combination of functions. A common example of such a function is *Average*, a pre-written formula which finds the **sum** of a set of numbers, **counts** how many numbers are in the set, and then **divides** to find the average. In this case the formula *average* is composed of the functions: sum, counting, and divide. To save time and work, functions can be embedded within formulas.

This section of the chapter focuses on formulas and provides some formulas that will make working with your workbook and worksheets faster.

- *Writing Formulas for Your Workbook*
- *Calculating Your Workbook*

Writing Formulas for Your Workbook
Actually the best use of spreadsheet is its ability to use formulas for mathematical calculations. Formulas can be used in two different ways indicated below.

- *Mathematical operations within cells and worksheets*
- *Link other worksheets and other workbook files*

4.6.1 Basic Formula Requirements

When writing a formula in Excel spreadsheet, there are three elements which must be included for it to work properly:

- An equals sign [=] at the beginning of the formula
- Operand(s) (e.g., values or cell references that will be used to create the result of the formula)
- Operant(s) or Operators (e.g., commands to add, subtract, multiply, divide or perform other actions upon the operands)

Formulas may be extremely simple or extremely complex, and some even contain functions within them. A very basic formula could appear like this:

=A1 + A2

Let say this formula is located at the cell address A3, the formula can be naturally re-written as A3 = A1 + A2. In this example, the cell references A1 and A2 are the operands, the [+] is the operant, and the selected cell (A3) would contain the sum of the values in cells A1 and A2. Below is an illustration of the operation:

Figure 4.8
Worksheet Showing
=A1+A2

Cell A3 contains two values: 15 and formula: =A1 + A2

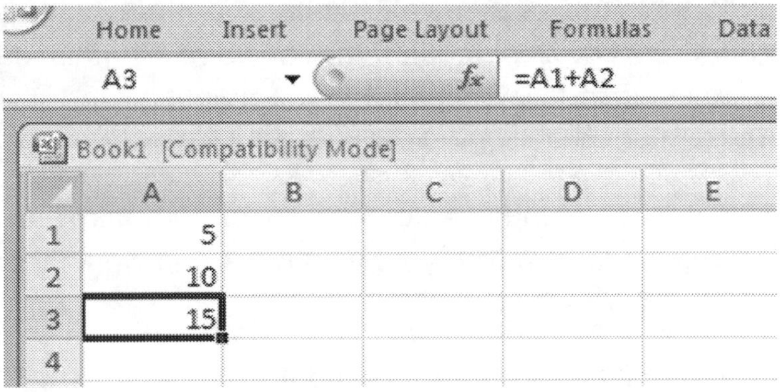

4.7 Creating a Formula for a Single Worksheet

Formulas can be basic or complex, depending on your needs. If you are creating a complex but fairly common formula (such as finding an average), it may be helpful for you to insert a function instead of creating the entire formula from scratch. Formulas for a single worksheet may be defined by simply making direct reference to cell addresses involved. When you want to create a formula for a single worksheet, you must follow the following steps:

1. Select the cell where the results should be displayed
2. To begin the function, type the equal sign [**=**]
3. Click the first cell to be included **OR** Type the cell reference to the first cell to be included. NOTE: Be sure to stay aware of whether you will need to use a relative or absolute cell reference.
4. Type the first operator EXAMPLE: Press [**+**].
5. Click the next cell to be included **OR** Type the cell reference to the next cell to be included
6. Repeat steps 4-5 as necessary to complete the formula
7. When finished, press [**Enter**] HINT: Be sure to press [Enter] before clicking away from the cell. If you don't, each cell that you click will be added to your formula.

The creation of the formula in figure 4.5 above went through these steps. However the [+] sign in the formula can be replaced with the **SUM** function, especially when you have to add up several cells.

Similarly the formula would begin with an equal sign [=] as   =SUM (A1:A3) with a defined range of cells.

   =SUM (A1:A3)

Figure 4.9
Worksheet Showing the use the SUM function:
=SUM(A1:A3)

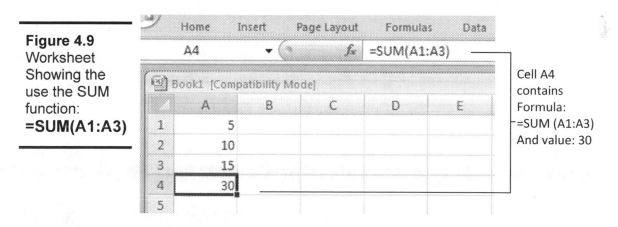

Cell A4 contains Formula: =SUM (A1:A3) And value: 30

In the above case instead of clicking on operator [+] you actually click on function (f_x) to select **SUM** from among the list of functions. Another way of displaying the function list is to type [=] and followed by an "**S**". Then Click OK button.

Figure 4.10
Insert Function
Dialog Box

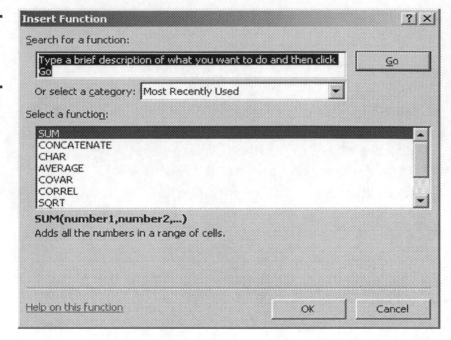

Specifying the range of cells. In this example the range is **A1:A3** which implies from cell A1 to A3.

Figure 4.11 Function Arguments: specifying the cell

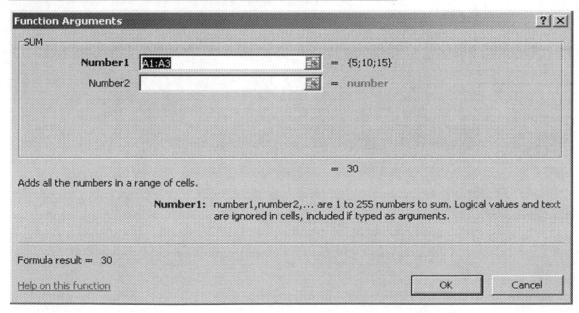

All formulas must be created following these steps:
1. Select the cell where the results should be displayed
2. To begin the function, press [=]

3. Click on function symbol (fx); select SUM.
4. Select the range. Here it is A1:A3. **OR** in the parentheses after the SUM type the beginning cell reference, and colon (**:**) and ending cell reference to specify the range.
5. Repeat steps 3–4 as necessary to complete the formula
6. When finished, press [**Enter**] HINT**:** Be sure to press [Enter] before clicking away from the cell. If you don't, each cell that you click will be added to your formula.

Another method of creating similar formulas must be created following these steps:
1. Select the cell where the results should be displayed
2. To begin the function, press [**=**]
3. Type the name of function. e.g., SUM and which is followed with beginning parentheses. NOTE**:** as soon as you start typing you will get all the sorted list of functions beginning with the letter you type, so will have to click on the desired function name.
4. Click on the beginning cell and drag it to the end of cell desired.
5. Close the parentheses and press Enter

Figure 4.12
Insert of SUM Function
In a Formula

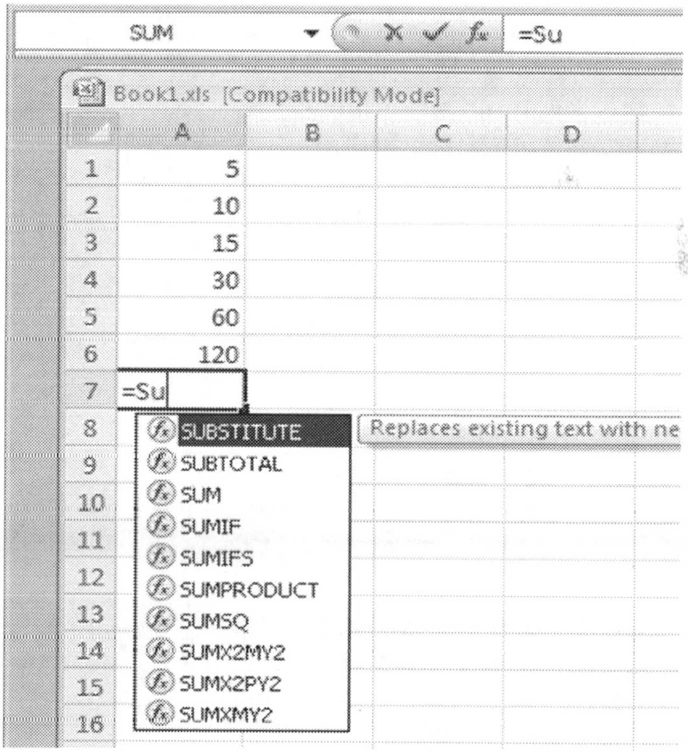

Notes:

The reader would notice that right after entering "=" you typed the character "S" which generated the list of all the functions that begins in "S" and the list shortens as you type along. You can choose to select the appropriate function from the list or type the full function name.

Figure 4.13
After Inserting the SUM Function
Comes the opening Parentheses

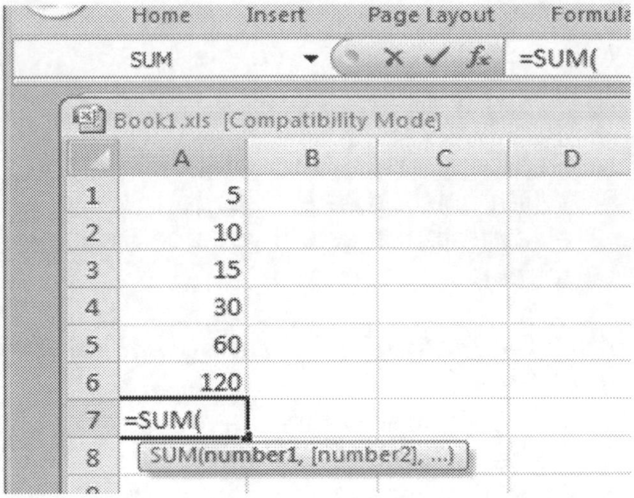

Notes:

All functions have open and close parentheses which take arguments or parameters. The reader would notice that right after entering **"=SUM("** Excel shows a tooltip as **SUM(number1,[number2],…)**

Figure 4.14
SUM Function and the Cell Range representing the parameters.

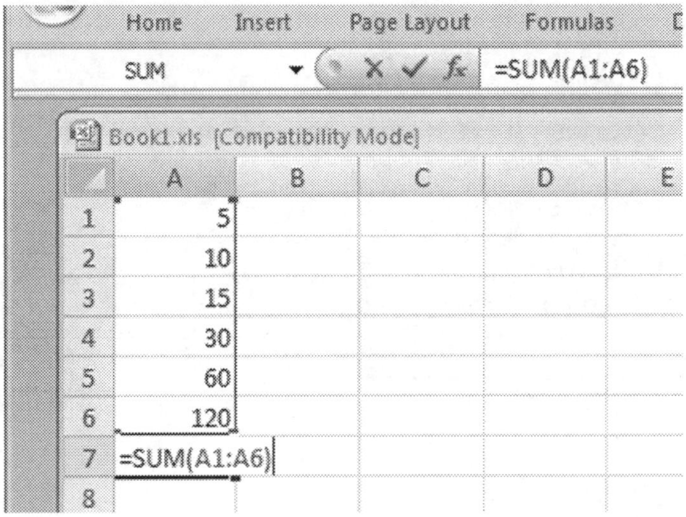

Notes:

The SUM function is finally defined as =SUM(Cell Range). In this example the function is given as **=SUM(A1:A6).**
The range was defined by clicking on A1 and dragging the mouse to A6, and typing the closing parentheses.

Figure 4.15
AVERAGE Function and the Cell Range representing the parameters.

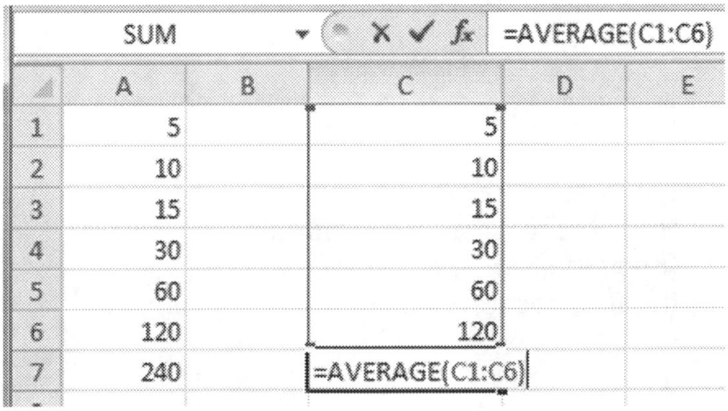

The AVERAGE function is defined as =AVERAGE(Cell Range). In this example the function is given as **=AVERAGE(A1:A6).**
After each case press **Enter**.

4.8 Writing Formula for Multiple Worksheet

While multiple worksheets can make your workbook more effective, writing formulas that include information across multiple worksheets is more complicated unlike writing formulas for a single worksheet. The advantage is that you can link between cells on one or more worksheets within the same workbook.

4.8.1 Using Special Characters

Five symbols can be used when creating a formula that links two or more separate worksheets. Each of these symbols must be placed directly into the formula to complete its respective function.

Character	Name	Use Within Formula
!	Exclamation point	Place between the worksheet name and cell reference (This implies referencing worksheet)
'	Apostrophe	Place around the filename and sheet name or when a sheet name contains a space EXAMPLE: 'Accounts 2010'!C4:C8
[ ]	Brackets	Place around a filename
:	Colon	Signifies a range (B3:C2 means B3 through C2)
+	Plus sign	Signifies a range (B3+C2 means B3 and C2)

NOTE: The following examples assume that the worksheets *Accounts* and *Payments* are located within the workbook *Accounts.xlsx*.

4.8.2 Creating a Link to a Single Worksheet in the Same Workbook

Excel allows you to create links to other worksheets, which enables you to include values from other worksheets in your formulas. These instructions focus on linking to a separate worksheet within the same workbook.

1. Select the cell where you want the formula to appear
2. To create the formula, use this format:
   =function_name(worksheet_name!cell_reference)
   EXAMPLES:
   (*with no spaces in sheet name*) **=SUM(Accounts!G19:G26)**
   (*with space in sheet name*) **=SUM('Accounts 2010'!G5:G8)**
3. To accept the formula, press **[Enter]**

Figure 4.16 Presentation of Worksheet named Accounts with highlighted range.

Workbook: Expenses.xlsx

G19				f_x	496.59	

	A	B	C	D	E	F	G
16				**2010**			
17							
18		Item No	Date	Name	Amount	Rate	Equivalent GH¢
19		1	1/7/2010	Yaw Sego	360	1.41882	496.59
20		2	2/13/2010	George Oteng Mensah	510	1.41544	707.72
21		3	3/27/2010	George Oteng Mensah	260	1.4048	351.2
22		4	3/27/2010	Emilia Konadu Sarfo	370	1.4048	505.73
23		5	6/6/2010	Eric Owusu Siaw	159	1.4045	210.69
24		6	6/23/2010	Postage for 3 Books	79.63	1.4045	111.84
25		7	7/15/2010	Philomena Mensah	209	1.41135	282.27
26					1947.63		2666.04
27							
28							

⊮ ◂ ▸ ⊨	Accounts	Accounts 2011	Summary	

Ready   Average: 666.5100838   Count: 8   Sum: 5332.08067

The above is an illustration of a Workbook named Expenses.xlsx containing three worksheets, Accounts, Accounts 2011, and Summary. The active worksheet is the Accounts. Looking at the Accounts worksheet status bar we will see the summary of the selected range G19:G26: Average =**666.51**, Counts =**8**, Sum=**5332.08**

Figure 4.17 Presentation of Worksheet named Accounts 2011 with highlighted range.

G5				f_x	1000	

	A	B	C	D	E	F	G
1							
2				**2011**			
3							
4		Item No	Date	Name	Amount	Rate	Equivalent GH¢
5		1	1/14/2011	Lucy Siaw Afriyie	675	1.48781	1000.00
6		2	1/24/2011	Lucy Siaw Afriyie	2325	1.48781	3400.00
7		3	2/10/2011	Bright	1500	1.48201	2223.00
8					4500		6623.00
9							
10							

⊮ ◂ ▸ ⊨	Accounts	Accounts 2011	Summary	

Ready   Average: 3311.50   Count: 4   Sum: 13246.00

The active worksheet is the Accounts 2011. Looking at the Accounts worksheet status bar we will see the summary of the selected range G5:G8: Average =**3311.50**, Counts =**4**, Sum=**13246.00**

Now, the Summary worksheet will combine the sums of both **Accounts** and "**Accounts 2011**" worksheets as illustrated below in figures 4.15 and 4.16.

Figure 4.18
Summary Worksheet Importing Values from the Cell ranges in Accounts and Accounts 2011 worksheets.

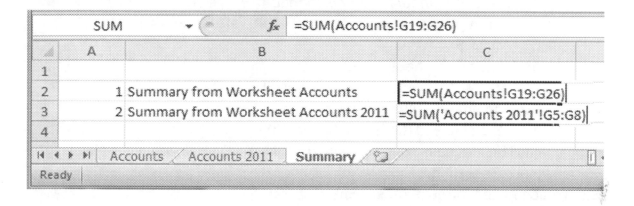

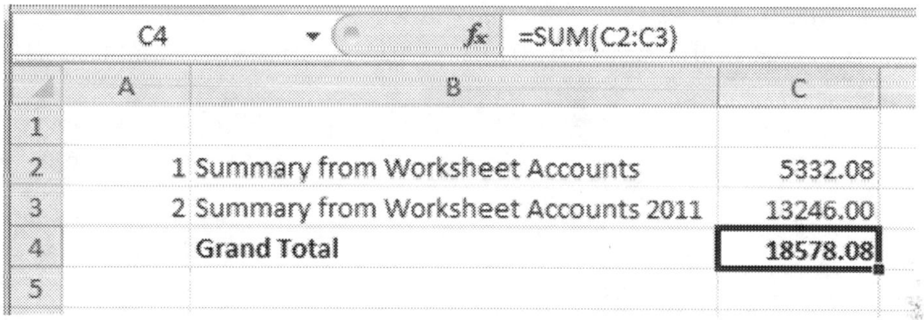

Figure 4.19
The Sum of the Summary Worksheet Imported values

4.8.3 Analysis of Formulas in Multiple Worksheets

1. =SUM(Accounts!G19:G26)
In the SUM parentheses is the defined cell range that begins with G19 and ends in G26 which is given by G19:G26). However the cell range does not bear references from the active worksheet but from another worksheet called Accounts within the current Expenses workbook. The reference to Accounts is indicated by placing an exclamation mark (!) after the worksheet name like this [Accounts!]. In this case the Cell range is defined by **Accounts!G19:26.**

2. =SUM('Accounts 2011'!G19:G26)
In the above formula since the worksheet has a compound name, it will therefore require the apostrophe that begins and closes the name.

4.8.4 Creating a Link to More than One Worksheet in the Same Workbook

Excel allows you to create links to more than one worksheet at a time. This method allows you to make calculations based on a selected range of worksheets.

1. *Select the cell where you want the formula to appear*
2. *To create the formula, use this format:*
   =function_name(worksheet range!cell_reference)
   EXAMPLES:
   (with spaces in sheet name)
       =SUM('Accounts 2011: Accounts'!D2:D10)
   (with no space in sheet name)
       =SUM(July2010:June2010!C4:C8)
   NOTE: Be sure to include a plus sign (**+**) or colon (**:**) between the worksheet range.
3. To accept the formula, press [**Enter**]

Figure 4.20 The Second Summary Worksheet Importing Values from the Cell ranges in both Accounts 2011 and 10Accounts worksheets.

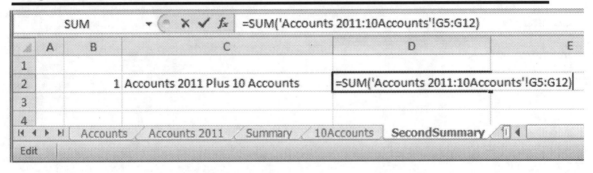

Figure 4.21 Sum of Accounts 2011 and 10Accounts worksheets is 18578.08

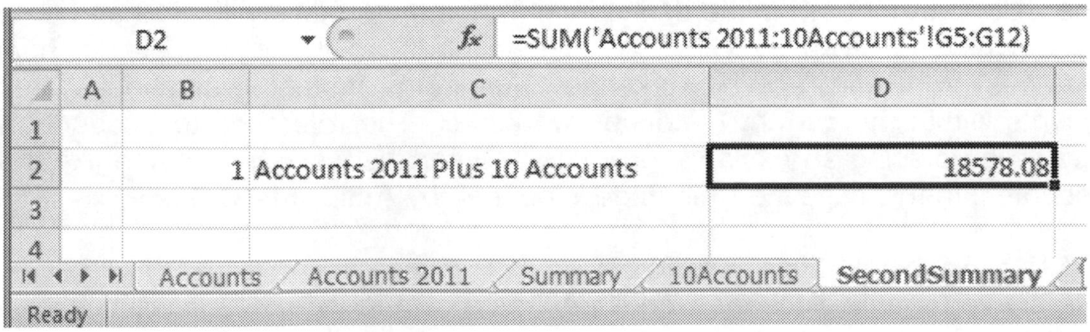

4.8.5 Writing Formulas for Other Workbook Files - From Same Directory
Formulas can also reference cells and worksheets from other workbooks.
1. Select the cell where you want the formula to appear
2. To create the formula, use this format:

=function_name('[workbook_name]worksheet_name'!cell_reference)
EXAMPLE:

=SUM('[10Accounts.xlsx]Payments'!F2:F8)

Figure 4.22 Sum of Payments in 10Accounts.xlsx workbook

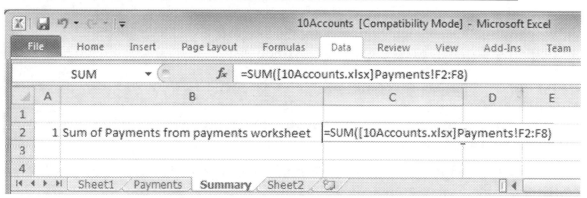

The values are referenced from Payments worksheet in 10Accounts workbook. The cells range of referenced is F2:F8.

NOTES: This assumes the two files you are working with are in the same directory.

Figure 4.23 Sum of Payments in 10Accounts.xlsx workbook showing results

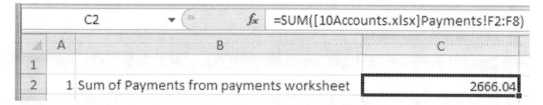

When the user press enter key after typing the formula in figure 4.19 above you will have the result shown in the cell address C2. The formula is shown in the formula bar when you click on the result cell C2 to make it the active cell.

4.8.6 Writing Formulas for Other Workbook Files- From Different Directory

Sometimes you will require referencing the range of cells from a different worksheet in a workbook residing in a different directory. There is no difference in the formula if your sheet name contains a space. If the two files you are working with are in different directories, you must include the file path in your formula. Use the following format:

=function_name('[file_path\workbook_name]worksheet_name'!cell_reference)

   EXAMPLE:

   =SUM('[E:\Bright\ICT\Volume2\10Accounts.xlsx]Payments'!F2:F8)

3. To accept the formula, press [**Enter**]

4.9 Using Range Names in Formulas

Using range names for some cells can be especially helpful if you cannot remember the cell location. Range names should not be assigned to every group of cells. Special groups, like assumptions and key totals, are good groups with which to use range names.

When using a range name in your formulas, the name will replace the traditional cell reference. For example, if the desired values are stored in cell *G5:G12*, which is named *PAY*, either reference can be used in a formula, as shown in the examples below.

Figure 4.24 Name Range

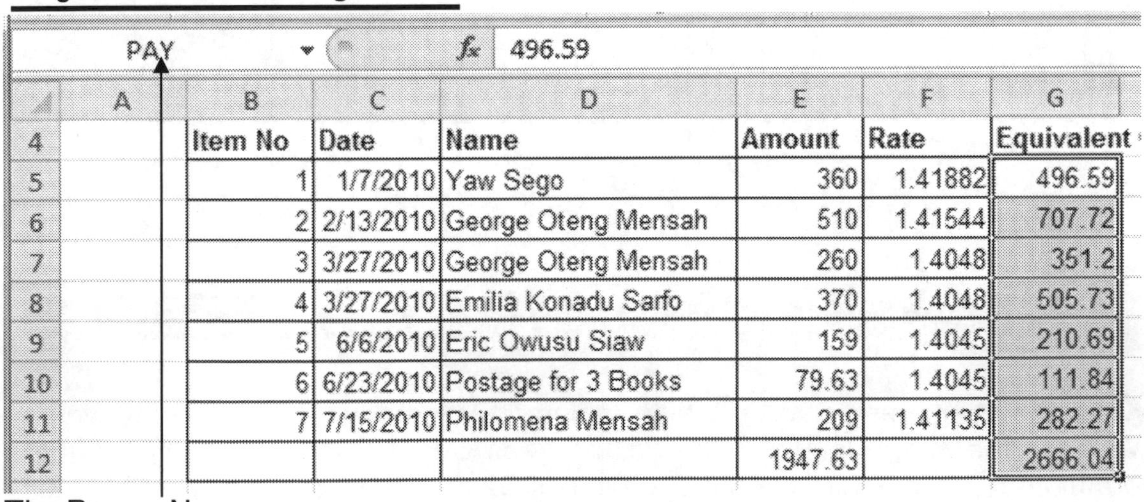

PAY	▼	f_x	496.59			
	A	B	C	D	E	F	G
4		Item No	Date	Name	Amount	Rate	Equivalent
5		1	1/7/2010	Yaw Sego	360	1.41882	496.59
6		2	2/13/2010	George Oteng Mensah	510	1.41544	707.72
7		3	3/27/2010	George Oteng Mensah	260	1.4048	351.2
8		4	3/27/2010	Emilia Konadu Sarfo	370	1.4048	505.73
9		5	6/6/2010	Eric Owusu Siaw	159	1.4045	210.69
10		6	6/23/2010	Postage for 3 Books	79.63	1.4045	111.84
11		7	7/15/2010	Philomena Mensah	209	1.41135	282.27
12					1947.63		2666.04

The Range Name

The selected range is **G5:G12** is named as **PAY**. To do so follow the steps below:

To create a range name.

1. Select the range as shown in the diagram above.
2. Right-Click on the selected range
3. Click on Define Name
4. Type the name for the range
5. Select the Scope (e.g. Workbook or Worksheets)
6. Refers to: defines the range by default. You can change at wish.

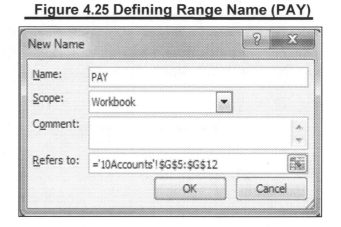

Figure 4.25 Defining Range Name (PAY)

EXAMPLE:

Cell Reference	Range Name Reference
=SUM(Expenses.xlsx!**G5:G12**) * 1500	= SUM(Expenses.xlsx!**PAY** * 1500

NOTE: Since the range does not change automatically in the formula, the referenced cells range is absolute. See figure 4.24 the referenced range is **='Accounts'!$G$5:$G$12.**

4.10 Calculating Your Workbook

By default, Excel recalculates all formulas every time you enter new information, in case the formulas are affected by the new information. When working with large workbooks and several calculations, you may find data entry slowing down (especially on older computers). To speed up data entry, you can change the calculation mode so that the workbook is recalculated only when you specify (and optionally, when you save your file). WARNING: Excel has an option for automatically calculating before you save your work, but not before you print. If you set up manual calculation, you will need to make sure that you recalculate before you print, and especially before others view your document.

4.10.1 Changing to Manual Calculation

To speed up data entry time, you can choose the *Manual Calculation* option. To choose this option, follow these steps:

1. From the *Ribbon*, select the **Formulas** command tab
2. In the *Calculations* group, click **OPTIONS**
3. Select **Manual**

Figure 4.26
Changing to Manual Calculation

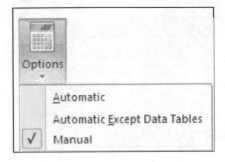

4.11 Using More Relative Addressing

How would you generate the relative address in the formula =A1*B1 to produce the results in figure 4.28 below in the next page?

Figure 4.27
Initial definition of formula using relative cell address

	A	B	C	D	E
1	5	18	90		
2	10	15			
3	15	4			
4	30	10			
5	60	8			
6	120	19			
7	240	12			
8					

C1 — *fx* =A1*B1

Book1.xls [Compatibility Mode]

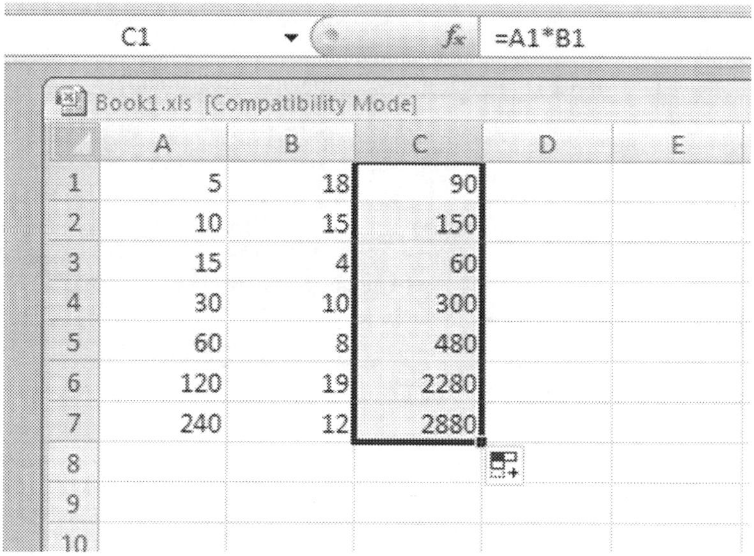

Figure 4.28
Results of formula
using relative cell
address

Define the formulas used
to compute the values in
Cells C2 to C7.

	C1	▼	f_x	=A1*B1

Book1.xls [Compatibility Mode]

	A	B	C	D	E
1	5	18	90		
2	10	15	150		
3	15	4	60		
4	30	10	300		
5	60	8	480		
6	120	19	2280		
7	240	12	2880		
8					
9					
10					

4.12 Visual Basic for Applications (VBA)

Like other Microsoft Office packages, Excel files can include advanced macros and even embedded programs. The language was originally WordBasic, but changed to Visual Basic for Applications as of Word 97.

Visual Basic for Applications (VBA) is an implementation of Microsoft's event-driven programming language, Visual Basic 6 which is now an object-oriented programming language, called Visual Studio.Net; and its associated integrated development environment (IDE), which is built into most Microsoft Office applications like Word, Excel, Access, etc. By embedding the VBA IDE into the applications, developers can build custom solutions using Microsoft Visual Basic. As its name suggests, VBA is closely related to Visual Basic and uses the Visual Basic Runtime, but it can normally only run code within a host application rather than as a standalone application. It can, however, be used to control one application from another that is using (object linking and embedding) OLE Automation. For example, it is used to automatically create Excel spreadsheet. To invoke the VBA IDE go through the following step:

1. Start Excel.
2. Press **ALT+F11** to start the Visual Basic editor.
3. On the **Insert** menu, click **Module**.
4. Enter the code in a module sheet:

Figure 4.29
VBA Integrated Development Environment (IDE)

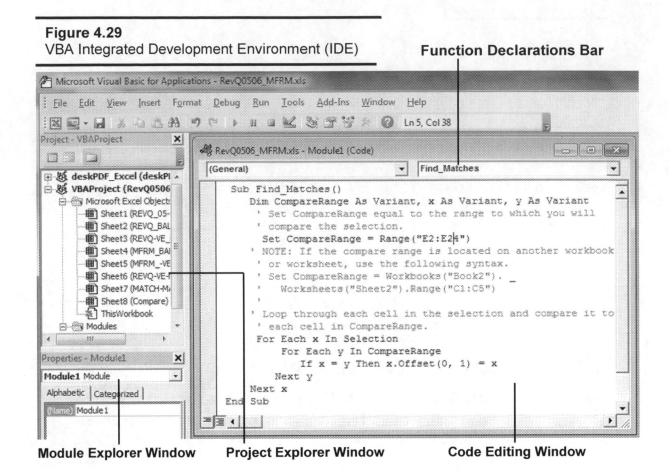

Function Declarations Bar

Module Explorer Window   **Project Explorer Window**   **Code Editing Window**

Debug in the standard menu bar is used to edit and correct errors in the program. **Run** in the standard menu bar is used to run the macro or program.

Use a Visual Basic macro

Microsoft provides programming examples for illustration only, without warranty either expressed or implied. This includes, but is not limited to, the implied warranties of merchantability or fitness for a particular purpose. This article assumes that you are familiar with the programming language that is being demonstrated and with the tools that are used to create and to debug procedures. Microsoft support engineers can help explain the functionality of a particular procedure. However, they will not modify these examples to provide added functionality or construct procedures to meet your specific requirements. To use a Visual Basic macro to compare the data in two columns, use the steps in the following example:

1. Start Excel.
2. Press **ALT+F11** to start the Visual Basic editor.
3. On the **Insert** menu, click **Module**.
4. Enter the following code in a module sheet:

```
1.  Sub Find_Matches()
2.      Dim CompareRange As Variant, x As Variant, y As Variant
3.        ' Set CompareRange equal to the range to which you will
4.        ' compare the selection.
5.      Set CompareRange = Range("E2:E23")
6.   ' NOTE: If the compare range is located on another workbook
7.        ' or worksheet, use the following syntax.
8.   ' Set CompareRange = Workbooks("Book2"). _
9.   '    Worksheets("Sheet2").Range("C1:C5")
10.  '
11.  ' Loop through each cell in the selection and compare it to
12.  ' each cell in CompareRange.
13.      For Each x In Selection
14.          For Each y In CompareRange
15.              If x = y Then x.Offset(0, 1) = x
16.          Next y
17.      Next x
18. End Sub
```

The above script will require some basic programming skills to understand. The part of this book will explain a few concepts in Section three under programming and data processing. But we will attempt to explain the statements. The line #1 statement is the name of function (**Sub Find_Matches( )**), and the end of function is indicated on line **#18**. Line **#2** is declaration of two variables **x**, and **y**. All the statements beginning with an apostrophes ['] are comments which are not executed. On line **#5** the variable **CompareRange** which holds the cell range E2:E23. Lines **#13** and **#14** are the beginning of For Loops. Line **#13** represents the iteration of each element selected from the Excel spreadsheet, and this element is stored in **x**. Line **#14** represents the second and inner iteration of each element in the range stored in the variable **CompareRange** (**E2:E23**) referenced in the Excel spreadsheet, and each element is stored in **y** for each iteration.

Figure 4.30
Spreadsheet Showing Three columns Selected, Matched and Compared items

	B1	▼	fx	SELECTED Column	
	A	B	C	D	E
1		SELECTED Column	MATCHED ITEM		COMPARED ITEM
2		C08-401137-01			C13-404636-01
3		C08-431147-01			C08-431147-01
4		C09-153136-01			C15-312544-05
5		C09-210146-01			C16-102469-13
6		C12-016820-01			C12-016820-01
7		C12-057652-01			C15-441584-13

Before running the above macro you must go to the worksheet and select one of the columns. Note: The defined macro takes in two arguments *x* and *y* representing the **Selected column** and **Compared Item** column respectively. In our case the elements in column **B** was selected to check against column **E**.

Figure 4.31
The Results of the Code Populating Matched Item Column

	B2	▼	fx	C08-401137-01	
	A	B	C	D	E
1		SELECTED Column	MATCHED ITEM		COMPARED ITEM
2		C08-401137-01	C08-401137-01		C13-404636-01
3		C08-431147-01	C08-431147-01		C08-431147-01
4		C09-153136-01			C15-312544-05
5		C09-210146-01			C16-102469-13
6		C12-016820-01	C12-016820-01		C12-016820-01
7		C12-057652-01			C15-441584-13
8		C12-145423-01			C17-663144-01
9		C12-179144-01	C12-179144-01		C14-260050-01
10		C13-023709-01			C13-438796-01
11		C13-219311-01			C17-578634-02
12		C13-295742-01	C13-295742-01		C13-295742-01
13		C13-341556-01	C13-341556-01		C13-341556-01

The above figure 4.28 is the representation of the results returned after running the macro. The elements in the Matched Item column are the matching items.

4.13 Assignment Questions

Answer the following project questions by showing all the appropriate steps that should be followed to arrive at the answer for each question.

1. Define the following terms:
   a. Function
   b. Formula
   c. Macro

2. A cell containing a formula in excel basically displays two parts. Name them

3. Given the expression 1200/25-275*0.52 entered in the cells A1, B1, C1, and D1 respectively. Write this expression into a formula in cell E1, in terms of the cells A1, B1, C1, and D1.

4. What is Relative reference of a formula? Show how to create a formula of relative reference by providing suitable examples.

5. What is Absolute reference of a formula? Show how to create a formula of absolute reference by providing suitable examples.

6. What is the difference between Relative and Absolute references of formula?

7. What do the following cell addresses imply?
   a. $B2
   b. B$2

8. What are the results for each of the following formulas, given B1=5, B2=12, B3=80, B4=8.
   a. =SUM(B1:B6)
   b. =IF(SUM(B1:B6) > 100

9. When writing a formula in Excel spreadsheet, there are three elements which must be included for it to work properly. List and define these three elements.

10. Describe how formulas must be created in excel spreadsheet.

11. Given the formula 'Accounts 2010'!C4:C8. Explain what this formula does.

12. Given the formula **=SUM(Accounts!G19:G26).** Explain what this formula does

4.14 Multiple Choice Questions

13. A reference such as $B$5 is called a relative reference
    A. True
    B. False

14. A number stored as 9123456 can be displayed in a cell as 9.123E+6.
    A. True
    B. False

15. A range of cells in Excel can be assigned any name and used in any formula.
    A. True
    B. False

16. The function that is represented pictorially as the Greek letter sigma is used to do the following function
    A. AutoCount
    B. AutoSum
    C. AutoValue

17. If you copy a formula, such as =$A$13+B13, down the column, the value that is in the cell A13 will remain unchanged down the column.
    A. True
    B. False

18. What feature helps me to put a list into alphabet order or to organize it by price?
    A. File > Save
    B. Data > Organize
    C. Data > Sort
    D. File > Open

19. Which of these would I have to do in order to find the average of a column of numbers? Select ALL that apply.
    A. Type =AVERAGE(
    B. Close parentheses) and press enter
    C. type A+B+C+D+E+F+G/7
    D. drag a box from the top to the bottom of the column of numbers to select them all
    E. Type =SUM(and Copy and paste cell total

20. **Which of these should I do to find the total of a column of numbers added together? Select ALL that apply**
    A. Close parentheses) and press enter
    B. Type A+B+C+D+E+F and press enter
    C. Type =SUM(
    D. Type =AVERAGE(
    E. Add them all together on another sheet of paper and enter it in the cell drag a box from the top to the bottom of the column of numbers to select them all

21. **The numbers, text, or cell references used by the function to return a value are**
    A. expressions
    B. arguments
    C. data
    D. values

22. **In the following formula: =IF(A1="YES","DONE","RESTART"), what happens if A1="NO"?**
    A. the formula returns the text "RESTART"
    B. the formula returns the text "DONE"
    C. the formula returns the text "NO"
    D. the formula returns the text "NO, RESTART"

23. **The _____ button is equivalent to using the sum button**
    A. COUNT
    B. ADD
    C. AutoSum
    D. AddSum

24. **FUNCTION(argument1,argument2, ...) is _____**
    A. the syntax of writing optional arguments.
    B. an example of a formula.
    C. the general syntax of all functions.
    D. the general syntax of all formulas.

25. **Formatting changes only the appearance of data- it does not affect the data itself.**
    A. True
    B. False

26. **If a formula contains several functions, Excel starts with the outermost function and then moves inward**
    A. True
    B. False

27. **As you begin to type a function name within a formula into a cell, a list of functions that begin with the letters you typed appears**
    A. True
    B. False

28. **If there are too many numbers after the decimal place displayed in a cell, creating a distraction from the data, you could make the data appear cleaner by:**
    A. reenter all the numbers
    B. decrease the column width
    C. decrease the font size
    D. Use the Number group to decrease the number of digits displayed

29. **If you have data that runs across five columns, from column A to column E, one way to center a title across the top of the data would be to:**
    A. type the data in A1 and Merge cells A1:A5
    B. type the data in A1 and Merge cells A1:E1
    C. type the data in C1
    D. choose Center from the Format menu

30. **If you have columns that are truncating your content, but you cannot increase the width of the worksheet and be able to print on one page, a solution for making the test visible without losing data would be to:**
    A. abbreviate all text
    B. reduce the font size to 8 pt
    C. click Wrap text
    D. delete one column

31. **The most efficient way to format several cells with a specific font, number format, alignment, font color would be to:**
    A. use Format Painter
    B. format each element using the Toolbar
    C. select all and use the Formatting dialog box
    D. apply a table style

32. **The Paste Options button allows you to_____.**
    A. keep source formatting
    B. copy formatting only
    C. copy values only
    D. all of the above

33. **Put the following five steps in the order in which you would perform them to use the Paste Special function:**

    1. Select and copy a range
    2. Click the Paste button arrow in the Clipboard group
    3. Specify exactly what you want to paste
    4. Click Paste Special to open the dialog box
    5. Select the range where you want to paste the Clipboard contents

    A. 1, 2, 4, 3, 5
    B. 1, 2, 4, 5, 3
    C. 1, 5, 2, 4, 3
    D. 1, 5, 2, 3, 4

34. **If you want to use your PivotTable to combine items into groups, which of the following would not be true?**
    A. Items that appear as row labels cannot be grouped
    B. Items that appear as column labels can be grouped
    C. If items are dates, they can be grouped automatically using the Grouping dialog box
    D. If items are numbers, they can be grouped manually using the Ctrl key to select items in a group and then choosing Group from the shortcut menu

35. The formula that will add the value of cell D4 to the value of C2 and then multiply by the value in B2 is _____.
   A. (D4+C2)*B2
   B. D4+C2*B2
   C. =(D4+C2)*B2
   D. =(B2*(D4+C2)

36. Cell A4 =2 and A5 = 4. You select both cells and drag the fill handle down to A8. The contents of cells A6, A7, and A8 are _____.
   A. 8,16,32
   B. 2,4,2
   C. 2,2,2
   D. 6,8,10

37. If a cell shows ####### , it means that _____.
   A. your formula has a syntax error
   B. the row is too short to show the number at the current font size
   C. the column is too narrow to show all the digits of the number
   D. either b or c

38. Given the formula =SUM('Accounts 2010'!G2:G8). The 'Accounts 2010' is_____
   A. Reference name for the range G2:G8
   B. The name for the workbook
   C. The name for the worksheet
   D. Label for the range G2:G8

39. What is Not true about the formula =SUM('[10Accounts.xlsx]Payments'!F2:F8).
   A. 'Payments' refers to the range name F2:F8
   B. 'Payments' refers to the worksheet
   C. '[10Accounts.xlsx]' refers to name of the workbook
   D. F2:F8 is the range of cells in Payments worksheet

40. Given the formula "=SUM('Accounts 2011:10Accounts'!D2:D10)". Which statement is false?
   A. ('Accounts 2011:10Accounts' refers to the range worksheets
   B. 'D2:D10' is a range in each worksheet Accounts 2011: 10Accounts
   C. Accounts 2011:10Accounts refers to name of cell range D2:D10
   D. D2:D10 is the range of cells in Account2011 and also 10Accounts

CHAPTER 5

Managing Worksheets

Objectives:

- o *Introduction: Modify width and height of columns; Insert row or column*
- o *Insert or delete cells in worksheet or Worksheets*
- o *Move data in worksheet or workbook*
- o *Change the color of gridlines, default fonts and Themes in a worksheet*
- o *Freeze or lock rows and columns; Hide or show worksheets or workbooks*
- o *Move or copy a worksheet*
- o *Switch to full or normal screen view*

5.0 Introduction

The introduction to managing worksheets will begin with 5 tips for working with columns, rows, and cells in Excel 2007/2010.

- • Tip 1. Modify width and height of columns
- • Tip 2. Insert row or column to add space
- • Tip 3. Hide columns or rows
- • Tip 4. Insert or delete cells in worksheet
- • Tip 5. Move data in worksheet

Tip 1: Modify width and height of columns

Modifying column width and row height can make a worksheet's contents easier to work with. You can change the width of a column or the height of a row in a worksheet by dragging the column or row's border to the desired position. Increasing a column's width or a row's height increases the space between cell contents, making it easier to select a cell's data without inadvertently selecting data from other cells as well.

NOTE: You can apply the same change to more than one row or column by selecting the rows or columns you want to change and then dragging the border of one of the selected rows or columns to the desired location. When you release the mouse button, all the selected rows or columns change to the new height or width.

Tip 2: Insert row or column to add space

You can also insert a row or column between the edge of a worksheet and the cells that contain the data to make it easier to work with a worksheet's contents. Adding space between the edge of a worksheet and cells, or perhaps between a label and the data to which it refers, makes the workbook's contents less crowded and easier to work with. You insert rows by clicking a cell and clicking the Home tab. Then, in the Cells group, click the Insert button's down arrow and click Insert Sheet Rows. Office Excel 2007/2010 inserts a row above the row that contains the active cell. You insert a column in much the same way by choosing **Insert Sheet Columns** from the Insert button's drop-down list. When you do this, Office Excel 2007/2010 inserts a column to the left of the active cell. When you insert a row, column, or cell in a worksheet with existing formatting, the Insert Options button appears. Usually the existing formatting will remain after inserting a row. Clicking the Insert Options button displays a list of choices you can make about how the inserted row or column should be formatted. The following table summarizes your options.

OPTION	ACTION
Format Same as Above	Applies the format of the row above the inserted row to the new row.
Format Same as Below	Applies the format of the row below the inserted row to the new row.
Format Same as Left	Applies the format of the column to the left of the inserted column to the new column.
Format Same as Right	Applies the format of the column to the right of the inserted column to the new column.
Clear Formatting	Applies the default format to the new row or column.

Tip 3. Hide columns or rows

You can temporarily hide a number of rows or columns by selecting those rows or columns and then, on the Home tab, in the **Cells** group, clicking the **Format** button, pointing to Hide & Unhide, and then clicking either **Hide Rows** or **Hide Columns**. The rows or columns you selected disappear, but they aren't gone for good, as they would be if you'd used Delete. Instead, they have just been removed from the display until you call them back. To return the hidden rows to the display, on the Home tab, in the **Cells** group, click the **Format** button, point to **Hide & Unhide**, and then click either **Unhide Rows** or **Unhide Columns**.

Tip 4. Insert or delete cells in worksheet

Likewise, you can insert individual cells into a worksheet. To insert a cell, click the cell that is currently in the position where you want the new cell to appear. On the **Home** tab, in the **Cells** group, click the Insert button down arrow and then click **Insert Cells** to display the **Insert** dialog box. In the Insert dialog box, you can choose whether to shift the cells surrounding the inserted cell down (if your data is arranged as a column) or to the right (if your data is arranged as a row). When you click **OK**, the new cell appears, and the contents of affected cells shift down or to the right, as appropriate. In a similar vein, if you want to delete a block of cells, select the cells, and on the Home tab of the user interface, in the **Cells** group, click the **Delete** button down arrow and then click Delete Cells to display the Delete dialog box—complete with option buttons that enable you to choose how to shift the position of the cells around the deleted cells.

NOTE: The Insert dialog box also includes option buttons you can select to insert a new row or column; the Delete dialog box has similar buttons that enable you to delete an entire row or column.

Tip 5. Move data in worksheet
If you want to move the data in a group of cells to another location in your worksheet, select the cells you want to move and position the mouse pointer on the selection's border. When the mouse pointer changes to a four-way arrow, you can drag the selected cells to the desired location on the worksheet. If the destination cells contain data, Office Excel 2007/2010 displays a dialog box asking if you want to overwrite the destination cells' contents. If you want to replace the existing values, click the **OK** button. If you don't want to overwrite the existing values, click the **Cancel** button and insert the required number of cells to accommodate the data you want to move.

5.1 Change the color of gridlines in a worksheet

By default, gridlines are displayed in worksheets using the color that is assigned to it automatically. To change the color of gridlines, you can use the following procedure.

1.   Select the worksheets for which you want to change the gridline color.

TO SELECT	HOW TO DO THE SELECTION
A single sheet	Click the sheet tab. If you don't see the tab that you want, click the tab scrolling buttons to display the tab, and then click the tab.
Two or more adjacent sheets	Click the tab for the first sheet. Then hold down **SHIFT** while you click the tab for the last sheet that you want to select.
Two or more nonadjacent sheets	Click the tab for the first sheet. Then hold down **CTRL** while you click the tabs of the other sheets that you want to select.
All sheets in a workbook	Right-click a sheet tab, and then click **Select All Sheets** on the shortcut menu.

2. Click the Microsoft Office Button 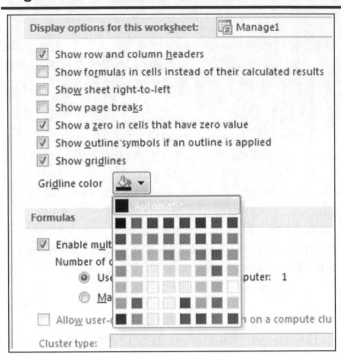, and then click Excel Options.
In Excel 2010 click File, and then click Excel Options.
3. In the Advanced category, under Display options for this worksheet, make sure that the Show gridlines check box is selected.
4. In the Gridline color box, click the color you want.

TIP: To return gridlines to the default color, click Automatic.

Figure 5.1 Gridline Color Scheme

Next Steps- Showing the Gridlines

After you change the color of gridlines on a worksheet, you may want to take the following next steps:

- *Make gridlines more visible:* To make the gridlines stand out on the screen, you can experiment with border and line styles. These settings are located on the **Home** tab, in the **Font** group. To learn exactly how to apply, remove, or create custom borders, see Apply or remove cell borders on a worksheet

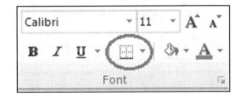

- *Print gridlines:* By default, Excel doesn't print gridlines on worksheets. If you want gridlines to appear on the printed page, select the worksheet or worksheets that you want to print. On the **Page Layout** tab, in the **Sheet Options** group, select the **Print** check box under Gridlines. To print, **press CTRL+P**.

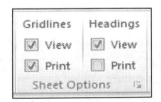

5.2 Change the default Font in Excel

By default, Microsoft Office Excel 2010 uses the **Body Font** in font size 11 (which is displayed as the **Calibri** font in font size 11 when you type data in a worksheet, header or footer, or text box) but you can change the default font and font size for all new workbooks that you create.

1. Click the Microsoft Office Button , or in Excel 2007/2010, click File, and then click Excel Options.
2. In the Popular category, under When creating new workbooks, do the following:
   • In the Use this font box, click the font that you want to use.
   • In the Font Size box, enter the font size that you want to use.

NOTE: To begin using the new default font and font size, you must restart Excel. The new default font and font size are used only in new workbooks that you create after you restart Excel; existing workbooks are not affected. To use the new default font, you can move worksheets from an existing workbook to a new workbook. For more information, see Move or copy a worksheet.

5.2.1 Change the default Theme

A theme is a quick and easy way to give a professional and modern look to an entire 2010 Microsoft Office system document. A document theme is a set of formatting choices that include a set of theme colors, a set of theme fonts (including heading and body text fonts), and a set of theme effects (including lines and fill effects). If you want to change fonts or line spacing in your 2010 Microsoft Office system documents, see:
   • Double-space the lines in a document
   • Adjust the spaces between lines or paragraphs
   • Change the font or font size in Excel
   • Change the font size
   • Change the default font for e-mail messages
   • Change the fonts

Every document that you create by using Microsoft Office PowerPoint 2010, Microsoft Office Word 2010, or Microsoft Office Excel 2010 has a theme inside it — even blank, new documents. The default theme is **Office Theme**, with a white background and dark, subtle colors. When you apply a new theme, Office Theme is replaced by a new look, such as the dark background and bright colors of the Metro theme. If you want a different default theme from the Office Theme, you can save time by pre-configuring your document with a different default theme. All content (such as text, tables, and **SmartArt graphics**) is dynamically linked to the theme, so changing the theme automatically changes the look of your content, unless you customize it.

Creating the default template from a new blank workbook

To change the default theme in Office Excel 2010, you need to create a new, default workbook template or a new, default worksheet template. A workbook template can contain multiple worksheets, whereas a worksheet template contains only one worksheet. Workbook and worksheet templates can contain default text, such as page headers, column and row labels, formulas, themes, and other formatting information. The default workbook template is automatically used to create new workbooks, and the default worksheet template is used to automatically create new worksheets.

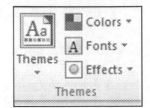

1. Click the Microsoft Office Button , and then click New.
   In Excel 2010 click File, and then click Excel Options.

2. Under Templates, click Blank and recent, and then under Blank and recent, double-click Blank Workbook.

   Keyboard shortcut: Press CTRL+N

3. On the Page Layout tab, in the Themes group, click Themes.

4. To apply a theme to the workbook that every new workbook will use, do one of the following:
   • To apply a predefined document theme, under Built-In, click the document theme that you want to use.
   • To apply a custom document theme that you created, under Custom, click the document theme that you want to use.

   NOTE: Custom is available only if you create one or more custom document themes. For more information about creating custom document themes, see Apply or customize a document theme.
   • To apply a document theme that is not listed, click Browse for Themes to find it on your computer or on a network location.
   • To search for other document themes on Microsoft Office Online, click More Themes on Microsoft Office Online.

5. Click the Microsoft Office Button , point to Save As, and then click Excel Workbook.

6. Browse to your **XLStart** folder, which is located in the directory where Office Excel 2007 or the 2007 Office release is installed (usually C:\Program Files\Microsoft Office\Office12), and then in the File name box, do one of the following:
   • To create a default workbook, enter **book.xltx**.
   • To create a default worksheet, enter **sheet.xltx**.

7. In the Save as type list, click Excel Template (***.xltx**), and then click Save.
   NOTE: Any template in the default **XLStart** folder opens automatically when you start Excel 2010.

Create the default template from an existing workbook

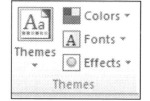

1. Click the Microsoft Office Button , in Excel 2010 click File, and then click New.
2. Under Templates, click New from existing, and then in the New from Existing Workbook dialog box, browse to the computer, network, or Internet location that contains the workbook that you want to use.
3. Click the workbook, and then click Create New.
4. On the Page Layout tab, in the Themes group, click Themes.
5. To apply a theme to the workbook that every new workbook will use, do one of the following:
   • To apply a predefined document theme, under Built-In, click the document theme that you want to use.
   • To apply a custom document theme, under Custom, click the document theme that you want to use.

   NOTE: Custom is available only if you create one or more custom document themes. For more information about creating custom document themes, see Apply or customize a document theme.

   • To apply a document theme that is not listed, click Browse for Themes to find it on your computer or on a network location.
   • To search for other document themes on Microsoft Office Online, click More Themes on Microsoft Office Online.

6. Click the Microsoft Office Button , or in Excel 2010 click File, and point to Save As, and then click Excel Workbook.
7. Browse to your **XLStart** folder, which is located in the directory where Office Excel 2010 or the 2010 Microsoft Office system is installed (usually C:\Program Files\Microsoft Office\Office12), and then in the File name box, do one of the following:
   • To create a default workbook, enter **book.xltx**.
   • To create a default worksheet, enter **sheet.xltx**.

8. In the Save as type list, click Excel Template **(*.xltx)**, and then click Save.
   NOTE: Any template in the default XLStart folder opens automatically when you start Excel 2010.

5.3 Change the Font or Font size in Excel

You can change the font or font size for selected cells or ranges in a worksheet. You can also change the default font and font size that are used in new workbooks.
   • Change the font or font size in a worksheet
   • Change the default font or font size for new workbooks

5.3.1 Change the font or font size in a worksheet

1. Select the cell, range of cells, text, or characters that you want to format.
2. On the Home tab, in the **Font** group, do the following:

- To change the font, click the font that you want in the **Font** box. [Calibri ▼]
- To change the font size, click the font size that you want in the **Font Size** box, [11 ▼] or click **Increase Font Size** A⌃ or **Decrease Font Size** A⌄ until the size you want is displayed in the **Font Size** box.

NOTES

- Small-caps and all-caps font options are not available in Microsoft Office Excel. For a similar effect, you can choose a font that includes only uppercase letters, or you can press CAPS LOCK and choose a small-sized font.

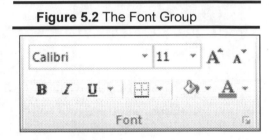

Figure 5.2 The Font Group

- If some of the data that you entered in a cell is not visible, and you want to display that data without specifying a different font size, you can wrap the text in the cell. If only a small amount is not visible, you might be able to shrink the text so that it fits.

5.3.2 Change the default font or font size for new workbooks

1. Click the **Microsoft Office Button** , and then click **Excel Options**. In Excel 2010, click File, and then click Excel Options.
2. In the Popular category, under When creating new workbooks, do the following:
   - In the **Use this font** box, click the font that you want to use.
   - In the **Font Size** box, enter the font size that you want to use.

NOTE: In order to begin using the new default font and font size, you must restart Excel. The new default font and font size are used only in new workbooks that you create after you restart Excel; existing workbooks are not affected. To use the new default font, you can move worksheets from an existing workbook to a new workbook. For more information, see Move or copy a worksheet.

5.3.3 Change the number of worksheets in a new workbook

By default, Microsoft Office Excel provides three worksheets in a workbook, but you can change the number of worksheets that appear by default in a new workbook.

1. Click the Microsoft Office Button , and then click Excel Options. In Excel 2010, click File, and then click Excel Options.

2. On the Popular tab, under When creating new workbooks, in the Include this many sheets box, enter the number of sheets that you want to include by default when you create a new workbook.

5.3.4 Change the width of all columns with one command

Problem: I have a large model set up in Excel. Some of the columns are hidden. I want to globally change the width of all unhidden columns to a width of 4. If I choose all columns in the worksheet and use Home >> Format dropdown >> Column Width, the hidden columns will unhide.

Figure 5.3 Change default column width

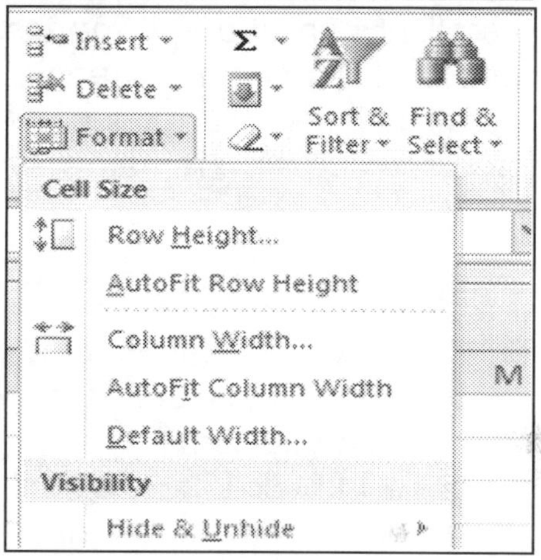

Strategy: To solve this problem, you can use Home >> Format dropdown >> Default Width, as shown in Figure 5.3.

The Default Width dialog allows you to enter one global column width. This change will affect all columns that have not been previously resized or hidden. The result is that you can change the width of all columns without unhiding the hidden columns.

Additional Details: Changing the default width will change the width of hidden columns, but will not unhide them. When they are later unhidden, they will have the new width.

Gotcha: The Default Width command does not change the widths of columns that have previously been changed. To see this in action, open a new workbook. Manually change **column C** to be 20 wide. Use Home >> Format dropdown and set Default Width to be 1 wide. All the columns except **C** will be changed.

Summary: You can use Default Width to globally adjust the width of all columns without unhiding hidden columns.
Commands Discussed: Home >> Format dropdown >> Default Width.
In **Excel 97-2003:** Format >> Column >>Standard Width

5.3.5 Freeze or lock rows and columns
To keep an area of a worksheet visible while you scroll to another area of the worksheet, you can lock specific rows or columns in one area by freezing or splitting panes.

When you freeze panes, you keep specific rows or columns visible when you scroll in the worksheet. For example, you might want to keep row and column labels visible as you scroll.

A solid line indicates that row 1 is frozen to keep column labels in place when you scroll. When you split panes, you create separate worksheet areas that you can scroll within, while rows or columns in the non-scrolled area remain visible.

Figure 5.4 Row 1 is frozen to keep column labels

	A	B	C
1	City	Date	Books Sold
4	Kumasi	Mar	120
5	Tamale	April	72
6	Sunyani	Mar	50
7	Takoradi	Feb	75
8	Koforidua	Jan	86

Sheet1 / SH

Freeze panes to lock specific rows or columns

1. On the worksheet, do one of the following:
   - To lock rows, select the row below the row or rows that you want to keep visible when you scroll.
   - To lock columns, select the column to the right of the column or columns that you want to keep visible when you scroll.
   - To lock both rows and columns, click the cell below and to the right of the rows and columns that you want to keep visible when you scroll.

2. On the View tab, in the Window group, click the arrow below Freeze Panes.

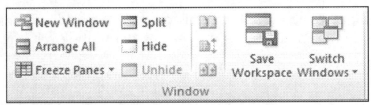

3. Do one of the following:
   - To lock one row only, click Freeze Top Row.
   - To lock one column only, click Freeze First Column.
   - To lock more than one row or column, or to lock both rows and columns at the same time, click Freeze Panes.

   NOTES
   - When you freeze the top row, first column, or panes, the Freeze Panes option changes to Unfreeze Panes so that you can unlock any frozen rows or columns.
   - You can freeze rows at the top and columns on the left side of the worksheet only. You cannot freeze rows and columns in the middle of the worksheet.

- The **Freeze Panes** command is not available when you are in cell editing mode or when a worksheet is protected. To cancel cell editing mode, press **ENTER** or **ESC**. For information about how to remove protection from a worksheet, see Protect worksheet or workbook elements.

Split panes to lock rows or columns in separate worksheet areas

1. To split panes, point to the split box at the top of the vertical scroll bar or at the right end of the horizontal scroll bar.

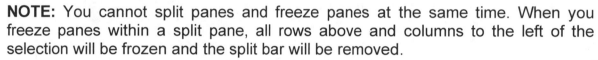

2. When the pointer changes to a split pointer ÷ or ◄╫►, drag the split box down or to the left to the position that you want.
3. To remove the split, double-click any part of the split bar that divides the panes.

NOTE: You cannot split panes and freeze panes at the same time. When you freeze panes within a split pane, all rows above and columns to the left of the selection will be frozen and the split bar will be removed.

5.4 Hide or show worksheets or workbooks

You can hide any worksheet in a workbook to remove it from view. You can also hide the workbook window of a workbook to remove it from your workspace. The data in hidden worksheets and workbook windows is not visible, but it can still be referenced from other worksheets and workbooks. You can display hidden worksheets or workbook windows as needed.

By default, all workbook windows of workbooks that you open are displayed on the taskbar, but you can hide or display them on the taskbar as needed.

5.4.2 Hide a worksheet

1. Select the worksheets that you want to hide.

2. On the Home tab, in the Cells group, click Format.
3. Under Visibility, click Hide & Unhide, and then click Hide Sheet.

5.4.3 Display a hidden worksheet

1. On the Home tab, in the Cells group, click Format.
2. Under Visibility, click Hide & Unhide, and then click Unhide Sheet.
3. In the Unhide sheet box, double-click the name of the hidden sheet that you want to display.

NOTE: You can unhide only one worksheet at a time.

If worksheets are hidden by Visual Basic for Applications (VBA) code that assigns the property **xlSheetVeryHidden**, you cannot use the Unhide command to display those hidden sheets. If you are using a workbook that contains VBA macros and you encounter problems when working with hidden worksheets, contact the owner of the workbook for more information.

5.4.4 Hide a workbook window

• On the View tab, in the Window group, click Hide.

> **NOTE:** When you exit Excel, you will be asked if you want to save changes to the hidden workbook window. Click **Yes,** if you want the workbook window to be hidden the next time that you open the workbook.

5.4.5 Display a hidden workbook window

1. On the View tab, in the Window group, click Unhide.

> **NOTE:** If Unhide is unavailable, the workbook does not contain hidden workbook windows.

2. Under Unhide workbook, double-click the workbook window that you want to display.

5.4.6 Hide or display workbook windows on the Windows taskbar

1. Click the Microsoft Office Button , click **Excel Options**, and then click the **Advanced category**.
   In Excel 2010, click File, click **Excel Options**, and then click the **Advanced category.**
2. Under Display, clear or select the Show all windows in the Taskbar check.

5.5 Insert or delete a worksheet

By default, Microsoft Office Excel provides three worksheets in a workbook, but you can insert additional worksheets (and other types of sheets, such as a chart sheet, macro sheet, or dialog sheet) or delete them as needed. You can also change the number of worksheets that appear by default in a new workbook. If you have access to a worksheet template that you created or one that is available on Office Online, you can base a new worksheet on that template.

The name (or title) of a worksheet appears on its sheet tab at the bottom of the screen. By default, the name is Sheet1, Sheet2, and so on, but you can give any worksheet a more appropriate name.

NOTE: Sheet tabs are displayed by default, but if you do not see them, verify that the Show sheet tabs check box is selected in the Advanced category of the Excel Options dialog box (File menu, Excel Options).

5.5.1 Insert a new worksheet

To insert a new worksheet, do one of the following:

- To quickly insert a new worksheet at the end of the existing worksheets, click the Insert Worksheet tab at the bottom of the screen.

- To insert a new worksheet in front of an existing worksheet, select that worksheet and then, on the Home tab, in the Cells group, click Insert, and then click Insert Sheet.

    TIP: You can also right-click the tab of an existing worksheet, and then click Insert. On the General tab, click Worksheet, and then click **OK.**

5.5.2 Insert multiple worksheets at the same time

1. Hold down **SHIFT**, and then select the same number of existing sheet tabs of the worksheets that you want to insert in the open workbook.
   For example, if you want to add three new worksheets, select three sheet tabs of existing worksheets.
2. On the Home tab, in the Cells group, click Insert, and then click Insert Sheet.

TIP: You can also right-click the selected sheet tabs, and then click Insert. On the General tab, click **Workshee**t, and then click **OK**.

5.5.3 Change the number of worksheets in a new workbook

1. Click the Microsoft Office Button, and then click Excel Options.
   In Excel 2010 click File, and then click Excel Options.

2. In the Popular category, under When creating new workbooks, in the Include this many sheets box, enter the number of sheets that you want to include by default when you create a new workbook.

5.5.4 Insert a new sheet that is based on a custom template

1. If needed, create the worksheet template that you want to base a new worksheet on.
2. **Right-click** the sheet tab of a worksheet, and then click Insert.
3. **Double-click** the template for the type of sheet that you want.

5.5.5 Rename a worksheet

1. On the Sheet tab bar, **right-click** the sheet tab that you want to rename, and then click **Rename.**

Active sheet

2. Select the current name, and then type the new name.
   TIP: You can include the name of the sheet when you print the worksheet.

5.5.6 Delete one or more worksheets

1. Select the worksheet or worksheets that you want to delete.
2. On the Home tab, in the Cells group, click the arrow next to Delete, and then click Delete Sheet.

   TIP: You can also right-click the sheet tab of a worksheet or a sheet tab of any selected worksheets that you want to delete, and then click **Delete.**

5.6 Move or copy a worksheet

This section describes how to move or copy worksheets and worksheet data to other locations as described under the following sub-topics:

- Move or copy worksheets to another location in a workbook
- Move or copy worksheets to another workbook
- Move or copy data to another worksheet or workbook
- Drag data between open workbook windows in Excel
- Drag data to another workbook that is open in a separate instance of Excel

5.6.1 Move or copy worksheets to another location in a workbook

It's easy to move or copy a whole worksheet (or sheet) to another location in a workbook. However, be aware that calculations or charts that are based on worksheet data might become inaccurate if you move the worksheet. Similarly, if a moved or copied worksheet is inserted between sheets that are referred to by a 3-D formula reference, data on that worksheet might be unexpectedly included in the calculation.

1. Select the worksheets that you want to move or copy.

   Keyboard shortcut: To move to the next or previous sheet tab, you can also press **CTRL+PAGE UP** or **CTRL+PAGE DOWN.**

2. On the Home tab, in the Cells group, click Format, and then under Organize Sheets, click Move or Copy Sheet.

   TIP: You can also right-click a selected sheet tab, and then click Move or Copy.

3. In the Move or Copy dialog box, in the Before sheet list, do one of the following:
   - Click the sheet before which you want to insert the moved or copied sheets.
   - Click move to end to insert the moved or copied sheets after the last sheet in the workbook and before the Insert Worksheet tab.

4. To copy the sheets instead of moving them, in the Move or Copy dialog box, select the Create a copy check box.

   NOTE: When you create a copy of the worksheet, the worksheet is duplicated in the workbook, and the sheet name indicates that it is a copy — for example, the first copy that you make of Sheet1 is named Sheet1 (2).

   Tips
   - To move sheets in the current workbook, you can drag the selected sheets along the row of sheet tabs. To copy the sheets, hold down CTRL, and then drag the sheets; release the mouse button before you release the CTRL key.
   - To rename the moved or copied worksheet, right-click its sheet tab, click Rename, and then type the new name in the sheet tab.
   - To change the color of the sheet tab, right-click the sheet tab, click Tab Color, and then click the color that you want to use.

5.6.2 Move or copy worksheets to another workbook

1. To move or copy worksheets to another workbook, make sure that the target workbook is open in the same instance of Microsoft Office Excel.

   NOTE: You cannot move or copy worksheets between workbooks that are open in separate instances of Excel. If a workbook is opened in a separate instance of Excel - for example, this can happen when you open that workbook from a Windows SharePoint Services site - make sure that you open that workbook in the same instance of Excel instead by browsing to it in the Open dialog box (Microsoft Office Button or File, Open).

2. In the workbook that contains the sheets that you want to move or copy, select the sheets.
   Keyboard shortcut: To move to the next or previous sheet tab, you can also press **CTRL+ PAGE UP** or **CTRL+ PAGE DOWN.**

3. On the Home tab, in the Cells group, click Format, and then under Organize Sheets, click Move or Copy Sheet.
   TIP: You can also right-click a selected sheet tab, and then click Move or Copy.

4. In the Move or Copy dialog box, in the To book list, do one of the following:
   - Click the workbook to which you want to move or copy the selected sheets.
   - Click new book to move or copy the selected sheets to a new workbook.

5. In the Before sheet list, do one of the following:
   - Click the sheet before which you want to insert the moved or copied sheets.
   - Click move to end to insert the moved or copied sheets after the last sheet in the workbook and before the Insert Worksheet tab.

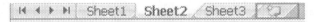

6. To copy the sheets instead of moving them, in the Move or Copy dialog box, select the Create a copy check box.
   NOTE: When you create a copy of the worksheet, the worksheet is duplicated in the destination workbook. When you move a worksheet, the worksheet is removed from the original workbook and appears in the destination workbook only.
   Tips
   - To rename the moved or copied worksheet in the destination workbook, **right-click** its sheet tab, click **Rename**, and then type the new name in the sheet tab.
   - Worksheets that you move or copy to another workbook will use the theme fonts, colors, and effects that are applied to the destination workbook.
   - To change the color of the sheet tab, **right-click** the sheet tab, click **Tab Color**, and then click the **color** that you want to use.

5.6.3 Move or copy data to another worksheet or workbook

Although moving or copying the actual worksheet is a fast and effective way to transfer data to another location, you can also move or copy all or part of the data in a worksheet to another worksheet. This method can be used to transfer data to a worksheet in a workbook that is open in a separate instance of Excel.

a. In a worksheet, select the data that you want to move or copy.

   NOTE: If the selection includes hidden rows or columns, Excel also copies the data in those hidden rows and columns. You may have to temporarily unhide rows or columns that you do not want to include, and then select each range of data that you do want to move or copy in separate operations. For information, see Hide or display rows and columns.

b. On the Home tab, in the Clipboard group, do one of the following:
   - To move the selected data, click **Cut** .
   - **Keyboard shortcut:** You can also press **CTRL+X.**
   - To copy the selected data, click Copy .
   Keyboard shortcut: You can also press **CTRL+C**.

3. Do one of the following:
   - Click the worksheet where you want to paste the data.
   - Switch to a workbook that is opened in another instance of Excel, and then click the worksheet where you want to paste the data.

4. Select the upper-left cell of the paste area.
   NOTE: Data in the paste area will be overwritten. Also, if the paste area contains hidden rows or columns, you might have to unhide the paste area to see all the copied cells.

5. On the **Home** tab, in the **Clipboard** group, click **Paste** .
   Keyboard shortcut: You can also press **CTRL+V.**
   TIP: To keep the column width that was originally specified for the data, click the arrow below Paste , click Paste Special, and then under Paste, click Column widths.

   NOTES
   - By default, Excel displays the Paste Options button on the worksheet to provide you with special options when you paste cells, such as Keep Source Formatting and Match Destination Formatting. If you do not want Excel to display this button every time that you paste cells, you can turn this option off.

1. Click the Microsoft Office Button , and then click Excel Options.
   In Excel 2010 click File, and then Excel Options.
2. In the Advanced category, under Cut, Copy, and Paste, clear the Show Paste Options buttons check box.

- When you copy cells, cell references are automatically adjusted. However, when you move cells, cell references are not adjusted, and the contents of those cells and of any cells that point to them might be displayed as reference errors. In this case, you will have to adjust the references manually.

5.6.4 Drag data between open workbook windows in Excel

If you open more than one workbook in the same instance of Excel, you can drag worksheet data between the workbook windows.

1. In Excel, open the workbooks between which you want to transfer worksheet data.
2. On the **View** tab, in the **Window** group, click **Arrange All**.
3. In the Arrange Windows dialog box, under Arrange, click the options that you want, and then click OK.
4. In one of the windows, select the data that you want to move or copy to another window.
5. Do one of the following:
   - To move the selected data, point to the border of the selection. When the pointer becomes a move pointer, drag the selected data to another window.
   - To copy the selected data, hold down CTRL while you point to the border of the selection. When the pointer becomes a copy pointer, drag the selected data to another window. Or select data>> copy>>point to new cell>>paste.

5.6.5 Drag data to another workbook that is open in a separate instance of Excel

If a workbook is open in another instance of Excel, you can drag worksheet data to it if it is visible on the taskbar.

1. Start an instance of Excel, and then open the workbook into which you want to drag worksheet data, or create a new workbook.
2. In another instance of Excel, open the workbook that contains the worksheet data that you want to transfer by dragging.
3. In a worksheet, select the data that you want to drag to a workbook that is visible on the taskbar.
4. Do one of the following:
   - To move the selected data, point to the border of the selection. When the pointer becomes a move pointer, drag the selected data to the workbook on the taskbar.
   - To copy the selected data, hold down CTRL while you point to the border of the selection. When the pointer becomes a copy pointer, drag the selected data to the workbook on the taskbar.

5.7 Show or hide columns and rows

You can hide a row or column by using the Hide command, but a row or column also becomes hidden when you change its row height or column width to 0 (zero). You can display either again by using the Unhide command.

You can either unhide specific rows and columns, or you can unhide all hidden rows and columns at once. The first row or column of the worksheet is tricky to unhide, but it can be done.

- Hide one or more rows or columns
- Display one or more hidden rows or columns
- Display all hidden rows and columns at once
- Unhide the first row or column of the worksheet

5.7.1 Hide one or more rows or columns

1. Select the rows or columns that you want to hide.
2. On the Home tab, in the Cells group, click Format.
3. Do one of the following:
   - Under **Visibility**, point to **Hide & Unhide**, and then click **Hide Rows** or **Hide Columns**.
   - Under **Cell Size**, click **Row Height** or **Column Width**, and then type **0** in the **Row Height** or **Column Width** box.
     TIP: You can also right-click a row or column (or a selection of multiple rows or columns), and then click **Hide**.

5.7.2 Display one or more hidden rows or columns

1. Do one of the following:
   - To display hidden rows, select the row above and below the rows that you want to unhide.
   - To display hidden columns, select the columns adjacent to either side of the columns that you want to unhide.
   - To display the first hidden row or column on a worksheet, select it by typing A1 in the Name Box next to the formula bar.
     TIP: You can also select it by using the **Go To** dialog box. On the Home tab, under Editing, click Find & Select, and then click Go To. In the Reference box, type A1, and then click OK.
2. How to select cells, ranges, rows, or columns
   On the Home tab, in the Cells group, click Format.
3. Do one of the following:

- Under Visibility, point to Hide & Unhide, and then click Unhide Rows or Unhide Columns.
- Under Cell Size, click Row Height or Column Width, and then type the value that you want in the Row Height or Column Width box.
  TIP: You can also right-click the selection of visible rows and columns that surround the hidden rows and columns, and then click *Unhide*.

5.7.3 Display all hidden rows and columns at once

1. To select all cells on a worksheet, do one of the following:
   - Click the Select All button.
   - Press CTRL+A.
     NOTE: If the worksheet contains data and the active cell is above or to the right of the data, pressing CTRL+A selects the current region. Pressing CTRL+A a second time selects the entire worksheet.

Select All button

2. On the Home tab, in the Cells group, click Format.

3. Do one of the following:
   - Under Visibility, point to Hide & Unhide, and then click Unhide Rows or Unhide Columns.
   - Under Cell Size, click Row Height or Column Width, and then type the value that you want in the Row Height or Column Width box.

5.7.4 Unhide the first row or column of the worksheet

1. To select the first hidden row or column on the worksheet, do one of the following:
   - In the Name Box next to the formula bar, type A1.
   - On the **Home** tab, in **the Editing** group, **click Find & Select**, and then click Go To. In the Reference box, type A1, and then click OK.

2. On the Home tab, in the Cells group, click Format.
3. Do one of the following:
   - Under Visibility, point to Hide & Unhide, and then click Unhide Rows or Unhide Columns.
   - Under Cell Size, click Row Height or Column Width, and then type the value that you want in the Row Height or Column Width box.

5.8 Switch to full or normal screen view

To view more data on the screen, you can temporarily switch to full screen view. Full screen view hides the Microsoft Office Fluent user interface Ribbon, the formula bar, and the status bar. To have access to the hidden elements again, you have to return to normal screen view.

- To switch to full screen view, on the View tab, in the Workbook Views group, click Full Screen.
- To return to normal screen view, right-click anywhere in the worksheet, and then click Close Full Screen.
  Keyboard shortcut: You can also press **ESC**.

5.8.1 View two or more worksheets at the same time

You can quickly compare two worksheets in the same workbook or in different workbooks by viewing them side by side. You can also arrange multiple worksheets to view them all at the same time.

- View two worksheets in the same workbook side by side
- View two worksheets of different workbooks side by side
- View multiple worksheets at the same time

5.8.2 View two worksheets in the same workbook side by side

1. On the **View** tab, in the **Window** group, click **New Window**.
2. On the **View** tab, in the **Window** group, click **View Side by Side**.
3. In the workbook window, click the worksheets that you want to compare.
4. To scroll both worksheets at the same time, click **Synchronous Scrolling** in the Window group on the **View** tab.
   NOTE: This option is available only when **View Side by Side** is turned on.
   Tips
   - If you resize the workbook windows for optimal viewing, you can click Reset **Window Position** to return to the original settings.
   - To restore a workbook window to full size, click **Maximize** at the upper-right corner of the workbook window.

5.8.3 View two worksheets of different workbooks side by side

1. Open both of the workbooks that contain the worksheets that you want to compare.
2. On the View tab, in the Window group, click View Side by Side.

NOTE: If you keep more than two workbooks open, Excel displays the Compare Side by Side dialog box. In this dialog box, under Compare Side by Side, click the workbook that contains the worksheet that you want to compare with your active worksheet, and then click **OK.**

3. In each workbook window, click the sheet that you want to compare.
4. To scroll both worksheets at the same time, click Synchronous Scrolling ▣ in the Window group on the View tab.

NOTE: This option is available only when View Side by Side is turned on.
Tips
- If you resize the workbook windows for optimal viewing, you can click Reset Window Position ▣ to return to the original settings.
- To restore a workbook window to full size, click Maximize ▣ at the upper-right corner of the workbook window.

5.8.4 View multiple worksheets at the same time

1. Open the workbook or workbooks that contain the worksheets that you want to view at the same time.
2. Do one of the following:

   - If the worksheets that you want to view are in the same workbook, do the following:

     a. Click a worksheet that you want to view.
     b. On the View tab, in the Window group, click New Window.
     c. Repeat steps 1 and 2 for each sheet that you want to view.
   - If the worksheets that you want to view are in different workbooks, continue with step 3.

3. On the **View** tab, in the Window group, click **Arrange All**.
4. Under Arrange, click the option that you want.
5. To view sheets only in the active workbook, select the Windows of active workbook check box.

TIP: To restore a workbook window to full size, click Maximize ▣ at the upper-right corner of the workbook window.

5.9 Where are my worksheet tabs?

If you can't see the worksheet tabs at the bottom of your Excel 2007/2010 workbook, refer to the following for possible causes and solutions.

CAUSE: The workbook window is sized in such a way that the tabs are hidden

SOLUTION: This problem sometimes happens after you unhook the workbook window from the Excel window (by using the **Restore Window** button in the trio of buttons on the title bar), and then inadvertently move the window beneath the status bar. This may also occur if your computer's screen resolution is higher than that of the person who last saved the workbook. To maximize the window so that you can see the tabs again, double-click the window's title bar.

If you still don't see the tabs, try this instead: On the **View** tab, in the **Window** group, click **Arrange All**. Under Arrange, click **Tiled**, and then click **OK**.

CAUSE: The Show sheet tabs setting is turned off.
SOLUTION: First, see if the option is, in fact, turned off. To do this, click the Microsoft Office button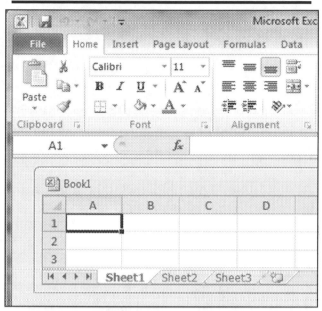, and then click **Excel Options**.

Figure 5.5 Workbook with three worksheets

Figure 5.6 Display options for worksheet

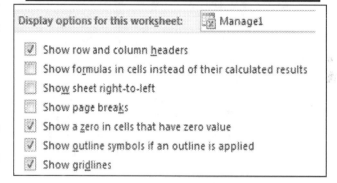

In the **Advanced** category, under Display options for this **Workbook**, look at the **Show sheet** tabs check box. Is it cleared? If so, select it, and then click **OK**.

In some cases, you may not see worksheet tabs after adding a macro sheet to a workbook. For more information, see Worksheet tabs disappear when you change some "Display options for this workbook" options and then add a macro worksheet to a workbook in Excel 2007/2010.

CAUSE: The horizontal scroll bar obscures the tabs.

SOLUTION: If you widen the horizontal scroll bar at the bottom of a worksheet, you may unintentionally hide some or all of the sheet tabs. If this happens, point to the button next to the left of the scroll bar.

Figure 5.7 Illustration of worksheet scroll bar

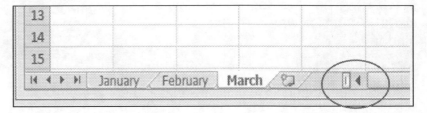

When your pointer becomes a double-headed arrow, drag it to the right until you see the tabs again.

CAUSE: The worksheet itself is hidden.

SOLUTION: To unhide a worksheet, right-click a visible tab on the worksheet, and then click Unhide. In the Unhide dialog box, click the sheet you want to unhide, and then click OK.

CAUSE: The formula box is resized.

SOLUTION: This problem sometimes happens after you unhook the workbook window from the Excel window (by using the Restore Window button in the trio of buttons on the title bar), and then adjust the size of the formula box in the formula bar. If the workbook window happens to be sized in a particular way when you enlarge the formula box, your worksheet tabs may disappear beneath the status bar. To restore the tabs, maximize the window by double-clicking its title bar.

Figure 5.8 Illustration to Unhide worksheet

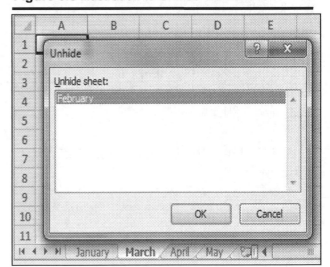

5.10 Assignment Questions (1- 22)

Answer the following project questions by showing all the appropriate steps that should be followed to arrive at the answer for each question.

1. What activities are involved in managing worksheets?

2. Describe the process of performing the following actions on a worksheet:
    a. Insert a new column
    b. Insert a new row
    c. Hide and unhide a column
    d. Hide and unhide a row

3. Describe the process of performing the following actions on a workbook:
    a. Insert a new worksheet
    b. Delete a worksheet.

4. In Excel the gridlines are visible in worksheets, but do not appear in print out by default.   Explain how you would print an Excel worksheet with gridlines.

5. What is the difference that exists between a workbook template and a worksheet template?

6. Describe how you will change the font size in workbooks.
    a. Does this change affect all worksheets under the workbook; True or False?

7. Briefly show the steps for the following operations
    a. View two worksheets in the same workbook side by side
    b. View two worksheets of different workbooks side by side
    c. View multiple worksheets at the same time

8. What will you do to switch normal screen to full screen view in worksheet?
    a. Show how to return to normal screen view.

9. Which steps will you take to display all hidden rows and columns at once?
    a. How will you hide the rows?

10. In one of your accounting assignments you do not want to display a few columns and rows.   Show how to hide one or more rows and columns.

11. Briefly describe the steps necessary to drag data to another workbook that is open in a separate instance of Excel

12. A document was saved to your disk and you want to open it.
    a. Which menu do you select?
    b. Given the path of the saved file as **C:\Bright\Expenses\Account.xlsx.** Show how to open this file in Excel spreadsheet.

13. The Formatting toolbar has been removed and you want to add it back to your window. Which menu do you select? Show the steps to follow.

14. You have selected the content of a cell that you want to remove from the worksheet. Describe which steps to follow to clear the contents of the cell.

15. Your spreadsheet is too wide, and you want to turn the page to landscape orientation for printing. Which menu do you select? Describe the process of achieving this objective

16. You have a three page spreadsheet, and where the printing stops on each page is critical. Which menu tools do you use to check where the Page Breaks are located?

17. You have placed comments in several cells and want to see all of them displayed at the same time. Explain how to go about it.

18. You have changed a worksheet and now want to save it with a different name. Briefly explain the most suitable way to achieve that objective?

19. You have finished for the day and want to quit Microsoft Excel. Which menu do you select?

20. Sheet one of a workbook is your grade book. You want to place a password on that sheet so students can not change the data. Which menu do you select?

21. A list of numbers just does not communicate as well as you want to. A chart should be put into your spreadsheet to clearly show the patterns you see in the data. Which menu do you select?

22. Where is that button? You have grown accustomed to a toolbar button in another Office application and want to add it to an Excel toolbar. Which menu do you select?

CHAPTER 6
Conditional Formatting and Data Analysis

Objectives:

- Introduction to Conditional Formatting and Data Analysis
- Conditional Formatting by Range of Values
- CountIF in Microsoft Excel 2007 to 2010
- SUMIF in Microsoft Excel 2007 to 2010
- Data Tables in Microsoft Excel 2007 to 2010
- Scenarios in Microsoft Excel 2007 to 2010
- Goal Seek in Microsoft Excel 2007 to 2010

6.0 Introduction

You can use something called Conditional Formatting in your Excel spreadsheets. Conditional Formatting allows you to change the appearance of a cell, depending on certain conditions. We will do is to color the Overall Averages on our Student Exam spreadsheet, depending on the grade. Here is the spreadsheet we will be working on.

Figure 6.1 Student Exam Spreadsheet

	A	B	C	D	E	F	G	H	I
1		Peter	Samuel	Lucy	Eric	Ernest	Agnes	George	Joe
2	Maths	76	90	53	58	61	78	88	66
3	English	55	86	79	71	57	85	90	78
4	Science	65	82	49	68	42	64	59	45
5	History	54	91	58	72	49	54	76	58
6	Geography	51	85	55	64	48	64	69	68
7	Art	67	63	49	62	39	90	65	64
8	Computer Science	61	95	46	59	51	91	89	52
9	French	45	91	68	36	35	52	93	58
10									
11	Overall Average	59.25	85.375	57.13	61.25	47.75	72.25	78.625	61.125

- Open up the Student Exam spreadsheet.
- Highlight the cells with Overall Grades, which should be cells **B11** to **I11**

6.1 Conditional Formatting by Range of Values

The Overall Averages range from **47** to **85**. We will color each grade, depending on a scale. A different color will apply to the following grades:

- 50 and below
- 51 to 60
- 61 to 70
- 71 to 80
- 81 and above

So five different bands, and a color for each. To set the Conditional Formatting in Excel, do the following:

- With your Overall Averages highlighted, click on the Home menu at the top of Excel
- Locate the Styles panel, and the Conditional Formatting item:

The Conditional Formatting menu gives you various options. The easiest one is the Color Scales option. Select one of these and Excel will color the cell backgrounds for you:

That is not quite what we are looking for, though. We would like to choose our own values. So click on More Rules, from the Color Scales submenu. You will see the following rather complex dialogue box:

Figure 6.2 Condition Formatting Menu

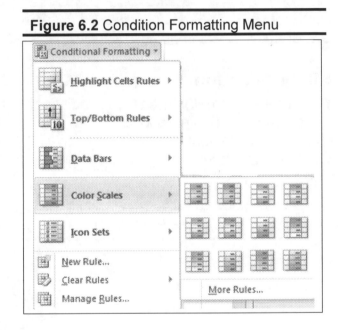

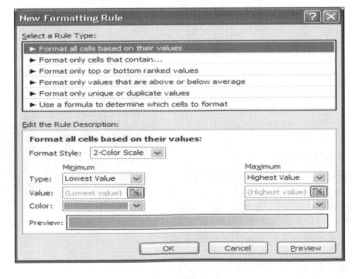

The one we want is the second option, **Format only cells that contain**... This will allow us to set up our values. When you click this option, the dialogue box changes to this:

1. Format only cells that contain...
2. Enter the range of values.
3. Click Format... button
4. Select the color.
5. Repeat the process from 1.

Figure 6.3 Dialogue Box For New Formatting Rule

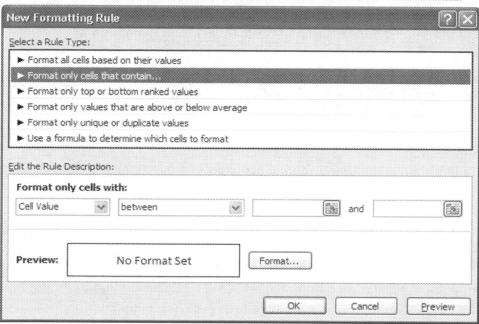

The part we are interested in is the bottom part, under the heading "**Edit the Rule Description.**" It says **Cell Value** and **Between**, in the drop down boxes. These are the ones we want. We only need to type a value for the two boxes that are currently blank in the image above. We can then click the Format button to choose a color. So type **0** in the first box and **50** in the second one:

Figure 6.4 Dialogue Box For Edit the Formatting Rule Description

Edit the Rule Description:

Format only cells with:

Cell Value   between   0   and   50

Preview: No Format Set   Format...

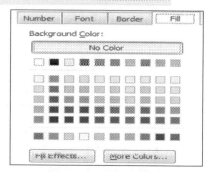

Then click the **Format button**. You will get another dialogue box popping up. This is just the **Format Cells**. You have met this before. Click on the Fill tab and choose a color. Click **OK** and you should see something like this under **Edit the Rule Description:**

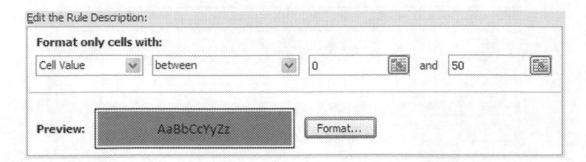

The Preview is showing the color we picked. So we've said, "If the **Cell Value** is between **0** and **50** then color the cell **Red**".

Click **OK** on this dialogue box to get back to Excel. You should find that one of the cells has turned red. To format the rest of the cells, click on **Conditional Formatting** on the Styles panel again. From the menu, click on **Manage Rules:**

You will get yet another complex dialogue box popping up! This one:

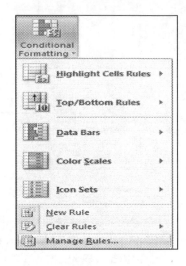

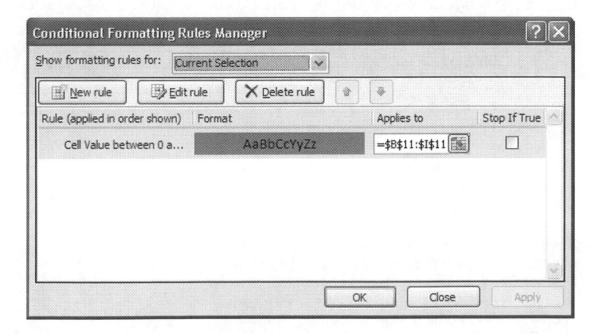

Our first rule is already there - Cell Value Between. The only thing we are doing here is adding New Rules, similar to the one we've just set up. Click the New Rule button then. You will see the exact same dialogue boxes you used to set up the first rule.

Set a new color for the next scores - **51** to **60**. Choose a color, and keep clicking OK until you get back to the **Rules Manager dialogue** box. It should now look something like this one.

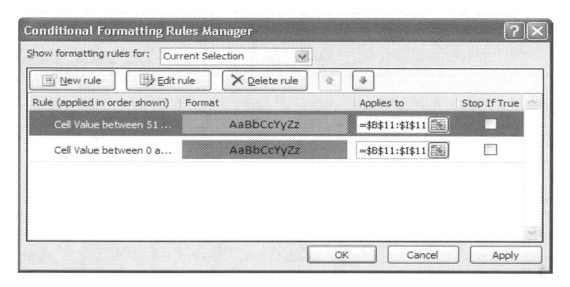

We now have two colors in our range. Do the rest of the scores, choosing a color for each. The scores are these, remember:
  *   50 and below
  *   51 to 60
  *   61 to 70
  *   71 to 80
  *   81 and above
When you have done them all, your dialogue box should have five colours:

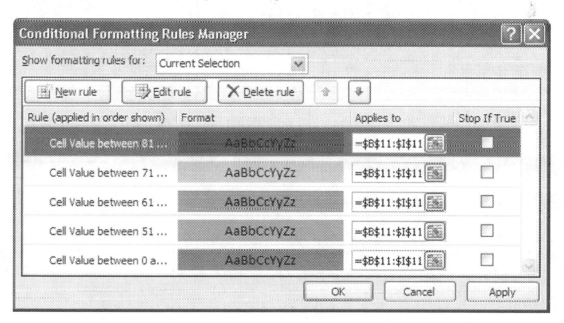

The colors above are entirely arbitrary, and you don't have to select the same ones we did. The point is to have a different color for each range of scores. But click OK when you're done. Your Overall Averages will then look something like this:

Figure 6.5 Conditional Formatting For Scores Ranges of the Spreadsheet

	A	B	C	D	E	F	G	H	I
1		Peter	Samuel	Lucy	Eric	Ernest	Agnes	George	Joe
2	Maths	76	90	53	58	61	78	88	66
3	English	55	86	79	71	57	85	90	78
4	Science	65	82	49	68	42	64	59	45
5	History	54	91	58	72	49	54	76	58
6	Geography	51	85	55	64	48	64	69	68
7	Art	67	63	49	62	39	90	65	64
8	Computer Science	61	95	46	59	51	91	89	52
9	French	45	91	68	36	35	52	93	58
10									
11	Overall Average	59.25	85.375	57.125	61.25	47.75	72.25	78.625	61.125

6.2 CountIF in Microsoft Excel 2007 to 2010

Formatting your spreadsheet in this way allows you to see at a glance relevant information. In the spreadsheet above, it's obvious who's failing - just look for the red cells! In the next part, we'll look at a useful function that counts things - **COUNT IF**.

Figure 6.6 Counting For Scores Ranges Above 70

	A	B	C	D	E	F	G	H	I	J	K
1		Peter	Samuel	Lucy	Eric	Ernest	Agnes	George	Joe		Num of Students Above 70
2	Maths	76	90	53	58	61	78	88	66		4
3	English	55	86	79	71	57	85	90	78		6
4	Science	65	82	49	68	42	64	59	45		1
5	History	54	91	58	72	49	54	76	58		3
6	Geography	51	85	55	64	48	64	69	68		1
7	Art	67	63	49	62	39	90	65	64		1
8	Computer Science	61	95	46	59	51	91	89	52		3
9	French	45	91	68	36	35	52	93	58		2
10											
11	Overall Average	59.25	85.375	57.125	61.25	47.75	72.25	78.625	61.125		3

=COUNTIF(B11:I11,">=70")

Another useful function that uses **Conditional Logic** is **CountIF**. This one is fairly straightforward. As its name suggests, it counts things! But it counts things **IF** a condition is met. For example, keep a count of how many students have an **A Grade**.

To get you started with this function, we will use our Student Grade spreadsheet and count how many students have a score of **70** or above. First, add the following label to your spreadsheet: "Number of Students with Grades Above 70%"

As you can see, we have put our new label at the start of the **K** column.
We can now use the **CountIF** function to see how many of the students scored **70** or above for a given subject.

The **CountIF** function looks like this: **COUNTIF(range, criteria)**

The function takes two arguments (the words in the round brackets). The first argument is range, and this means the range of cells you want Excel to count. Criteria means, "What do you want Excel to look for when it's counting?".
So click inside cell K2, and then click inside the formula bar at the top. Enter the following formula: **=CountIf(B2:I2, ">= 70")**

The cells B2 to I2 contain the Math scores for all 8 students. It's these scores we want to count. Press the enter key on your keyboard. Excel should give you an answer of 4:

Figure 6.7 Composition of Counting Formula For Scores Ranges Above 70

K2		f_x	=COUNTIF(B2:I2, ">= 70")	
	A	J	K	L
1			Num of Students Above 70	
2	Maths		4	
3	English			
4	Science			

(If you are wondering where the **columns B** to **I** have gone in the image above, we have hidden then for convenience sake!). To do the rest of the scores, you can use **AutoFill**. You should then have a **K** column that looks like this:

By using **CountIF**, we can see at a glance which subjects students are doing well in, and which subjects they are struggling in.

	A	J	K
1			Num of Students Above 70
2	Maths		4
3	English		6
4	Science		1
5	History		3
6	Geography		1
7	Art		1
8	Computer Science		3
9	French		2
10			
11	Overall Average		3

Exercise
Add a new label to the L column. In the cells L2 to L9, work out how many students got **below 50** for a given subject. You should get the same results as in the image below: **=COUNTIF(B11:I11,"<=50")**

Figure 6.8 Counting Formula For Scores Above 70 and Scores Below 50

	A	J	K	L
1			Num of Students Above 70	Num of Students Below 50
2	Maths		4	0
3	English		6	0
4	Science		1	3
5	History		3	1
6	Geography		1	1
7	Art		1	2
8	Computer Science		3	1
9	French		2	3
10				0
11	Overall Average		3	1

6.3 SUMIF in Microsoft Excel 2007 to 2010

In this part, we will look at a function **SumIF,** which is similar to **CountIF**. Another useful Excel function is **SumIF**. This function is like **CountIf**, except that it adds one more argument:

SUMIF(range, criteria, sum_range)

Range and criteria are the same as with **CountIF** - the range of cells to search, and what you want Excel to look for. The **Sum_Range** is like range, but it searches a new range of cells. To clarify all that, here's what we'll use **SumIF** for. (Start a new spreadsheet for this.)

Five people have ordered goods from us. Some have paid us, but some have not.

The five people are Kofi, Kwame, Adjoa, Abena, and Kwabena. We will use **SumIF** to calculate how much in total has been paid to us, and how much is still owed.
So in **Column A**, enter the names. In Column B enter how much each person owes.

Figure 6.9 SumIF Formula For Paid and Unpaid Cost

	A	B	C
1	Customer	Total Goods Ordered	Has Paid
2			
3	Kofi	$150.00	TRUE
4	Kwame	$135.00	FALSE
5	Adjoa	$128.00	FALSE
6	Abena	$145.00	TRUE
7	Kwabena	$166.00	FALSE

In **Column C**, enter **TRUE** or **FALSE** values. **TRUE** means they have paid up, and **FALSE** means they have not. Add two more labels:
Total Paid, and **Still Owed**. Your spreadsheet should look something like this one.

Figure 6.10 SumIF Formula For Paid and Unpaid

	A	B	C
1	Customer	Total Goods Ordered	Has Paid
2			
3	Kofi	$150.00	TRUE
4	Kwame	$135.00	FALSE
5	Adjoa	$128.00	FALSE
6	Abena	$145.00	TRUE
7	Kwabena	$166.00	FALSE
8			
9	Total Paid		
10	Still Owed		

In cells B9 and B10, we'll use a **SumIF** function to work out how much has been paid in, and how much is still owed. Here's the **SumIF** function again:
SUMIF(range, criteria, sum_range)

So the range of cells that we want to check are the **True** and **False** values in the C column; the criteria is whether they have paid (**True**); and the **Sum_Range** is what we want to add up (in the B column).
In cell B10, then, enter the following formula:

=SUMIF(C3:C7, TRUE, B3:B7)

When you press the enter key, Excel should give you the answer:

Figure 6.11 SumIF Showing Paid and Unpaid Amounts

B9	▼	f_x	=SUMIF(C3:C7,TRUE,B3:B7)

condition_format [Compatibility Mode]

	A	B	C
1	Customer	Total Goods Ordered	Has Paid
2			
3	Kofi	$150.00	TRUE
4	Kwame	$135.00	FALSE
5	Adjoa	$128.00	FALSE
6	Abena	$145.00	TRUE
7	Kwabena	$166.00	FALSE
8			
9	Total Paid	$295.00	
10	Still Owed	$429.00	

So **$295** is what has been paid in. But we told **SumIF** to first check the values in the cells **C3** to **C7** (range). Then we said look for a value of TRUE (**criteria**). Finally, we wanted the values in the **B** column adding up, if a **criteria** of **TRUE** was indeed found (**sum_range**).

Exercise
Use **SumIF** to work out how much is still owed. Put your answer in cell B10.

6.4 Data Tables in Microsoft Excel 2007 to 2010

In Excel, a Data Table is a way to see different results by altering an input cell in your formula. As an example, we are going to alter the interest rate, and see how much a $10,000 loan would cost each month. The interest rate will be our input cell. By asking Excel to alter this input, we can quickly see the different monthly payments. Want to know how much we would pay back each month if the interest was 24 percent per year. But other banks may be offering better deals. So we will ask Excel to calculate how much we would pay each month if the interest rate was 22 percent a year, 20 percent a year, and 18 percent a year.

The formula we need is the Payment - **PMT( )**. Here it is again:

> **PMT(rate, nper, pv, fv, type)**

We only need the first three arguments. So for us, it's just this:

> **PMT(rate, nper, pv)**

Rate means the interest **rate**. The second argument, **nper**, is how many months you have got to pay the loan back. The third argument, **pv**, is how much you want to borrow. Let's make a start then. On a new spreadsheet, set up the following labels:

Figure 6.12 PMT Formula Showing Interest Loan Amount

	A	B	C	D
1	Payment Terms			
2				
3	Interest Rate	24.00%		
4	Num of Months	60		
5	Loan Amount	$10,000.00		

So we'll put our starting interest rate in cell B3 (rate), our loan length in cell B4 (**nper**), and our loan amount in cell **B5** (**pv**). Enter the following in cells B3 to B5.
So you need to enter **24.00%** in cell **B3**, **60** in cell B4, and **$10,000** in cell **B5**. We will enter our formula now. Click inside cell D2 and enter the following:

> **=PMT(B3 / 12, B4, -B5)**

Cell B3 is the interest rate. But this is for the entire year. In the formula, we're diving whatever is in cell **B3** by **12**. This will get us a monthly interest rate. **B4** in the formula is the number of months, which is **60** for us. **B5** has a minus sign before it. It's a minus figure because it's a debt. When you press the enter key on your keyboard, Excel should give you an answer of **$287.68.**

Now that we have our function in place, we can create an **Excel Data Table**. First, though, we need to tell Excel about those other interest rates. It will use these to work out the new monthly payments. Remember, Excel is recalculating the **PMT** function. So it needs some new values to calculate with. So enter some new values in cells **C3**, **C4**, and **C5**. Enter the same ones as in the image above.

Figure 6.13 PMT Formula Showing 1 Month Pay

D2		*fx*	=PMT(B3/12,B4,-B5)	
	A	B	C	D
1		Payment Terms		
2				$287.68
3	Interest Rate	24.00%	22.00%	
4	Num of Months	60	20.00%	
5	Loan Amount	$10,000.00	18.00%	

We have put the **PMT** function in cell D2 for a reason. This is one Row up, and one Column to the right of our first new interest rate of 22%. The new monthly payments are going to go in cells D3 to D5. Excel needs the table setting out this way.

So that **Excel** can work out the new totals, you have to highlight both the new values and the Function you are using. So highlight the cells C2 to D5. Your spreadsheet should look like this:

Figure 6.14 PMT Formula – Highlighted C2:D5

	A	B	C	D
1		Payment Terms		
2				$287.68
3	Interest Rate	24.00%	22.00%	
4	Num of Months	60	20.00%	
5	Loan Amount	$10,000.00	18.00%	

As you can see, the cells C2 to D5 are now highlighted. This includes our new interest rate values in the C column, and our **PMT** function in cell D2. We can now create an **Excel Data Table**. This will work out new monthly payments for us. So do this:

- From the Excel menu bar, click on Data
- Locate the Data Tools panel
- Click on the "What if Analysis" item:

When you click on the "**What if Analysis**" item, you'll see the following menu.

Click on Data Table, and you'll see this small dialogue box:

Figure 6.15 Data Table Input Box

In the dialogue box, there is only a **Row input cell** or a **Column input cell**. We want Excel to fill downwards, down a column. So we need the second text box on the dialogue box "**Column input cell**". If we were filling across in rows, we would use the "**Row** input cell" text box.

The Input Cell for us is the one that contains our original interest rate. This is the cell you want Excel to substitute. So click inside the **Column input cell box** and enter **B3.** Click **OK.** When you do, Excel will work out the new monthly payments as shown in figure 6.13

So if we could get an **18** percent interest rate, our monthly payments would be **$253.93**.

If you click inside any of the cells D3 to D5, then look at the formula bar, you will see this:

Figure 6.16 Automatically Calculated Amount

	A	B	C	D
1	Payment Terms			
2				$287.68
3	Interest Rate	24.00%	22.00%	$276.19
4	Num of Months	60	20.00%	$264.94
5	Loan Amount	$10,000.00	18.00%	$253.93

$$\{=TABLE(,B3)\}$$

That's Excel's way of telling you that a Table has been created, based on the input cell **B3**. We will try one more Data Table in the next part. We will try an easier formula, this time

6.5 Scenario - A Second Data Table in Microsoft Excel 2007 to 2010

We will do one more Data Table, just so that you get the hands-on experience. This time, we will use a more simple formula than **PMT**, and we will use **Rows** instead of **Columns**. This is the scenario:

You have 150 items that you want to sell on EBay. Your unique selling point is this - All items are only $5.50 each! **Except**, you feel $5 may be a bit expensive for the goods you are selling. What you want to know is

Figure 6.17 Scenario Initial Data Table

	A	B	C	D	E
1	Number of Items	150			
2	Unit Price	$5.50			
3	Discounted Price	$0.00	$5.00	$4.00	$3.50
4	Profits				

how much profit you will make if you reduce your prices to $5, how much if you reduce to $4.00, and how much for a reduction to $3.50. Assume that everything gets sold. To start creating your Table, construct a spreadsheet like the one above. Make sure that you start on a new sheet.

In cell B1 is the number of items we want to sell is 150. Cell **B2** has the original price of $5.50. And the Discounted Price Row has our new values. Cell B3 has a 0 because there is no discount for $5.50. Row 4 is where our Profits will be entered. The formula to work out the profits is simply the Number of Items multiplied by the Price Per Item. So click inside cell B4 and enter the following formula:

= B1 * B2

Your spreadsheet will then look like this:

Figure 6.18 Scenario Initial Data Table

	A	B	C	D	E
1	Number of Items	150			
2	Unit Price	$5.50			
3	Discounted Price	0	$5.00	$4.00	$3.50
4	Profits	$825.00			

So if we manage to sell all our items at $5.50, we will make $825. We are a bit dubious, though. Realistically, all our items will not sell at this price. Let's use an **Excel Data Table** to work out how much profit we would make at the other prices.

Again, we put the answer in cell B4 for a reason. This is because when you want Excel to calculate a **Data Table in Rows**, the formula must be inserted one **Column** to the Left of your first new value, and then one Row down. Our first new value is going in cell C3. So one column to the left takes us to the B column. One row down is **Row 4**. So the formula goes in cell **B4**. Next, click inside cell **B3** and highlight to cell **E4**. Your spreadsheet should now look like this one:

Excel is going to use our formula in cell B4. It will then look at the new values on Row 3 (not counting the zero), and then insert the new totals for us. To create a Data Table then, do the following:

Figure 6.19 Scenario - Highlighted Calculated Cells

	A	B	C	D	E
1	Number of Items	150			
2	Unit Price	$5.50			
3	Discounted Price	0	$5.00	$4.00	$3.50
4	Profits	$825.00			

- From the Excel menu bar, click on Data
- Locate the Data Tools panel
- Click on the "What if Analysis" item
- Select Data Table from the menu

Just like last time, you will get the **Data Table dialogue** box. The one we want now, though, is **Row Input Cell**. But what is the Input Cell this time?

Ask yourself what you are trying to work out, and what you want Excel to recalculate. You want to work out the new prices. The formula you entered was:

= B1 * B2

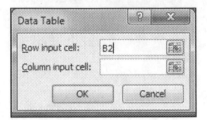

Excel is going to be changing this formula. You only need to decide if you want Excel to alter the B1 or the B2. B1 contains the number of items; B2 contains the price of each item. Since we're trying to work out the profits we'd get if we change the price, we need Excel to change B2. So enter B2 for the Row Input Cell:

When you click OK, Excel will work out the new profits:

Figure 6.20
Scenario – Results of Calculated Cells

	A	B	C	D	E
1	Number of Items	150			
2	Unit Price	$5.50			
3	Discounted Price	0	$5.00	$4.00	$3.50
4	Profits	$825.00	$750.00	$600.00	$525.00

So setting a price of $3.50 per item, you would make $525 profit. You would make $600 at $4.00 per item, and $750 if you sell for $5.00.

Hopefully, Data Tables were not too difficult to create. But they are very useful tools when you want to analyse values that can change. In the next section, we will take a look at scenarios.

6.6 Scenarios in Microsoft Excel 2007 to 2010

Scenarios come under the heading of "**What-If Analysis**" in Excel. They are similar to tables in that you are changing values to get new results. For example, What if I reduce the amount I am spending on grocery? How much will I have left then? Scenarios can be saved, so that you can apply them with a quick click of the mouse.

An example of a scenario you might want to create is a family budget. You can then make changes to individual amounts, like grocery, clothes, or fuel, and see how these changes effect your overall budget.

We will see how they work now, as we tackle a family budget. So, create the spreadsheet below:

The value in cell B13 in the figure 6.21 is just a SUM function, and is your total debts. The figure in D3 is how much you have to spend each month (not a lot!). The figure in D14 is how much you have left after you deduct all your debts.

With only $343 spending money left each month, clearly some changes have to be made. We will create a scenario to see what effect the various budgets cuts have.

Figure 6.21 Scenario - Highlighted Calculated Cells

	A	B	C	D
1		The Family Budget		
2		EXPENSES		INCOME
3	Car Loan	525		3500
4	Mortgage	1250		
5	Fuel Bills	150		
6	Credit Cards	65		
7	Grocery	385		
8	Electric Bill	250		
9	Clothes	175		
10	Phone Bill	300		
11	Water Bill	57		
12				
13	Total Expenses	3157		
14	Income Left			343

- From the top of Excel click the Data menu
- On the Data menu, locate the Data Tools panel
- Click on the **What if Analysis** item, and select **Scenario Manager** from the menu:

When you click **Scenario Manager**, you should the following dialogue box: When you click Scenario Manager, you should see the following dialogue box:

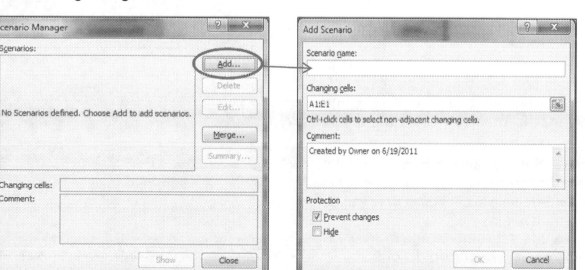

We want to create a new scenario. So click the Add button. You will then get another dialogue box popping up:

The A1:E1 in the image is just whatever cell you had selected when you brought up the dialogue boxes. We will change this. First, type a Name for your Scenario in the Scenario Name box. Call it **Family Budget.**

Excel now needs you to enter which cells in your spreadsheet will be changing. In this first scenario, nothing will be changing (because it's our original). But we still need to specify which cells will be changing. Let's try to reduce the Grocery bill, the Clothes Bill, and the Phone bill.

These are in cells **B7** to **B10** in our spreadsheet. So in the Changing Cells box, enter **B7:B10**. Do not forget to include the colon in the middle! But your Add **Scenario** box should look like this:

Click OK and Excel will ask you for some values:
We don't want any values to change in this first scenario, so just click **OK**. You will be taken back to the **Scenario Manager** box. It should now look like this:

Now that we have one scenario set up, we can add a second one. This is where we'll enter some new values - our savings.
Click the Add button again. You will get the **Add Scenario** dialogue box

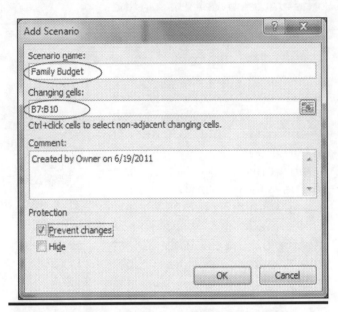

Figure 6.22 Scenario Original Values

back up. Type a new Name, something like Budget Two.

The Changing Cells area should already say B7:B10. So just click **OK.**

You will be taken to the Scenario Values dialogue box again. This time, we do want to change the values. Enter the same ones as in the image below:

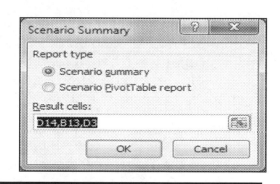

These are the new values for our Budget. Click OK and you'll be taken back to the Scenario Manager. This time, you'll have two scenarios to view:

These values are modified due to budget constraint. B7: 285, B8: 125, B9: 105 and B10: 210.

Figure 6.23 The Modified Values

As you can see, we have our Original Budget, and Budget Two. With Budget Two selected, click the Show button at the bottom. The values in your spreadsheet will change, and the new budget will be calculated. The image below shows what it looks like in the spreadsheet:

Click on the Original Budget to highlight it. Then click the Show button. The first values will be displayed!

Click the Close button on the dialogue box when you're done.

So a Scenario offers you different ways to view a set of figures, and allows you to switch between them quite easily.

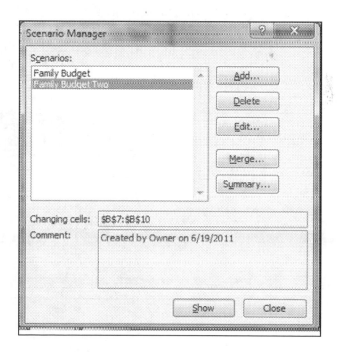

How to Create a Report from a Scenario. Another thing you can do with a scenario is create a report.

To create a report from your scenarios, do the following:

- Click on Data from the Excel menu bar
- Locate the Data Tools panel
- On the Data Tools panel, click What if Analysis
- From the What if Analysis menu, click Scenario Manager
- From the Scenario Manager dialogue box, click the Summary button to see the following dialogue box:

Figure 6.24 The Modified Budget Values

▲	A	B	C	D
1		**The Family Budget**		
2		EXPENSES		INCOME
3	Car Loan	525		3500
4	Mortgage	1250		
5	Fuel Bills	150		
6	Credit Cards	65		
7	Grocery	285		
8	Electric Bill	125		
9	Clothes	105		
10	Phone Bill	210		
11	Water Bill	57		
12				
13	Total Expenses	2772		
14	Income Left			728

What you are doing here is selecting cells to go in your report. To change the cells, click on your spreadsheet. Click individual cells by holding down the **CTRL key** on your keyboard, and clicking a cell with your left mouse button. Select the cells **D14, B13** and **D3**. If you want to get rid of a highlighted cell, just click inside it again with the **CTRL key** held down. Click **OK** when you have selected the cells. Excel will then create your Scenario Summary:

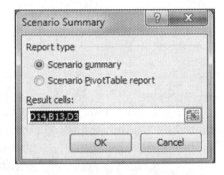

Figure 6.25 The Scenario Summary for two Budgets				

Scenario Summary		Current Values:	Family Budget	Family Budget Two
Changing Cells:				
	$B$7	285	385	285
	$B$8	125	250	125
	$B$9	105	175	105
	$B$10	210	300	210
Result Cells:				
	$D$14	728	343	728
	$B$13	2772	3157	2772
	$D$3	3500	3500	3500

Notes: Current Values column represents values of changing cells at time Scenario Summary Report was created. Changing cells for each scenario are highlighted in gray.

6.7 Goal Seek in Microsoft Excel 2007 to 2010

Goal Seek is used to get a particular result when you are not too sure of the starting value. For example, if the answer is 72, and the first number is 9, what is the second number? Is it 9 multiplied by 8, or 9 multiplied by 7? You can use Goal Seek to find out. We will try that example to get you started, and then have a goal at a more practical example.

Create the following Excel spreadsheet:

Figure 6.26
Excel spreadsheet
of multiplying Cells
B1 by B2

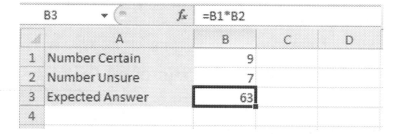

In the spreadsheet above, we know that we want to multiply the number in **B1** by the number in **B2**. The number in cell **B2** is the one we are not too sure of. The answer is going in cell **B3**. Our answer is wrong at the moment, because we have a Goal of 72. To use Goal Seek to get the answer, try the following:

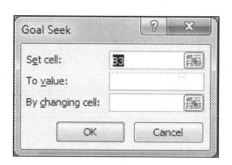

- From the Excel menu bar, click on **Data**
- Locate the Data Tools panel and the What if Analysis item. From the What if Analysis menu, select Goal Seek
- The following dialogue box appears:

The first thing Excel is looking for is "**Set cell**". This is not very well named. It means "Which cell contains the Formula that you want Excel to use". For us, this is cell B3. We have the following formula in B3: **= B1 * B2**
So enter **B3** into the "**Set cell**" box, if it's not already in there.

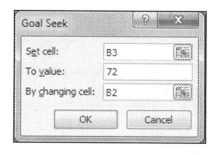

The "**To value**" box means "What answer are you looking for"? For us, this is **72**. So just type 72 into the "**To value**" box.

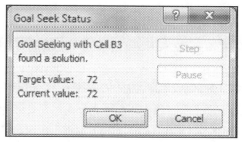

The "**By Changing Cell**" is the part you are not sure of. Excel will be changing this part. For us, it was cell B2. We weren't sure which number,when multiplied by 8, gave the answer 72. So type B2 into the box.

You Goal Seek dialogue box should look like ours below:

Click OK and Excel will tell you if it has found a solution:

Figure 6.27 Goal Seek Value of 72

	A	B	C	D
	B3	f_x =B1*B2		
1	Number Certain	9		
2	Number Unsure	8		
3	Expected Answer	72		

Click OK again, because Excel has found the answer. Your new spreadsheet will look like this one. As you can see, Excel has changed cell B2 and replace the 7 with a 8 - the correct answer.

6.7.1 More Goal Seek in Microsoft Excel 2007 to 2010

We will now try a more practical example.

Consider this problem:

Your business has a modest profit of 30,000. You've set yourself a new profit Goal of 45,000. At the moment, you're selling 2000 items at 15 each. Assume that you will still sell 2000 items. The question is, to hit your new profit of 45,000, by how much do you have to raise your prices?

Create the spreadsheet below, and we will find a solution with Goal Seek.

Figure 6.28 The Spreadsheet Showing the Original Cell Values

	A	B	C	D	E	F
	J6			f_x		
1	Current Sales Figures			Futures Sales Figures		
2	Items Sold	2,000		Items Sold	2,000	
3	Unit Price	$15.00		Unit Price	$15.00	
4	Profits	$30,000.00		Profits	$30,000.00	
5						

The spreadsheet is split into two: **Current Sales**, and **Future Sales**. We'll be changing the Future Sales with Goal Seek. But for now, enter the same values for both sections. The formula to enter for **B4** is this: **= B2 * B3**

And the formula to enter for E4 is this: **= E2 * E3**

The current Unit Price per item is 15.00. We want to change this with Goal Seek, because our prices will be going up to hit our new profits of 30,000.

So try this:
- From the Excel menu bar, click on Data
- Locate the Data Tools panel and the What if Analysis item. From the What if Analysis menu, select Goal Seek
- The following dialogue box appears:

For "**Set cell**", enter **E4**. This is where the formula is. The "**To Value**" is what we want our new profits to be. So enter **45000**. The "By changing cell" is the part we're not sure of. For us, this was the price each item needs to be increased by. This was coming from cell **E3** on our spreadsheet. So enter **E3** in the "By changing cell" box. Your Goal Seek dialogue box should now look like this:

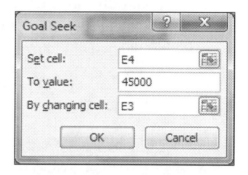

Click OK to see if Excel can find an answer:

Excel is now telling that it has indeed found a solution. Click OK to see the new version of the spreadsheet:

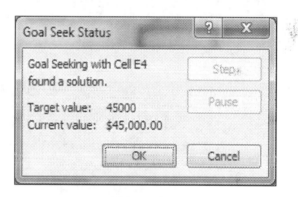

Figure 6.29 The Spreadsheet Showing Calculated Goal

	E4		f_x	=E2*E3	
	A	B	C	D	E
1	Current Sales Figures			Futures Sales Figures	
2	Items Sold	2,000		Items Sold	2,000
3	Unit Price	$15.00		Unit Price	$22.50
4	Profits	$30,000.00		Profits	$45,000.00

Our new Unit Price is $30. Excel has also changed the Profits cell to $60,000.

Exercise: You have had a meeting with your staff, and it has been decided that a price change from $25 to $35 is not a good idea. A better idea is to sell more items. You still want a profit of $75,000. Use Goal Seek to find out how many items you will have to sell to meet your new profit figure.

6.7 Assignment Questions

Answer the following project questions by showing all the appropriate steps that should be followed to arrive at the answer for each question.

1. What is Conditional Formatting in Excel spreadsheets? What is the purpose of Conditional Formatting? Demonstrate your answer with suitable example.

2. Given the table of students grades below:

	A	B	C	D	E	F	G	H	I
1		Peter	Samuel	Lucy	Eric	Ernest	Agnes	George	Joe
2	Maths	76	90	53	58	61	78	88	66
3	English	55	86	79	71	57	85	90	78
4	Science	65	82	49	68	42	64	59	45
5	History	54	91	58	72	49	54	76	58
6	Geography	51	85	55	64	48	64	69	68
7	Art	67	63	49	62	39	90	65	64
8	Computer Science	61	95	46	59	51	91	89	52
9	French	45	91	68	36	35	52	93	58
10									
11	Overall Average	59.25	85.375	57.125	61.25	47.75	72.25	78.625	61.125

   a. Using the table conditionally format the following criteria by highlighting each category by different colors
   50 and below   as red
   51 to 60   as blue
   61 to 70   as green
   71 to 80   as orange
   81 and above   as purple

   b. Explain how to obtain your results.

3. Show how to create new formatting rules based on the above criteria.

4. What is the purpose of COUNTIF()? *(Refer to above table)*
   a. What will be the evaluated results of =COUNTIF(B11:I11,">=70")?

5. What is the purpose of =SUMIF(C3:C7, TRUE, B3:B7)
   a. What does C3:C7 represent?
   b. What does TRUE represent?
   c. What does B3:B7 represent?

6. You have had a meeting with your staff, and it has been decided that a price change from $25 to $35 is not a good idea. A better idea is to sell more items. You still want a profit of $75,000. Use Goal Seek to find out how many items you will have to sell to meet your new profit figure.

7. Define Scenarios and "**What-If Analysis**" in Excel
    a. How do you create a Scenario?
    b. What is the purpose of "**What-If Analysis**"?

8. Describe the use of Goal Seek in Microsoft Excel 2007/2010.

6.8 Multiple Choice Questions

9. After defining alternative values in a scenario, you can replace the spreadsheet's original values with the alternative values by clicking the following button:
   Select the one best answer.
    A. Add.
    B. Delete.
    C. Show.
    D. Collapse Dialog.
    E. Undo.

10. The button shown in the following graphic is referred to as:

A. Expand Dialog.
B. Error Options.
C. Auto Fill Options.
D. Show.
E. Evaluate

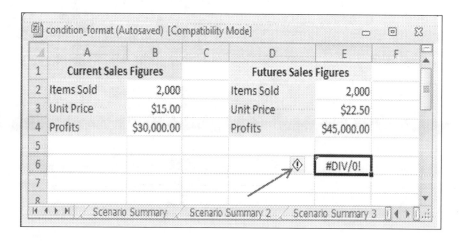

11. You can use the following Excel tool to work with a group of cells that are related, either directly or indirectly, to the formula in a target cell:
Select the one best answer.
 A. Goal Seek.
 B. Solver.
 C. Scenarios.
 D. Data Analysis.
 E. Subtotals.

12. While working in Excel, you can specify a graphic as a background for your worksheet by clicking the following:
Select the one best answer.
 A. Insert menu, Name, and then Paste.
 B. Edit menu, Fill, and then Across Worksheets.
 C. Page Layout, Background, and then select File.
 D. Insert menu, Picture, and then From File.
 E. Data menu, Import External Data, and then Import Data.

13. Given the formula **=PMT(B3 / 12, B4, -B5)** for future payment calculations. What do the following represent?
 A. B3/12 is rate
 B. B4 is rate
 C. –B5 is pv
 D. B4 is pv

14. You need to create a unique data format for your workbook. To accomplish this from the Format Cells dialog box, as illustrated in the following graphic, you would select the following option from the Category list:

 A. General.
 B. Custom.
 C. Number.
 D. Special.
 E. Scientific.

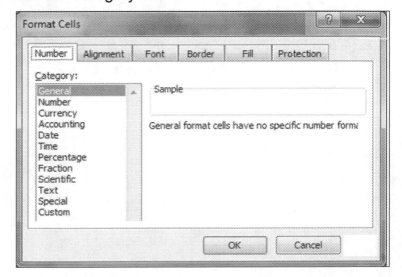

15. You need to change the color of data contained in specific cells in a spreadsheet, as illustrated in the following graphic, by using conditional formats. Place the following five steps in the order required to accomplish this.

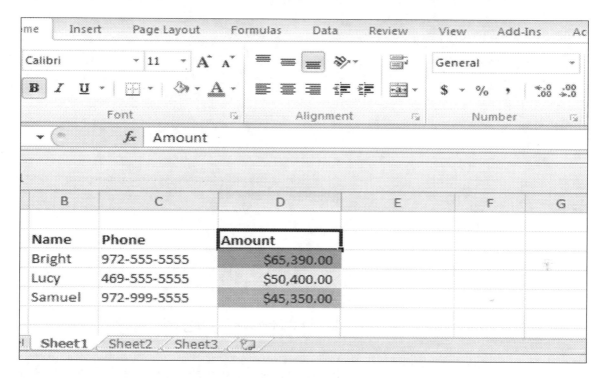

You need to change the color of data contained in specific cells in a spreadsheet, as illustrated in the following graphic, by using conditional formats. Place the following five steps in the order required to accomplish this.
Enter a number in each box below.

[1] Click Apply and OK.
[2] Click the Home tab, and then click Conditional Formatting.
[3] Click on Rules Manager
[4] Select the cells to be formatted.
[5] Specify the value range for the condition.

	1	2	3	4	5
A.	3	5	4	2	1
B.	4	2	3	5	1
C.	5	3	4	1	2
D.	1	3	2	4	5

16. You need to create a scenario based on data contained in specific cells in a spreadsheet, as illustrated in the following graphic:

	A	B	C	D
1		The Family Budget		
2		EXPENSES		INCOME
3	Car Loan	525		3500
4	Mortgage	1250		
5	Fuel Bills	150		
6	Credit Cards	65		
7	Grocery	385		
8	Electric Bill	250		
9	Clothes	175		
10	Phone Bill	300		
11	Water Bill	57		
12				
13	Total Expenses	3157		
14	Income Left			343

In the process the Scenario Values dialog box is displayed as shown below.

By using the expenses column in the table above, insert the corresponding values for
1. $B$7 =?
2. $B$8 =?
3. $B$9 =?
4. $B$10=?

Scenario Values

Enter values for each of the changing cells.

1:	$B$7	
2:	$B$8	
3:	$B$9	
4:	$B$10	

Add   OK   Cancel

    1   **2**   **3**   **4**
A. 150, 1250, 175, 57
B. 250, 300, 175, 57
C. 385, 250, 175, 300
D. 385, 250, 175, 150

CHAPTER 7

Working With Tables in Excel

Objectives:

○ *Introduction to Tables in Excel Spreadsheet*
○ *Creating a Table, and Working with Table Size*
○ *Working with the Total Row, and Working with Table Data*
○ *Summarizing a Table with a PivotTable*
○ *How To Create A Pivot Table In Excel 2010*
○ *Insert Slicer In Pivot Tables & Create Charts – Excel 2010*
○ *Types of Charts in Excel 2010*

7.0 Introduction: Working with Tables in Excel 2010

The Excel data is only useful if you can make sense of the numbers. As had been already discussed in volume one of Concise ICT Fundamentals, information is data which had been processed to a meaningful form. In order to organize your data into meaningful format, or to easily readable and understandable tables, you need to know the essentials of creating and working with tables in Excel 2010. Use tables to help you manage your data.

7.1 Creating a Table in Excel 2010

Tables can be created in Excel 2010 to help manage and analyze related data. The main purpose of an Excel table is to store lots of information in a consistent manner, making it easier to format, sort, and filter **worksheet** data instead of to calculate new values as in Data tables.

An Excel table is not the same as a **data table** that can be used for what-if analysis. You use a data table to show how changing one or two variables in **formulas** affects the results of those formulas. You can use one of two ways to create a table. You can either insert a table in the default table style or you can format your data as a table in a style that you choose.

Insert a table

1. On a worksheet, select the range of cells that you want to include in the table. The cells can be empty or can contain data.
2. On the Insert tab, in the Tables group, click Table.
3. **Keyboard shortcut**. You can also press **CTRL+L** or **CTRL+T**.
4. If the selected range contains data that you want to display as table headers, select the **My table has headers check box**.
5. Click OK

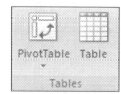

In this example, the check box "My table has headers" is checked. So the table shows a default column headers column1..column5 in addition to the specified the column headers.

Here the check box "My table has headers" is not checked. So the table shows a default column headers column1..column5 in addition to the specified column headers.

Figure 7.1 Table With "**My table has Header** is not Checked

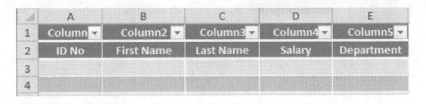

Figure 7.2 Table With "My table has Header is Checked

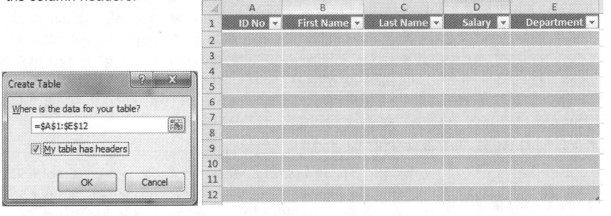

Table headers display default names if you do not select the My table has headers check box. You can change the default names by typing the text that you want.

NOTE: If you do not want to display table headers, you can turn them off later. For more information about how to turn table headers off, see Turn Excel table headers on or off. Tips:

- After you create a table, the Table Tools become available, and a Design tab is displayed. You can use the tools on the Design tab to customize or edit the table.
- Unlike lists in Office Excel 2003, a table does not have a special row (marked with *) for quickly adding new rows. For more information about how to add or insert rows in a table, see Add or remove table rows and columns in an Excel table.

1. Enter your table's column headings.

Click the blank cell where you want to start the new table and then enter the column headings (such as ID No, First Name, Last Name, Salary, Department, and so on) in separate cells within the same row. Column headings are also known as *field names*. The column headings should appear in a single row without any blank cells between the entries.

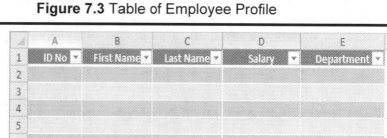

Figure 7.3 Table of Employee Profile

2. Enter the first row of data immediately below the column headings you typed in Step 1.

These entries constitute the rows, or *records,* of the table. A record constitutes data in a row.

Figure 7.4 Table of Employee Profile with Data Records

	A	B	C	D	E
1	ID No	First Name	Last Name	Salary	Department
2	27699	Bright	Siaw Afriyie	25,000	CIS
3	82449	Lucy	Ankomah	17,500	HR
4	28879	Samuel	Siaw Afriyie	15,000	MD
5	89244	Eric	Owusuh Siaw	20,000	GIS
6	74826	Ernest	Siaw Afriyie	18,000	Police

3. Click the Table command button in the Tables group of the Insert tab.

Excel displays a marquee around all the cells in the new table. The Create Table dialog box appears, listing the address of the table in the **"Where Is the Data for Your Table text"** box. (If the address displayed here is incorrect, drag in the worksheet to select the correct range.)

4. Click the "My Table Has Headers" check box to select it.

These headers are the column headings entered in the first step.
Excel inserts and formats the new table and adds filter arrows (drop-down buttons) to each of the field names in the top row.

Another way to insert a table is to click the Format as Table button in the Styles group on the Home tab and then select a table style of your choice in the gallery that appears. Use this method if you want to apply a different table style as you create a table. If you want to convert an existing Excel table back to a normal range of cells, select any cell in the table and then click the "**Convert to Range**" button on the Table Tools Design tab. All data and formatting is preserved.

7.2 Create Data Form and Add Records to an Excel 2010 Table

After you have created an Excel 2010 table, you can choose from several methods for adding records to the table. Before you add records, the range must already be formatted as a table. To format a worksheet range as a table, select a cell in the range and then click the **Table** button on the **Insert tab**.

The most direct way to add new data is to press the Tab key when the cell cursor is in the last cell of the last record (row). Doing this causes Excel to add another row to the table, where you can enter the appropriate information for the next record.
Another way to add records to an Excel table is to use a data form. The Form button is not included on the Excel 2010 **Ribbon**, but you can add this button to the **Quick Access toolbar.** To do this and access the data form, follow these steps:

1. **Click the arrow at the right end of the Quick Access toolbar and select More Commands.**
   The Excel Options dialog box appears with the Quick Access Toolbar options displayed in the right pane.
2. **In the Choose Commands From drop-down list, select All Commands.**
   You will see a long, alphabetical list of all the commands available in Excel.
3. **Select the Form button in the list box, click Add, and click OK.**
   The Form button appears at the end of the Quick Access toolbar.
4. **Position the cell cursor in the table and click the Form button on the Quick Access toolbar.**

   The data form lists the field names down the left side of the form with the entries for the first record in the text boxes next to them.
5. **Click the New button in the data form.**
   Excel displays a blank data form, which you get to fill in.

Figure 7.5 Customizing the Quick Access Toolbar Dialogue Box

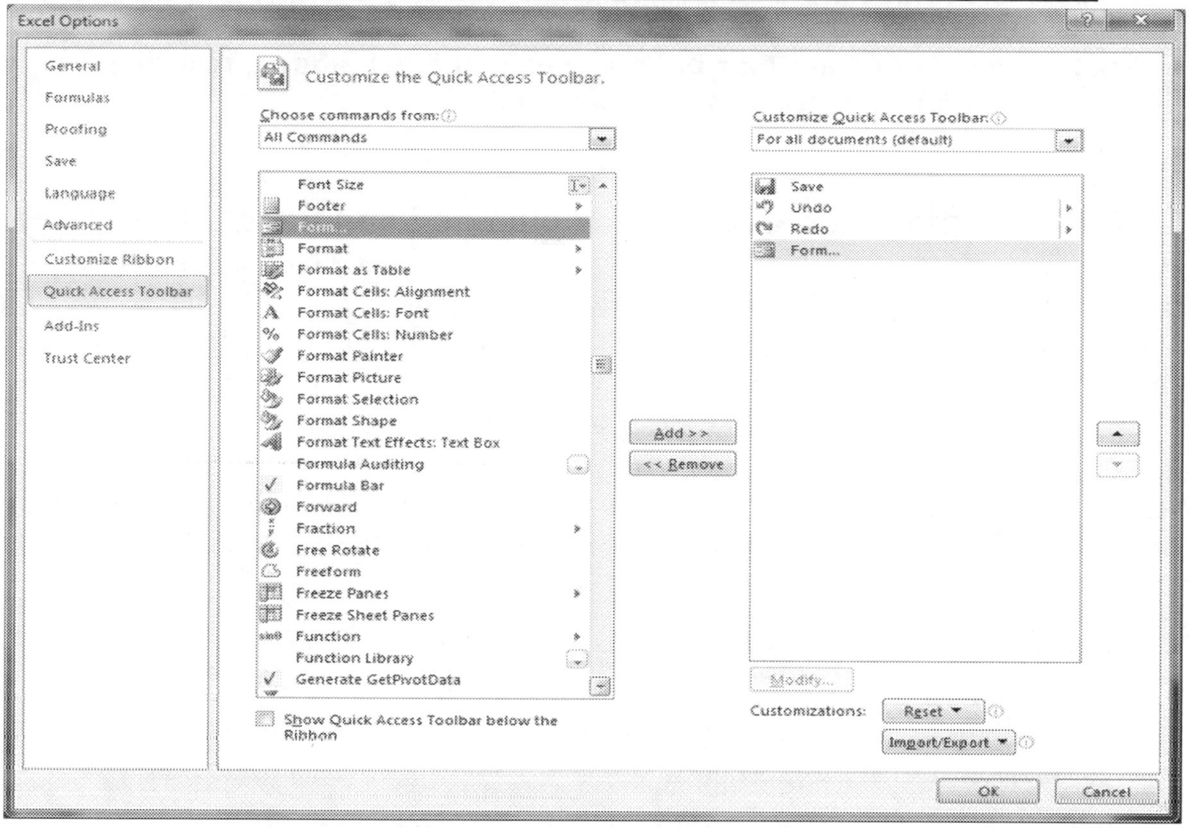

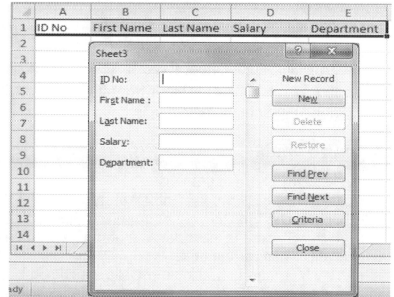

6. **Type the information for the first field and press Tab to move to the next field.** Continue typing data for each field in the record.

To obtain the form like the one illustrated here you must do the following:

1. You must type in the fields in a row.
2. Select all the typed fields.
3. then, click on the form icon from the Quick Access Tool bar

Figure 7.6 Data Form showing the labeled fields

7. Press Enter to complete the record.
Excel adds the record to the table and displays another blank data form.
8. Press Esc or click the Close button when you finish adding records.
Your table will be updated with the new records.

7.3 Add or remove table rows and columns in an Excel table

After you create a Microsoft Office Excel table in your worksheet, you can easily add table rows and columns. You can quickly add a blank row at the end of the table, include adjacent worksheet rows or worksheet columns in the table, or insert table rows and table columns anywhere you want.

You can delete rows and columns as needed. You can also quickly remove rows that contain duplicate data from a table.
NOTE: Adding and removing table rows and columns is different from adding and removing worksheet rows and columns. To add and remove worksheet rows and columns; see Insert or delete cells, rows, and columns.

a. Add a blank row at the end of the table
- Press **TAB** in the last cell of the last row to add a blank row at the end of the table.
   NOTE: If a total row is displayed in the table, pressing **TAB** in the last cell of the total row does not add a new row.

b. Include a worksheet row or worksheet column in a table
Do one of the following:
- To include a worksheet row in the table, type a value or text in a cell that is directly below the table.
- To include a worksheet column in the table, type a value or text in a cell that is directly adjacent to the right of the table.
- To include worksheet rows or worksheet columns by using the mouse, drag the resize handle at the lower-right corner of the table down to select rows and to the right to select columns.

7.4 Resize a table

1. Click anywhere in the table.
   TIP: This displays the Table Tools, adding the **Design** tab.
2. On the **Design** tab, in the Properties group, click Resize Table.
3. In the Select the new data range for your table box, type the range that you want to use for the table.
   TIP: You can also click the Collapse Dialog button ▨ at the right end of the Select the new data range for your table box and then select the range that you want to use for the table on the worksheet.

When you finish, click the Collapse Dialog button again to display the entire dialog box.

TIP: To resize a table by using the mouse, drag the triangular resize handle at the lower-right corner of the table up, down, to the left, or to the right to select the range that you want to use for the table.

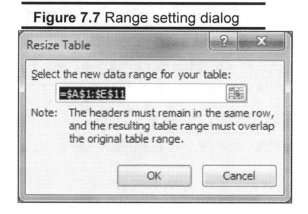

Figure 7.7 Range setting dialog

Turning a table back into an ordinary range

If the need arises to turn a table back into an ordinary worksheet range, select any cell or block of cells within the table. Then click Convert To Range in the Tools group on the Design tab. Click Yes to answer the confirmation prompt. Note that after you change a table into a regular range, the formatting turns into regular cell formatting. This can cause unexpected behavior if you ever turn the range back into a table.

TIP: An easy way to tell whether a range is a table is to select a cell in the range and look at the Ribbon. If you see a Table Tools tab, then the current list has been converted to a table.

Naming a table

When you designate a range as a table, Excel assigns a name to that table and displays the name in the **Properties group** on the Design tab.

7.5 Using Data Form to Find Records in an Excel 2010 Table

When you work with Excel 2010 tables, you can use keystrokes or a data form to move through table records until you find the one you want to edit or delete. In larger tables, you can use search criteria in the data form to look up a record. These methods also work with a normal range of data — one that has not been converted to a table using the Table button on the Insert tab.

a. How to find records in a table manually

When you click the Form button on the Quick Access toolbar, it will generate a form with populated data as shown below. You then have to use the following techniques to navigate records in the data form.

Figure 7.8 Form with populated data

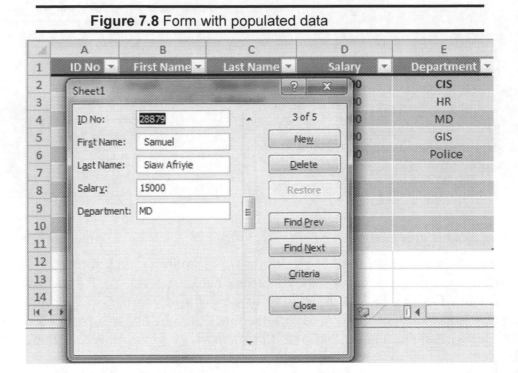

- **Next record:** Press the down-arrow key, press Enter, click the Find Next button, or click the down scroll arrow at the bottom of the scroll bar.

- **Previous record:** Press the up-arrow key, press **Shift+Enter**, click the Find **Prev** button, or click the up scroll arrow at the top of the scroll bar.

- **First record:** Press **Ctrl+up-arrow** key, press **Ctrl+PgUp**, or drag the scroll box to the very top of the scroll bar.

- **New, blank data form:** Press **Ctrl+down-arrow** key, press **Ctrl+PgDn**, or drag the scroll box to the very bottom of the scroll bar.

b. *How to use search criteria to find table records*

For larger Excel tables, use the Criteria button in the data form to find records. Follow these steps:

1. Click the Form button in the Quick Access toolbar to open the data form. Remember that you must add this button to the Quick Access toolbar.

2. Click the Criteria button in the data form.
   Excel clears all the field entries in the data form (and replaces the record number with the word *Criteria*) so that you can enter the criteria to search for in the blank text boxes.

3. Enter criteria in one or more fields of the data form. You can use wildcards (such as a? for a single character and * for multiple characters) and comparison operators (such as < and >=) as well as text and values.

For example, if you are searching for a record in an employee table and you know that the person's last name begins with **S** and they are located in **Siaw**, you would type *S** in the Last Name field and *Siaw* in the Location field to locate the record.

Use the **Criteria** button to search records based on known data.

4. Click the Find Next button or the *Find Prev* button.
Excel finds the first record that matches the specified criteria. Repeat this step as needed until you find the desired record.

The first record in the table that meets the criteria.

5. Click the Form button to return to the data form or click Close to close the data form.

The first record that meets the criteria will be displayed. When you press "Find Next" button it will display the next searched record until the last item.

Figure 7.9 Form Showing Searching Criteria

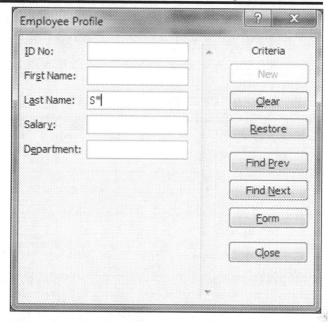

Figure 7.10 Form Showing Search Results

7.6 Edit Records in an Excel 2010 Table

As you work with Excel 2010 tables, you will often find the need to edit or delete records and perform routine maintenance on the table. You can edit the records manually in the worksheet or use a data form to make the necessary changes.

For example, you can use the data form to locate a record you want to change and then edit the particular fields. You can also use the data form to find a specific record you want to remove and then delete it from the table.

1. Locate the record you want to edit by displaying it in the data form.
   You can scroll through the records or use the Criteria button to search based on the criteria you enter in the specified fields.

2. To edit a field in the current record, move to that field by pressing Tab or **Shift+Tab** and replace the entry by typing a new one.

   Change Salary from 25,000 to 50,000

   Alternatively, press the left-arrow key or right-arrow key or click the I-beam cursor to reposition the insertion point and then make your edits. To clear a field, select it and then press the Delete key.

Figure 7.11 Form Showing Edited Field

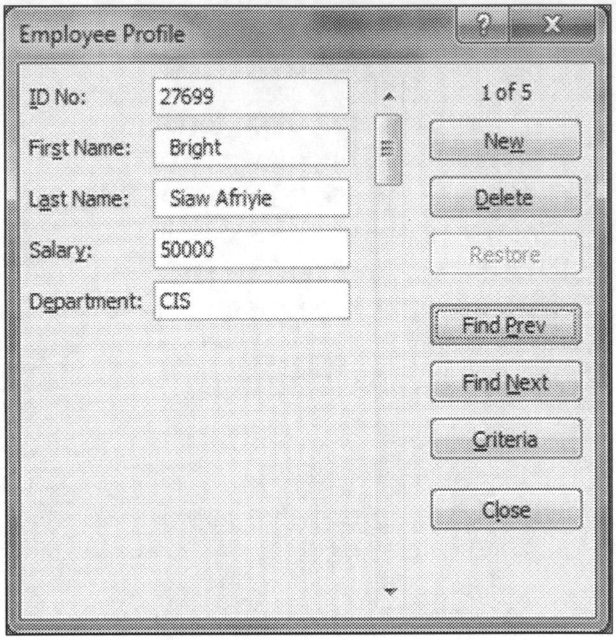

3. If you want to delete the entire record from the table, click the Delete button in the data form and click OK.

   Keep in mind that you cannot use the Undo feature to bring back a record you removed with the Delete button in a data form. As a precaution, always save a back-up version of the worksheet before you start deleting records.

4. Click Close to close the data form.

7.7 Apply a Table Style to an Excel 2010 Table

In Excel 2010, you can apply a predefined table format to a cell range. The Format as Table feature displays an extensive Table gallery with formatting thumbnails divided into three sections — Light, Medium, and Dark — each of which describes the intensity of the colors used by the various formats.

1. **Click any cell within the group of cells you want to format as a table.**
   If you select multiple nonadjacent cells before you click the Format as Table button, the formats in the Table gallery are not available. This feature works with one contiguous group of cells.

2. **On the Home tab, in the Styles group, click the Format as Table button.**
   A gallery of table formats appears. You can also build your own custom table format by clicking the New Table Style button below the table formats.

3. **Click a thumbnail in the gallery.**
   Excel makes its best guess as to the cell range of the table to apply it to (indicated by the marquee around its perimeter) and the Format As Table dialog box appears.

4. **If the cell range for the table is incorrect, drag through the range in the worksheet.**
   The table range appears in the "**Where Is the Data for Your Table?**" text box.

Figure 7.12 Table Showing Different Color Style

	A	B	C	D	E
1	ID No ▾	First Name ▾	Last Name ▾	Salary ▾	Department ▾
2	27699	Bright	Siaw Afriyie	50,000	CIS
3	82449	Lucy	Ankomah	17,500	HR
4	28879	Samuel	Siaw Afriyie	15,000	MD
5	89244	Eric	Owusuh Siaw	20,000	GIS
6	74826	Ernest	Siaw Afriyie	18,000	Police

5. **Click OK.**

Excel formats the table with the style you selected, and the Table Tools Design contextual tab appears at the end of the Ribbon. Use the options on this tab to change the table style or modify other table settings. When you finish selecting and/or customizing the formatting of your data table, click a cell outside of the table to remove the Design contextual tab from the Ribbon. If you later decide that you want to further experiment with the table's formatting, click any of the table's cells to redisplay the Design contextual tab at the end of the Ribbon.

7.8 Filter Records in an Excel 2010 Table with AutoFilter

Use the AutoFilter feature in Excel 2010 to hide everything in a table except the records you want to view. Filtering displays a subset of a table, providing you with an easy way to break down your data into smaller, more manageable chunks. Filtering does not rearrange your data; it simply temporarily hides rows that don't match the criteria you specify.

1. **Click inside a table, and then choose Filter in the Sort & Filter group of the Data tab (or press Ctrl+Shift+L).**

   Filter arrows appear beside the column headings. If the data is formatted as an Excel table, skip this step; you should already see the filter arrows.

2. **Click the filter arrow beside the column heading for the column you want to filter.**
   Excel displays a drop-down list which includes one of each unique entry from the selected column.

3. **Remove the check mark from Select All.**
   All items in the list are deselected.

4. **Select the check box for the entry you want to filter and then click OK.**
   You can select multiple check boxes to filter on two or more items. Excel displays only the records that match your selections.

5. **(Optional) Repeat Steps 2–4 as needed to apply additional filters to other columns in the filtered data.**
   You can apply filters to multiple columns in a table to further isolate specific items. Notice that the filter arrows on filtered columns take on a different appearance to indicate that a filter is in use.

   To remove filters and redisplay all table data, click the Clear button on the Data tab. If multiple columns are filtered, you can click a filter arrow and select Clear Filter to remove a filter from that column only. To remove the filter arrows when you're done filtering data, choose **Filter** in the **Sort & Filter** group of the **Data** tab (or press **Ctrl+Shift+L**).

7.9 Filter Numbers in an Excel 2010 Table

If you are working with a large table of data in Excel 2010, you can apply number filters to columns that contain values to temporarily hide unwanted values. Excel provides several options for filtering numeric data, including filtering for top or bottom values (using the Top 10 option) or filtering for values that are above or below the average in a column that contains numeric data.

Excel 2010 tables automatically display filter arrows beside each of the column headings. To display the filter arrows so that you can filter data, format a range as a table using the Table button on the Insert tab. Or, you can click the Filter button in the Sort & Filter group on the Data tab.

Filtering for top or bottom values
Follow these steps to filter for the top or bottom numbers in a table:
   1. Click the filter arrow for the numeric column by which you want to filter data.
      The filter drop-down list appears.

2. Point to Number Filters in the drop-down list.
3. Choose Top 10 in the resulting menu. The Top 10 AutoFilter dialog box appears.

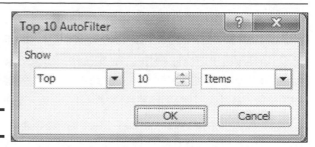

Figure 7.13 Top 10 AutoFilter

Use the Top 10 **AutoFilter** dialog box to filter on top or bottom values in a table.

4. From the first option, select whether you want the Top (highest) or Bottom (lowest) values.
5. In the second option, select the number of items you want to see (from 1 to 500). This spin box displays a default value of 10.
6. In the third option, select whether you want to filter the items by their names or by their percentiles.
   For example, choose to list the top 10 customers per their sales dollars, or list the top 10% of your customer base.
7. Click OK.
   Excel displays the records that match your criteria.

Filtering for above- or below-average values
Use these steps to filter a table for above-average or below-average values in a column:
1. Click the filter arrow for the numeric column by which you want to filter data.
   The filter drop-down list appears.
2. Point to Number Filters in the drop-down list.
3. **Choose Above Average** or **Below Average** in the resulting menu to filter by numbers that meet either condition.
   Only the records with values above or below the total average (for that column) appear in the filtered list.

A Below Average filter applied to a column of numeric data in a table.

To remove filters and redisplay all table data, click the Clear button on the Data tab. If multiple columns are filtered, you can click a filter arrow and select Clear Filter to remove a filter from that column only. To remove the filter arrows when you're done filtering data, choose Filter in the Sort & Filter group of the Data tab (or press **Ctrl+Shift+L**).

Filtering by Date in an Excel 2010 Table

If your Excel 2010 table includes columns with dates or times, you can filter the table to display a subset of the data with the dates or times you specify. The rows that do not match the criteria you specify are hidden temporarily.

Excel 2010 tables automatically display filter arrows beside each of the column headings. To display the filter arrows so that you can filter data, format a range as a table using the Table button on the Insert tab. Or, you can click the Filter button in the Sort & Filter group on the Data tab.

1. Click the filter arrow for the date column by which you want to filter data.
   The filter drop-down list appears.
2. Point to Date Filters in the drop-down list.

Figure 7.14 Date Filters

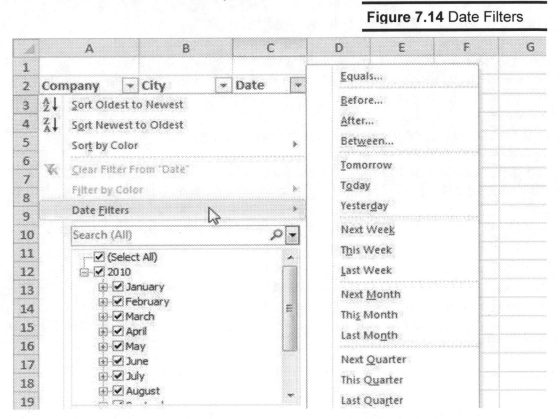

You see an extensive list of date filters.
3. Select a date filter.
   To filter by a date range, select **Between**. If you select a Common filter, you see the Custom AutoFilter dialog box. If you select a dynamic filter, Excel immediately applies the filter.
4. If the Custom AutoFilter dialog box appears, enter a date or time in the box on the right and click OK.
   Optionally, click the Calendar button to select a date.

To remove filters and redisplay all table data, click the Clear button on the Data tab. If multiple columns are filtered, you can click a filter arrow and select **Clear Filter** to remove a filter from that column only. To remove the filter arrows when you're done filtering data, choose Filter in the **Sort & Filter** group of the **Data** tab (or press **Ctrl+Shift+L**).

How to Filter an Excel 2010 Table by Color

If you've applied color to fonts or cells in an Excel 2010 table, you can filter the table to display a subset of the data with the colors you specify. The rows that do not match the criteria you specify are hidden temporarily.

Excel 2010 tables automatically display filter arrows beside each of the column headings. To display the filter arrows so that you can filter data, format a range as a table using the Table button on the Insert tab. Or, you can click the Filter button in the Sort & Filter group on the Data tab.

1. **Click the filter arrow for the column by which you want to filter data.**
   The filter drop-down list appears.

2. **Point to Filter by Color in the drop-down list.**
   A submenu of color options appears. You can filter by Cell (background) Color or by Font Color. The submenu you see depends on the color choices in your data.

3. **Select an option.**
   Excel displays the table using the filter you requested.
   To remove filters and redisplay all table data, click the Clear button on the Data tab. If multiple columns are filtered, you can click a filter arrow and select Clear Filter to remove a filter from that column only. To remove the filter arrows when you're done filtering data, choose Filter in the Sort & Filter group of the Data tab (or press **Ctrl+Shift+L**).

Using Advanced Table Filtering in Excel 2010

With Excel 2010's advanced filtering methods, you can specify complex filtering criteria and designate a specific area of your worksheet to manage your criteria selections when filtering table data. Use the following directions to filter data that has been formatted as a table in Excel 2010.

1. *Make sure the AutoFilter is turned off.*
   Click the Filter button on the Data tab, if necessary.

2. *Select the first four rows of the worksheet.*
   This is where you will insert the criteria range.

3. ***Right-click the selected rows and choose Insert.***
   Your table moves down four rows, and you get four empty rows to work with.

4. ***Select the header row in the table, and click the Copy button on the Home tab.***
   A marquee appears around the copied area.

5. ***Click cell A1, and then click the Paste button on the Home tab.***
   This copies the header row of your table to the first blank row in the worksheet. You now have a criteria range ready to enter filter selections.

6. ***In the first blank row of the criteria range, enter the data you want to match.***
   For example, if you want to locate any entries for the state of Indiana, type **IN** directly under the State heading.

7. ***Enter any additional filter criteria.***
   If you want Excel to find data that meets more than one restriction, enter the additional criteria in another field on the first criteria row. This is called an AND filter. If you want Excel to find data that meets at least one of the criteria (an OR filter), enter the filter data on the second row of the criteria range.

8. ***Click any cell in the main part of the table.***
   You should not have any of your filter criteria selected before you begin the next step.

9. ***Click the Advanced button in the Sort & Filter group of the Data tab.***
   Excel displays the Advanced Filter dialog box.

10. ***Select the Filter List, In-Place option in the Action section.***
    If you want the filter results to appear in another location in the current worksheet, select Copy to Another Location instead (and then specify the location in the Copy To text box).

11. ***Verify the table range in the List Range box.***
    Make sure Excel recognizes the entire table.

12. ***Specify the criteria range including the header row, but not any blank rows.***
    You can type the range address or drag to select the range in the worksheet. Be sure to specify only the rows that contain filtering information. If you include blank rows in your criteria range, Excel includes them in the filtering process. The effect is that no data is filtered out, so all records are returned.

13. ***Click OK to display the search results.***
    The tables display the filtered results. The records that don't fit the criteria are hidden.

14. *When you're ready to view all data records again, click the Clear button on the Data tab.*

All the hidden records reappear.

When you're specifying criteria for a range of dates or numbers, you can use Greater Than, Greater Than Or Equal To, Less Than, or Less Than Or Equal To as operators in your criteria range. For example, to find sales greater than or equal to 10,000, enter **>=10000** in the Sales criteria row.

7.9.1 How to Import Online Data into Excel 2010 with a Web Query

In Excel 2010, you can use Web queries to import data directly from various Web pages that contain financial and other types of statistical data that you need to work with in a worksheet.

1. **Click the From Web button in the Get External Data group on the Data tab.**

Excel opens the New Web Query dialog box containing the Home page for your computer's default Web browser.

2. **To select the Web page containing the data you want to import into Excel, you can do either of the following.**

Either type the **URL** in the Address text box at the top of the **New Web Query** dialog box and click the **Go button**, or use the Search feature to find the Web page containing the data you wish to import. Excel indicates which tables of information you can import by using a yellow box with an arrowhead pointing right.

7.10 Excel 2010 - Pivot Tables

The Pivot Table concept is not new in Excel 2010, it was already present in Excel 2007 but some noteworthy improvements have been made to it. We will discuss the following in this section:

- What is a Pivot Table?
- How to create a Pivot Table in Excel 2010
- What's New in the Excel 2010 Pivot tables

What Is A Pivot Table?

The Pivot tables are used to summarize, analyze, explore and present your data. A Pivot table is a way to extract data from a long list of information and present it in a more meaningful and user friendly understandable format. For example, let's say that we have the data of student scores in a spreadsheet you could turn this into a pivot table, and then view only the Math scores for each pupil.

Excel pivot tables are very useful and powerful feature of MS Excel.

They can be used to summarize, analyze, explore and present your data. In plain English, it means, you can take the sales data with columns like salesman, region and product-wise revenues and use pivot tables to quickly find out how products are performing in each region. In this tutorial, we will learn what is a pivot table and how to make a pivot table using excel.

Uses of Pivot Tables

There are numerous uses of pivot tables that we can talk about them until Christmas. Here are some example uses of pivot tables:

- Summarizing data like finding the average sales for each region for each product from a product sales data table.
- Listing unique values in any column of a table
- Creating a pivot report with sub-totals and custom formats
- Making a dynamic pivot chart
- Filtering, sorting, drilling-down data in the reports without writing one formula or macro.
- Transposing data – i.e. moving rows to columns or columns to rows.
- Linking data sources outside excel and be able to make pivot reports out of such data.

7.10.1 How To Create A Pivot Table In Excel 2010

Here are the steps to create a Pivot table in Excel 2010.

Step 1: First of all, make sure to select the data range for which you want to make the pivot table.

Step 2: Insert the Pivot Table by going to the Insert tab and then clicking the Pivot Table icon.

Figure 7.15 Selected Range of Cells for Pivot Table

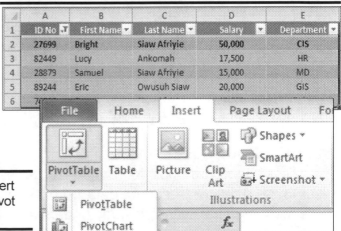

Figure 7.16 The Menu Showing Insert tab and Pivot Table (Pivot Table Pivot Chart) & Table

Step 3: Select the target cells where you want to place the pivot table. For beginners, select the New Worksheet option.

Figure 7.17 Create Pivot Table Step 3

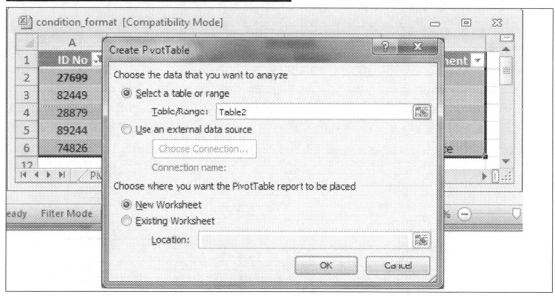

Figure 7.18 The Pivot Table

Step 4: The new worksheet will open and you will be able to see the pivot table that you just created. You can now generate the report from this table and can perform various operations on this table for better visualization and presentation of data.

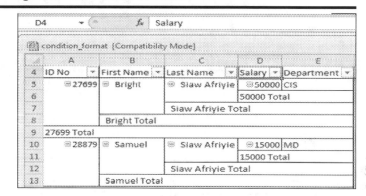

In the right side, you will see the Pivot Table Panel which contains many useful options to work with the Pivot table. The panel contains fields to add to report. In this example the fields are:
ID No, First Name, Last Name, Salary, and Department.

It might be a bit difficult to understand how this works. But believe me, if you have seen any reports or worked with any other reporting systems, then the idea of pivot tables, pivot reports and pivot charts becomes quite simple to you.

Figure 7.19 The Pivot Table Panel

7.10.2 Insert Slicer In Pivot Tables & Charts – Excel 2010

Through Excel, now you can filter down your data in much more detail, pick out every little detail that you would not afford to ignore. By using Slicers you will be able to depict the datasheet fields more comprehensively. Excel 2010 include this feature for the first time, which lets you to slice your data by showing you only the element stored in the tables. Real usage of Slicers can be seen with pivot table. Unlike Pivot table, which pivots down the datasheet, it makes you to compare and evaluate the data from different perspectives. This post will explain how you can use Slicer with Pivot Table and Charts. To begin with, launch Excel 2010, and open a datasheet, containing Pivot Table.

Figure 7.20 The Pivot Table

	A	B	C	D	E
1	ID No	First Name	Last Name	Salary	Department
2	27699	Bright	Siaw Afriyie	50,000	CIS
3	82449	Lucy	Ankomah	17,500	HR
4	28879	Samuel	Siaw Afriyie	15,000	MD
5	89244	Eric	Owusuh Siaw	20,000	GIS
6	74826	Ernest	Siaw Afriyie	18,000	Police

Figure 7.21 The Pivot Table

First Name	Salary
⊟ Bright	50000
Bright Total	
⊟ Eric	20000
Eric Total	
⊟ Ernest	18000
Ernest Total	
⊟ Lucy	17500
Lucy Total	
⊟ Samuel	15000
Samuel Total	
⊞ (blank)	
Grand Total	

Figure 7.22 The Generated Chart From Pivot Table

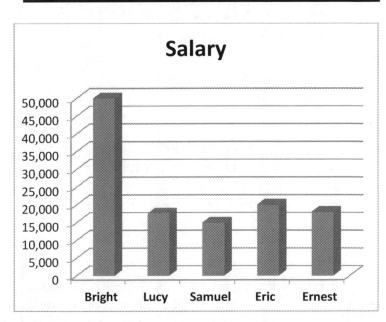

The above chart is generated by performing the following steps:

1. Select the first name and salary columns
2. Click on Insert tab

3. Click on chart
4. Select the type of chart

1. Creating Slicers

Now we want to create slicers for each category present in Pivot table. For this, select the whole Pivot table, and navigate to Options tab, click Insert Slicer.

Upon click, Insert Slicers dialog will appear, containing fields of the Pivot table. Select the desired one from the list to view respective Pivot table and chart, and click OK.

The chart can be one of the different types listed below:

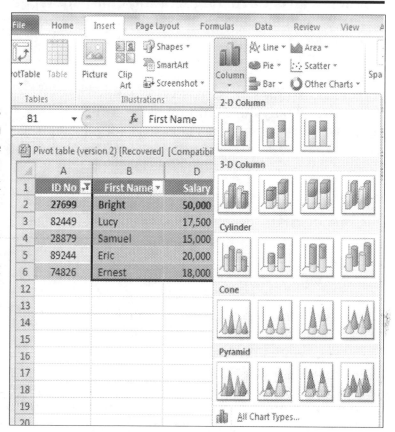

Figure 7.23 The Generated Pivot Table

1. Column charts
2. Line charts
3. Pie charts
4. Bar charts
5. Area charts
6. XY (scatter) charts
7. Stock charts
8. Surface charts
9. Doughnut charts
10. Bubble charts
11. Radar charts

1. Column charts

Data that is arranged in columns or rows on a worksheet can be plotted in a column chart. Column charts are useful for showing data changes over a period of time or for illustrating comparisons among items.

In column charts, categories are typically organized along the horizontal axis and values along the vertical axis.

Column charts have the following chart subtypes:
Clustered column and clustered column in 3-D Clustered column charts compare values across categories. A clustered column chart displays values in 2-D vertical rectangles. A clustered column in 3-D chart displays the data by using a 3-D perspective only. A third value axis (depth axis) is not used.

Column charts have the following chart subtypes:

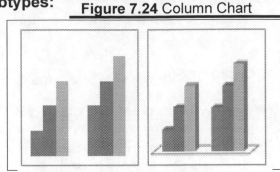

Figure 7.24 Column Chart

2. Line charts

Data that is arranged in columns or rows on a worksheet (worksheet: The primary document that you use in Excel to store and work with data. Also called a spreadsheet. A worksheet consists of cells that are organized into columns and rows; a worksheet is always stored in a workbook.) can be plotted in a line

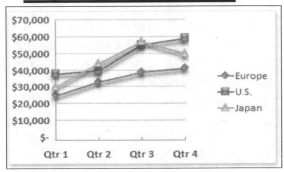

Figure 7.25 Line Chart

chart. Line charts can display continuous data over time, set against a common scale, and are therefore ideal for showing trends in data at equal intervals. In a line chart, category data is distributed evenly along the horizontal axis, and all value data is distributed evenly along the vertical axis.

3. Pie charts

Data that is arranged in one column or row only on a worksheet (worksheet: The primary document that you use in Excel to store and work with data. Also called a spreadsheet. A worksheet consists of cells that are organized into columns and rows; a worksheet is always stored in a workbook.) can be plotted in a pie chart.

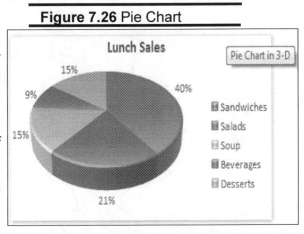

Figure 7.26 Pie Chart

Pie charts show the size of items in one data series (data series: Related data points that are plotted in a chart. Each data series in a chart has a unique color or pattern and is represented in the chart legend. You can plot one or more data series in a chart. Pie charts have only one data series.), proportional to the sum of the items. The data points (data points: Individual values plotted in a chart and represented by bars, columns, lines, pie or doughnut slices, dots, and various other shapes called data markers. Data markers of the same color constitute a data series.) in a pie chart are displayed as a percentage of the whole pie.

4. Bar charts

Data that is arranged in columns or rows on a worksheet (worksheet: The primary document that you use in Excel to store and work with data. It's also called a spreadsheet. A worksheet consists of cells that are organized into columns and rows; a worksheet is always stored in a workbook.) can be plotted in a bar chart. Bar charts illustrate comparisons among individual items.

Bar charts have the following chart subtypes:

Clustered bar and clustered bar in 3-D Clustered bar charts compare values across categories. In a clustered bar chart, the categories are typically organized along the vertical axis, and the values along the horizontal axis. A clustered bar in 3-D chart displays the horizontal rectangles in 3-D format; it does not display the data on three axes.

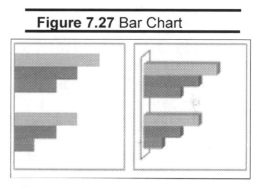

Figure 7.27 Bar Chart

5. Area charts

Data that is arranged in columns or rows on a worksheet can be plotted in an area chart.

Area charts emphasize the magnitude of change over time, and can be used to draw attention to the total value across a trend.

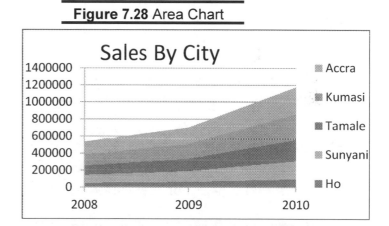

Figure 7.28 Area Chart

For example, data that represents profit over time can be plotted in an area chart to emphasize the total profit. By displaying the sum of the plotted values, an area chart also shows the relationship of parts to a whole.

6. XY (scatter) charts

Data that is arranged in columns and rows on a worksheet can be plotted in an **xy** (scatter) chart. Scatter charts show the relationships among the numeric values in several data series, or plot two groups of numbers as one series of **xy** coordinates.

A scatter chart has two value axes, showing one set of numeric data along the horizontal axis (x-axis) and another along the vertical axis (y-axis). It combines these values into single data points and displays them in irregular intervals, or clusters. Scatter charts are typically used for displaying and comparing numeric values, such as scientific, statistical, and engineering data.

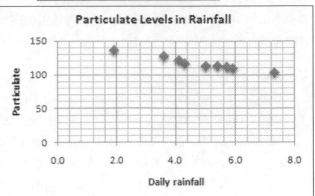

Figure 7.29 Scatter Chart

7. Stock charts

Data that is arranged in columns or rows in a specific order on a worksheet can be plotted in a stock chart. As its name implies, a stock chart is most often used to illustrate the fluctuation of stock prices. However, this chart may also be used for scientific data. For example, you could use a stock chart to indicate the fluctuation of daily or annual temperatures. You must organize your data in the correct order to create stock charts.

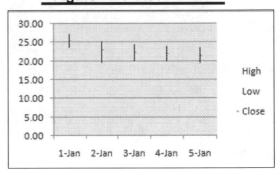

Figure 7.30 Stock Chart

The way stock chart data is organized in the worksheet is very important. For example, to create a simple high-low-close stock chart, you should arrange your data with High, Low, and Close entered as column headings, in that order.

8. Surface charts

Data that is arranged in columns or rows on a worksheet can be plotted in a surface chart. A surface chart is useful when you want to find optimum combinations between two sets of data. As in a topographic map, colors and patterns indicate areas that are in the same range of values.

You can use a surface chart when both categories and data series are numeric values.

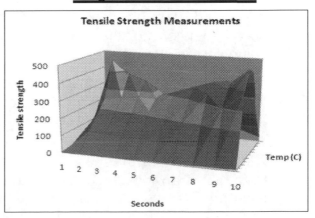

Figure 7.31 Surface Chart

9. Doughnut charts

Data that is arranged in columns or rows only on a worksheet can be plotted in a doughnut chart. Like a pie chart, a doughnut chart shows the relationship of parts to a whole, but it can contain more than one data series (data series: Related data points that are plotted in a chart. Each data series in a chart has a unique color or pattern and is represented in the chart legend. You can plot one or more data series in a chart. Pie charts have only one data series.).

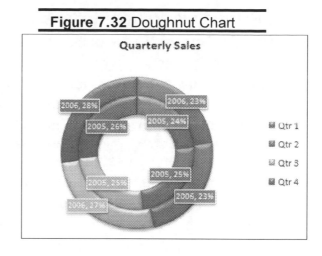

Figure 7.32 Doughnut Chart

Note: Doughnut charts are not easy to read. You may want to use a stacked column or stacked bar chart instead

10. Bubble charts

Data that is arranged in columns on a worksheet so that **x** values are listed in the first column and corresponding **y** values and bubble size values are listed in adjacent columns, can be plotted in a bubble chart. For example, you would organize your data as shown in the following example.

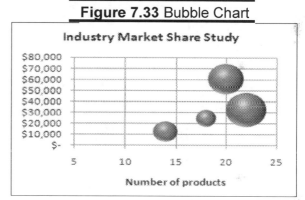

Figure 7.33 Bubble Chart

11. Radar charts

Data that is arranged in columns or rows on a worksheet can be plotted in a radar chart. Radar charts compare the aggregate values of several data series (data series: Related data points that are plotted in a chart. Each data series in a chart has a unique color or pattern and is represented in the chart legend. You can plot one or more data series in a chart. Pie charts have only one data series.).

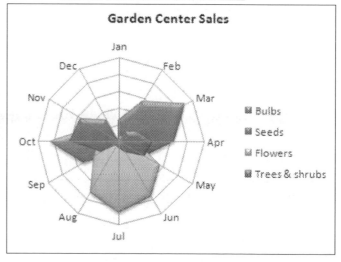

Figure 7.34 Radar Chart

7.11 Print a worksheet in landscape or portrait orientation

By default, Microsoft Excel prints worksheets in portrait orientation (taller than wide). You can change the page orientation to landscape (wider than tall) on a worksheet-by-worksheet basis. If you always want to print worksheets in landscape orientation, you can create a template, change the page orientation from portrait to landscape, and then use that template as the basis for all future workbooks.

Note: Because you can set page orientation on a worksheet-by-worksheet basis, it is possible to print some worksheets in a workbook in one orientation (such as portrait orientation) and other worksheets in the same workbook in the opposite orientation (such as landscape orientation). Simple set the orientation for each worksheet as appropriate, and then print the entire workbook.

Change the page orientation in the worksheet

1. Select the worksheet or worksheets for which you want to change the orientation.
2. On the Page Layout tab, in the Page Setup group, click Orientation, and then click Portrait or Landscape.

Note: If you don't have a printer set up, the Orientation option will appear dimmed, and you won't be able to select it. To resolve this, you must set up a printer. The option also appears dimmed when you're in the process of editing the contents of a cell. To resolve this, press **ENTER** to accept the changes or **ESC** to cancel the changes.

Tip: To see the borders of printed pages more distinctly, you can work in Page Layout view (View tab, Workbook Views group).

Change the page orientation when you are ready to print

1. Select the worksheet, worksheets, or worksheet data that you want to print.
2. Click the File tab.
3. Click Print.
4. Keyboard shortcut: You can also press **CTRL+ P.**
5. In the Page Orientation drop-down box, under Settings, click Portrait Orientation or Landscape Orientation.
6. When you are ready to print, click **Print**.

7.12 Define or clear a print area on a worksheet

If you print a specific selection on a worksheet frequently, you can define a print area that includes just that selection. A print area is one or more ranges of cells that you designate to print when you don't want to print the entire worksheet. When you print a worksheet after defining a print area, only the print area is printed. You can add cells to expand the print area as needed, and you can clear the print area to print the entire worksheet. A worksheet can have multiple print areas. Each print area will print as a separate page.

Set one or more print areas
1. On the worksheet, select the cells that you want to define as the print area. You can create multiple print areas by holding down CTRL and clicking the areas that you want to print.
2. On the Page Layout tab, in the Page Setup group, click Print Area, and then click Set Print Area.
    Note: The print area that you set is saved when you save the workbook.

Add cells to an existing print area
1. On the worksheet, select the cells that you want to add to the existing print area.
    Note: If the cells that you want to add are not adjacent to the existing print area, an additional print area is created. Each print area in a worksheet is printed as a separate page. Only adjacent cells can be added to an existing print area.
2. On the Page Layout tab, in the Page Setup group, click Print Area, and then click Add to Print Area.

Clear a print area
Note: If your worksheet contains multiple print areas, clearing a print area removes all the print areas on your worksheet.

1. Click anywhere on the worksheet for which you want to clear the print area.
2. On the Page Layout tab, in the Page Setup group, click Clear Print Area.

7.13 Assignment Questions

Answer the following project questions by showing all the appropriate steps that should be followed to arrive at the answer for each question.

1. What is a Table in Excel spreadsheet?
   a. Describe how you create tables in Excel
   b. What is a data table?
   c. What difference exists between a data table and table in Excel?

2. You want to insert a Table in Excel spreadsheet. Place the following five steps in the order required to accomplish this. Enter a number in each box below.

   [   ] On a worksheet, select the range of cells that you want to include in the table. The cells can be empty or can contain data.

   [   ] Click OK

   [   ] If the selected range contains data that you want to display as table headers, select the **My table has headers check box**.

   [   ] On the Insert tab, in the Tables group, click Table.

3. To create a Data Form and Add Records to an Excel 2010 Table, you must do the following to add the form icon.

   a. Write the steps to add the Form button on the Quick Access toolbar.
   b. Explain the steps to create the Form as presented in this diagram.
   c. How was the labels (FirstName, LastName, Emp.Id, No. of Hours, Rate, and Wages) are displayed in worksheet

4. How do you add the following items to a table?
    a. To add a blank row at the end of the table.
    b. To include a worksheet row in the table.
    c. To include a worksheet column in the table.
    d. To include worksheet rows or worksheet columns by using the mouse.

5. For larger Excel tables, we can use the Criteria button in the data form to find records.
    a. How to use search criteria to find table records? Explain each step involved..

6. What is a Pivot Table?
    a. Name seven uses of Pivot Tables.
    b. Describe how to create a Pivot Table in Excel 2010.

7. You want to insert Filter in a Table in Excel spreadsheet. Place the following five steps in the order required to accomplish this objective. Enter a number in each box below.

    [   ] Click the filter arrow beside the column heading for the column you want to filter.

    [   ] Click inside a table, and then choose Filter in the Sort & Filter group of the Data tab (or press Ctrl+Shift+L).

    [   ] Select the check box for the entry you want to filter and then click OK.

    [   ] Remove the check mark from Select All.

8. What is a Chart in Excel?
    a. Explain how to create a bar chart.
    b. Explain how to create a line chart.
    c. Explain how to create a pie chart.

9. What is the page orientation for a selected worksheet?
    a. How do you change a page orientation?
    b. How do you change a page orientation to landscape?

10. Explain the steps for setting a print area in a worksheet.

7.14 Multiple Choice Questions

11. You are currently editing an Excel workbook, and you need to link a PowerPoint presentation to your workbook. Place the following five steps in the order required to accomplish this objective. Enter a number in each box below and select the correct answer.

[ ] 1. Click on the Insert menu in Excel, and then click Object.

[ ] 2. Select the Link to file check box.

[ ] 3. Click OK.

[ ] 4. Click the Create from File tab, and then click Browse.

[ ] 5. Click on the desired PowerPoint presentation file, and then click the Insert button.

Order->	1	2	3	4	5
A.	3,	1,	4,	5,	2
B.	1,	4,	5,	2,	3
C.	2,	5,	3,	4,	1
D.	5,	3,	2,	1,	4

12. You need to consolidate data from three different worksheets and display the sum in a single worksheet. The three worksheets are all open in Excel, and the primary worksheet in which you want to consolidate the data is currently visible on your screen. Place the following five steps in the order required to accomplish this consolidation task. Enter a number in each box below and select the correct answer.

[ ] 1. When the All references list has been populated as desired, switch back to the primary worksheet, and click OK.

[ ] 2. On the active worksheet, select the cell in which the first value of the consolidated data list will need to be displayed.

[ ] 3. To begin defining the data range for consolidation, select the desired range of cells from a worksheet, and click Add to add the range to the All references list.

[ ] 4. Click the Data menu, click Consolidate, and in the Function box of the Consolidate dialog box, select Sum.

[ ] 5. Verify the desired ranges are selected in all worksheets, and click Add to add each range to the All references list.

Order->	1	2	3	4	5
A.	2,	4,	3,	4,	1
B.	5,	4,	1,	2,	3
C.	3,	2,	5,	4,	1
D.	5,	3,	2,	1,	4

13. After defining alternative values in a scenario, you can replace the spreadsheet's original values with the alternative values by clicking the following button:
   - A. Add.
   - B. Delete
   - C. Show
   - D. Collapse Dialog
   - E. Undo.

14. You need to summarize the existing Employee Salaries and Expenses scenarios, as illustrated in the following graphic. Place the following five steps in the order required to accomplish this. Enter a number in each box below

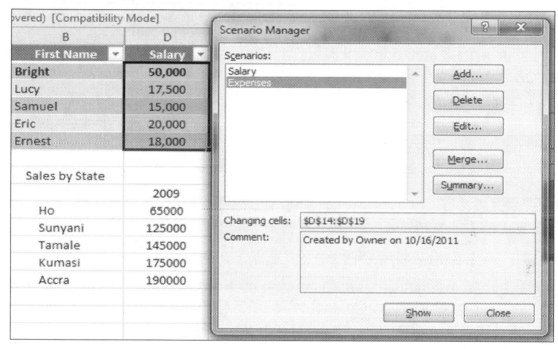

[   ] 1. Click the Expand Dialog button, and click OK.
[   ] 2. Click the Collapse Dialog button in the Scenario Summary dialog box.
[   ] 3. In the Scenario Manager dialog box, click Summary.
[   ] 4. Define the cells that will contain the summary of the two scenarios.
[   ] 5. To delete the contents of the Results cells box, press Delete.

Order-> 1 2 3 4 5
    A. 2, 4, 3, 4, 1
    B. 5, 4, 1, 2, 3
    C. 3, 2, 5, 4, 1
    D. 5, 3, 2, 1, 4

15. You are editing an Excel worksheet, and you need to import an external data list that is in text format. Place the following five steps in the order required to successfully import the data into the worksheet that you're currently using. Enter a number in each box below.

[   ] 1. In the Import Data dialog box, verify that the Existing worksheet option is selected, click OK, and then on the External Data toolbar, click the Close button.

[   ] 2. In the Open dialog box, select the text file, and then click Open.

[   ] 3. Click the Data menu, point to Import External Data, and then click Import Data.

[   ] 4. In the Data Preview box, verify that the data type of each column is set to General, and then click Finish.

[   ] 5. In the Text Import Wizard, verify that the Delimited option is selected, and then click Next. In the first section, verify that the Tab check box is selected, and then click Next.

Order-> 1 2 3 4   5
    A. 2, 4, 3, 4,   1
    B. 3, 2, 5, 4,   1
    C. 4, 2, 5, 3,   1
    D. 5, 3, 2, 1,   4

16. You need to create a chart from the SalesData worksheet, illustrated in figure 7.23 above, and then apply a border and shadow to the chart. Place the following five steps in the order required to accomplish this. Enter a number in each box below.

[   ] 1. Click the Shadow check box to insert a checkmark, and then click OK.

[   ] 2. In the Format Chart Area dialog box, click the Weight arrow, and then click the border you want to apply.

[   ] 3. Select the data and then, on the Standard toolbar, click the Chart Wizard button.

[   ] 4. Click the Format menu, and then click Selected Chart Area.

[   ] 5. Accept the default values, and then click Finish.

Order-> 1 2 3 4   5
    A. 3, 5, 4, 2,   1
    B. 3, 2, 5, 4,   1
    C. 4, 2, 5, 3,   1
    D. 5, 3, 2, 1,   4

17. You are working on a PivotTable, as illustrated in the following graphic. You need to create a PivotChart from this existing PivotTable, and then change the chart type to Area. Place the following five steps in the order required to accomplish this. Enter a number in each box below.

[   ] 1. Click the Chart menu and then click Chart Type. In the Chart Type dialog box, click the Custom Types tab.

[   ] 2. Specify the name and the description of the chart in the Name and Description boxes, respectively, and then click OK.

[   ] 3. On the PivotTable toolbar, click the Chart Wizard button.

[   ] 4. Click the Standard Types tab, in the Chart type area, click Area, and then click OK.

[   ] 5. In the Select from area, click User-defined, and then click Add.

    Order-> **1** **2** **3**   **4**   **5**
        A. 3, 5, 4,   2,   1
        B. 3, 1, 5,   2,   4
        C. 4, 2, 5,   3,   1
        D. 5, 3, 2,   1,   4

18. While editing an Excel worksheet, you need to create a new data source and define it so that you can import product data into the worksheet. Place the following five steps in the order required to accomplish this. Enter a number in each box below.

[   ] 1. Assign a default table for the data source, and then click OK.

[   ] 2. In Excel, click the Data menu, point to Import External Data, and then click New Database Query.

[   ] 3. Verify that <New Data Source> is selected, and then click OK.

[   ] 4. Click the Select button, choose the target database, and then click OK.

[   ] 5. Type a name for the data source, select a driver for the type of database you need to access, and then click the Connect button.

    Order-> **1** **2** **3**   **4**   **5**
        A. 3, 5, 4,   2,   1
        B. 2, 3, 5,   1,   4
        C. 2, 3, 5,   4,   1
        D. 5, 3, 2,   1,   4

19. To keep yourself updated about the latest sales figures, you decided to publish your sales data PivotTable on the Web, and make the PivotTable interactive so that you can modify the data. Assuming that the PivotTable is currently open in Excel on your computer, place the following five steps in the order required to accomplish this. Enter a number in each box below.

[   ] 1. Click PivotTable in the Choose list, and select the AutoRepublish every time this workbook is saved check box.

[   ] 2. Click the File menu, and then click Save as Web Page.

[   ] 3. Type a file name in the File name box, and then click Selection: Sheet.

[   ] 4. Select the Open published web page in browser check box, and then click Publish.

[   ] 5. Select the Add Interactivity check box, and then click Publish.

Order-> 1   2   3   4   5
    A. 3, 5, 4, 2,   1
    B. 4, 3, 5, 1,   2
    C. 2, 3, 5, 4,   1
    D. 2, 3, 5, 1,   4

20. You are editing a worksheet containing data shown in the image below. To share the data with other organizations, you decide to add a schema to your worksheet. Place the following four steps in the order required to accomplish this. Enter a number in each box below.

[   ] 1. Choose the schema document you want to add.

[   ] 2. Click the Data menu, point to XML, and then click XML Source.

[   ] 3. Click Open, and then click OK.

[   ] 4. In the XML Source task pane, click XML Maps, and then click Add.

Order-> 1   2   3   4
    A. 3, 1, 4, 2,
    B. 4, 3, 2, 1,
    C. 2, 3, 2, 4,
    D. 2, 4, 1, 3,

SECTION II

POWERPOINT

APPLICATION

SUMMARIZED OBJECTIVES:

This is a one chapter section that covers several sub-chapters describing the use of Microsoft PowerPoint Application. The student will learn the fundamental concept of PowerPoint presentation. The student will be able to identify what is a good PowerPoint presentation and learn how to create a presentation from the scratch or from a template. This section discusses the inserting of slide master, normal slides, and how to navigate from a slide to another. To customize slides, student will learn how to change slide background, themes, colors, fonts and theme effects. Students will be able to edit and save a presentation. This chapter will explain how to produce PowerPoint handouts, insert hyperlink, tables and images. To crown it all the section teaches final embellishment of a presentation that includes adding sound to PowerPoint, and animations.

The Objectives

Chapter 8: Introduction to PowerPoint Application

8.0 Presentation Basics

8.1 What Makes A Good PowerPoint Presentation

8.1.1 Creating a New Presentation
8.1.1a Creating a New Blank Presentation
8.1.1b Creating a New Presentation from a Template
8.1.2 Inserting Slides and Selecting a Layout
8.1.2.1 Creating a PowerPoint Template
   The PowerPoint Slide Master
   Changing the Background
8.1.2.2 Applying A Theme

8.1.3 Slide Master Layouts
8.1.4 Create A PowerPoint Theme
8.1.4.1 Theme Colors
8.1.4.2 Theme Fonts
8.1.4.3 Theme Effects
8.1.4.4 Saving Your PowerPoint Theme
8.1.5 Opening a presentation
8.1.6 Navigation of Presentation
8.1.7 Using Undo, Redo and Report
      1. Undo a single action
      2. Undo multiple actions
      3. Redo an action
      4. Repeat an action
8.1.8 Saving a Presentation
8.1.9 Using Print Preview
8.1.10 Printing a Presentation
8.1.10.1 PowerPoint Handouts
8.1.11 Closing a Presentation

8.2. Insert PowerPoint Hyperlink

8.2.1 Insert A Table In PowerPoint 2010
8.2.2 Insert Images In Microsoft PowerPoint 2010

8.3 Creating A Quiz In PowerPoint

8.3.1 Creating A Multiple Choice PowerPoint Quiz
8.3.1.1 The Question Slide
8.3.1.2 The Right Answer Slide

> ## Chapter 8: Introduction to PowerPoint Application

8.4 Creating Multimedia Presentations

8.4.1 Animating Slides
8.4.2 Animation Painter
8.4.3 PowerPoint Animations
8.4.4 Applying A PowerPoint Animation
8.4.5 Previewing an Animation

8.5 Assigning A Sound File To An Object

8.5 Assigning A Sound File To An Object
8.5.1 Add Sound To PowerPoint
8.5.1.1Inserting A Sound File As An Object

8.6 Working with Tables, Charts, and Diagrams

8.6 Working with Tables, Charts, and Diagrams
8.6.1 Inserting and Formatting a Table
8.6.1.1 Creating Tables
8.6.1.2 Formatting Tables
8.6.1.3 Importing Excel Worksheets
8.6.1.4 Inserting a Link in A Slide

8.6.2 Inserting and Formatting a Chart
8.6.2.1 Creating Organization Charts
8.6.2.2 Formatting Organization Charts
8.6.2.3 Create an organization chart with pictures
8.6.2.4 Add or delete boxes in your organization chart
8.6.2.5 Delete boxes in your organization chart
8.6.2.6 Change a solid line to a dotted line

8.6.3 Change the hanging layout of your organization chart
8.6.4 Change the colors of your organization chart
8.6.4.1 Change the background color of a box in your organization chart

8.7 Assignment and Exercises

CHAPTER 8

Working With Presentation in PowerPoint

Objectives:

- *Introduction to PowerPoint Application*
- *Presentation Basics, Creating a New Presentation, and Slide Master Layouts*
- *Insert PowerPoint Hyperlink*
- *Creating A Quiz In PowerPoint*
- *Creating Multimedia Presentations*
- *Assigning A Sound File To An Object*
- *Working with Tables, Charts, and Diagrams*
- *Assignments, Exercises, and Multiple Choice Quizzes*

8.0 Presentation Basics

After creating a document, it will make sense to find a way to present it in a professional manner. In fact, you can do many great things with a presentation, such as formatting, animation, etc. In this section the student will learn about more basic tasks, like how to create a presentation and save it. We are going to teach how the most basic commands and functions you can perform in PowerPoint, such as open, save, and close a presentation. Students will also learn how to insert a new slide and navigate between slides in a presentation. Every sub-topic will begin with exercise.

8.1 What Makes A Good PowerPoint Presentation

When thinking of what makes a good PowerPoint presentation, there are basically two areas that the mind is drawn to:

1. the technical use of PowerPoint (how you can present your images in the best possible way etc.), and
2. the practical aspects of delivering that presentation (how big is your audience and can the members at the back see the screen?).

The following is an overview that covers both aspects and serves as a good starting point for anyone who has to give a presentation with little previous experience to help them.

A good PowerPoint presentation must possess the following attributes:
- ✓ Must target precisely at your audience. Your viewers will be turned off by presentations that do not communicate effectively using language they understand, or that present information that they don't find useful.

✓ Must tightly focus on its subject, with no irrelevant topics clouding the discussion. Avoid going off on unplanned tangents.

✓ Must structure well with slides that follow a logical sequence that your audience finds easy to follow.

✓ Must have a good balance between images and text and other forms of media.

✓ Must use themes (colors, fonts and effects) that are appropriate for the subject and that reinforce the presentation's message.

✓ Must use artwork (charts, images, video, shapes, etc.) that support the message and that don't distract or confuse. If you want to show the growth of your company in the last financial year – use a colorful chart! Charts are simple to use and they present information in an easy to digest way.

✓ Must present information in the most appropriate format. Data should be presented in tables where appropriate, or charts if they transmit the message more effectively. And do not forget that there is a large selection of chart types to choose from.

✓ May use sound and video only where it enhances the presentation. Too much is worse than none at all.

✓ May employ animations (including transitions) only where appropriate. If you go overboard, you can distract your audience and take the focus away from the presentation's subject.

✓ Must be accompanied by handouts for the members of the audience to take away. They then have something concrete to refer to later when they try to recall the facts presented.

✓ Must afford time at the end for a question and answer session in which the audience can clarify any matters they are unsure of.

The above is more of a bulleted checklist, whereas what follows describes in more in-depth how to create a good presentation.

Think About Your Audience
The most important element of your PowerPoint presentation is.... your audience. Never neglect your audience.

Different audiences respond differently to the same presentation. A presentation that you are using to pitch an idea to someone will have a very different feel to a presentation you are using to share information with colleagues. In the former case, you are trying to "sell" the idea to someone and you want them to be seduced by the benefits of "buying", but in the latter you are sharing information that your colleagues need to accomplish a task – you do not need them to buy into something as the decision has already been made.

If you have a desired response as a goal, for example selling a product, then you will want to use language that sells the product. You might emphasize features and benefits.

There are also some practical considerations, such as audience size. The larger the audience, the bigger your screen must be so that everyone in the room can see the presentation. If you do not have a large screen, you may need to make fonts bigger, and that may mean breaking information into more slides with less information on each. Similar consideration should be given to any audio that is used – can people at the back of the room hear it comfortably?

Find out what kind of background, knowledge and experiences the members of your audience have. People who are already familiar with the subject matter will not need so much background information and ongoing explanation as people who are new to the subject.

Always rehearse your presentation. You might think that you know your presentation off by heart because you created every slide, but you will not know how it hangs together until you present it. Always rehearse, and preferably to a real live human being who gives you feedback.

8.1.1 Creating a New Presentation

One of the basic commands you need to know is creating a new presentation in PowerPoint.   A new blank presentation appears by default whenever you open the PowerPoint program.

You can also create a new presentation using a template. A template is pre-designed presentation that you can use if you don't have the time or creative ability to design your own presentation from scratch.

8.1.1a Creating a New Blank Presentation

1. Click the office Button in PowerPoint 2007.
   Click File tab menu in PowerPoint 2010.
   Select New.

> **Exercise:** Create a new blank presentation. Create a second new presentation using the Contemporary Photo Album template.

Figure 8.1 A Blank Presentation

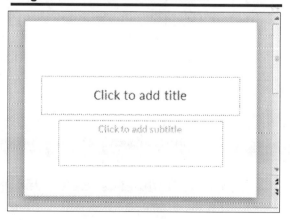

The New Presentation dialog box appears. By default, the Blank Presentation option is already selected. To add a title, click to add title box. Do the same for the subtitle and the content of presentation. You can copy and paste from a Word document.

Figure 8.2 The New Presentation dialog box

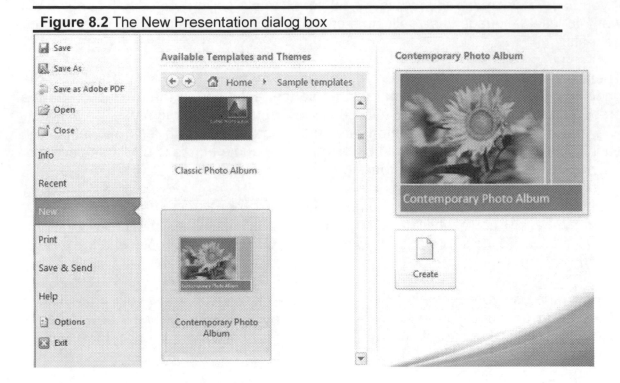

2. Make sure the **Blank Presentation** options selected and click **Create.**
A new blank presentation appears in the program window.
Other ways to **Create a Blank Presentation**. Press <**Ctrl**>+<**N**>

8.1.1b Creating a New Presentation from a Template

1. Click the office Button in PowerPoint 2007 or Click File tab menu in PowerPoint 2010. Select New.
The New Presentation dialog box appears.
There are five options when it comes to creating a new presentation from a template:

- **Installed Templates:** Select this option to select from the templates that were installed on your computer with Microsoft Office. Once you have found a template that you like, click Create.

- **My templates:** Select this option to select a template that you have created or saved on your computer.

- **New from existing:** If you want to base your new presentation on an existing one, select this option.

- **Microsoft Office Online:** Under Microsoft Office Online, click a category to view the templates associated with it. Once you've found a template that you like, click Download.

- **Installed Themes:** Select this option to select from the themes that were installed on your computer with Microsoft Office.

2. Select the desired options in the New Presentation dialog box and **Create** when you are finished.

Tips

The AutoContent Wizard, available in previous versions of PowerPoint, is not available in PowerPoint 2007 or 2010. However, most of the themes and layouts that existed in the AutoContent Wizard are available via the templates found in PowerPoint 2007/2010.

8.1.2 Inserting Slides and Selecting a Layout

This part will explain how to insert a new slide, how to select a layout for the new slide, and how to delete a slide.

Exercise: Open a new blank presentation, if necessary. Insert a new slide into the blank presentation. Insert another new slide, this time using the Two Content layout.

Insert a new slide

Inserting a new slide is quick and easy.

Figure 8.3 The Slides group on Home tab

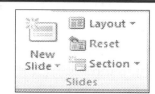

- Click the **Home** tab in the Ribbon and click the **New Slide** button in the Slides group.

A new slide is added to the presentation.
Other Ways to Insert a new slide:

Press **<Ctrl> + <M>** or **right-click** slide on the Slides tab in the Outline pane and select New Slide from the contextual menu.

Select a layout

If you do not like the layout that has been assigned to the new slide by default, choose a new one. PowerPoint 2007 or 2010 gives you nine different layouts to choose from, and you can even create your own custom layouts (more on this later).

The layout name tells you which types of text and/or object placeholders are included in the layout; for example, the Title and Content layout contains a title placeholder and a body text placeholder.

1. Click the Home tab on the Ribbon and click the Layout button in the Slides group. The layout gallery appears.
2. Select the layout you want to use. The new layout is applied to the slide.

    Other Ways to Select a Layout:

    On the Slides tab in the Outline pane, right-click the slide whose layout you want to change. Select Layout from the contextual menu and select a layout from the list.

    Tip: If you do not find a layout that meets your needs perfectly, you can always modify, move, or delete placeholders.

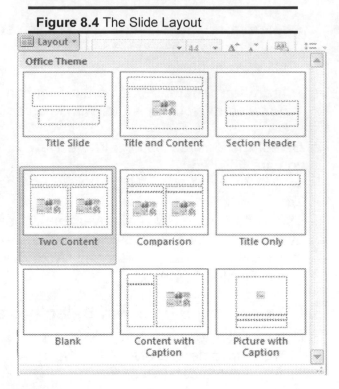

Figure 8.4 The Slide Layout

Insert a new slide using the layout gallery
You can insert a new slide and select a layout at the same time using the Layout gallery.

1. Click the Home tab on the Ribbon and click the New Slide button list arrow in the Slides group. The Layout gallery appears, listing the available layout you have to choose from.
2. Select a layout from the list. A new slide with the selected layout is inserted into the presentation.

Delete a Slide
If you decide you do not a slide, you can delete it.

1. Navigate to the slide you want to delete
2. Click the **Home** tab on the Ribbon and click the **Delete** button in the Slides group.

    Other ways to Delete a Slide: On the Slides tab in the Outline panel select the slide you want to delete and press **<Delete>**.

8.1.2.1 Creating a PowerPoint Template
Creating your own PowerPoint template is a good idea if you plan to use the same color scheme, fonts, effects and layout designs on future presentations. PowerPoint 2010 comes with a variety of stylish templates on which you can base your presentation (learn how to Create A PowerPoint 2010 Presentation From A

Template), and there are many more you can download from **office.com**, but sometimes you need something a little different. Creating your own template gives you the ability to define precisely the look and feel you want.

When creating a PowerPoint template, it's up to you how much detail you define. Some people simply specify a background image that will be used on each slide in their presentation. However, you can actually define the following:

✓ Your own theme (including color schemes, fonts and effects)
✓ A unique background (an image, pattern or color)
✓ The layout of each slide type (title slide layout, title and content layout etc.)

All the settings for your template are defined within the slide master. With the slide master, you can control how all the slides in a presentation look. In fact, making changes to the slide master even after your presentation is created will affect all the slides in that presentation.

The PowerPoint Slide Master

To modify the slide master:

Click **View >> Master Views >> Slide Master**.

The slide master tab appears on the ribbon, giving you the tools you need to make changes to the slide master. Along the left hand side of the workspace, there is a vertical panel that contains the design elements that comprise your template. At the very top is the slide master, and below that and indented are all the different slide layouts that you can use (for example, title slide layout, title and content layout etc.).

Changing The Background

Let's first of all look at applying a background to our template using the slide master. The beauty of using the slide master for this is that you only have to do it in one place and it affects all slides. To modify the background:

1. Select the top level **slide master** on the left hand side of the workspace and then;
2. Click **Slide Master >>Background >> Background Styles**.
   Here, we can see some of the backgrounds that come with PowerPoint 2010.

There are solid color backgrounds and gradient backgrounds available, but we're looking for something that delivers a bigger impact. We are going to use an image for our background, so click Format Background. When the Format Background window opens, select the Fill category on the left and then select Picture or text fill.

Figure 8.5 The Background Styles

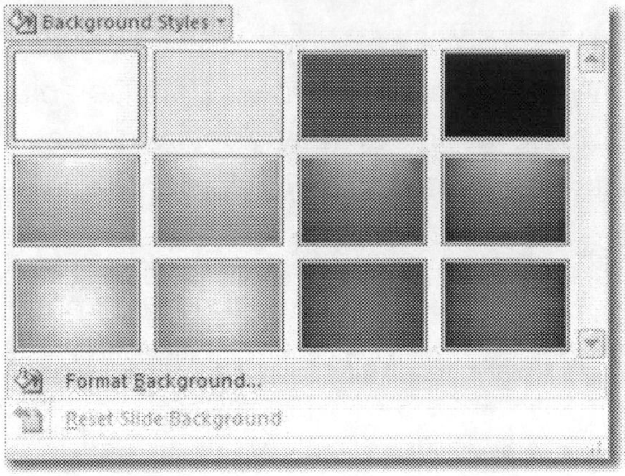

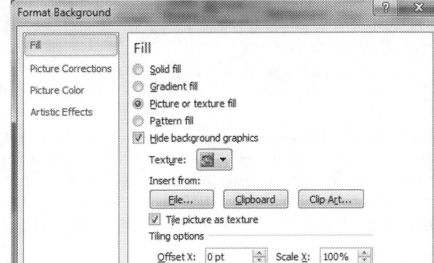

1. Under Insert from, click **File,** and
2. Navigate to where your image is.

Figure 8.6 The Background Style Format Dialog Box

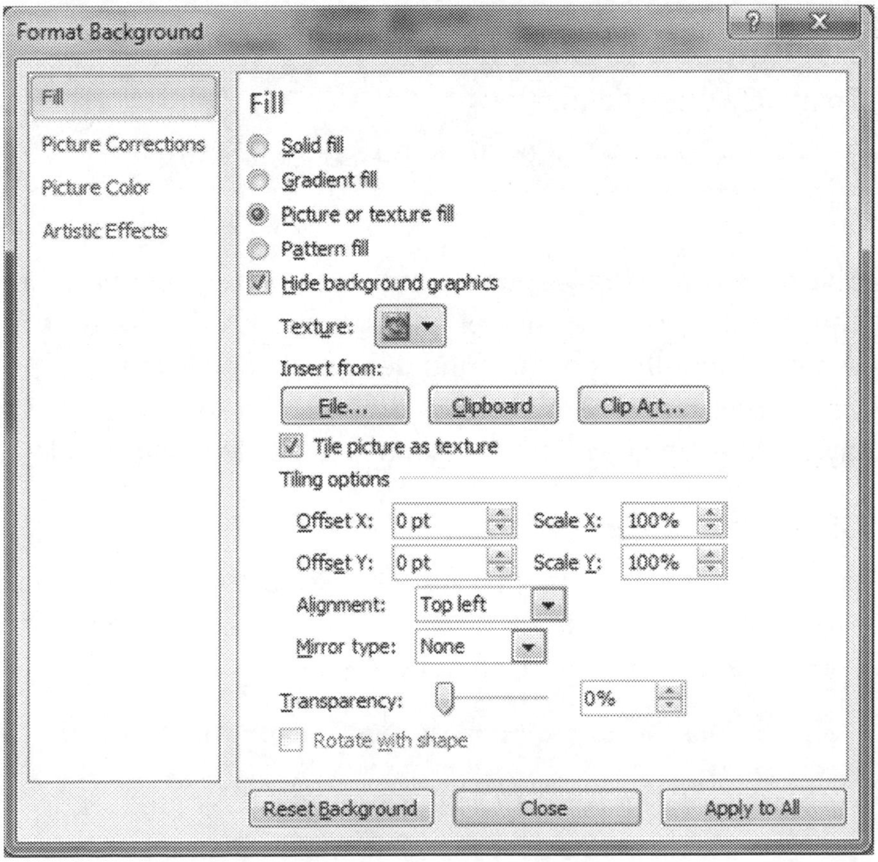

(*It is a good idea to use an image that has large dimensions. You can use the ones around 1,500 pixels wide by 1,000 pixels high.*)

3. Select the image and click Insert. Close the Format Background window.

Over on the left you can see that the background image has been applied to the slide master and all the slide layouts included.

8.1.2.2 Applying A Theme

PowerPoint **Themes** consist of colors, fonts and effects. You could create a new theme for the template you are creating, but let's keep it simple here and use an existing theme. Learn how to create a PowerPoint theme.

Ensure that you are still working in the **Slide Master** tab and look in the Edit Theme group. This is where we can change the theme elements.

Each set of colors, fonts and effects is linked to a theme name. That is, if you click on the Colors button, you will see a list of color combinations that are used by the themes named to the right of the selection panel. For example, you'll notice that there is a set of colors that are used in the Concourse theme. If we now click on the Fonts button, we can see a combination of fonts that are also used in the Concourse theme. You have probably already guessed that when we click on the effects button, there are also effects that are used by this theme too. You can, of course mix and match colors, fonts and effects from different themes, but when doing so, you are not guaranteed the same kind of coherence between the different elements.

Select the theme colors, fonts and effects, you want to use for this template.
Each set of colors, fonts and effects is linked to a theme name. That is, if you click on the Colors button, you will see a list of color combinations that are used by the themes named to the right of the selection panel. For example, you'll notice that there is a set of colors that are used in the Concourse theme. If we now click on the Fonts button, we can see a combination of fonts that are also used in the Concourse theme.

You have probably already guessed that when we click on the effects button, there are also effects that are used by this theme too. You can, of course mix and match colors, fonts and effects from different themes, but when doing so, you are not guaranteed the same kind of coherence between the different elements.

Select the theme colors, fonts and effects which you want to use for this template.

Figure 8.7 Theme Menu

8.1.3 Slide Master Layouts

So far, we have been looking at the "global" settings for our PowerPoint template that we set up against the top slide (the slide master) in the left hand panel. The background and theme defined here affect all slides in our presentation. However, we have further control over how each particular slide type looks too. Below the top slide, and indented, are all the slide layout types. We can modify how each one looks in a similar way.

Let's select one of the slide layouts below the Slide Master and see what we can do. The default Title and Content Slide Layout, for example, has two placeholder text boxes for the title and text. We can style those in any way we please, including changing the font used, the font size, color and background for the text. We can even add new placeholder text boxes and style those. Any changes we make will affect all title and content slides we add to a presentation based on this template.

Saving Your Template
Once you have finished making your template, you will need to save it so that you can use it for future presentations. First of all, exit the Master View by clicking on Close Master View, to the far right of the Slide Master tab.

Now, Click the **File** tab **>> Save As**. Give your masterpiece a name and change the Save as type to be PowerPoint Template (***.potx**).

The default location to save templates is a folder within the Microsoft PowerPoint "file system" called Templates. Putting it there will ensure that it is visible for selection within My Templates when you create a new presentation based on a template.
Note that from PowerPoint 2007 onwards, all PowerPoint file formats have an "**x**" at the end. That means that PowerPoint 2007 and PowerPoint 2010 templates have the **.potx** extension, whereas templates created before PowerPoint 2007 have the **.pot** extension.

8.1.4 Create A PowerPoint Theme
PowerPoint 2010 comes with a nice selection of ready-made PowerPoint themes for you to use on your new presentations. And if you can't find one that's just right, you can even create your own.
A theme comprises the following:

✓ Color schemes
✓ Fonts
✓ Effects

When we say that we're going to create a new PowerPoint theme, we mean that we will create a new color scheme, create a combination of fonts, select an effect and then save all those settings as a new PowerPoint theme.

8.1.4.1 Theme Colors
To create a new color scheme:

Click Design >> Themes >> Colors >> Create New Theme Colors

You can see in the Create New Theme Colors window that there are a number of different elements we must assign colors to.

You can assign those colors by clicking on the color selector to the right of each element. At the bottom of the window there is an input box where you should give the color scheme a name. Once you're done, click Save.

Figure 8.8 Creating Color Theme Dialog Box

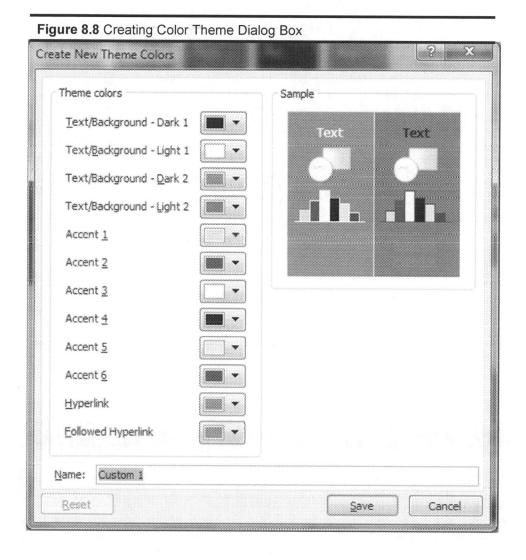

8.1.4.2 Theme Fonts

Now we are ready to create a combination of fonts. Note that we're not creating new fonts, as the fonts already exist. We're just selecting the fonts that we want to use in our new theme.

Click Design >> Themes >> Fonts >> Create New Theme Fonts

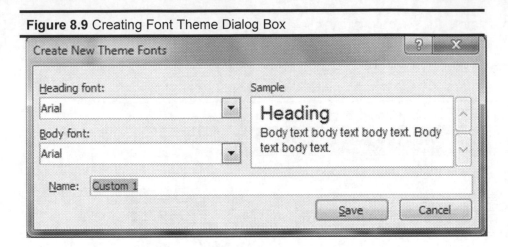

Figure 8.9 Creating Font Theme Dialog Box

Here, all we have to do is select what font we want to appear for our headings and what font we want to appear for our body text. Type in a name for your font selection in the name box and click Save.

8.1.4.3 Theme Effects

Theme effects are sets of lines and fill effects. You cannot create a new theme effect, but you can select one of the pre-made effects to apply to the PowerPoint theme you are in the process of creating.

Click Design >> Themes >> Effects >> and click on the effect you want to use

8.1.4.4 Saving Your PowerPoint Theme

Now that you have created your PowerPoint theme, it's time to save it. Staying in the Themes group on the Design tab, click the **More** button (to the bottom right of the themes gallery) and then click Save Current Theme.

Give the theme a name by typing it in the File name box. If you don't change the default location to save it to (i.e. the Document Themes folder) then you will see this new theme in your themes gallery. Note that the file extension used is **.thmx**. This is the file extension used for PowerPoint themes. Click **Save**.

8.1.5 Opening a presentation

Opening a presentation that you or someone else has previously created and saved is one of the most basic and common tasks in Microsoft PowerPoint.

1. Click the Office Button and select Open, in PowerPoint 2007. Or click on File and Open in PowerPoint 2010. The Open dialog box appears. Other Ways to Open a Presentation: Press **<Ctrl> + <O>**

2. Navigate to the location where the file you want to open is stored. The Open dialog box has several controls that make it easy to navigate to locations and find files on your computer:

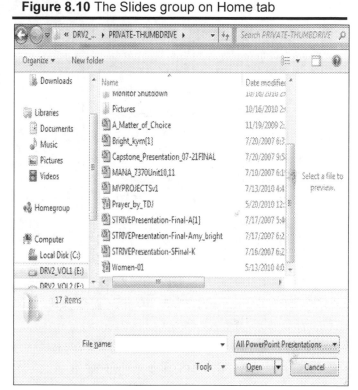

Figure 8.10 The Slides group on Home tab

   - **Address bar:** Click a link in the Address bar to open it. Click the arrow to the right of a link to open a list of folders within that location. Select a folder from the list to open it.

   - **Favorite Links:** Shortcuts to common locations on your computer, such as the desktop and Documents Folder.

   - **Search box:** This searches the contents – including subfolders – of that window for the text that you type.

   If a file's name, file content, tags, or other file properties match the searched text, it will appear as you enter text in the search box.

3. Select the file you want to open and click **Open**. The presentation appears in the program window.
   Tip: To open a presentation that has been used recently, click the **Office Button** and select a presentation from the Recent Documents list.

8.1.6 Navigation of Presentation

Before you start entering information into a presentation, you need to learn how to move around in one. This lesson shows you several ways to navigate through your presentations

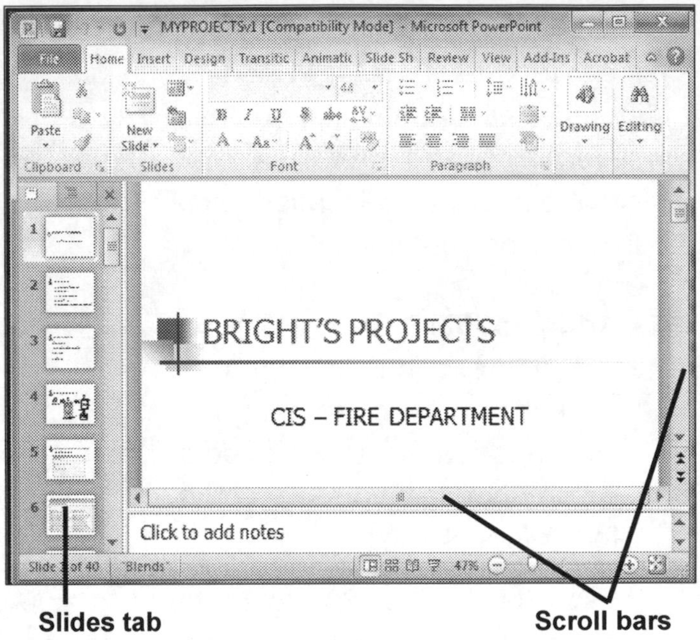

Scroll Bars

The scroll bars are the most basic way to move between slides in a presentation. The vertical scroll bar is located along the right side of the window and is used to move up and down in a presentation. The horizontal scroll bar is located along the bottom of the Slide pane, and is used to move them left to right when a slide doesn't fit entity in the window.

Figure 8.11 Presentation: Slides tab & Scroll bar

Slides tab   Scroll bars

- When you click the Scroll Up or Scroll Down, buttons, PowerPoint move up or down one slide.
- Click and drag the scroll box to move quickly around a presentation.

Navigation keystrokes

You can also use keystroke shortcuts, or navigation keystrokes, to move around in a presentation:

Table 8-1 Short Cut Keys

<Home>	Jumps to the beginning of line.
<End>	Jumps to the end of line
<Page Up>	Jumps to the previous of slide
<Page Down>	Jumps to the next slide
<Ctrl>+<Home>	Jumps to the beginning of the presentation
<Ctrl>+<End>	Jumps to the end of the presentation

Slide tab

You can use the Slides tab in the Outline pane to quickly jump to a specific slide in a presentation.

- On the Slides tab in the Outline pane, click the slide you want to navigate to.
- PowerPoint jumps to select slide.

8.1.7 Using Undo, Redo and Report

You do not need to be afraid of making mistakes in PowerPoint because you can use Undo feature to erase your actions. This lesson will show you how to use the Undo, Redo, and Repeat commands.

1. Undo a single action

Click the Undo button on the Quick Access Toolbar.

Your last action is undone. For example, if you had deleted an item and then decided you wanted to keep it after all, using Undo would make the item reappear.

Other Ways to Undo:
Press **<Ctrl> + <Z>**

Exercise: Delete the last slide in the presentation, then undo this action

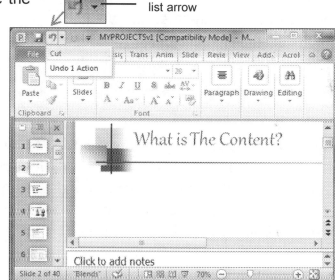

2. Undo multiple actions

The Undo feature saves up 100 of your previous actions, making it easy for you to undo multiple actions.

1. Click the Undo button list arrow on the Quick Access Toolbar.

   A list of your most recent actions appears. This list must be used in order; for example, if you delete a slide, insert a title, and then change the font color, you cannot undo the title without first undoing the font color.

   Tip: You can undo up to 100 of your previous actions in PowerPoint, even after saving the presentation.

2. Click the action that you want to undo.

   PowerPoint undoes the selected action and all actions that were performed after it (all actions that appear above it in the list.

3. Redo an action

If you change your mind, you can "redo" the action that you just undid. Here is how:

Click the Redo button on the Quick Access Toolbar.
>**Other Ways to Redo an Action:**
>Press **<Ctrl> + <Y>**
>Tip: Click the Redo button multiple times to redo multiple actions.

4. Repeat an action

Repeat is different from Redo, because Repeat repeats your last command or action (if possible). For example, let's say you want to delete several slides. Rather than deleting each slide one by one by clicking the **<Delete>** key repeatedly, you could delete one slide and then use the Repeat command to delete all the others.

- Click the Repeat button on the Quick Access Toolbar
- Other Ways to Repeat a Command: Press <F4>

Tip: The Redo and Repeat buttons toggle between the two commands. The Redo button only appears when you have just used the Undo command. Once you have redone all the actions that were undone the button changes back to the Repeat button.

Repeat button

Figure 8.12
Repeat button on the Quick Access Toolbar

8.1.8 Saving a Presentation

Once you have created a presentation, you need to save it if you ever intend on using it again. This lesson will show you how to save a presentation, how to save any changes made to a presentation, and how to save presentation under a different file name, location, and format.

Exercise: Open a new, blank presentation in PowerPoint. Save the presentation with the file name "Test Presentation". Make a few changes to the presentation and save the presentation again with a new name: "Test2 Presentation"

Tips: By default all presentations created in PowerPoint 2007 are saved using the new PowerPoint XML, format (**.pptx**). This format is much smaller in file size and makes it easier to recover damaged or corrupted file.

Saving a new presentation

Figure 8.13 Presentation: Save As Dialog Box

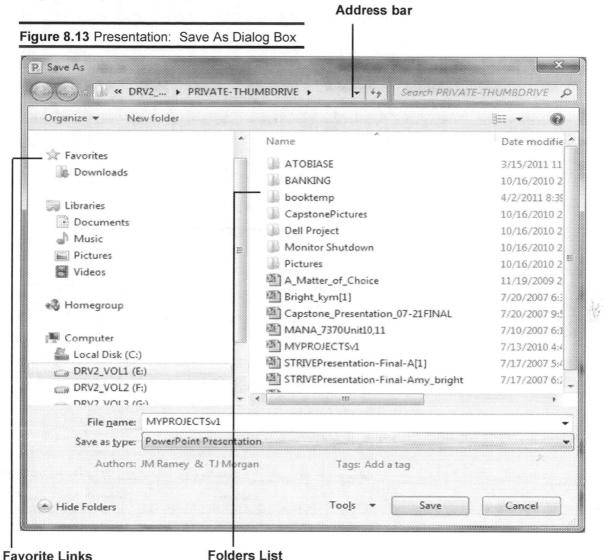

Favorite Links   **Folders List**

1. In PowerPoint 2007, Click the **Office Button** and select **Save As.**
   *Or In PowerPoint 2010, Click **File**Tab and Select **Save*** (The Save As dialog box appears)

   Other Ways to Save:
   Click the **Save** button on the Quick Access Toolbar, or press **<Ctrl> + <S>**

2. Specify the drive and/or folder where you want to save the presentation.
   The Save As dialog box has several controls that make it easy to navigate to locations on your computer:

- **Address bar:** Click a link in the Address bar to open it. Click the arrow to the right of a link to open a list of folders within that location. Select a folder from the list to open it.

- **Favorite Links:** Shortcuts to common locations on your computer, such as the Desktop and Documents Folder.

- **Folder List:** View the hierarchy of drives and folders on your computer by expanding the Folders list.

3. Type a name for the presentation in the File name text box.

4. Click Save.

Saving Presentation Changes

Click the **Office Button** and select **Save**. *Or In PowerPoint 2010, Click **File**Tab and Select **Save***
PowerPoint saves any changes that have been made to the presentation.

Other Ways to Save Changes:
Click the **Save** button on the Quick Access Toolbar, or press **<Ctrl> + <S>**

Saving a Presentation under a different name and/or Location

When you save a presentation under a different name or location, you are essentially creating a new file. The original file is saved with its original name and/or in its original location, and a copy of the file is saved with the new name and/or in the new location.

1. Click the File tab and select **Save As**.
   The Save As dialog box appears

2. Enter a different name or the file in the File name text box and/or navigate in the new location where you want to save the file.

3. Click Save.

   The original presentation is replicated and saved under the new name, and original presentation without changing the original.

Save a Presentation in a different File Format

Just as some people can speak several languages, PowerPoint can read and write in other file formats. Saving a presentation in a different file format makes it easier to share information between programs,

1. Click the File tab and select Save As. (The Save As dialog box appears.)
2. Click the Save as type list arrow and select a file format.
3. Click Save.

   Tip: In order to save a file in **.pdf** or **.xps** format, you need to install an add-in. To do this, open the File menu, point to **Save As**, and select **Find add-ins for other file formats** from the menu.

Table 8-2 Presentation: Save As Dialog Box

File Extension	File Description
.pptx	Presentations created in PowerPoint 2007 to 2010 saved in this XML-enabled format by default.
.ppt	Presentations that were created in PowerPoint 97-2003 are saved in this format.
.pdf	This format preserves document formatting and enables file sharing across any platform.
.xps	XPS Document Format is a new Microsoft electronic paper format used to exchange documents in their final form.
.potx	Saves a presentation as a template that you can use to format future presentations.
.pot	Templates that were created in PowerPoint 97-2003 are saved in this format.
.thm	Saves the presentation as an Office theme.
.pps/.ppsx	Saves the presentation so that it opens in Slide Show view rather than Normal view.
.html	Saves the presentation as a Web page.
.wmf	Windows Metafile. Saves a slide as a 16-bit graphic.
.emf	Enhanced Windows Metafile. Saves a slide as a 32-bit graphic.
.rtf	Rich Text Format. Saves the presentation as text-only document.
.sldx	An autonomous slide file.

8.1.9 Using Print Preview

Print Preview allows you to see what a presentation will look like when printed.

1. Click the **File** tab and point to **Print** list arrow
   A list of **Print** options appears.
   Tip: If you accidentally click Print dialog box will appear. Click the Close button to close this dialog box and try again.

2. In PowerPoint 2010, as soon as you select Print the **Print Preview** function is activated to display the presentation.

Exercise: View the presentation in Print Preview. Zoom in on the presentation. Close Print Preview.

Notice that the Ribbon changes to display only the Print Preview tab.

3. When you are finished previewing the presentation, click the **Close Print Preview** button in the Preview group on the Print Preview tab.

Print Preview closes and you return to your presentation when you select any of the menu tab.

Tips: To zoom in on a slide, click the slide with the 🔍 pointer. To zoom out, click the slide again.

You can print directly from Print Preview by clicking the **Print** button in the Print group.

Figure 8.14 Presentation shown in Print Menu

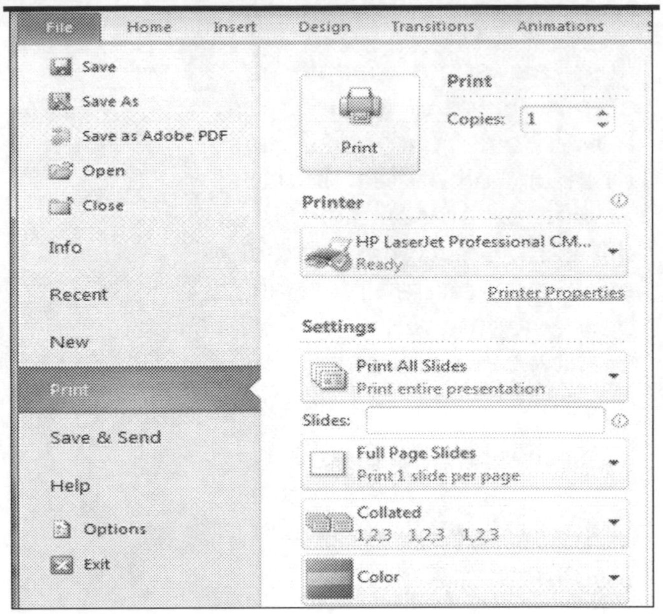

Figure 8.15 Presentation shown in Print Preview

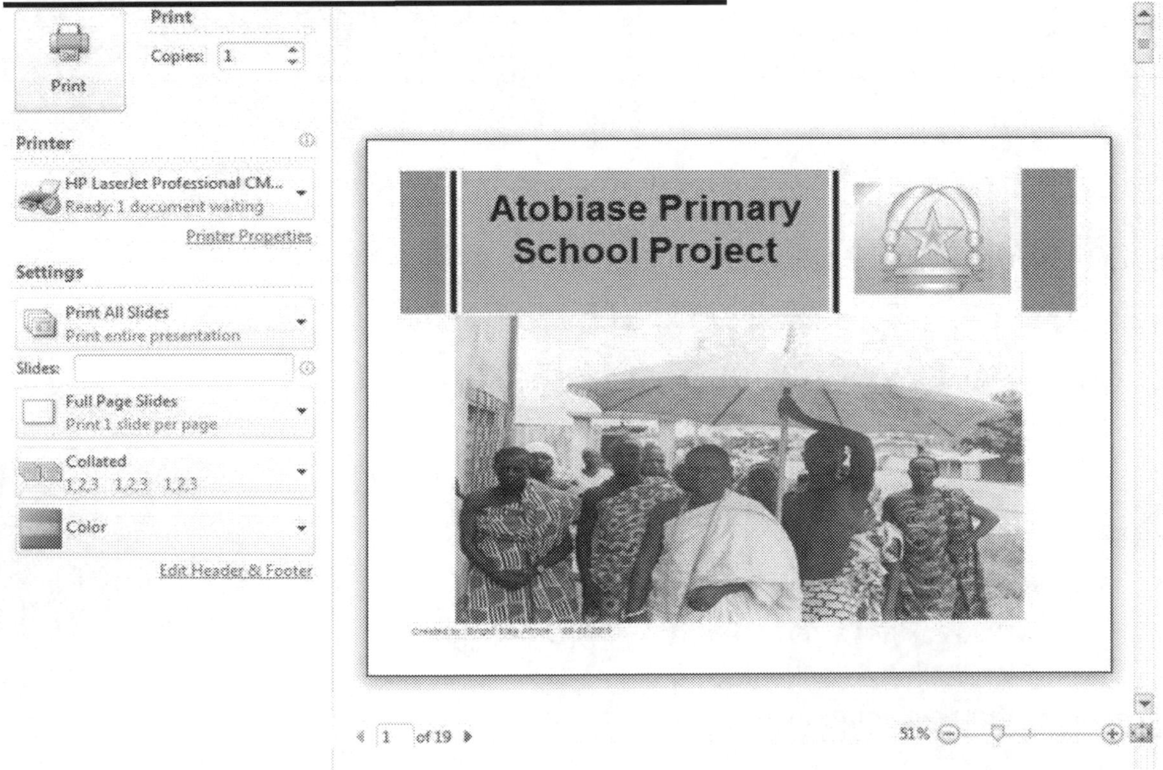

8.1.10 Printing a Presentation

There are two ways to print in PowerPoint 2007 or 2010:

- **Standard Print:** Opens the Print dialog box where you can select a printer, how many copies you want to print, and other options.
- **Quick Print:** Sends the presentation directly to the default printer without making any changes.

Standard Print

1. Click the File and select Print. The Print dialog box appears.
   Other Ways to Open the Print Dialog Box:
   Press **<Ctrl> + <P>**
2. Specify the print options for the presentation.
3. Click OK.
   The Print dialog box closes and the presentation is sent to the printer.

Quick Print

1. Click the File and point to the Print list arrow.
2. Select Quick Print from the list. PowerPoint sends the presentation to the default printer

8.1.10.1 PowerPoint Handouts

PowerPoint handouts are simply printouts of the slides within your presentation. They are useful to your audience as they provide a way for viewers to refer back to slides that have been and gone. Also, members of the audience can take printed handouts away with them to read again later.

How many slides are printed on each page is totally within your control.

Click the **File** tab **>> Print**, and then in the Settings section click on the second drop down list.

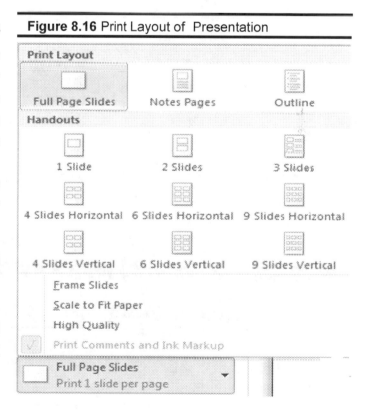

Figure 8.16 Print Layout of Presentation

In the Handouts section you can see all the different arrangements available for the slides printed on each page.

You can see a preview of what each printed page will look like on the right.

At the bottom of the **Print** screen you should be able to see a link that says **Edit Header & Footer**. After clicking that link, the **Header** and **Footer window** is displayed.

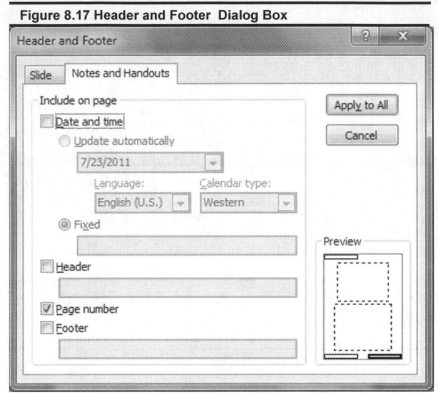

Figure 8.17 Header and Footer Dialog Box

Using this window, we can control whether the date and time is printed on each handout. If we check the box to include the date and time on each page, we can then select whether the date and time printed is now or a fixed value that we can type in. Moving down the Header & Footer window, we can also elect to print three things:

✓ **a header and also the text that displays in the header**
✓ **page numbers**
✓ **a footer and also the text that displays in the footer**

Once you have made your selections, click Apply to All.

8.1.11 Closing a Presentation

When you have finished working on a presentation, you need to close it.

Click the **File** tab and select Exit. The Presentation closes.
Other Ways to Do Close:
Click the Close button in the upper right-hand corner of the program window, or press
<Ctrl>+<W>.
Tip: If you have more than one presentation open, clicking the close button only closes the current presentation. If you only have one presentation open onscreen, clicking the Close button closes the PowerPoint program will.

8.2. Insert PowerPoint Hyperlink

Being able to add hyperlinks to your Microsoft PowerPoint presentation is a very useful facility. You can add hyperlinks to the following:

- ✓ A file or web page
- ✓ A custom show or location in the current presentation
- ✓ A specific slide in a different presentation
- ✓ An email address
- ✓ A new file

To add a hyperlink, first of all you need some text or an object to add the hyperlink to.

Select the text or object and then **click Insert >> Links >> Hyperlink.**
When the Insert Hyperlink dialogue appears you have different options, depending on what you want the destination of the link to be.

Figure 8.18 Hyperlink Inserting Dialog Box

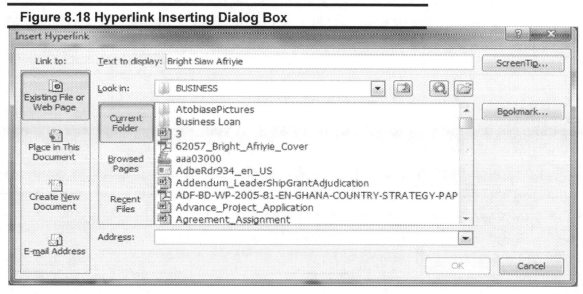

Use the following:

- **A file or web page** – Under *Link to*, click *Existing File or Web Page* and navigate to its location on your hard drive. Select it and click OK.
- **A custom show or location in the current presentation** – Under *Link to* click *Place in This Document*. You are presented with what looks like a file explorer panel for the slide in your presentation, including elements that are on each slide. Select a slide or element and click OK.
- **A specific slide in a different presentation** – Under *Link to*, click *Existing File or Web Page* and navigate to its location on your hard drive. Select it and click OK.
- **An email address** – Under *Link to*, click *E-mail Address*. Type in the email address and subject reference.
- **A new file** – Under *Link to*, click *Create New Document*. Type in the name of the new document and select either *Edit the new document later* or *Edit the new document now*.

Whichever destination for your hyperlink you choose, you can specify a tooltip (text that appears when you hover over the link) by clicking the **Screen Tip** button next to your display text at the top.

Figure 8.19 Hyperlink Screen Tip Insert Dialog Box

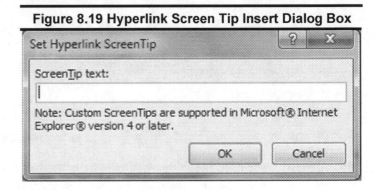

In the dialogue box that opens, type in your screen tip and click OK.

When you run your presentation, clicking on the hyperlink will take you to the resource that you specified above.

8.2.1 Insert A Table In PowerPoint 2010

Using tables is a great way to set out information in your PowerPoint presentation. In addition to presenting tabular data, tables are often used for laying out a slide. Once you have removed the borders and shading from the table and cells, the audience will never know that there is a table there.

There are a few ways of inserting a table in your presentation:

1. Click on the table icon on a content palette.
2. Use the Insert tab in the ribbon.

Using the content palette is probably the easiest method. Content palettes are found on slides of the following types:

- ✓ Title and Content
- ✓ Two Contents
- ✓ Comparison
- ✓ Content with Caption

When adding any of these kinds of slides, you will see a group of icons in the Centre, like this:

Figure 8.20 Insert tab Showing Table Icon

The table icon is circled in the image above. If you click on that icon, the Insert Table window will open. You can use this to specify how many columns and rows you want your table to have. Click OK when you've made you selections and the table will be inserted.

The style of the table entered fits the theme that the presentation is using (read more about PowerPoint Themes). Here is how the table I just inserted looks:

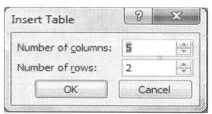

8.2.2 Insert Images In Microsoft PowerPoint 2010

The presence of images in your PowerPoint presentation can help to capture the attention of the members of your audience and to engage them. To insert an image into your presentation in PowerPoint 2010, first of all select the slide you want the image to appear on. Then click **Insert >> Images >> Picture**. When the Insert Picture dialogue box opens, navigate to the location of the image on your hard drive, select it and click Insert.

Figure 8.21 Picture and images Icon

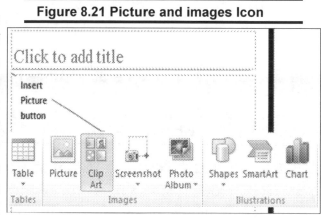

The image is inserted onto the slide and because it is selected, the Picture Tools contextual tab appears in the ribbon. There are several interesting things you can do to manipulate the image immediately, such as:

✓ Reposition the image on the slide using the arrow keys.

✓ Scale the image up or down by holding down shift while you press the arrow keys. The up arrow and right arrow keys make the image bigger, whilst the left arrow and down arrows make the image smaller.

✓ Rotate the image by hovering over the round green handle at the top of the image – then click and drag left or right.

✓ Resize the image by clicking and dragging on the resize handles at the corners of the image and halfway along each edge. Dragging on the corner handles maintains the proportions of the image, while dragging the handles along the edges will "squash" the image.

8.3 Creating A Quiz In PowerPoint

It is pretty easy to create a quiz in PowerPoint. To create a multiple choice style of PowerPoint quiz, you need to follow these five simple steps:

1. Create a slide with a question and some multiple choice answers. Each answer will become a clickable link.
2. Create a "Correct Answer" slide. This will congratulate the student and move them onto the next question.
3. Create a "Wrong Answer" slide that will berate the student for getting the answer wrong and will invite them to take the question again.
4. Create hyperlinks from all the wrong answers on the question slide to the "Wrong Answer" slide.
5. Create a hyperlink from the correct answer to the "Correct Answer" slide.

The above steps will create all you need for one question. You need to repeat the process for each question you want to include in your quiz. Be warned that, although it is a simple concept to understand, creating a PowerPoint quiz with 20 questions may take quite a while, especially if you are going to include images in the quiz.

8.3.1 Creating A Multiple Choice PowerPoint Quiz

Let's work through an example of a multiple choice PowerPoint quiz. In our example we will create all the slides you need for the first question. Open PowerPoint and by default you should have a blank presentation in front of you with the default title slide.

Click in the title box and type in the title "Geography Test". Groan all you like, this is a geography test!

8.3.1.1 The Question Slide

The first question is "**What is the capital of Ghana?**" For this question we need to add a Title and Content slide. If you have not yet added any slides to the presentation, then clicking the top half of the New Slide button (*Home tab, Slides group*) will give you the slide layout you want – title and content. *If you have added a slide to this presentation already, then the new slide will be of the same layout as the last one added.* In this case, click the bottom half of the New Slide button and choose Title and Content. Read more about PowerPoint slide layouts.

Click into the title text box and type in the question "*What is the capital of Ghana?*"

Inserting a Picture:
Now, click on the Insert Picture (*Ghana map*) from **File icon** in the center of the slide. Navigate to where a suitable image is on your hard drive. Try and find one that illustrates the question well. We inserted this map of Ghana:

What is the capital of Ghana?

We now need to add several wrong answers and one right answer. To do this, we will insert text boxes and type the following answers:
- ✓ Kumasi (wrong!)
- ✓ Cape Coast (wrong!)
- ✓ Tamale (wrong!)
- ✓ Accra (right!)

To insert a text box, go to the Insert tab, and in the Text group click on the Text Box button. Drag out a box and type an answer in it. The box may not fit the text snugly, but do not worry. Just click on the drag handles that you see at the corners and halfway along each edge of the text box and drag to resize the text box.
Add more text boxes to contain all the wrong answers and the right answer too. You should end up with something like this:

What is the capital of Ghana?

We are going to leave the question slide for now and come back to it later.
The Wrong Answer Slide

Add another title and content slide for the "***Wrong Slide***". In the title text box, type something like "Wrong answer!". In the content text box, type "Try again". This is where it starts to get interesting. We are going to turn the "Try again" text into a hyperlink that leads back to the question slide.

Select the "Try again" text and then click **Insert >> Links >> Hyperlink**. In the Insert Hyperlink window, select Place in This Document. When you do this, PowerPoint displays all the slides in your presentation that you can link to.

Figure 8.22 Inserting Hyperlink in PowerPoint

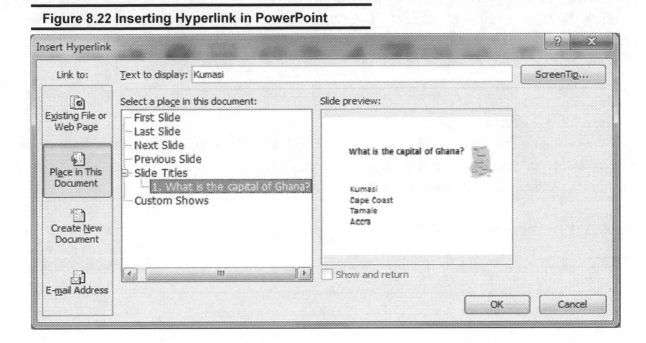

Click the question slide (it should display the text "***What is the capital of Ghana***" in the window). Click OK and the hyperlink is added. The linked text should appear blue with an underline by default. Read more about adding hyperlinks in PowerPoint.

Now let's go back to the question slide and link all the wrong answers to the "**wrong slide**". Select the question slide in the Slides panel on the left and select the text box for the first wrong answer. Insert a hyperlink to the "**Wrong answer**" slide. Do the same for all the wrong answers. This means that when the person taking the quiz clicks on a wrong answer, they will be shown the "Wrong Answer" slide and they will be invited to try again.

Figure 8.23 Inserting Hyperlink To link Wrong Answers

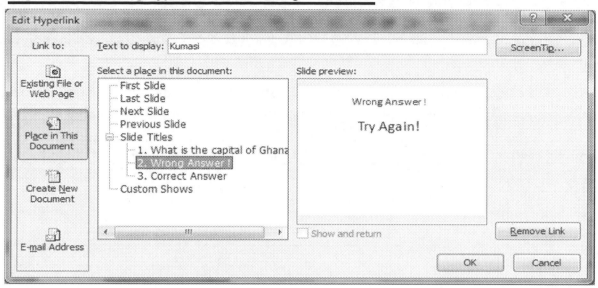

8.3.1.2 The Right Answer Slide

We need to sort out the right answer now, and the first thing to do is create a "*Right answer*" slide. Select the wrong answer slide so that the next slide you add is inserted after it and click the New Slide button on the Home tab. Type a congratulatory message in the title text box, like "**Yes, It is correct!**". In the content text box, type the text "**Next question**". Later you will need to add a hyperlink to this piece of text that leads to the next question slide.

Figure 8.24 Inserting Hyperlink To link Correct Answer

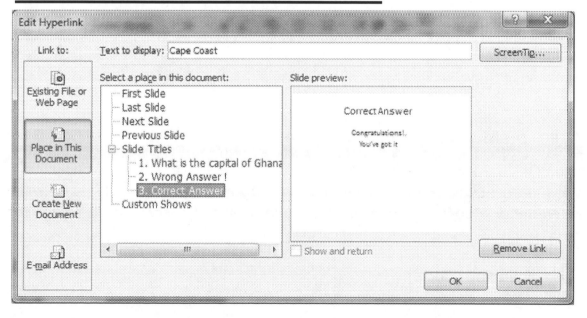

Go back to the question slide we created earlier and add a hyperlink to the text box that holds the right answer is Accra. Make the hyperlink point to the "*Right answer*" slide. That is the first question complete. Now rinse and repeat for all the questions in your PowerPoint quiz.

When you run the slideshow, the cursor will appear as a hand when it hovers over each answer on the question slide, indicating that each answer is a clickable link.

Figure 8.25 Presentation Showing Hyperlinks To link Wrong and Correct Answers Slides

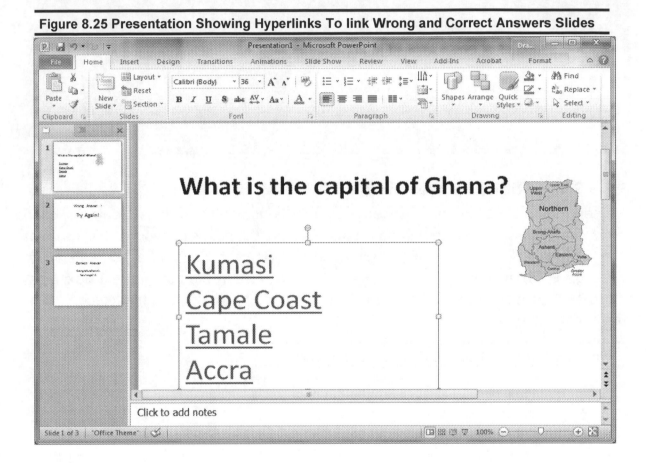

8.4 Creating Multimedia Presentations

Microsoft Office PowerPoint 2007/2010 enables you to transform a slide show into a multimedia presentation by animating text and objects, adding transitions between slides, and adding sounds and movie clips. The multimedia presentation covers the following:

1. Animate slides.
2. Add transition effects.
3. Insert and play sounds and movies.

8.4.1 Animating Slides

The easiest way that you can apply animation effects to a slide show is by using the Slide Design task pane, which provides professionally designed animations divided into three categories: Subtle, Moderate, and Exciting.

We will learn about the following:

a. Apply an animation scheme to a slide.
b. Animate multiple slides.
c. Animate the text in a slide.
d. Modify text animation settings and text animation levels.
e. Change the order in which objects animate.

Types of Animation

The most common animation effects that you can apply include the following:

- You can animate text so that it appears on the screen one paragraph, word, or letter at a time.
- If a slide has more than one level of bullet points, you can animate each level separately.
- You can animate objects, such as shapes.
- If an object contains text, you can animate the text only, the object only, the object and the text simultaneously, or the object and text separately.
- You can change the order of how text or shapes appear.
- You can animate charts that were created by using Microsoft Graph or imported from Microsoft Excel; for example, you can animate each data series in a chart to appear at a different time.

Built-in Animation Effects

PowerPoint has a wide variety of built-in effects that you can use to make your slides more interesting. Most of these animations have associated sound effects.

You can apply a built-in animation effect in Slide Sorter view or in Normal view. If you are in Slide Sorter view, PowerPoint applies the effect to every object on the slide, except the title and background objects. If you are in Normal view, you must select the object that you want to animate and then apply the effect.

Custom Animation Effects

You can create your own custom animation scheme in Normal view. Custom animations enable you to move multiple objects simultaneously, move objects along a path, and sequence all of the effects on the slide. You can add your animation scheme to each slide individually or easily apply it to all of the slides in a presentation.

Adding Transition Effects

A transition is the visual effect of a slide as it dynamically appears and dissolves during a slide show presentation. Transition effects can increase the impact of a presentation by varying how one slide replaces another.

About Transitions

You can apply a transition to one slide at a time, or apply the same transition to a group of slides. However, each slide can have only one transition.
The transition can have any of the following effects on a slide's entrance:

i.   Dragging the slide into view from one of several directions.
ii. Dissolving from the outer edges or the center and gradually revealing the slide.
iii. Opening like a vertical blind to reveal the slide.

Tip: If you apply both a transition effect and an animation effect to a slide, the transition effect occurs first, followed by the animation effect.
You can also specify the following:

- The speed of the transition.
- The sound of the transition.
- The direction in which the transition appears and dissolves.
- When the transition occurs.

8.4.2 Animation Painter

If you have used PowerPoint's Format Painter before, you'll find the Animation Painter is strangely familiar. The animation painter is new to PowerPoint 2010. It copies existing animations and "*paints*" them on new objects. This means that the time you spend constructing a complicated animation does not need to be duplicated for each object you want to apply it to. You create the animation once, and with a couple of clicks you can copy that animation to new objects.

When you apply an animation to an object, there are a variety of settings and adjustments to help you fine-tune it for a more polished effect. Being able to copy all those features can be a real timesaver.

Instead of wandering about this new feature, let us just use it in an example.

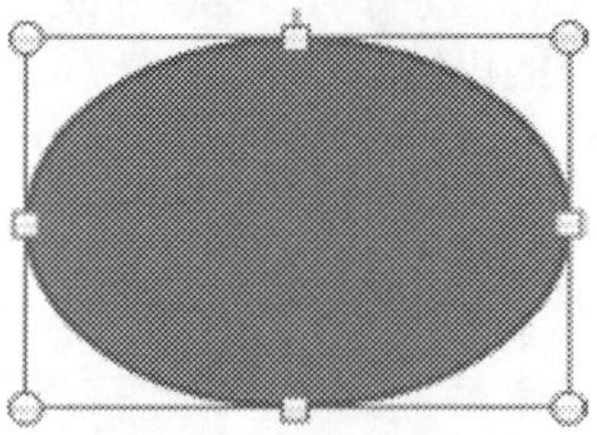

Figure 8.26 Oval Image

i. *Draw out an ellipse by:*
Clicking **Insert >>Illustrations>>Shapes>>Oval**.
OK, it's an oval not an ellipse! Click and drag on the slide to drag out your oval.
ii. Let us add an animation to the oval by:
Clicking ***Animations >> Add Animation** (More button) **>> Bounce**.*
iii. *Let us add a second animation:*
Select the oval *again and this time click the* **Add Animation button** *(in the Advanced Animation group)* **>> Spin**.

We now have both the Bounce and Spin animations added to the oval, and they will play in that order. If you had simply selected a different animation from the gallery instead of using the Add Animation button, the new animation would have replaced the old one, instead of being added. You can tell that there are two animations present because of the telltale symbols displayed next to the oval:

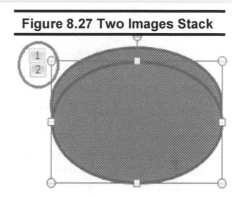
Figure 8.27 Two Images Stack

We can preview the animations by clicking on the **Preview** button in the **Preview** group. We will now alter the timings of these animations.

1. Select the Bounce animation (the first one) by clicking the 1 in the image above.
2. In the **Timing** group in the ribbon, change the **Duration** from 2.00 to 1.00. That will speed things up!
3. Click the **Preview** button to see how fast it is now.

Currently, both animations are triggered by the presenter clicking the left mouse button. This is fine for the first animation but let us change the second animation to start when the first one finishes. That will make the animations look smoother.

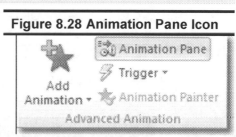
Figure 8.28 Animation Pane Icon

1. Click the **Animation Pane** button in the **Advanced Animation group**.
2. In the **animation pane**, double click the second animation. (*That's the Spin animation*)
3. In the window that opens click on the **Timing** tab and change the **Start** drop down selection to be **After Previous**. (That means that the second animation will start after the first one finishes.)
4. Click **OK** to close the window.

Figure 8.29 Animation Pane

Figure 8.30 Spinning Timing Dialog Box

8.4.3 PowerPoint Animations

Animations can emphasize points you want to make and can help make the information in your PowerPoint 2010 presentations more memorable to your audience. They can also engage viewers and capture their attention. Of course, if you go overboard with your animations, your audience may feel overwhelmed and just switch off. Use them sparingly. Animations do not just exist by themselves. You need to apply them to an object. This object is usually a piece of text, but can be other things like a chart, a picture or even a video.

Animations come in 4 flavors:

1. **Entrance** – these animations make your object appear on your slide. For example, your object might float in.
2. **Emphasis** – these animations bring audience attention to the animated object. For example, Pulse makes your object grow and shrink like a beating heart (just once though!).
3. **Exit** – with an exit animation, your object leaves the slide. Fly out is an exit animation.
4. **Motion Path** – motion path animations are a little more complex, but not much. The animated object follows a path that you define. We'll look at these in more detail later.

8.4.4 Applying A PowerPoint Animation

To apply an animation to an object in your presentation, first of all select it. Now click the Animations tab and you should see a selection of animations in the Animation group. To see the entire collection of animations, click on the **More** button.

When you click the **More button**, you get to see the following large collection of animations:

You can use Live Previews to see what an animation will look like before applying it: all you have to do is hover over the thumbnail image of the animation to see it play once. To actually add the animation, just click on it. If you decide that you want to remove the animation, click on the **None button** at the top of the animations list.
Any slides that use animations will display a whooshing star in the top left hand corner of the slide in the slides pane. This animation symbol will be familiar to you if you've ever added transitions to your slides.

8.4.5 Previewing an Animation

PowerPoint provides several ways for you to preview animations. First of all there is the live preview you see when you hover over an animation in the animations gallery. After an animation has been applied, though, you can preview it in the following ways:

- Click on the animation symbol in the image above.
- Click the Preview Animations button in the Preview group on the Animations tab.

If you click on the top half of the Preview button, the animation will play. If, however, you click on the bottom half of the button, you'll see some preview options (see image above). The top option (Preview), simply plays the animation. The **AutoPreview** option controls whether animations are played automatically when added to an object, and it affects whether a live preview is displayed too. You will probably want this option checked so that you can see what the animation looks like when previewed and applied.

Adding animations can be very easy, as we have seen above. We can also get as complicated as we like! Check out the following PowerPoint animation tutorials (coming soon):

- Motion Path Animations
- The Animation Pane
- Advanced Animation Controls

8.5 Assigning A Sound File To An Object

Instead of inserting a sound file and having it appear as an icon, you can assign the sound file to an object. The sound will play when the object is clicked. There is a big drawback to this method. You can only use **.wav** files.

- The first step is to insert an object. For this example, let's insert a picture. While the picture is still selected, click the **Insert** tab and then click **Action** (in the *Links* group).

Figure 8.31 Action Settings Dialog box

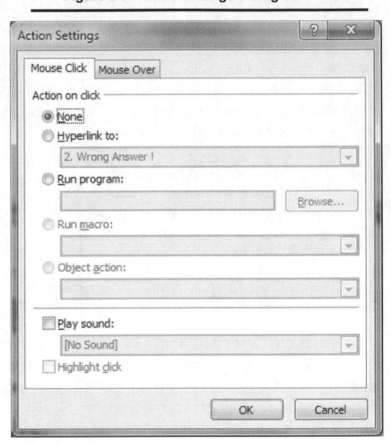

✓ In the Action Settings panel, make sure you're on the Mouse Click tab, check the Play sound box at the bottom and then select a sound. There are some ready-made sounds for you to select from the list, but you can also choose your own sound file – as long as it's a **.wav** – by selecting Other Sound. If you select Other Sound, the Add Audio dialogue box will open, and you'll have to navigate to where the sound file is on your hard drive, select it and then click OK.

The **.wav** will play to give you a preview of what it sounds like.

✓ Click OK on the Action Settings window.

✓ When you insert a sound file directly into a PowerPoint presentation, the sounds playback controls are visible. When you associate a sound file with an object, however, these controls are hidden.

✓ Because we selected the Mouse Click tab on the Action Settings window, the sound only plays when you click the image. Also, when you run your presentation, you'll notice that the cursor changes to a hand, indicating that the image is clickable.

8.5.1 Add Sound To PowerPoint

Sound and music can make a big difference to the delivery of your PowerPoint presentation to your audience. It can make the impact more dramatic and enhance your message – if used wisely. As with animations, you should not overwhelm your audience with sound! Use only where it will help to get your message across. You can use music and sounds in the following ways:

1. Insert a sound file onto a slide. The sound then plays when a trigger occurs such as the sound icon being clicked or the slide being shown.
2. Associate a sound with an object. Similar to above, the sound will play when the object is clicked, or something else happens to the object. You can use objects like pictures or charts here.
3. Associate a sound with an animation effect. The sound will play when the animation happens.
4. Associate a sound with a slide transition. The sound will play when the next slide appears.
5. Add a music file that plays continuously in the background, like the soundtrack to a movie.

Sound in PowerPoint is a big subject, so we have split this tutorial up into 5 sections. The first section – how to insert a sound file as an object – is here. Use the links at the bottom to jump to the other sections.

8.5.1.1Inserting A Sound File As An Object

Figure 8.32 Clip Art Dialog box

When inserting a sound file as an object, you will see an audio icon that displays controls for playing, pausing and rewinding. There are two sources of sound file you can use: those on your computer's hard drive and those in Clip Art. Let us look at Clip Art sounds first.

Open up the Clip Art panel by **clicking Insert >> Clip Art** (in the Images group). The Clip Art panel should appear to the right. As we are interested in sounds and music, change the Results should be drop down selector to be Audio. Type in something to search for and click Go.

If you want to preview what the file sounds like, right click on it in the Clip Art panel and select **Preview/Properties**. If you left click on a sound file, that will add it to your slide. When you have a sound file on your slide, you will see the sound icon.

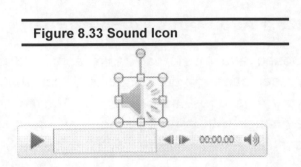

Figure 8.33 Sound Icon

When selected, the icon displays some playback controls beneath it that let you play the sound and rewind it. You can actually hide this icon by checking the **Hide During Show** box in the Audio Options group on the Playback tab. Some people even drag the icon off the slide so that it's hidden. The choice is yours.

To delete the sound file from the slide, select it and press the delete key.

To insert a sound file that exists on your computer's hard drive, follow the steps below:
1. Click **Insert >> Audio** (in the Media group).
2. Navigate to where the file exists on your hard drive
3. Select it and then click Insert.

The same sound icon, together with the same playback controls are displayed on the slide.

8.6 Working with Tables, Charts, and Diagrams

Often you will want to strengthen your presentations by using facts and figures that are bes presented in a table, chart, or diagram. These objects are easy to place on slides that have a content placeholder.

8.6.1 Inserting and Formatting a Table

When you want to display information in an organized and easy-to-read format, a table is often your best choice. If the table already exists in another format, you can import it into PowerPoint or embed it as an object in a slide. We will learn about inserting a table into a slide, formatting a table, inserting a Microsoft Excel worksheet as an embedded object, and formatting an embedded Excel worksheet.

8.6.1.1 Creating Tables

As described under 8.2.1. a table is a simple two-dimensional organization of rows and columns. The intersection of a row and a column is a cell. The first row is commonly used for column headings, and the leftmost column often contains row headings.

To create a table, you select a slide layout that includes a content placeholder, and then click the placeholder's Insert Table button and specify the number of columns and rows. After you create the table's structure, you type text in the cells just as you would in a paragraph, using the TAB key to move the insertion point from cell to cell.

8.6.1.2 Formatting Tables

As shown in the following graphic, you can format cells, columns, rows, or the entire table. Using buttons on the Formatting toolbar or the specialized Tables and Borders toolbar, you can merge and split cells, add color and borders, and change text alignment.

8.6.1.3 Importing Excel Worksheets

PowerPoint's table capabilities are adequate for the display of simple information that is unlikely to change. However, if your data involves calculations or information that is likely to change, you will probably want to maintain it in an Excel worksheet.

You can embed a worksheet, or a table created in another program, as an object in a slide. As a result, the worksheet or table becomes part of the presentation and can be edited from within PowerPoint, as shown in the following graphic.

To insert work and graph, do the following:

1. Click insert tab
2. Click on Object
3. Select the object type
4. Select create from
5. Click on browse to navigate to the file you want to import.
6. Click Ok.

Figure 8.34 Insert Object Dialog Box

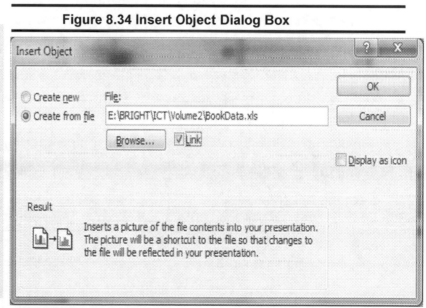

Figure 8.35 below is the result of the above process.

Figure 8.35 Excel Data and Graph imported into a Slide

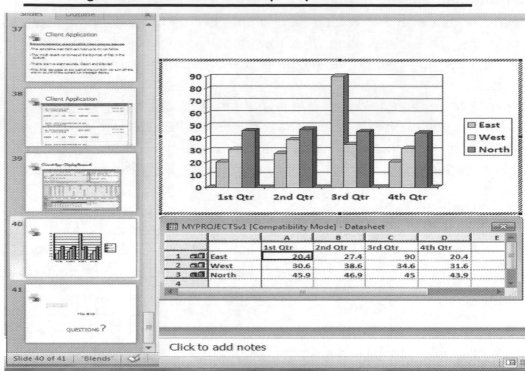

8.6.1.4 Inserting a Link in A Slide

Alternatively, you can link the slide to the source worksheet file so that you are not required to keep the data updated in more than one place. To insert a linked Excel chart or data source in PowerPoint 2010, do the following:

1. Open the Excel workbook that has the chart that you want.
   Notes:
   - The workbook must be saved before the chart data can be linked in the PowerPoint file.
   - If you move the Excel file to another folder, the link between the chart in the PowerPoint presentation and the data in the Excel spreadsheet breaks.

2. Select the chart.
3. On the **Home tab**, in the **Clipboard** group, click **Copy**.
4. Open the PowerPoint presentation that you want and select the slide that you want to insert the chart into.

5. On the **Home** tab, in the **Clipboard** group, click the arrow below **Paste**, and then do one of the following:

- If you want the chart to keep its look and appearance from the Excel file, select **Keep Source Formatting & Link Data** 🗐.

- If you want the chart to use the look and appearance of the PowerPoint presentation, select **Use Destination Theme & Link Data** 🗐

Tip: When you want to update the data in the PowerPoint file, select the chart, and then under Chart Tools, on the Design tab, in the Data group, click Refresh Data.

8.6.2 Inserting and Formatting a Chart

You can use charts to present numerical information visually when it is important for your audience to understand trends and patterns. To create a chart on a slide, you can use Microsoft Graph.

Creating Charts

You can create charts using Microsoft Graph in the following ways:

1. **Double-click** a chart placeholder on a slide
2. Click **the Insert Chart** button on the Standard toolbar
3. Click **Chart** on the Insert menu

Graph then displays a datasheet containing sample data that is plotted by default as a column chart, as shown in the following graphic.

Figure 8.36 Graph

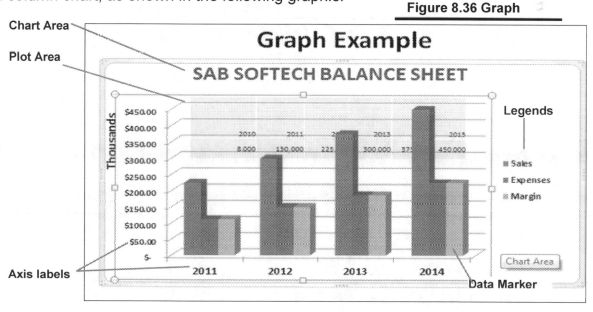

In a datasheet, each cell is identified by its column letter and row number, as in A1. To perform most tasks on the datasheet, you must first select a cell or a block of cells, called a range. To select cells, you can do the following:

1. To select a single cell, simply **click the cell**.
2. To select a range of cells, click the first cell, hold down the **SHIFT key**, and then click the **last cell**.
3. To select a row or column, click its **control box**.
4. To select the entire datasheet, click the **gray box** in the uppermost-left corner of the datasheet.

To enter data into the datasheet, you can do the following:

1. Type data into the datasheet
2. Import information from another program, such as Microsoft Excel
3. Copy and paste a specified range of data or a complete worksheet into the datasheet

As you enter data in the datasheet, the chart on the PowerPoint slide updates to reflect the new values.

Formatting Charts

After data is entered, you can change the chart's type to show the data in different ways. As shown in the following graphic, Graph offers 11 types of charts, each with several two-dimensional and three-dimensional sub-type variations.

After you select a chart type, you can format the elements of the chart to display the elements the way that you want them to appear. Some of these elements are shown in the following graphic.

Figure 8.37 Chart Types and Format

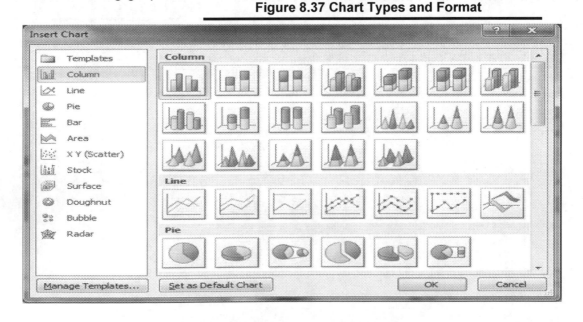

8.6.2 Inserting and Formatting an Organization Chart

An Organization chart is a diagram used to depict such information as hierarchies or processes. PowerPoint has diagramming tool that enables you to easily create organization charts, as well as cycle, radial, pyramid, Venn, and target diagrams.

8.6.2.1 Creating Organization Charts

An organization chart graphically represents the management structure of an organization, such as department managers and non-management employees within a company. By using a SmartArt graphic in Excel, Outlook, PowerPoint, or Word, you can create an organization chart and include it in your worksheet, e-mail message, presentation, or document. To create an organization chart quickly and easily, you can type or paste text in your organization chart and then have the text automatically positioned and arranged for you.

When you add an **assistant box** to an organization chart layout, such as Organization Chart, a bullet with a line attached indicates the assistant box in the Text pane.

You can use an organization chart to show the relationships among the elements of an organization—for example the relationship between a manager and her subordinates or between a parent company and its subsidiaries, as shown in the diagram below.

Figure 8.38 Organizational Chart for Executives

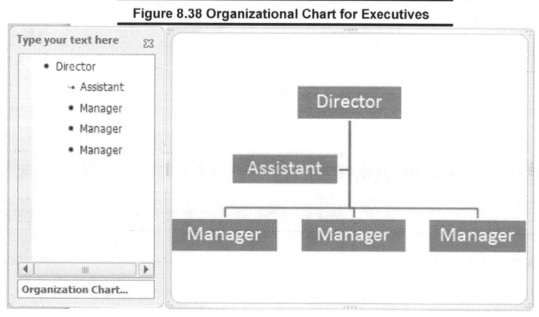

Although you can use other hierarchy layouts to create an organization chart, the assistant box and the hanging layouts are available only with organization chart layouts. To quickly add a designer-quality look and polish to your SmartArt graphic, you can change the colors of your organization chart or apply a SmartArt Style to your organization chart. In PowerPoint 2010 presentations, you can also animate your organization chart.

You can create an organization chart above by following the steps below:
Creating an organization chart

1. In your document, presentation, spreadsheet, or e-mail message, on the **Insert tab**, in the Illustrations group, click **SmartArt**.

Figure 8.39 Example of the Illustration group on the Insert tab in PowerPoint 2010.

---

2. In the Choose a **SmartArt Graphic gallery**, click Hierarchy, click an organization chart layout (such as Organization Chart), and then click OK.

3. To enter your text, do one of the following:
   - Click in a box in the SmartArt graphic, and then type your text.
     NOTE: For best results, use this option after you add all of the boxes that you want.
   - Click [Text] in the Text pane, and then type your text.
   - Copy text from another location or program, click [Text] in the Text pane, and then paste your text.
     NOTE: If the Text pane is not visible, click the control. You can rearrange boxes by dragging them.

8.6.2.2 Formatting Organization Charts

After creating an organization chart, you can double-click the chart to edit it at any time. When select the hierarchy by default, an organization chart appears in a traditional hierarchy, with one director at the top and subordinates below, but you can change the chart style by using tools such as the Smart tools, Design, Format under Smart Styles group, shown in the graphic below.

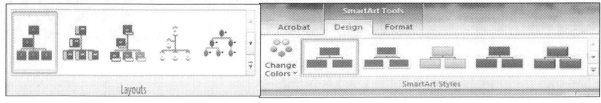

You can format the chart boxes and their connecting lines individually. You can also change the chart box color, shadow, border style, border color, or border line style by clicking buttons on the Drawing toolbar.

8.6.2.3 Create an organization chart with pictures

Create an organization chart with pictures
1. In your document, presentation, spreadsheet, or e-mail message, on the Insert tab, in the Illustrations group, *click SmartArt*.

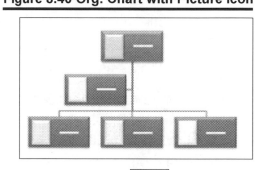

Figure 8.40 Org. Chart with Picture icon

2. In the Choose a *SmartArt Graphic* gallery, click Hierarchy, and then *double-click* Picture Organization Chart.

3. To add a picture, in the box where you want to add the picture, *click the picture icon*, locate the folder that contains the picture that you want to use, *click the picture file*, and then *click Insert*.

4. To enter your text, do one of the following:

A picture icon

- Click in a box in the **SmartArt graphic**, and then type your text.
  NOTE: For best results, use this option after you add all of the boxes that you want.
- Click **[Text]** in the Text pane, and then type your text.
- Copy text from another location or program, click **[Text]** in the Text pane, and then paste your text.
  NOTE: If the Text pane is not visible, click the control.

8.6.2.4 Add or delete boxes in your organization chart

To add a box to your organization chart follow the steps below:
1. Click the SmartArt graphic that you want to add a box to.
2. Click the existing box that is located closest to where you want to add the new box.
3. Under **SmartArt Tools**, on the **Design** tab, in the **Create Graphic** group, click the arrow under **Add Shape**, and then do one of the following:

Figure 8.41 Create Graphic Pane

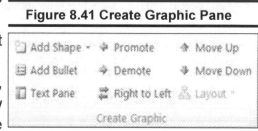

NOTE: If you do not see the **SmartArt Tools** or **Design** tabs, make sure that you have selected the SmartArt graphic. You may have to double-click the SmartArt graphic to select it and open the **Design** tab.

- To insert a box at the same level as the selected box but following it, click **Add Shape After**.
- To insert a box at the same level as the selected box but before it, click **Add Shape Before**.
- To insert a box one level above the selected box, click **Add Shape Above**.

The new box takes the position of the selected box, and the selected box and all the boxes directly below it are each demoted one level.

- To insert a box one level below the selected box, click Add Shape Below.
- To add an assistant box, click Add Assistant.

The assistant box is added above the other boxes at the same level in the **SmartArt graphic**, but it is displayed in the Text pane after the other boxes at the same level. Add Assistant is available only for organization chart layouts. It is not available for hierarchy layouts, such as Hierarchy.

8.6.2.5 Delete boxes in your organization chart

To delete a box, click the **border** of the box you want to delete, and then **press DELETE** key.

NOTES

- When you need to add a box to your relationship graphic, experiment with adding the shape before or after the selected shape to get the placement you want for the new shape.
- **To add a shape from the Text pane:**
  1. At the shape level, place your cursor at the end of the text where you want to add a new shape.
  2. Press **ENTER**, and then type the text that you want in your new shape.
  3. To add an assistant box, press **ENTER** while an assistant box is selected in the Text pane.
- Although you cannot automatically connect two top-level boxes with a line in the organization chart layouts, such as **Organization Chart**, you can imitate this look by adding a box to the top level to your SmartArt graphic and then drawing a line to connect the boxes.

- To move a box, click the box that you want to move and then drag the box to its new location. To move or "**nudge**" the box in very small increments, hold down CTRL while you press the arrow keys on your keyboard.

8.6.2.6 Change a solid line to a dotted line

To show a dotted-line reporting relationship between two boxes, change the style of the line between the two boxes.

1. Click the **SmartArt graphic** whose line you want to change.
2. **Right-click** the line, and then click Format Shape on the shortcut menu.
3. Click **Line Style**, and then select the **Dash** type that you want.

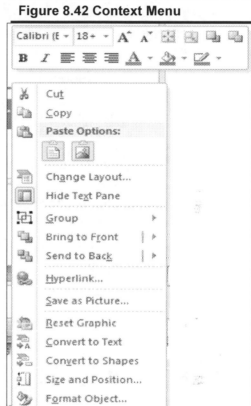

Figure 8.42 Context Menu

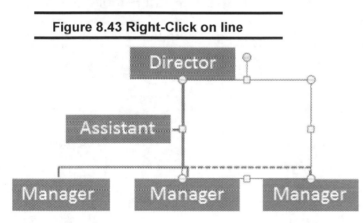

Figure 8.43 Right-Click on line

8.6.3 Change the hanging layout of your organization chart

A hanging layout affects the layout of all boxes below the selected box.

1. Click the box in the organization chart that you want to apply a hanging layout to.
2. Under SmartArt Tools, on the Design tab, in the Create Graphic group, click Layout, and then do one of the following:

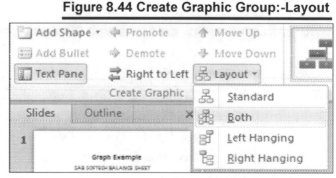

Figure 8.44 Create Graphic Group:-Layout

NOTE: If you do not see the **SmartArt Tools** or **Design** tabs, make sure that you have selected a SmartArt graphic. You may have to double-click the SmartArt graphic to select it and open the Design tab. *The SmartArt graphic is the designed chart.*

- To center all of the boxes below the selected box, click **Standard.**
- To center the selected box above the boxes below it and arrange the boxes below it horizontally with two boxes in each row, click **Both.**
- To arrange the selected box to the right of the boxes below it and left-align the boxes below it vertically, click **Left Hanging**.

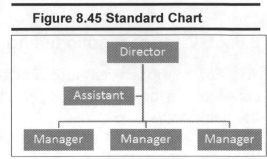

Figure 8.45 Standard Chart

- To arrange the selected box to the left of the boxes below it and right-align the boxes below it vertically, click **Right Hanging**.

Below are the results of clicking on Both, Left Hanging, and Right Hanging:

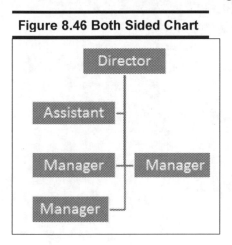

Figure 8.46 Both Sided Chart

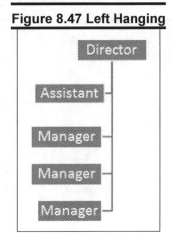

Figure 8.47 Left Hanging

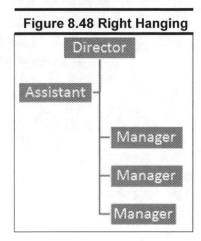

Figure 8.48 Right Hanging

8.6.4 Change the colors of your organization chart

You can apply color combinations that are derived from the theme colors to the boxes in your SmartArt graphic.

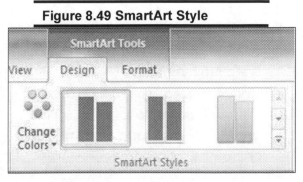

Figure 8.49 SmartArt Style

3. Click the **SmartArt graphic** whose color you want to change.
4. Under **SmartArt Tools**, on the **Design** tab, in the **SmartArt Styles** group, click Change Colors.

If you do not see the SmartArt Tools or Design tabs, make sure that you have selected a SmartArt graphic. You may have to double-click the SmartArt graphic to select it and open the Design tab.

5. Click the color combination that you want.

TIP: When you place your pointer over a thumbnail, you can see how the colors affect your SmartArt graphic.

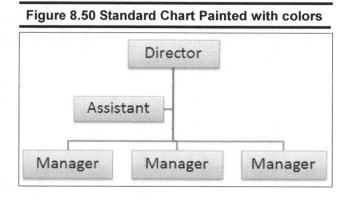

Figure 8.50 Standard Chart Painted with colors

8.6.4.1 Change the background color of a box in your organization chart

We want to change the background color of a box in our organization chart, so we need to follow the four steps below to achieve that purpose:

1. Right-click the border of a box, and then click **Format Shape** on the shortcut menu.
2. Click the **Fill** pane, and then click **Solid** fill.
3. Click **Color** ⬛▾ , and then click the color that you want.
4. To specify how much you can see through the background color, move the **Transparency** slider, or enter a number in the box next to the slider. You can vary the percentage of transparency from 0% (fully opaque, the default setting) to 100% (fully transparent).

8.7 Assignment and Exercises

Answer the following project questions by showing all the appropriate steps that should be followed to arrive at the answer for each question.

1. What is the purpose of PowerPoint Presentation?
   a. What is a good PowerPoint Presentation about?
   b. Why is it important to think about your audience when creating a PowerPoint presentation?

2. Itemize all the five options for creating a new presentation from a template.
    a. Describe the purpose of each of options.
    b. Explain the steps for creating a fresh presentation.

3. Why is it important to use Slide Masters in creating a PowerPoint presentation?
    a. What is the effect of modifying a slide master?

4. What do we call Color Schemes, Fonts, and Effects in PowerPoint?
    a. Briefly explain the steps for creating each of the above (color Schemes, Fonts, Effects).

5. Itemize three ways for opening a PowerPoint Presentation.
    a. For each of the three ways listed above explain the steps involved in opening a presentation in PowerPoint 2010.

6. You created a PowerPoint presentation and saved it in the name of C:\Bright\Townppt.ppt. You modified this presentation and wanted to save it in different location and name.
    Assuming the location and the name you want to save the presentation in are "C:\Lucy\" and Atobiase.ppt.
    Show the steps you will take to accomplish this objective.

7. You finished creating a PowerPoint Presentation, and you want to print the presentation with some notes. Demonstrate the steps to accomplish this objective.

8. What is PowerPoint Hyperlink?
    a. What is the process of implementing a Hyperlink in PowerPoint Presentation?

9. Briefly describe how to perform the following:
    a. Inserting a table in PowerPoint Presentation.
    b. Inserting a picture in PowerPoint Presentation.

10. What is the purpose of creating multimedia presentations?
    a. Name three basic ways multimedia can be created in PowerPoint.
    b. Describe each of these basic ways can be created in PowerPoint.

11. What are the steps for creating the standard Organization chart in PowerPoint presentation?

8.8 Exercises And Multiple Choice Questions

12. Which view should you select when you want to be able to easily rearrange the slides in a presentation?

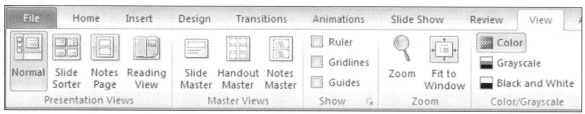

Select the one best answer.
- A. Normal.
- B. Notes Page.
- C. Show Slides and Record Timings.
- D. Slide Sorter.
- E. Slide Show.

13. Text that is entered in the Notes pane is displayed in which views?
Select all answers that apply.

- A. Normal And Notes Page.
- B. Show Slides And Record Timings.
- C. Slide Sorter.
- D. Slide Show.
- E. None of the above

14. The order of two bullet points on a slide needs to be reversed. Place the steps in the correct order to accomplish this task. Select all answers that apply.
Enter a number in each box below.
[   ] 1. Double-click the word Rules.
[   ] 2. Click the bulleted list to select its object.
[   ] 3. Hold down the left mouse button, and drag Rules below Overview

A. 2, 3, 1
B. 2, 1, 3
C. 1, 2, 3
D. 3, 2, 1

15. Match the labeled buttons with their actions.

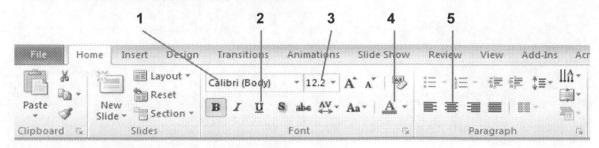

Enter a number in each box below.
[   ] Change the alignment of the text.
[   ] Change the color of the text.
[   ] Change the font of the text.
[   ] Change the size of the text.
[   ] Underline the text.

A. 5, 4, 1, 3, 2
B. 2, 4, 5, 3, 1
C. 1, 5, 3, 4, 2
D. 4, 1, 2, 5, 3

16. When you click Apply in the dialog box, the slide background changes to white, and the bullet text becomes invisible. How can you make the text visible again? Select all answers that apply.

A. Cut the text from the original slide, and paste the text onto a new slide.
B. Click the Undo button on the Standard toolbar.
C. Retype the text on a new slide.
D. Change the color of the bullet text.
E. Change the background to a color other than white.

17. Your company's financial information needs to be identified as confidential. Sequence the steps required to insert COPYRIGHT in the footnote section of every slide. Enter a number in each box below.
[   ] In the Master Layout group, click the Footer check box to insert a check mark.
[   ] Click outside the text box.
[   ] Click the Footer text box, and type COPYRIGHT
[   ] Click the View menu, and then click Slide Master.

A. 3, 2, 4, 1
B. 2, 3, 1, 4
C. 4, 1, 3, 2
D. 2, 4, 3, 1

18. To draw the shape shown in the graphic below, in what order must you perform the steps?   Enter a number in each box below.

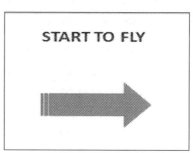

[   ] 1. Move the pointer over the slide.
[   ] 2. On the Drawing toolbar, click Shapes, click Block Arrows, and then click the arrow shape you want.
[   ] 3. Create a new title-only slide, and if necessary, display the Drawing toolbar.
[   ] 4. Hold down the mouse button, and drag to create an arrow the size you want.

    A. 3, 2, 4, 1
    B. 2, 3, 1, 4
    C. 3, 2, 1, 4
    D. 2, 4, 3, 1

19. Place the following steps in the order required to add an embedded Microsoft Excel worksheet to a PowerPoint slide.
Enter a number in each box below.
[   ] 1. Click Create from file.
[   ] 2. Click Browse, navigate to the folder where the worksheet file is stored, and click OK.
[   ] 3. Click the placeholder on the slide where you want to add the embedded worksheet.
[   ] 4. Click OK.
[   ] 5. Click the Insert menu, and then click Object.

    A. 5, 1, 3, 4, 2.
    B. 3, 5, 1, 2, 4
    C. 4, 1, 3, 5, 2.
    D. 1, 5, 4, 2, 3

20. Your PowerPoint presentation was packaged by using the Package for CD feature. When you test the package on a different computer, the PowerPoint Viewer shows the presentation. The most likely reason is that:
Select the one best answer.
    A. The presentation file is too big.
    B. PowerPoint is not installed on the computer.
    C. The embedded graphics are missing.
    D. The fonts used in the presentation are missing.

21. A presenter wants to make annotations on slides during a presentation. When annotations are added to a slide, which of the following statements are true?
Select all answers that apply.

   A. You can change the color of the pen tool only before the slide show starts.
   B. Comments made by using the pen tool are automatically saved with the slide when the presentation ends.
   C. You can erase one annotation or all annotations on a slide.
   D. You can change the shape of the pen tool at any time.
   E. When you move to the next slide, your annotations are erased.

22. A member of a review committee does not have PowerPoint available, and needs to review your presentation in Microsoft Word. What is the correct sequence of steps to export your presentation as a Word document?
Enter a number in each box below.
[　] 1. Click the File menu, click Send To, and then click Microsoft Office Word.
[　] 2. Open the presentation in PowerPoint.
[　] 3. Click OK.
[　] 4. Select the page layout.
[　] 5. In Word, review and save the document.

   A. 2, 1, 4, 3, 5
   B. 3, 4, 1, 5, 2
   C. 1, 5, 4, 3, 2
   D. 4, 2, 1, 5, 3

23. What will be the results of the selections made in the Print dialog box shown below? Select all answers that apply.
   A. All slides will be printed.
   B. Handouts will be printed for all slides.
   C. All slides will be framed.
   D. Each slide will be on a separate page.
   E. All slides will be printed in color.

24. What is the best type of hyperlink to create when you need comments about the slide show presentation to be sent to you? Select the one best answer.

   A. Link to Existing File or Web Page.
   B. Link to Place in This Document.
   C. Link to Create New Document.
   D. Link to E-mail Address.

SECTION III

DATA PROCESSING

SUMMARIZED OBJECTIVES:

In this lesson, we will learn how raw data is converted into useful information. We will explain the importance of computer in carrying out the various data processing activities. Discussion about hierarchy of data is also included in this lesson. The word "data" is the plural of datum which means fact, observation, assumption or occurrence. On the other hand, information can be defined as data that has been transformed into a meaningful and useful form for specific purposes.

Student will learn about Data processing which is the process through which facts and figures are collected, assigned meaning, communicated to other and retained for future use. Students will be able to differentiate between Data and Information. Thorough discussion of the Concept of Data Processing is covered. It will cover a series of actions or operations that converts data into useful information. In data processing system, we include the resources that are used to accomplish the processing of data. We will discuss the involvement of the arrangement of data items in a desired sequence. Students will be able to explain various data processing activities: Sorting, Comparison, Data Processing Life Cycle and Data Organization. This lesson explains data elements, records, files and databases and creation of Tables for Data Entry Generating Data Entry forms from a defined table. We will discuss Structured Query Language (SQL).

The Objectives

CHAPTER 9
Data Processing - Using Microsoft Access Database
9.0 Define Data Processing, Data and Information

9.1 Concepts of Data Processing
    9.1.1 Collection
    9.1.2 Conversion
    9.1.3 Manipulation
    9.1.4 Managing the Output Results
    9.1.5 Communications

9.2 The Data Processing Cycle
    9.2.1 Input
    9.2.2 Processing
    9.2.3 Output
    9.2.4 Storage

9.3 The Data Organization
    9.3.1 Data Item
    9.3.2 Field
    9.3.3 Record
    9.3.4 File
    9.3.5 Database

9.4 Variable and Fixed Length Records
    9.4.1 Fixed Length Records
    9.4.2 Variable Length Records

9.5 Logical Versus Physical Record

9.6 Lesson Summary

9.7 Creating Tables For Data Entry
    9.7.1 Creating Database in MS. Access
    9.7.2 Creating Table under a Database in MS. Access

9.8 Creating Data Entry Form

9.9 Structured Query Language.
    9.9.1 Sorting On Field Name.
    9.9.2 Filtering Data On Credit Field.

9.10 Assignment Questions and Quizzes

CHAPTER 9

Data Processing - Using Microsoft Access Database
The Objectives:

○ Define Data Processing: Data Processing, Data and Information
○ Define the Concept of Data Processing
○ Explain various data processing activities: Sorting, Comparison, etc.
○ Data Processing Life Cycle
○ Data Organization
○ Explain data elements, records, files and databases.
○ Creating Tables for Data Entry Generating Data Entry forms from a defined table
○ Structured Query Language (SQL)

9.0 Define Data Processing, Data and Information

Data processing *is a process used to enter data into a computer in order to summarize, analyze or convert it into other usable information.* It may involve recording, sorting, calculating and disseminating and storing data. The process may be automated and run on a computer. Because data is most useful when well-presented and actually informative, data-processing systems are often referred to as information systems. Data-processing systems typically manipulate raw data into information, and likewise information systems typically take raw data as input to produce information as output. The Data processing usually can be performed by using database management systems, such as Microsoft Access, SQL Server, Oracle, Dbase or FoxPro, Excel Spreadsheet.

Data Processing software refers to a class of programs that organize and manipulate data, usually large amounts of numeric data. Accounting programs are the typical examples of data processing applications. In contrast, word processors, which manipulate text rather than numbers, are not usually referred to as data processing applications. All software is divided into two general categories: data and programs. Programs are collections of instructions for manipulating data. Data can exist in a variety of forms -- as numbers or text on pieces of paper, as bits and bytes stored in electronic memory, or as facts stored in a person's mind.

Data: Strictly speaking, *data* is the plural of *datum*, a single piece of information. Data are representations of facts pertaining to people, things, ideas and events. Data are represented by symbols such as letters of the alphabets, numerals or other special symbols. In practice, however, people use data as both the singular and plural form of the word. The term data is often used to distinguish binary machine-readable information from textual human-readable information. For example, some applications make a distinction between data files (files that contain binary data) and text files (files that contain ASCII data).

In database management systems, data files are the files that store the database information, whereas other files, such as index files and data dictionaries, store administrative information, known as metadata.

Information: Information can be defined as *data that has been transformed into a meaningful and useful form for specific purposes*. In some cases data may not require any processing before constituting information. However, generally, data is not useful unless it is subjected to a process through which it is manipulated and organized, its contents analyzed and evaluated. Only then data becomes information.

There is no definite rule for determining when data becomes information. A set of letters and numbers may be meaningful to one person, but may have no meaning to another. Information is identified and defined by its users. For example, when you purchase something in a departmental store, a number of data items are put together, such as your name, address articles you bought, the number of items purchased, the price, the tax and the amount you paid. Separately, these are all data items but if you put these items together, they represent information about a business transaction.

Processing: A Process is an executing program. The term is used loosely as a synonym of task. Processing is performing some useful operations on data. Basically, data is nothing but unorganized facts and which can be converted into useful information. This process of converting facts to information is *Processing*.

Data Entry: The process of entering data into a computerized database or spreadsheet. Data entry can be performed by an individual typing at a keyboard or by a machine entering data electronically.

9.1 Concepts of Data Processing

Each organization, regardless of its size or purpose, generates data to keep a record of events and transactions that take place within the business. Generating and organizing this data in a useful way is called data processing. In this lesson, we shall discuss about various terms such as data, information, data processing and data processing system.

As discussed above, data processing consists of those activities which are necessary to transform data into information. Man has in course of time devised certain tools to help him in processing data. These include manual tools such as pencil and paper, mechanical tools such as filing cabinets, electromechanical tools such as adding machines and typewriters, and electronic tools such as calculators and computers. Many people immediately associate data processing with computers. As stated above, a computer is not the only tool used for data processing; it can also be done without computers. However, computers have outperformed people for certain tasks. There are some other task for which computer is a poor substitute for human skills and intelligence. Regardless to the type of equipment used, various functions and activities which need to be performed for data processing can be grouped under five basic categories: Collection, Conversion, Manipulation, Storage (Managing the Output Results) and Communication and Reproduction. The various activities under each of the five categories are summarized in Table 9-1

Table 9-1 Shows the Five Categories of Data Processing

Collection	Conversion	Manipulation	Storage	Communication
Originating	Coding	Sorting	Storing	Sharing or
Measuring	Classifying	Calculating	Retrieving	Distributing
Recording	Verifying	Summarizing		Reproduction
Comparing	Transforming	Comparing		

To describe each of the data processing activity let us take a look at employee weekly time sheet shown below which is the source of document for a payroll application.

Table 9-2 Shows Employee Time Sheet

Department 6 Employees Time Sheet for Week ending 22/08/2011							
HOURS WORKED							
Emp. No.	Name	Mon	Tues	Wed	Thurs	Fri	Total Hours
1049	Samuel	8	8	8	8	8	40
1120	Bright	8	8	8	6	8	38
1195	Lucy	8	8	5	6	8	35
1264	Ernest	8	6	8	8	5	35
1295	George	8	8	8	5	7	36
1298	Joe	8	5	8	5	8	34

9.1.1 Collection

Data Collection consists of originating, measuring, recording, and comparing. Data originates in the form of events transaction or some observations. This data is then recorded in some usable form. Data may be initially recorded on paper source documents in table 9-2 and then converted into a machine usable form for processing. Alternatively, they may be recorded by a direct input device in a paperless, machine-readable form. Data collection is also termed as data capture. The 6 or 8 hours is a measure of day's work, and differentiating one day from another is done by comparison.

9.1.2 Conversion

As described above data conversion consists of Coding, Classifying, Verifying, and Transforming. Once the data is collected, it is converted from its source documents to a form that is more suitable for processing. The data is first codified by assigning identification codes. A code consists of numbers, letters, special characters, or a combination of these. For example, an employee may be allotted a code as 1029, his category as **A**-class, etc. It is useful to codify data, when data requires classification. To classify means to categorize, i.e., data with similar characteristics are placed in similar categories or groups. For example, one may like to arrange accounts data according to account number or date. Hence a balance sheet can easily be prepared. After classification of data, it is verified or checked to ensure the accuracy before processing starts.

After verification, the data is transcribed from one data medium to another. For example, in case data processing is done using a computer, the data may be transformed from source documents to machine sensible form using magnetic tape or a disk.

9.1.3 Manipulation

Once data is collected and converted, it is ready for the manipulation function which converts data into information. Manipulation consists of the following activities:

a. Sorting	c. Summarizing
b. Calculation	d. Comparison

(a)Sorting

It involves the arrangement of data items in a desired sequence. Usually, it is easier to work with data if it is arranged in a logical sequence. Most often, the data are arranged in alphabetical sequence. Sometimes sorting itself will transform data into information. For example, a simple act of sorting the names in alphabetical order gives meaning to a telephone directory. The directory will be practically worthless without sorting. Business data processing extensively utilizes sorting technique. Virtually all the records in business files are maintained in some logical sequence. Numeric sorting is common in computer-based processing systems because it is usually faster than alphabetical sorting.

(b)Calculating

Arithmetic manipulation of data is called calculating. Items of recorded data can be added to one another, subtracted, divided or multiplied to create new data

Calculation is an integral part of data processing. For example, in calculating an employee's pay, the hours worked multiplied by the hourly wage rate gives the gross pay as shown in Table 9-3 below. Based on the total earning, income-tax deductions are computed and subtracted from gross-pay to arrive at net pay.

Table 9-3 Shows Employee Weekly Payroll Summary Report

Weekly Payroll Summary Report 26/08/2011				
Emp. No.	Name	Hours Worked	Pay Rate	Gross Wages
1049	Samuel	40	15.50	620.00
1120	Bright	38	20.50	779.00
1195	Lucy	35	18.00	630.00
1264	Ernest	35	15.75	551.25
1295	George	36	12.50	450.00
1298	Joe	34	15.00	510.00

(c)Summarizing

To summarize data is to condense or reduce masses of data to a more usable and concise form as shown in Table 9-4 For example, you may summarize a lecture attended in a class by writing small notes in one or two pages.

When the data involved are numbers, you may summarize by counting or accumulating the totals of the data in a classification or by selecting strategic data from the mass of data being processed. For example, the summarizing activity may provide a general manager with sales-totals by major product line, the sales manager with sales totals by individual salesman as well as by the product line and a salesman with sales data by customer as well as by product line.

Table 9-4 Payroll Summary for Week of 22-08-2011

Name	Hours Worked	Gross Wages
Samuel	40	620.00
Bright	38	779.00
Lucy	35	630.00
Ernest	35	551.00
George	36	450.00
Joe	34	510.00

(d)Comparing

To compare data is to perform an evaluation in relation to some known measure. For example, business managers compare data to discover how well their companies are doing. They may compare current sales figures with those for last year to analyze the performance of the company in the current month. A computer also possesses the ability to perform logic operations. For example, if we compare two items represented by the symbols A and B, there are only three possible outcomes:

A is less than **B** (A< B);   **A** is equal to **B** (A=B): or
A is greater than **B** (A > B).   **A** is different from **B** (A<>B):

There is a fourth outcome different from ("**<>**") which is the combination of less than "<" and greater than ">"

A computer can perform such comparisons and, depending on the result, follow a predetermined path to complete its work. This ability to compare is an important property of computers.

9.1.4 Managing the Output Results

Once data has been captured and manipulated the storing and retrieving activities may be carried out:

(a)Storing

To store is to hold data for continued or later use. Storage is essential for any organized method of processing and re-using data. The storage mechanisms for data processing systems are file cabinets in a manual system, and electronic devices such as magnetic disks/magnetic tapes in case of computer based system. The storing activity involves storing data and information in organized manner in order to facilitate the retrieval activity. Of course, data should be stored only if the value of having them in future exceeds the storage cost.

(b)Retrieving

To retrieve means to recover or find again the stored data or information.
Retrieval techniques use data storage devices. Thus data whether in file cabinets or in computers can be recalled for further processing. Retrieval and comparison of old data gives meaning to current information.

9.1.5 Communication

Communication is the process of sharing information. Unless the information is made available to the users who need it, it is worthless. Thus, communication involves the transfer of data and information produced by the data processing system to the prospective users of such information or to another data processing system. As a result, reports and documents are prepared and delivered to the users. In electronic data processing, results are communicated through display units or terminals.

Another way of data communication is data ***Reproduction***. To reproduce is to copy or duplicate data or information. This reproduction activity may be done by hand or by machine.

9.2 The Data Processing Cycle

The data processing activities described above are common to all data processing systems from manual to electronic systems. These activities can be grouped in four functional categories, viz., data input, data processing, data output and storage, constituting what is known as a data processing cycle.

The Data Processing Cycle is a perfect example of Information processing cycle which was discussed in *volume 1, page 10* of this series. It follows I-P-O (Input-Process-Output) method of processing data.

9.2.1 Input

The term input refers to the activities required to record data and to make it available for processing. The input can also include the steps necessary to check, verify and validate data contents. Input can also be described as the collection of raw data from the outside world meant to put into an information system. In computing input devices may include keyboards, mouse, flatbed scanners, bar code readers, joysticks, digital data tablets, electronic cash registers, modems, and microphones.

Figure 9-1 Data Processing Cycle

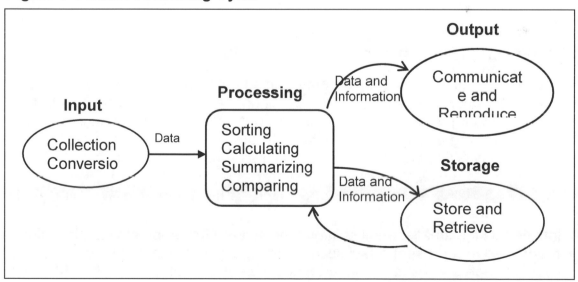

9.2.2 Processing

The term processing denotes the actual data manipulation techniques such as classifying, sorting, calculating, summarizing, comparing, etc. that convert data into information. All these are performed by the central processing unit of a computer system and other integrated circuits in the computer in collaboration with software packages installed in computers which are the ultimate instructors for any processing that may occur in the computer.

9.2.3 Output

It is a communication function which transmits the information, generated after processing of data, to persons who need the information. Sometimes output also includes decoding activity which converts the electronically generated information into human-readable form. The payroll summary in Table 9-4 is an example of output information from the payroll data. Examples of output devices are computer monitors, printers, LCD projectors, speakers, etc.

9.2.4 Storage

It involves the filing of data and information for future use. The above mentioned four basic functions are performed in a logical sequence as shown in Fig. 9-1 in all data processing systems. The information is stored in bytes (8-bits) in storage devices such hard disk drives, floppy drives, CD-ROM, DVD, or pen drives. Each of these devices has volume capacities that may range from kilobytes, megabytes, gigabytes, terabytes, to petabytes and more. For further reading refer to volume 1, chapter 2 under storage devices.

9.3 The Data Organization

So far we have discussed the concept of data processing, data processing cycle and the components of a computer. We will now focus attention on how data is organized before processing in a computer. Data can be arranged in a variety of ways however organizing data in a hierarchical way is generally the best way to go. Data can classified as data items, fields, records, files, or databases.

9.3.1 Data Item

A data item is the smallest unit of information stored in computer file. It is a single element used to represent a fact such as an employee's name, item price, etc. In the payroll application shown in table 9-3 above, the employee number **1049** is a data item and the name **Samuel** is a data item. In other words, each field value or a column value in a table is a data item.

9.3.2 Field

Data items are physically arranged as fields in a computer file. A field may have three distinct properties: data-type, and length.

a. Data-type

The data-type is the description of the data item. The basic data types can be classified into four categories:

1. Number: Number, auto-number, currency, etc.
2. String: Text, Characters
3. Date/Time: Date and Time
4. Boolean: Yes/No or True/False

All data item in a field can be described under any one of the four categories.

b. Length

The number of character space required to store a data item. The field length can be fixed or variable. For example in table 9-3 all individuals in the payroll application have 4-digit employee numbers, 4-digit field is required to store the particular data item. Hence, it is a fixed field.

In contrast, since customer's name varies considerably from one customer to another, a variable amount of space must be available to store this element. This can be called as variable field.

9.3.3 Record

A record is a collection of related data items or fields. Each record normally corresponds to a specific unit of information. When information is arranged in tabular form, the information contained in a row is considered a record. For example, various fields in the record, illustrated in figure 9-2 are employee number, employee's name, hours worked, pay rate and gross wages. This is the data used to produce the payroll register report. The first record contains all the data concerning the employee **Samuel**. The second record contains all the data concerning the employee **Bright**. Each subsequent record contains all the data for a given employee.

Figure 9-2
Table showing
Fields and Records

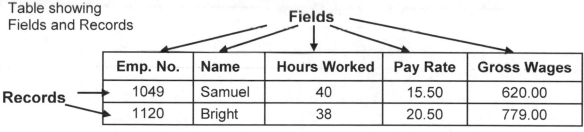

Emp. No.	Name	Hours Worked	Pay Rate	Gross Wages
1049	Samuel	40	15.50	620.00
1120	Bright	38	20.50	779.00

9.3.4 File

The collection of records is called a file. A file contains all the related records for an application. Therefore, the payroll file shown in Table.9-4 contains all records required to produce the payroll register report. Files are stored on some medium, such as floppy disk, magnetic tape or magnetic disk. The size of file is measured in bytes.

9.3.5 Database

The collection of related files is called a database. A database contains all the related files for a particular application. Typical database in modern times is relational in which one or several tables or files are regrouped under a database.

9.4 Variable and Fixed Length Records

As a field length can be fixed or variable, the same applies to records. Records can be of fixed or variable length. Figure 9-3 is an illustration that depicts a File with Fixed Length Records and Variable Length.

Figure 9-3 Fixed and variable length records

File with Fixed length Records

Record #1	Record #2	Record #3	Record #4
120 bytes	120 bytes	120 bytes	120 bytes

← ——————————— **480 bytes** ——————————— →

File with Variable Length Records

Record #1	Record #2	Record #3	Record #4
120 bytes	108 bytes	160 bytes	172 bytes

← ——————————— **560 bytes** ——————————— →

9.4.1 Fixed Length Records

In this case, all the records in a file have the same number of bytes. Such a file is called a flat file. If all the records are expected to contain essentially the same quantity of data, then fixed length records are used. It follows therefore in this case that all the fields in a record have fixed length.

9.4.2 Variable Length Records

In this case, records vary in length. Use of variable length records conserves storage space when the quantity of information, of various records in a file, differs significantly. The records are therefore composed of field of variable length.

9.5 Logical Versus Physical Record

A logical record contains all the data related to a single entity. It may be a payroll record for an employee or a record of grades secured by a student in a particular examination. A physical record refers to a record whose data fields are stored physically next to one another. It is also the amount of data that is treated as a single unit by the input-output device. Portions of the same logical record may be located in different physical records or several logical records may be located in one physical record. For example, in case of magnetic tape and number of logical records are stored in the form of a block to increase the data transfer speed and this block is referred to as a physical record.

9.6 Lesson Summary

In this lesson, we have learnt how raw data is converted into useful information. The importance of computer in carrying out the various data processing activities has been explained. Discussion about hierarchy of data is also included in this lesson.

1. (a) The word "data" is the plural of datum which means fact, observation, assumption or occurrence. On the other hand, information can be defined as data that has been transformed into a meaningful and useful form for specific purposes.

(b) Data processing is the process through which facts and figures are collected, assigned meaning, communicated to other and retained for future use. It is a series of actions or operations that converts data into useful information. In data processing system, we include the resources that used to accomplish the processing of data.

2. (a) It involves the arrangement of data items in a desired sequence.
(b) It means to condense or reduce masses of data to a more usable and concise form.

9.7 Creating Tables For Data Entry

Have discussed the concept behind data processing, we will now discuss the application of these concepts in data processing. We now proceed by using a relational database such as Microsoft (Ms.) Access Database Management System. As had been discussed under data organization, Ms Access will permit the creation of a database which regroups all the related tables or data files. For instance to efficiently process students records, you will probably need at least four different data files or tables such as student profile, courses, activities and grades. Each of these tables will be composed of various fields.

Another powerful feature in Ms. Access is that based on the fields in a table, it can generate a data entry form so data can be entered into the table.

9.7.1 Creating Database in MS. Access

Creating a table begins with creating a database and naming it in MS Access.

Figure 9-4 Dialog for Creating A Database (Donation.accdb) In MS Access

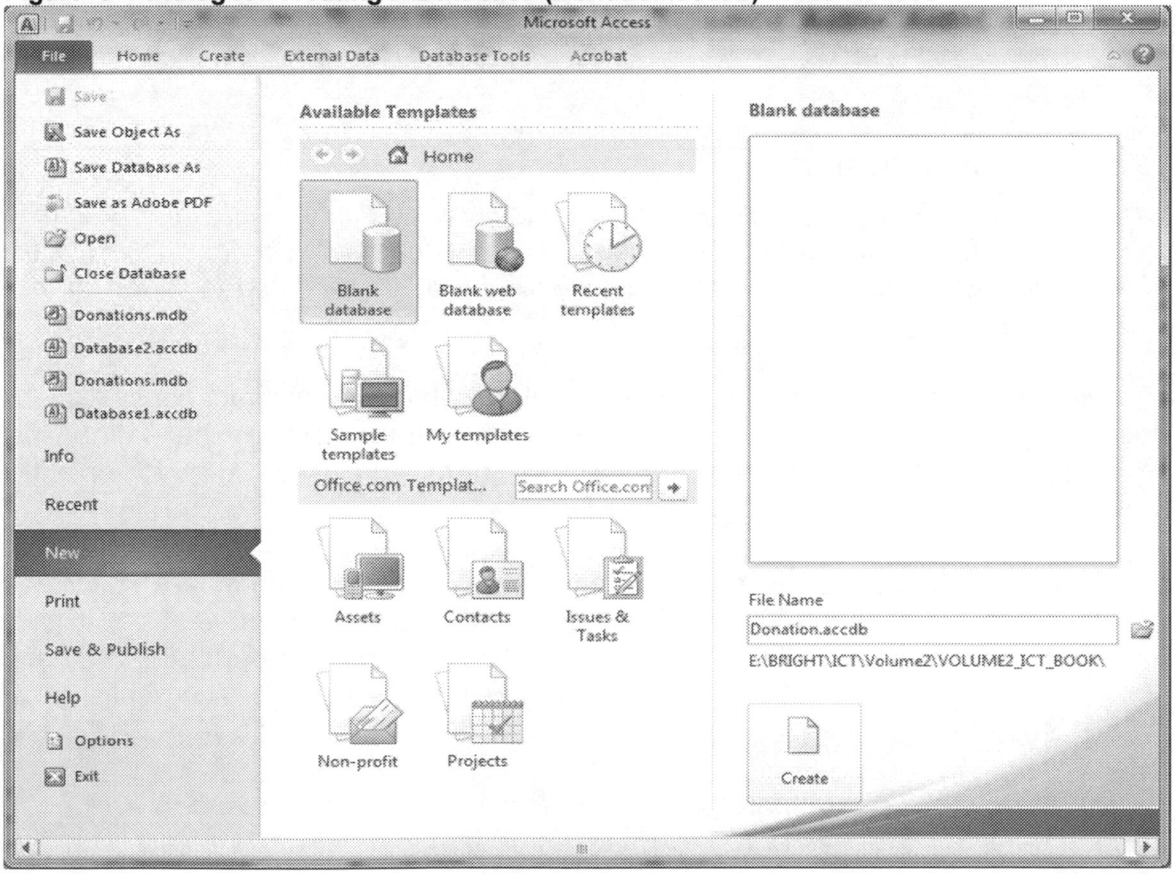

1.   Run MS Access Application and Click on File
2.   Click on New >> Blank database >> Enter the Database Name
3.   Click on Create

Figure 9-5 Dialog for Inserting the Database name In MS Access

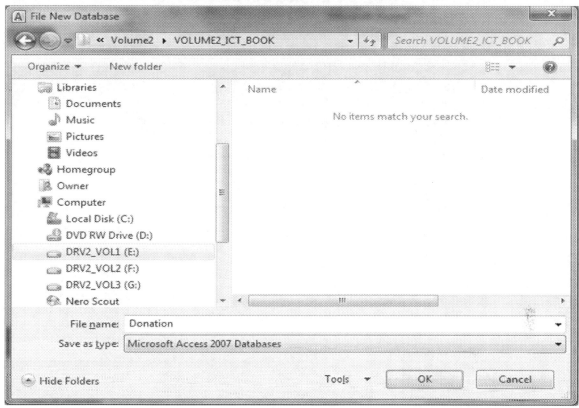

1. Under File name type the Database file name.
2. Navigate to the folder where you want to save the database file
   In this example the file path is **E:\Bright\ICT\Volume2\Volume2_ICT_Book**
3. Click on Save as type and select the file type:
   a. Microsoft Access 2007 Databases
   b. Microsoft Access Databases (2002-2003 format)
   c. Microsoft Access Databases (2000 format)
   d. Microsoft Access Project
4. Click Ok.

Also the table below shows the file extension matching the type of Access file.

Table 9-5 Description of File Types in MS Access Database

No	File Extension	Description
1	*.accdb	Microsoft Access 2007 Databases
2	*.mdb	Microsoft Access Databases (2002-2003 format)
3	*.mdb	Microsoft Access Databases (2000 format)
4	*.adp	Microsoft Access Project

9.7.2 Creating Table under a Database in MS. Access

The table named Donations is defined by the field names and data types.

Figure 9-6 Dialog for Creating Table (Donations) in Donation Database in MS Access

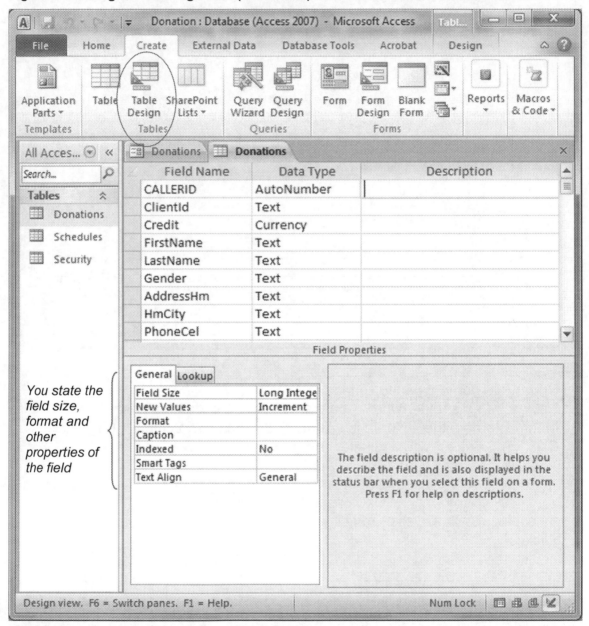

1. Click Create tab >> Table Design
2. Add Field >> Select Data type

As shown in the figure 9-6 the "Donations" table displays the Field names and the Data type.

After entering the field name and the data type the next thing to do is to set the field properties.

1. Click on the field name in figure 9-7. In this example "**FirstName**" field was selected
2. And set the field properties in figure 9-8.
   a. Field Size is 30 (by default is 255)
   b. Allow Zero Length is Yes
   c. Etc.

Figure 9-7 Field Names & Data Type   **Figure 9-8 Field Properties**

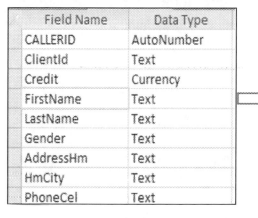

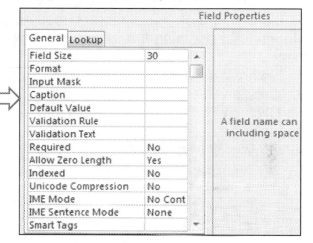

In summary the table 9-6 below shows the summary of the Donation table comprising the Field Name, Data Type, and Field Size.

Table 9-6 The Summary of Donations table Specifications

No	Field Name	Data Type	Field Size
1	CallerId	AutoNumber	Integer
2	ClientId	Text	10
3	Credit	Currency	2 Decimals Pts
4	FirstName	Text	30
5	LastName	Text	35
6	Gender	Text	6
7	AddressHm	Text	50
8	HmCity	Text	50
9	PhoneCel	Text	15

LOOKUP

While surfing the web, you have probably used a site, such as an airline, where you were required to type data into fields. Some of those fields, such as the State field, may have had a down-arrow as part of the field. When you clicked the down-arrow, a list appeared. This is an example of a lookup. A lookup is a data entry timesaver, an input mechanism to streamline data entry, and a data input watchdog. A lookup (a text box, combo box, or list box) provides limited choices to the individual who is entering data into a table or a form. A lookup prevents misspellings and data entry errors.

9.8 Creating Data Entry Form

Having discussed how to create database and related tables, we will now take a look at creating a data entry form based on the defined tables. Data entry form is a window that contains labels and input fields matching the fields in tables that facilitates the user's data entry.

1. Select the table
2. Click on Create
3. Click on Form to generate the form as shown in figure 9-9.

Figure 9-9 Donations Entry Form

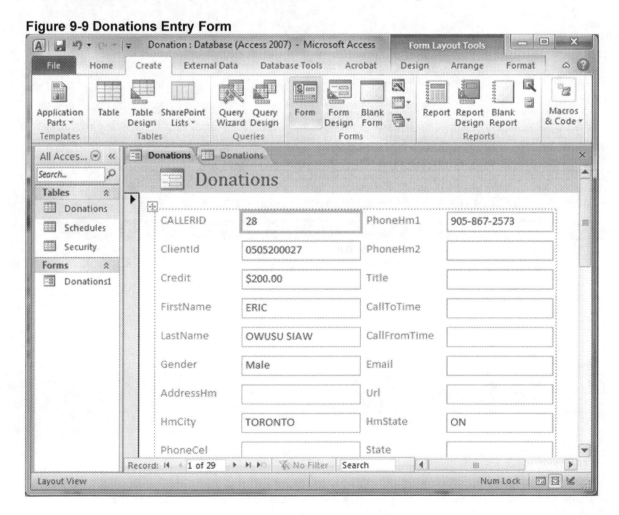

The form illustrated above is composed of fields that constitute an input of a record at a time. The field labeled "CALLERID" is autonumber data field which implies that the input into this field is automatically computed. The record shows this autonumber to be "28" in the above figure 9-9.

The list of records are shown in tabular form below. The list is sorted on "Credit" in descendant order.

Figure 9-10 Sort & Filter Group

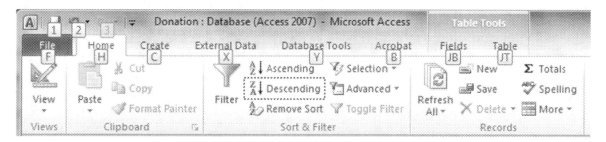

1. Select the field to be sorted
2. Click Z-A Descending in Sort & Filter group

Figure 9-11 The List of Records Sorted on Credit Field in Descending Order

CALLERID	ClientId	Credit	FirstName	LastName	Gender	AddressHm	HmCity
28	0505200027	$200.00	ERIC	OWUSU SIAW	Male		TORONTO
45	0506160011	$100.00	RICKEY	LEWIS	Male		DALLAS
23	0505190022	$100.00	JOHN	ODURO ASANTE	Male	MARYLAND	MARYLAND
36	0506160006	$100.00	AKWASI	SARFO	Male		BRONX
12	0505190011	$60.00	PETER	OWUSUH AMOAKO	Male	1869 MORRIS AV	BRONX
42	0506160008	$50.00	ERIC	OWUSU SIAW	Male		TORONTO
15	0505190014	$50.00	ROSE	ANTWI-MENSAH	Female	2544 VALENTINE AVE	BRONX
43	0506160009	$50.00	KOJO	NKANSAH	Male		DALLAS
44	0506160010	$50.00	MICHAEL	BOLSTIC	Male		DALLAS
19	0505190018	$50.00	CHRISTIANA	BOAKYE	Female	3525 DECATUR AVE	BRONX
16	0505190015	$50.00	AUGUSTINA	ANTWI GYAMBRA		1305 SHERIDAN AVE	BRONX
22	0505190021	$50.00	MARY	OWUSU ASANTE	Female	249 KINGSBRIDGE RD	BRONX
13	0505190012	$50.00	PETER	ABOAGYE	Male	1869 MORRIS AV	BRONX
14	0505190013	$50.00	MAXWEL	OSEI AMOAKO		1869 MORRIS AV	BRONX
20	0505190019	$50.00	LOVE	YEBOAH	Female	85 MACCULAN AVE	BRONX
35	0506160005		RITTA	ADDAE	Female		MONTREAL

9.9 Structured Query Language.

Once the data is entered into the database you can now manipulate them to present the desired information.

A query is essentially a question. An example might be: Which of our customers are located in Dallas? A query locates information that you can view, change, or analyze in various ways. Running a query displays the required information. There are two types of views associated with a query.

9.9.1 Types of Queries

Queries must be structured in a specific way to achieve the desired result. Each type of question has a corresponding type of query. Basically there two categories or types of queries which are listed below:

a. Primary query types
b. Secondary query types

1. Primary query types:

i. **Select:** Retrieves data from one or more tables and displays the results in a datasheet where you can update the records (with some restrictions). You can use this query to group records and calculate sums, counts, averages, and other types of totals.

ii. **Crosstab:** Use this query to calculate and restructure data for easier analysis. Crosstab queries calculate the sum, average, count, or other types of total for data that is grouped by two types of information — one down the left side of the datasheet and another across the top.

iii.**Parameter:** A parameter query displays a dialog box prompting you for information, such as the criteria for retrieving records or a value you want to insert in a field. You can design the query to prompt you for specific information. For example, you can design it to prompt you for two dates. Access will then retrieve all records falling between those two dates.

2. Secondary query types:

i. **Action:** An action query changes or moves records in just one operation. There are four types of action queries: Delete, Update, Append, and Make-Table.

ii. **AutoLookup:** A multi-table query that automatically looks up and fills in information related to a specified value. When you enter a query in AutoLookup join field, or in a form, report, or data access page based on the query, Microsoft Access looks up and fills in existing information related to that value. A join is an association between a field in one table or query and a field of the same data type in another table or query.

Joins tell the program how data is related. Records that don't match may be included or excluded, depending on the type of join. A data access page is an Access-published web page that has a connection to a database. From this page you can view, add to, edit, and manipulate the data stored in the database.

iii. **SQL (Structured Query Language):** A query you create by using an SQL statement

This manipulation may be achieved through a process known as the Structured Query Language or SQL. In the above list I just followed a manual process by selecting the field to be sorted, and clicking Z-A Descending in Sort & Filter group. All these steps create a SQL script as follows:

SELECT * ORDER BY Credit DESC   (The * implies all the fields)
The above is equivalent to the statement below:

SELECT Callerld, Clientld, Credit, FirstName, LastName, Gender, AddressHm, HmCity ORDER BY Credit DESC

9.9.1 Sorting On FirstName Field.
We will begin by manually sort the FirstName field in ascending order.
1. Select the field to be sorted (FirstName field)
2. Click A-Z Ascending in Sort & Filter group
3. You will get the list below:

Figure 9-12 The List of Records Sorted on FirstName Field in Ascending Order

CALLERID	Clientid	Credit	FirstName	LastName	Gender	AddressHm	HmCity
36	0506160006	$100.00	AKWASI	SARFO	Male		BRONX
16	0505190015	$50.00	AUGUSTINA	ANTWI GYAMBRA		1305 SHERIDAN AVE	BRONX
19	0505190018	$50.00	CHRISTIANA	BOAKYE	Female	3525 DECATUR AVE	BRONX
28	0505200027	$200.00	ERIC	OWUSU SIAW	Male		TORONTO
42	0506160008	$50.00	ERIC	OWUSU SIAW	Male		TORONTO
23	0505190022	$100.00	JOHN	ODURO ASANTE	Male	MARYLAND	MARYLAND
43	0506160009	$50.00	KOJO	NKANSAH	Male		DALLAS
20	0505190019	$50.00	LOVE	YEBOAH	Female	85 MACCULAN AVE	BRONX
22	0505190021	$50.00	MARY	OWUSU ASANTE	Female	249 KINGSBRIDGE RD	BRONX
14	0505190013	$50.00	MAXWEL	OSEI AMOAKO		1869 MORRIS AV	BRONX
44	0506160010	$50.00	MICHAEL	BOLSTIC	Male		DALLAS
12	0505190011	$60.00	PETER	OWUSUH AMOAKO	Male	1869 MORRIS AV	BRONX
13	0505190012	$50.00	PETER	ABOAGYE	Male	1869 MORRIS AV	BRONX
45	0506160011	$100.00	RICKEY	LEWIS	Male		DALLAS
15	0505190014	$50.00	ROSE	ANTWI-MENSAH	Female	2544 VALENTINE AVE	BRONX

The SQL script will as follows:
SELECT * ORDER BY FirstName ASC   (The * implies all the fields). Or

SELECT CallerId, ClientId, Credit, FirstName, LastName, Gender, AddressHm, HmCity ORDER BY FirstName ASC

9.9.2 Filtering Data On Credit Field.

Filter is the process of searching particular data using a certain condition or criteria. For example let's search for all those who donated $50.00.

Manual process:
1. Select Credit filed
2. A-Z Ascending
3. Click on Filter
4. Check $50.00
5. Click Ok

Figure 9-13 Filter on Credit Field = "$50.00"

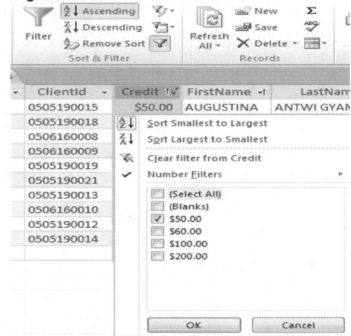

1. SQL Script:
SELECT * WHERE
Credit ="50.00" ORDER BY
FirstName ASC

2. SQL Script:
SELECT * WHERE
Credit >="100.00" ORDER BY
Credit DESC

Figure 9-14 Result of SQL #1 or Filter on Credit Field = "$50.00

CALLERID	ClientId	Credit	FirstName	LastName	Gender	AddressHm	HmCity
16	0505190015	$50.00	AUGUSTINA	ANTWI GYAMBRA		1305 SHERIDAN AVE	BRONX
19	0505190018	$50.00	CHRISTIANA	BOAKYE	Female	3525 DECATUR AVE	BRONX
42	0506160008	$50.00	ERIC	OWUSU SIAW	Male		TORONTO
43	0506160009	$50.00	KOJO	NKANSAH	Male		DALLAS
20	0505190019	$50.00	LOVE	YEBOAH	Female	85 MACCULAN AVE	BRONX
22	0505190021	$50.00	MARY	OWUSU ASANTE	Female	249 KINGSBRIDGE RD	BRONX
14	0505190013	$50.00	MAXWEL	OSEI AMOAKO		1869 MORRIS AV	BRONX
44	0506160010	$50.00	MICHAEL	BOLSTIC	Male		DALLAS
13	0505190012	$50.00	PETER	ABOAGYE	Male	1869 MORRIS AV	BRONX
15	0505190014	$50.00	ROSE	ANTWI-MENSAH	Female	2544 VALENTINE AVE	BRONX

Figure 9-15 Result of SQL #2 or Filter on Credit Field >= "$100.00

CALLERID	ClientId	Credit	FirstName	LastName	Gender	AddressHm	HmCity
28	0505200027	$200.00	ERIC	OWUSU SIAW	Male		TORONTO
45	0506160011	$100.00	RICKEY	LEWIS	Male		DALLAS
23	0505190022	$100.00	JOHN	ODURO ASANTE	Male	MARYLAND	MARYLAND
36	0506160006	$100.00	AKWASI	SARFO	Male		BRONX

9.10 Assignment Questions

Answer the following project questions by showing all the appropriate steps that should be followed to arrive at the answer for each question.

1. Define the following terms:
   a. Data Processing
   b. Data
   c. Information

2. Differentiate between the following :
   a. Data and Information
   b. Data processing and Data processing system

3. Define the following terms briefly:
   a. Sorting
   b. Summarizing

4. Identify various data processing activities.
5. Define the various steps of data processing cycles
6. Describe what you have learnt from this chapter?

7. Identify various activities involved in manipulation.
8. Write down the various computer processing operations briefly.
9. How data is organized before processing on a computer starts? Discuss briefly.
10. Data processing activities are grouped under how many basic categories?
    a. Name these basic categories.
    b. Briefly explain each category.

11. How many steps are involved in data processing cycle?
    a. Name these steps
    b. Briefly describe each step.

12. Define the following terms
    a. Data Field
    b. Data Type
    c. Field Properties
    d. Field size

13. Briefly describe the following processes
    a. How to create Access Database.
    b. How to create Access Table
    c. How to create Access Data Entry Form

14. Under which condition should you select "**Yes**" for "**Allow Zero Length**" under field property?

15. Demonstrate how to sort data in ascending order.

16. A project assignment:

    We want to model a data processing program for students' records in Opoku Ware School. The student database should comprise at least four different data files or tables such as student profile, courses, activities and student grades. The student profiles must comprise the student number, name, address, cell phone, Credit hours accumulated and GPA. The courses will cover course number, course title, course description, and pre-requisite. Activities constitute student number, course number, grade level, and semesters. Student grade is composed of course number, grade percentage, grade letter equivalent, and grade points.

    a. Create the database and call it StudentRecords.
    b. Define the summary characteristics of each of the tables.
    c. Base on (b) create each data table with the appropriate fields and field sizes.
    d. Identify the key fields and designate primary key and foreign.
    e. Define the link between any related data tables.
    f. Generate the data entry forms for the related data tables.
    g. Produce a report view that will constitute student's transcript. (Students Number, Name, Address, Semester, all courses the student had taken, grade points for each course and GPA.

9.11 Multiple Choice Questions

17. Which of the following buttons indicate Design view?
    Select the one best answer.

    A   B   C   D   E

18. In Access, each new field created must be assigned a data type. Match the data types for each of the 5 fields indicated below.
    Enter a number in each box below arranging from top to bottom.

    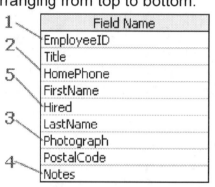

    [ ] OLE Object.
    [ ] Memo.
    [ ] Autonumber.
    [ ] Date/Time.
    [ ] Text.
    A. 1, 3, 5, 4, 2
    B. 3, 4, 1, 5, 2
    C. 5, 1, 3, 2, 4
    D. 2, 5, 4, 1, 3
    E. 3, 4, 1, 2, 5

19. You have the Atobiase Donation's Contacts database open and you need to add a new contact by using the Contacts form. Select the correct sequence of steps to achieve this. Enter a number in each box below.

    [5] 1. In the form, enter text in the box for the new contact.
    [3] 2. On the Database window toolbar, click Open.
    [1] 3. In the Database window, click Forms.
    [4] 4. On the form toolbar, click the New Record button.
    [2] 5. Under Forms, click Contacts.

    A. 1, 2, 5, 4, 3
    B. 3, 4, 1, 5, 2
    C. 5, 1, 4, 2, 3
    D. 3, 5, 2, 4, 1
    E. 3, 1, 4, 2, 5

20. Importing fixed-width text and delimited text by using the Import Text Wizard follow almost the same sequence. From the following steps, identify the step that occurs only when importing fixed-width text. Select the one best answer.

    A. Import as a new table or into an existing table.
    B. Specify field options.
    C. Choose between delimiter characters or fixed-width fields.
    D. Adjust the field breaks.
    E. Let Access add primary key.

21. What result would you expect the query statement below?
    SELECT * WHERE EmpId Like '%02%' ORDER BY LastName ASC
    Select the one best answer.
    A. List of EmpId 02 in ascending order of EmpId.
    B. List of EmpId 02 in ascending order of Lastname
    C. List of all EmpId containing 02 and ascending order of LastName.
    D. List of EmpId 02 and ascending order of LastName.
    E. List of all EmpId containing 02 and ascending order of EmpId

22. The Following query was performed on the data in the graphic below.
    SELECT * WHERE Credit >="105.00" ORDER BY Credit DESC

Donations					
CALLERID ▾	ClientId ▾	Credit ▾	FirstName ▾	LastName ▾	Gender ▾
28	0505200027	$200.00	ERIC	OWUSU SIAW	Male
45	0506160011	$100.00	RICKEY	LEWIS	Male
23	0505190022	$100.00	JOHN	ODURO ASANTE	Male
36	0506160006	$100.00	AKWASI	SARFO	Male
12	0505190011	$60.00	PETER	OWUSUH AMOAKO	Male
42	0506160008	$50.00	ERIC	OWUSU SIAW	Male
15	0505190014	$50.00	ROSE	ANTWI-MENSAH	Female
43	0506160009	$50.00	KOJO	NKANSAH	Male

Select the answer for the result:
    A. Akwasi Sarfo would be displayed
    B. Rickey Lewis would be displayed
    C. Eric Owusu Siaw would be displayed
    D. All donors below Eric Owusu Siaw would be displayed
    E. All donors giving money more than John Oduro Asante would displayed.

23. Files, such as index files and data dictionaries, store administrative information are known as:
    A. metadata
    B. Database
    C. Data Records
    D. Information
    E. Files

24. Data that has been transformed into a meaningful and useful form for specific purposes is:
    A. Datum
    B. Data Field
    C. Information
    D. Record
    E. Database

25. Sorting and Calculating may be classified under data processing as:
    A. Collection
    B. Conversion
    C. Manipulation
    D. Storage
    E. Communication

26. In data comparison A greater than B is equivalent to:
    A. A < B
    B. A > B
    C. B > A
    D. A = B
    E. A<> B

27. What does the description of data item represent?
    A. Field
    B. Data-type
    C. Record
    D. File
    E. Datum

28. To retrieve data from one or more tables and displays the results in a datasheet is a primary query type. Which query command is used for this purpose
    A. Crosstab
    B. Action
    C. Select Parameter
    D. Auto Lookup
    E. Data Table

29. A query script in database is generally created in:
    A. Uniform modeling language
    B. Structured Query Language
    C. Select Query Language
    D. Crosstab Query Language
    E. Selective Structured Language

30. Which one of the following does NOT represent File Type of Ms. Access Database?
    A. *.accdb
    B. *.mdb
    C. *.dbm
    D. *.adp
    E. None of the above

SECTION IV

BASIC CONCEPT

OF PROGRAMMING

USING

VISUAL STUDIO.NET

SUMMARIZED OBJECTIVES:

This is a one chapter section that covers several sub-chapters teaching the basic concepts of programming. The student will learn the fundamental concepts and the elements of programming. The student will learn basic computer systems analysis leading to creation of computer algorithms, data flow charts for a computer project. The student will be able to create simple programs. This section discusses the fundamental concepts of object oriented programming (oop). Students will be able to identify various types of classes, objects, and methods. The chapter discusses data types, variables, constants, arrays, functions, procedures, and constructors and their applications in loops, and conditional decisions in programs. The student will acquire knowledge on dot net platform particularly in Microsoft Visual Basic dot Net programming environment while working with classes, data and how to store information.

The Objectives

➤ **Chapter 10: Basic Concepts of Programming**

10.0 Overview of Basic elements of Programming

10.1 What is Computer Programming?
10.1.1 Computer Algorithms
10.1.2 Expressing Algorithms
10.1.3 Variables

10.2 Programming languages
10.2.1 Creating a Simple Program
10.2.2 Analysis
10.2.3 Designing
10.2.4 Coding
10.2.5 Testing

10.3 Application of Programming Methodology

10.4 Basic Object Oriented Concepts
10.4.1 Abstract Classes and Methods in Visual Basic.Net
10.4.2 Object: 3 Key characteristics of Object

10.5 Programming Concept in Visual Basic.Net
10.5.1 Visual Basic.Net – Object-Oriented Language Concepts

10.6 Visual Studio Integrated Development Environment (IDE)

10.7 How to Store Information
10.7.1 Object Access Concept
10.7.2 Review on the Code of Calculator Program

10.8 General Visual Basic (VB) Language Reference
10.8.1 Data type
10.8.2 Data Type Summary
10.8.2 Constant

The Objectives

> **Chapter 10: Basic Concepts of Programming**

10.9 Arrays
10.9.1 How an array is defined in Visual Basic.Net
10.9.2 Navigating Through Array Elements
10.9.3 Navigating Through Multi-Dimension Array

10.10 Instantiating Classes
Defining Class Employee
Instantiating Class Employee with keyword NEW

10.11 Storing Data in Text File

10.12 User- Defined Types
10.12.1 Data Types Conversion

10.13 Assignments and Exercises

CHAPTER 10

Basic Concept of Programming

The Objectives:

- Overview of Basic Elements of Programming
- Introduction to Concept of Programming
- Basic Elements Of Programming
- Computer Systems Analysis: Algorithms, Flowcharts
- Creating Simple Programs
- Data Types, Variables, Constants and Arrays
- Loops and Conditional decisions in programs
- Object Oriented Programming Concepts
- Visual Basic dot Net Programming environment

10.0 Overview of Basic elements of Programming

This section will focus on discussions pertaining to the basic principles readers would need to know about computer programming. It will outline the key elements on programming methodologies providing some highlights on analysis, designing, coding and testing procedures.

10.1 What is Computer Programming?

In a nutshell, programming means writing down a series of instructions that tell a computer what you want it to do. These instructions have the following properties:

- *Computation proceeds in discrete steps.*
- *Each step is precisely defined to provide sufficient computing details.*
- *The order in which steps are performed may be important.*
  A set of instructions with these properties is said to be an **algorithm**. *The steps in an algorithm can be short and simple, but they need not be redundant.*
- *Some steps may involve a series of smaller steps.*
- *Some steps may involve making decisions.*
- *Some steps may repeat.*

Algorithms are common in the real world. A cooking recipe is an algorithm, and so it is for a set of instructions that explains how to build a bookcase or read your email on the internet. Let's attempt to prepare one of my favorite dishes popularly known as "**Fufu**" and palm-nut soup. Fufu meal has two parts, the soup or gravy and pounded yam or mashed potatoes. It's usually preferable to begin with the preparation of soup.

Preparing Palm-Nut Soup:

1. Clean 2 lbs of meat
2. Chop the meat into 10 pieces
3. Chop 1 onion and 2 fresh tomatoes
4. Add:
    1. chopped meat and vegetable in a deep saucepan
    2. ½ tablespoonful of seasoning spices
    3. 1½ tablespoonful of salt.
5. Steam at 350 F for 10 minutes
6. Add 40 oz canned palm nut juice.
7. Allow it to boil for 25 minutes while stirring in every 5 minutes.
8. Now add ¾ liter of water
9. Allow to cook for 25 minutes

Preparing Fufu:

1. Slightly warm ¼ liter of water
2. Soak 2 tablespoons of potato starch in warm water
3. Stir thoroughly to obtain a homogenous mixture
4. Soak ½ lb of mashed potatoes in ½ liter of cold water
5. Add products of steps 3 and 4 and stir to obtain a mixture
6. In a plastic container cook in microwave for 10 minutes
7. Or cook in a cooking pot at 350° F and stir every 1½ minutes for 10-15 minutes.
8. Stir and beat to make it more palatable
9. Mold into serving sizes with soup.
10. Serve at once

This recipe satisfies most of the requirements for an algorithm:
- Algorithm involves discrete steps.
- It also involves a decision making, and how often one is required to stir to obtain a homogenous mixture.

Although this recipe is detailed enough for an experienced cook, it might pose some problems for a novice. A computer is the ultimate novice—it does exactly what you tell it to do, even if you tell it to do something that's blatantly wrong. For that reason, our "*recipes*" (*algorithms*) will need to be much more precise than a Joy of cooking recipe.

10.1.1 Computer Algorithms

As was discussed in chapter one in volume one, computer like any other machine follows the **I-P-O** process. This means computer follows the famous *input – process – output* method which clearly outlines the principle of algorithm. Computer algorithms often involve obtaining data inputs, performing calculations, and producing outputs. Let's consider a simple problem that can be solved by a computer: calculating the biweekly salary of an employee. Here are some of the steps that best represent the salary calculating process:

1. *Display a message asking the user to enter the timesheet information and wage rates.*
2. *Obtain the input entered by the user.*
3. *Convert the user's inputs into appropriate numerical forms.*
4. *Calculate the biweekly salary, using the following formula*
      S = (Hours) x (Rate)
5. *Convert salary calculated into character form and display the result.*

I have divided the algorithm into discrete steps. Most of these steps are reasonably precise, although it's not clear exactly at this stage how we are going to display the information to the user and obtain the user's input. That will depend on what type of program we eventually write. In a GUI application, input usually takes the form of clicking a button, making a choice from a menu, or typing characters into a box. In a text-based application, input comes from the keyboard. Another issue that's a bit fuzzy is **step 3:** *converting the user's input to numerical form.* What action do we take if the input is not in the form of a number? It would be nice to assume that users never make mistakes, but that's rarely the case in the real world. We'll have to decide whether the flow of the algorithm should stop at that point, or whether it should inform the user of the problem and ask for new input.

10.1.2 Expressing Algorithms

There are a number of ways to express algorithms; we will use three of them in this book: Natural Languages, Programming Languages, and Pseudo-code

- **Natural languages**. Algorithms can be written in a natural (human) language— recipes in cookbooks are expressed in this way. The advantage of natural language is that anyone who understands the language can read the algorithm. However, natural languages often lack the precision that we will need for expressing algorithms. Also, computers have troubles understanding natural languages.

- **Programming languages**. In order for a computer to be able to execute our algorithm, we will need to express it in a programming language. Programming languages provide the necessary precisions that are simple enough for computers to understand and interpret. (Whether they're simple enough for humans to understand is another matter.)

- **Pseudo-code**. Pseudo-code is a mixture of natural language and a programming language. An algorithm written in pseudo-code is more precise than one written in natural language but less precise than one written in a programming language. On the other hand, a pseudo-code algorithm is often easier to read (and to write) than one expressed in a programming language. Usually as best practice a clear programming details will often be expressed in a form of a pseudo-code, before translating into an actual programming language. In this way algorithms and pseudo-codes guide the programmers to avoid serious semantic errors that can be overlooked during coding. Semantic errors occur mostly during runtime when all syntax errors are correct but the logic of processing is incorrect, resulting in an unexpected output.

10.1.3 Variables

Variables are memory locations where data are stored during the execution of a program. Our payroll algorithm for an example will have to store four items of data in runtime:

- The input entered by a user
- The hours worked
- The wage per hours
- The Salary value

These are the locations that are used to store data within a program, and they are known as variables. Variables are given names by the programmer. We can choose whatever names we want, subject to the rules of the programming language. It is best to choose a name that suggests what data the variable stores. For example, we might store the Salary amount in a variable named *BiweeklySalary*, *SalaryTemp*, or just Salary. Shorter names are usually less descriptive and therefore undesirable. "*Sal*" would be worse than *Salary*, and *S* would be even worse still. Using a name that's completely unrelated to the value that it represents (such as *a* or *x*) would be in unspeakably poor taste; names such as these provide no useful information to anyone who might read the program in the future. When choosing a name for a variable, pick one that suggests what data the variable stores. Avoid names that are too short, and unrelated to the values intended for storage in the variables, or have more than one obvious interpretation.

Another example of a simple algorithm is the **Fahrenheit-to-Celsius** algorithm illustrated below. Each variable will store a particular type of data. In the Fahrenheit-to-Celsius algorithm, the user's input will be a sequence of characters. The **Fahrenheit** and **Celsius** temperatures, on the other hand, will be numbers, possibly with digits after the decimal point. We will need to use the user input names for Fahrenheit, and Celsius, also known as the variables in the Fahrenheit-to-Celsius algorithm. Here's what the algorithm looks like with the variables added:

1. Display a message asking the user to enter a Fahrenheit temperature.
2. Obtain the input entered by the user and store it into user input.
3. Convert user Input into numerical form and store the result into Fahrenheit.
4. Calculate the equivalent Celsius temperature using the formula
    ```
    Celsius = (Fahrenheit-32) x (5/9)
    ```
5. Convert the value of Celsius to a *string format* and display the result.

10.2 Programming languages

So far, we now know that algorithms are usually expressed in a natural language like English, with the help of an occasional mathematical formula. That's not good enough for a computer to make most of it though. However, in order to create working programs, we'll need to express our algorithms in a highly precise manner in languages that are specifically designed for computers, popularly known as programming language, compiler or interpreter. The reader will recall that these programming languages were briefly discussed under compiler and programming languages in chapter 3, volume one. To fully make sense of programming languages, I have selected visual basic programming language to illustrate our examples. In the sub-topic below we will learn the elements of creating a simple program in Visual Basic.Net.

10.2.1 Creating a Simple Program

In this sub-section we are going to learn how to create a simple addition calculator program in Microsoft Visual Basic.Net programming language. Since this book is not specifically designed for programming, readers are encouraged to consult any visual basic.net programming book for further reading. It is also important to note that visual basic.net is an object oriented programming language and as such we are most likely to come across terms like objects, attributes, controls, forms, and others. Traditionally a typical computer program development will involve four major stages: Analysis, Designing, Coding and Testing.

10.2.2 Analysis

Analysis is the process that involves project planning, gathering the relevant information and defining the problem and system requirements. Here is where programmers become more aware of their actual task. In other words the system specifications would be thoroughly analyzed and made clear to both programmers and the client or the end-user. From my personal experience, the system analysis is the most important process of all software development. Incorrect analysis may lead to technically unsounded and unreliable system and all subsequent efforts would have been wasted.

10.2.3 Designing

The design process is the second stage in software development. Using the product of the analysis, a designer will be able to identify all the major program components including modules, procedures and functions. At this stage a designer would be able to determine whether the proposed project would be feasible or not. The detail steps of programming and the scope of the project would have been uncovered by now. It is at this stage that algorithms, flowcharts and pseudo-codes are derived for each major module. The pseudo-code covers more important details providing a functional and final analysis reflecting the previously defined algorithm and the flowchart. The pseudo-code is more of a literal language expression, which provides an explicit outline to the programming language expressions. All these are considered logical design.

The logical design is the process of software design where the detailed components, functions and architecture are determined independent of the platform of development.

The Physical design is the process of software design in which the detailed components, functions and architecture are determined specific to the platform of development.

10.2.4 Coding
Having determined the specific platform, you are now ready for coding. The coding or programming process is the direct translation of the pseudo-code (a natural language expression) to a specific computer programming language like the C/C++, Visual Basic.Net, Java, Fortran Pascal, and so on. As in general there are rules governing the expression of any language, the computer programming languages are no exception. In a natural language expression this rule is known as *grammar*. Likewise in computer science each programming language expression is also governed by the special rule known as *syntax*. Wrong syntax will generate an error message. The most important job of a compiler or an interpreter may rest upon the ability to *analyze* the programming language syntax, before running the program.

10.2.5 Testing
Testing may be the final stage crowning all software programming projects. Usually a testing strategy pre-defined in the process of analysis may be used as the major testing guidelines. Testing is a confirmative process designed to validate the predefined objectives of a programming project. For an example, in the simple addition calculator, the basic testing strategy will likely be as follows:
Unit Test; Integration test; Stress test; Regression test, and acceptance test.

Unit test: is the test performed by the programmer to correct various such as compile errors, syntax errors and runtime errors, etc. Below are examples of the testing strategy:

    a. Test if the user input is calculable.

    b. Test for the size of the user input within the range of a number system.

    c. Test for the size of the calculated results.

    d. Test for the accuracy of the mathematical formula.

Stress/Volume test: this is to ensure the program can support current and future volumes. Volume testing is running a program with thorough volumes similar to those that would be encountered in real time operating conditions. Stress testing is performed to determine whether the program can function when subjected to volumes larger than what would usually be expected. The areas that are stress tested may include input transactions, internet tables, storage space, output, communications, and computer capacity.

Regression testing: is the execution of a standard battery of tests performed to ensure that unchanged portions of the program are not affected by program changes or new development. Test scripts should generally remain the same from execution to execution.

Acceptance test: this test is performed by end-user to ensure the program meets the requirements determined by the users.

10.3 Application of Programming Methodology

The application of the above programming methodology will be demonstrated by creating a simple "**Addition Calculator Program**". Now using the programming approach discussed above we want to create a simple addition calculator program. In other words, our programming method would embrace all the four stages illustrated above. These stages may include analysis, design, coding and testing.

1. Analysis

Under analysis, we will define the problem and propose a solution at the same time.

A. Definition of Problem

The current project is focused on the creation of a simple add machine. The program would permit the input of two numbers, and on selecting results or "**Add(=)**" sign the machine would calculate the sum of the two numbers and display the results in a text box. In the event that the machine was unable to calculate the two numbers an error message would be displayed.

B. The Proposed Solution to The Defined Problem

Given the above problem, the addition program is a typical example of a *binary* arithmetic operation. This program therefore will require three major variables including *operand#1*, *operand#2* and the *results*. The program will also make the necessary conversions to the appropriate numeric data-type. Since this project is a simple adding machine the value of our result will not be stored permanently. The following global algorithm will reflect the processing of the solution.

Adding Algorithm

```
1.  Begin
2.  Initialize operands
3.  Input Operand#1
4.  Input Operand#2
5.  Calculate Sum(Operand#1, Operand#2 )
6.  Display Results
7.  End
```

2. Design

Using the derived algorithm a pseudo-code can be generated. Here the lines of expressions in a natural language are exploded to accommodate the essential details. Pseudo-code is closer to a programming language. It is important to remember that the pseudo-code can be easily transformed into any programming language.

A. Pseudo-code

1. *Begin*
2.   *Do*
3.   *Set Operand#1 -> 0*
4.   *Set Operand#2 -> 0*
5.   *Input -> A*
6.   *Input -> B*
7.   *If A and B = Valid Then*
8.   *Operand#1= ConvertToNumeric(A)*
9.   *Operand#2= ConvertToNumeric(B)*
10.   *Results = Operand#1 + Operand#2*
11.   *Display Results*
12.   *End if*
13.   *Until Done*
14.   *End*

B. Data Flow Chart

The visual representation of the pseudo-code also known as the *flow chart* can be generated. Some designers generate the data flow chart from the pseudo-code.

FLOW CHART FOR SIMPLE ADDING CALCULATOR

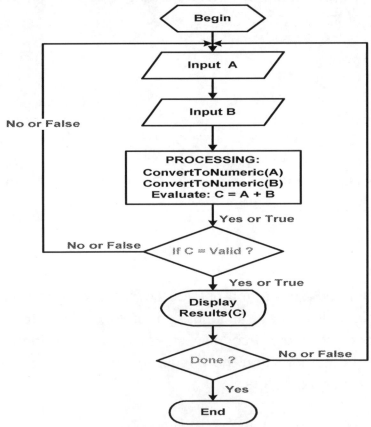

Figure 10-1
Data Flow Chart
Of A Simple Add
Machine

3. Coding The Add Machine Program

Once the pseudo-code has been finalized Coding process will begin. The coding process involves the translation of the pseudo-code to a selected computer programming language. At this level the language *syntax* will strictly be respected. In our example, we will choose Microsoft Visual Basic programming language since it's the most popular programming tool. More programming syntax will be discussed further down this chapter, but for now the reader may note that an *apostrophe comma* (') beginning a statement means a comment. Therefore the compiler will skip that statement during compilation and program execution.

Adding Block Procedure

```
Public Class Calculator
 Private Sub BtnAdd_Click(sender As System.Object, e As System.EventArgs)
 Handles BtnAdd.Click
 Dim Op1 As Single
 Dim Op2 As Single
   'Convert text in Op1 and Op2 to numbers
   Op1 = Val(TextOperand1.Text)
   Op2 = Val(TextOperand2.Text)
   'Two numbers added and reverted to text string
   'txtResult.Text = Str(Op1 + Op2)
   TextResults.Text = Format(Op1 + Op2, "###,###,###.##")

 End Sub

 Private Sub BtnCancel_Click(sender As System.Object, e As
 System.EventArgs) Handles BtnCancel.Click
  End
 End Sub
End Class
```

Since Visual Basic.Net is an object-oriented programming language the above block of code by itself is not complete. The interface that allows user interaction with the computer machine is missing. We will therefore introduce a second concept that will further clarify the hidden hitches in the event-driven programming. We will call this part an interface masking. This is where visual objects will be used to present information to guide users, in how to interact with the program.

10.4 Basic Object Oriented Concepts

The Object Oriented Programming concept is basically centered on the terms object, message, class inheritance and encapsulation. This lesson explains these key concepts behind object-oriented programming, design, and development. Below are the basis for understanding key object-oriented terminology and concepts.

1. An Object

An object is a software bundle of variables and related methods. Software objects are often used to model real-world objects you find in everyday life. In OOP terminology, we say that an Object is an instance of a class. Multiple objects that are instances of the same class have access to the same methods, but often have different values for their instance variables.

2. Messages

Software objects interact and communicate with each other using messages.

3. Class

A class is a blueprint or prototype that defines the variables and the methods common to all objects of a certain kind.   A Class can also be defined as a template for an object that contains variables to describe the object and methods to describe how the object behaves. Classes can inherit variables and methods from other classes. (i.e. Class is template or a blueprint from which object is actually made).

4. Abstract Class

An abstract class is a class that cannot be instantiated, but must be inherited from. An abstract class may be fully implemented, but is more usually partially implemented or not implemented at all, thereby encapsulating common functionality for inherited classes.

5. Base Class

A Base class is a class from which all other classes are built. Example in C#:

```
abstract class MyBaseC        //Abstract class
   {  protected int x = 100;
      protected int y = 150;
      public abstract void MyMethod();   //Abstract method
      public abstract int GetX  { get; } // Abstract property
      public abstract int GetY  { get; } // Abstract property
   }
class MyDerivedC: MyBaseC
    {public override void MyMethod()
       { x++;   y++; }
     }
```

6. Sub Class

A Sub Class is a class further down the class hierarchy than another class, its superclass. Creating a new class that inherits from an existing one is often called sub-classing. A class can have as many subclasses as necessary.

7. Super Class

A Super Class is a class further up the class hierarchy than another class, its subclass. A class only can have one superclass immediately above it, but that class also can have a superclass, and so on.

8. Inheritance

Inheritance is the general concept of extending a base class. Extending a base class creates a new class that carries all properties and methods. The resulting class can be modified, kept as it is or add new methods. A class inherits state and behavior from its superclass. Inheritance provides a powerful and natural mechanism for organizing and structuring software programs.

9. Encapsulation

Encapsulation is combining data and behavior in a package and hiding the implementation. The way of making encapsulation work is to have programs that never directly access instance variables (fields) in a class (Reusability, Black Box and Reliability). How do we access data?
Programs should interact with this data only through the object's methods.

10. Instance

Instance is the same thing as an object. Each object is an instance of some class. It is an object created from a class.

11. Extends

A class that builds on another class

12. Method

Method is a group of statements in a class that defines how the class' objects will behave. Methods are analogous to functions in other languages, but must always be located inside a class.

13. Class Method

Class method is a method that operates on a class itself rather than on specific instances of a class.

14. Instance Method

Instance method is a method that operates on instances of that class rather than on the class itself. Because instance methods are much more common than class methods, they are often are just called methods.

15. Class Variable

Class variable is a variable that describes an attribute of a class instead of specific instances of the class.

16. Instance Variable

Instance variable is a variable that describes an attribute of a class instead of the class itself.

17. Interface

Interface is a specification of abstract behavior that individual classes can the implement.

18. Package

Package is a collection of classes and interfaces. Classes from packages other than "**java.lang**" must be explicitly imported or referred to by their full package and class name.

10.4.1 Abstract Classes and Methods in Visual Basic.Net

In the examples below we have been using so far under this lesson, **Person**, **Employee**, and **Customer** have all been classes that can be created using the **New** operator. However, there may be situations where a **base class** (or the abstract class) should never be created. There can only be instances of the **Employee** type and **Customer** type and never an instance of the **Person** type. This implies the class **Person** should never be created, or **Person** might have a Private constructor to make it impossible to create. However, Person can also be designated as an **abstract** type. An **abstract** type is the same as a regular (or concrete) type in all respects except for one:

An abstract type can never directly be created or instantiated using the **New** operator. In the following example, **Person** is now declared as an abstract type, using the **MustInherit** modifier in visual basic.net. (In C#: *Abstract* Class Person.   In VB.Net *MustInherit* Person)

VB.Net Code 10-1

```vbnet
    MustInherit Class Person
      Public Name As String
      Public Address As String
      Public City As String
      Public State As String
      Public ZIP As String

      Sub Print()
        Console.WriteLine(Name)
        Console.WriteLine(Address)
        Console.WriteLine(City & ", " & State & " " & ZIP)
      End Sub
    End Class

    Class Customer
      Inherits Person

      Public CustomerID As Integer
    End Class

    Class Employee
      Inherits Person

      Public EmployeeID As Integer
      Public Salary As Double
      Public Hours As Double
    End Class
```

Just because a class is abstract and cannot be created, it does not mean that it cannot have constructors. An abstract class may have constructors to initialize methods or pass values along to base class constructors.

Abstract classes are special in that they can also define abstract methods. Abstract methods are **overridable** methods that are declared with the **MustOverride** keyword and provide no implementation. A class that inherits from a class with abstract methods must provide an implementation for the abstract methods or must be abstract itself. For example, the Person class could define an abstract **PrintName** method that each derived class has to implement to display the person's name correctly.

VB.Net Code 10-2

```
MustInherit Class Person
   Public Name As String
   Public Address As String
   Public City As String
   Public State As String
   Public ZIP As String

   MustOverride Sub PrintName()

   Sub Print()
     PrintName()
     Console.WriteLine(Address)
     Console.WriteLine(City & ", " & State & " " & ZIP)
   End Sub
End Class

Class Customer
   Inherits Person

   Overrides Sub PrintName()
     Console.Write("Customer ")
     Console.WriteLine(Name)
   End Sub

   Public CustomerID As Integer
End Class

Class Employee
   Inherits Person

   Overrides Sub PrintName()
     Console.Write("Employee ")
     Console.WriteLine(Name)
   End Sub

   Public Wage As Double
   Public Hours As Double
   Public Salary As Double
End Class
```

In this example, **Person.Print** can call the **PrintName** method, even though Person supplies no implementation for the method, because it is guaranteed that any derived class that can be instanced must provide an implementation.

10.4.2 Object: 3 Key characteristics of Object

Object's Behavior, Object's State, and Object's Identity

1. **Behavior:** the behavior of an object is defined by the messages it accepts. All objects that are instances of the same class share a family resemblance by supporting similar behavior.

2. **State:** the state of an object is the information it stores about what it currently looks like. The state changes over time and this change must be a consequence of messages sent to the object to keep encapsulation rule.

3. **Identity:** the same class. Note: Individual objects that are instances of a class always differ in their identity and usually differ in state. **Identity:** It is information that provides a distinct identity of an object. Example: two orders may be different though they may be instances of

4. **Objects:**

New *class( );*	Create new instance
New *class(arg,arg, arg . . .);*	New instance with parameters
New *type(arg, arg , arg . . .);*	Create new instance of an anonymous class
Primary.new type(arg,arg,arg. . .)	Create new instance of an anonymous class
	Instance variable
object.variable	
	Class variable
object.classvar	
	Class variable
Class.classvar	
	Instance method(no args)
object.method( )	
	Instance method(with args)
object.method(arg, arg, arg…)	
	Class method(no args)
object.classmethod( )	
	Class method(with args)
object.classmethod(arg, arg, arg…)	
	Class method(no args)
Class.classmethod( )	
	Class method(with args)
Class.classmethod(arg, arg, arg…)	

10.5 Programming Concept in Visual Basic.Net

In a simple addition calculator we will need to simulate the ordinary arithmetic method of adding two numbers and displaying the results. Let's assume the adding equation is for example:

Equation (1) . . . . . .   525 + 1200 = 1,725

The next step is to think computer machine. That is to visualize this equation in terms of a computer machine as shown below. The two most important aspects are *variables* and *values.* The values in equation(1) are 525, 1200, 1,725. They are called values because they are literals or **constants**. The variables are labeled A, B and C. They are variables because their respective values can be changed at any time during the program execution. In the example below the variable **A** contains the value **525**, **B** contains the value **1200**, and **C** contains the value **1,725**.

In the computer machine the variables A, B, and C are the identification names or labels of memory address. The computer refers to these memory addresses by the variable names.

Variables ——→ **A**   **+**   **B**   **=**   **C**

Values ——→ | 525 | **+** | 1200 | **=** | 1,725 |

Figure 10-2   A Simple Add Machine

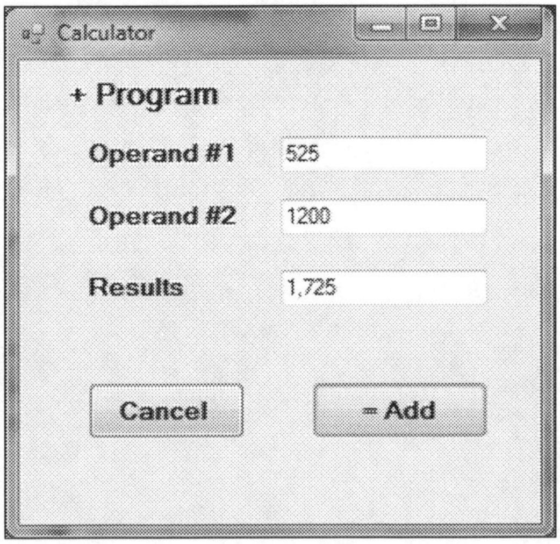

A and B are Operands and C is the result. Putting values into the variables or memory is popularly known as *data input*. And drawing values from the variables or memory is also called *data output*. Now for our calculator machine to work, it will require a declaration of some objects that will represent these variables in the memory.

10.5.1 Visual Basic.Net – Object-Oriented Language Concepts

In Visual Basic.Net the main object that allows users to interact with the computer machine is called **Form.** A form is an *object* because it is the visual representation of a form *class*. A class is therefore a general definition of a specific type of object, also known as a template. For example **Samuel** is a **boy**. A boy is the name for the class young male persons under the age of eight. Samuel is an **object** since he is a physical representation of the class **boy.** In the object oriented jargon we will also say Samuel is an *instance* of the class boy (young male person under eight). Similarly, it will be safer to say that a Form object is an instance of a Form class. A Form like any other object has *attributes* or *properties* and *characteristics* or *methods.* On a form, one can place other smaller objects known in visual basic as *Controls.* Example of controls are Text box or input box (e.g. Text), Label or display control like the "**+** *Program*" and a Button control called *command button.* Each object has a name and a display title called *caption or text.* The concept of object oriented design is very important in today's software development. The beauty of it is the re-usability of programs already created and stored in a special library. The creation of an object from a class is a good example of already created programs called class that can generate an instance called object. To visually represent our simple add calculator will require a form object and sub-objects known as controls already described above.

Table 10-1 A List of Objects and Properties For Add Calculator Program

Objects	Properties		Methods
	Name	Text or Caption	*Event Triggers*
Form	Calculator	Calculator	
Button	BtnAdd	=Add	`BtnAdd_Click`
Text	TextOperand1	Value	
Text	TextOperand2	Value	
Text	TextResults	Value	
Label	Label1	+ program	
Label	Label2	Operand#1	
Label	Label3	Operand#2	
Label	Label4	Results	

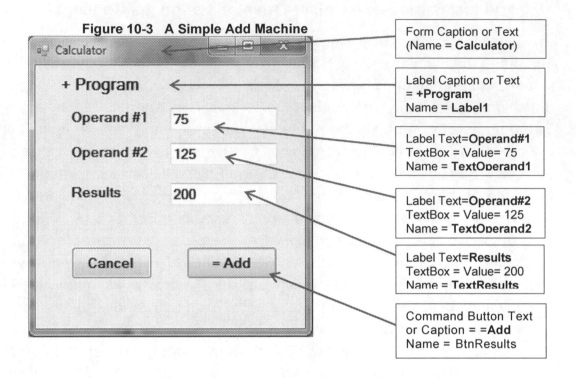

Figure 10-3   A Simple Add Machine

10.6 Visual Studio Integrated Development Environment (IDE)

The following illustration shows the Visual Studio integrated development environment (IDE). This is development environment for visual basic.net, C# (pronounced C-sharp), J# (pronounced J sharp) and ASP.Net (Active Server Pages). This topic provides a brief overview of many of the features and tools included in Visual Studio for application development. The Visual Studio product family shares a single integrated development environment (IDE) that is composed of several elements: the Menu bar, Standard toolbar, various tool windows docked or auto-hidden on the left, bottom, and right sides, as well as the editor space. The tool windows, menus, and toolbars available depend on the type of project or file you are working in.

The first thing to look for are the menu items under "**Recent Templates**" to view the programming languages listed under "**Installed Templates.**" The list comprises Visual Basic, Visual C#, Visual C++, Visual F#, Other Project Types, Database, and Test Project. When you select Visual Basic as indicated below the next column will list the type of applications that can be created in visual basic. In our example I selected **Windows Forms Application**.

Figure 10-4: IDE with General Development Settings applied

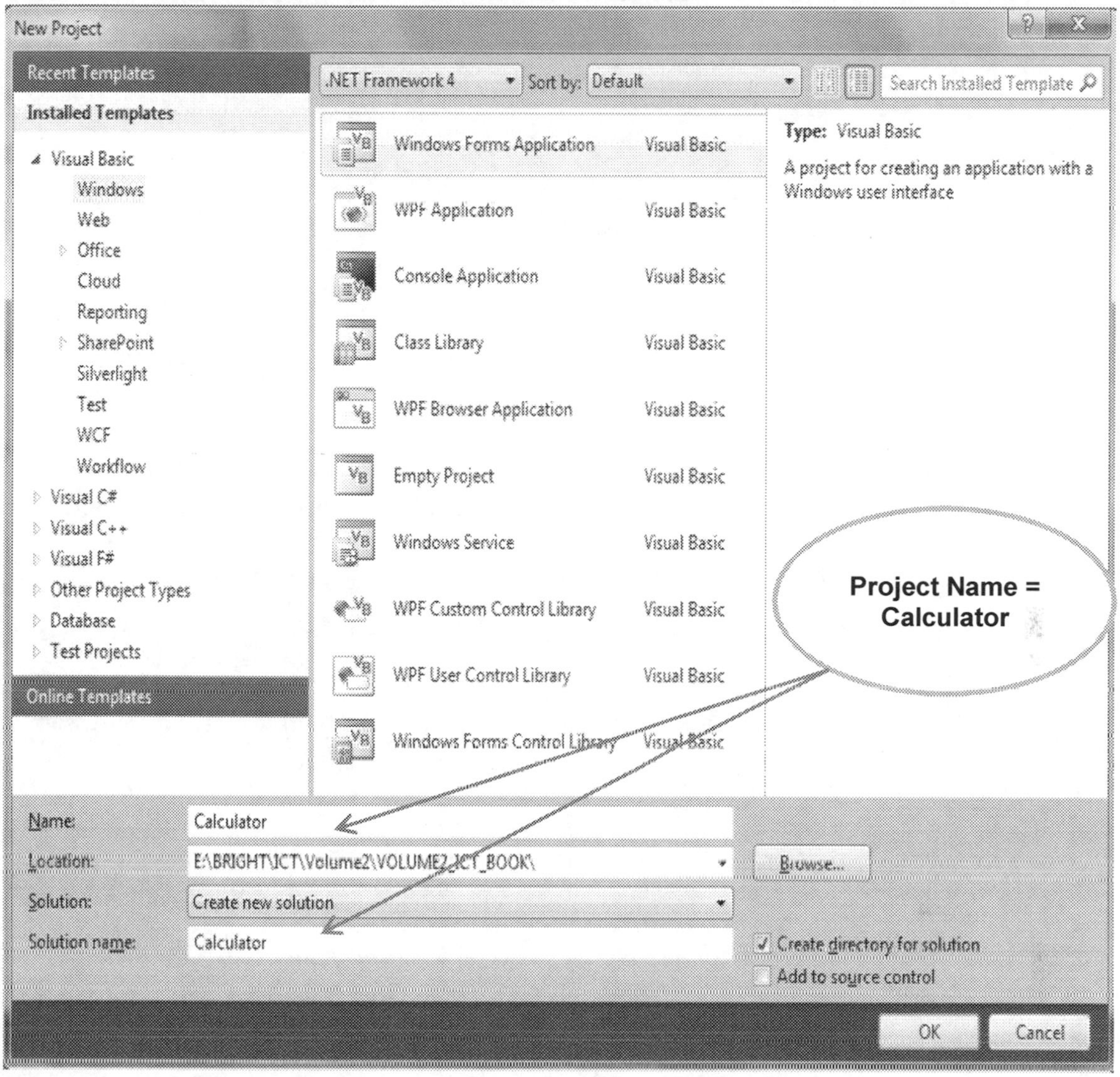

The above figure 10-4 is the initial window for creating a project called Solution. This project is windows form application in Visual Basic so would proceed as follows:

Click on **Visual Basic >> Windows** >> **Windows Forms Application**
Now type the **Solution name >> Folder Location >> Click OK**.
Initially a default form named Form1 will be obtained.

Figure 10-5: Blank Form

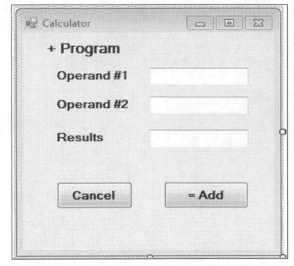

Figure 10-6: Customized Form (Calculator)

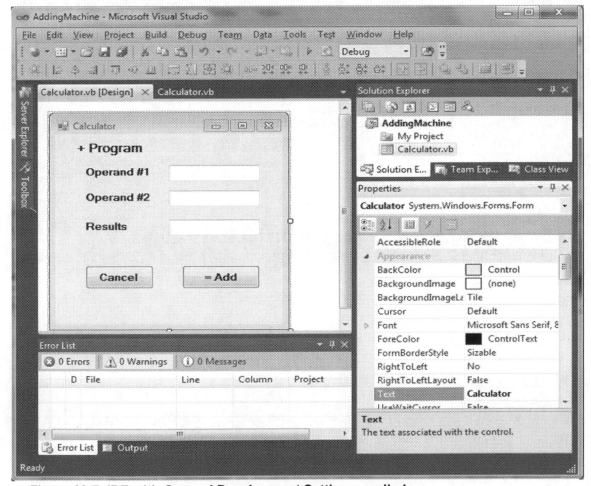

Figure 10-7: IDE with General Development Settings applied

The figure 10-7 above is an illustration of Visual Studio 2010 IDE which is ready for windows program development. The IDE is divided into four parts:
1. Design Window
2. Solution Explorer
3. Property Explorer
4. Output and Messages window.

1. The **design window** is where the form is customized. It is also provide an area for the code to be inserted. In the above figure the Calculator.vb is displayed in this windows. The code as indicated below also goes here:

Figure 10-8: IDE with Design Windows Showing the Code

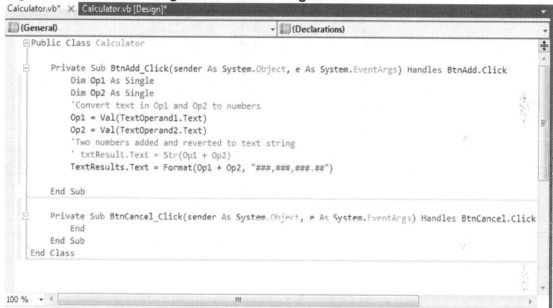

2. **Solution Explorer** is the area where the solution name, and all the module names (forms, classes, resources) are listed. In our example the solution name is **AddMachine** and the form name is **Calculator.vb**.

3. **Property Explorer** is used for listing all the properties of the selected object in the designed window. In the above example since the form object was selected in the property window the value for selected Text property is Calculator. This where all the property values of controls such as forms, labels, textbox, listbox, etc., can be set or changed. The property can be object name, object caption or text, object font size or color.

4. Output and Messages window displays error list, and output messages.

Figure 10-9: Design Toolbox

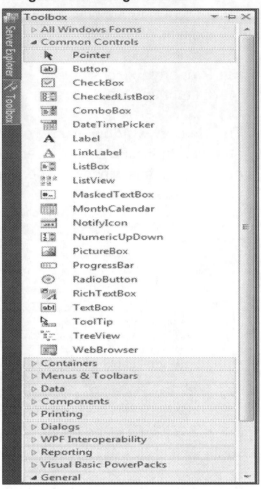

Another important window to take note of is the Toolbox. The Toolbox contains the objects which are also known as Controls. Controls are objects that can be placed on forms.

When a control is needed it's a matter of selecting the control from the toolbox and drag onto the form.

For example, if you want to put a TextBox on a form as shown in figure 10-6 above you can follow the steps below:

1. Click on TextBox
2. While selected drag it onto the form
3. Now click on the control
4. Set the values for the properties. E.g. Text, Name, Font Size, Color, etc.

10.6.1 Visual Studio (IDE) Menu Bar

The figure below is an illustration of a menu bar of Visual Studio IDE. We will discuss a few menu items such as File, Project, Build, Debug, and Run.

The **File** menu reflects standard windows file menu, like new project, open existing project, connection to database, save project, and print project.

Project menu item is used for manipulating the project such as Add new project, Add an existing project, Add user control or reference to built-in libraries.

Figure 10-10 Visual Studio IDE Menu Bar

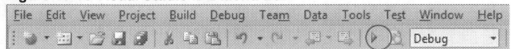

Build menu item is used when the program is complete to compile and build the runtime version of the source code. Under the build item there are build, publish and configuration manager.

Debug menu item is very important tool for the programmer for it is used to correct the programming errors.

Run   ▸   is used to run the source program for testing.

10.7 How to Store Information

For a program to run, programmers must define variables so they can be stored in the memory. In Chapter 2 of Volume one, we discussed memories as temporary storage devices which are very critical to program execution. In our example we will only calculate numbers and display the results without storing the values on a permanent disk. The Visual Basic programming language is a highly typed language. Variables must be predefined to determine which types they belong. A type is a description of data and therefore known as data type. A data type can be a byte, boolean, character, string, integer, single, double, currency etc. Such definitions allow the compiler to safely determine the size of memory space needed for each variable. Data type is more important in modern programming languages, so a sub-topic had been set aside to discuss it later in this chapter. The language grammar used for programming is known as the **syntax**. The syntax for defining a variable in visual basic is as follows.

> **Dim** *variable-name* **As** *Typename*

> **Example: Dim *Operand1* As *Integer***

Note: The keyword **Class** is used to declare a class. The keyword **Sub** is used to declare a subroutine or a ***procedure***. The keyword **Function** is used to declare a ***function.***

A procedure and a function are the same except that only a function can return values of a given data type after execution. Again a class, a variable, a procedure or a function can be declared as public, private, static, or global to promote the access restrictions. Therefore procedures that are triggered from the user-interface interaction must have an ***event*** function attached to it. An event can be a **Click, KeyPress, KeyUp, KeyDown, Load, GotFocus** etc.

10.7.1 Object Access Concept

A Visual Basic Program is contained in a project (or solution in .NET). The project may carry three major types of modules, Form modules, Standard program modules, and Class modules. All these three modules work together to form one complete application.

Public keyword declaration implies any other object can directly access members of this module from anywhere in the program.

Private keyword declaration implies no other object can directly access members of this module from anywhere in the program except the module itself. The table below shows how Visual Basic project is bundled.

Table 10-2 Presents A List of Object Access Levels In Visual Basic

Module	File Type	Public Access		Private ccess	
		IN Module	Outside	IN Module	Outside
Solution	*.sln				
Project	*. vbproj				
Form	*.vb	Yes	No	Yes	No
Std Module	*.Bas	Yes	Yes	Yes	No
Class Module	*.Cls	Yes	Yes	Yes	No
Sub	-	Yes	No	Yes	No
Function	-	Yes	No	Yes	No

Figure 10-11 The Class Module for in the Adding program

```
Imports System
Imports System.Windows.Forms
Public Class Calculator
    Private Sub BtnAdd_Click(sender As System.Object, e As
    System.EventArgs)  Handles BtnAdd.Click
     Dim Op1 As Single
     Dim Op2 As Single
       'Convert text in Op1 and Op2 to numbers
       Op1 = Val(TextOperand1.Text)
       Op2 = Val(TextOperand2.Text)
       'Two numbers added and reverted to text string
       'txtResult.Text = Str(Op1 + Op2)
       TextResults.Text = Format(Op1 + Op2, "###,###,###.##")
     End Sub

    Private Sub BtnCancel_Click(sender As System.Object, e As
    System.EventArgs) Handles BtnCancel.Click
        End
    End Sub
   End Class
```

The **Imports** keyword includes the system libraries such as Systems, Windows, and Forms code so they can be used in the program.

The block begins with **Public Class** declaration and ends in **End Class.**

The *Op1* and *Op2* local variables are **private** to the sub procedure *BtnAdd_Click*. No other sub procedure has access to these variables. On the other hand the form module objects like the *TextResults* and *BtnAdd_Click* are **private** to the form object but are also public to all member procedures and functions in the form module. This explains for why *txtResult.text* was not explicitly declared in *BtnAdd_Click()* sub procedure but was accessible. The figure 10-12 below illustrates this access restriction concept.

Figure 10-12 Access Restriction Concept

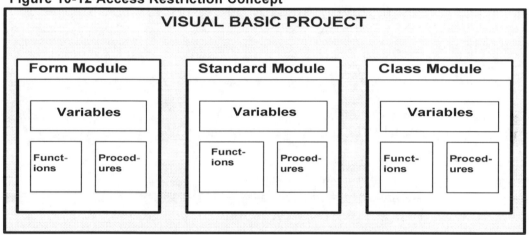

Note: The **Syntax** for a procedure and a function declaration in a standard module would look like the following:

```
Imports [Class Libraries]
Public Class ClassName
    Sub ProcedureName([Variable Declarations])
        [Statements]
    End Sub
  Function FunctionName([Variable Declarations]) As TypeName
     [Statements]
     Return (expression of TypeName)
  End Function
  Function CalculateSquare(ByVal anynumber As Integer)As Integer
        Dim intTemp As Integer
        IntTemp = anynumber * anynumber
        Return (intTemp)
  End Function
End Class
```

Below is the syntax for accessing object and properties of the object.

Object access: `ObjectName.Property`

10.7.2 Review on the Code of Calculator Program

Below are some important notes on the program in figure 10-11 program:

1. Objects are called in a program by their names with their properties. Example: **TextOperand1.Text**, **TextOperand2.Text, TextResult.Text** (TextOperand1=Object; Text= property)

2. The Object Command Button with Caption "`Add(=)`" triggers a **Sub** procedure. Since the procedure is triggered by a mouse click it is automatically named: **`BtnAdd_Click()`**. That's `ObjectName+_Type of Event`

3. The procedure is **private** and, it is Sub procedure for no value is returned.

4. The values for TextOperand1.Text and TextOperand2.Text are initially string types and are converted to float types before adding them. For example: Op1 = **Val**(txtOperand1.Text) and Op2 = **Val**(txtOperand2.Text)

5. The result is reconverted from float type to string type to make it possible to appear in the textbox. Example: **txtResult.Text = Str(Op1+Op2)**, or with special format **TextResults.Text = Format**(Op1+Op2,"###,###,###.##").

10.8 General Visual Basic (VB) Language Reference

Under this section, I have included a few visual basic language reference for further reading. These references which I obtained from the Microsoft website will provide an extra learning material to readers who are interested in visual basic.Net programming. I hope by now the reader would be able to create and run visual basic programs from both Salary and Celsius-Fahrenheit algorithm examples discussed earlier in this chapter. We will briefly discuss Data types, Arrays, Loops and a few other key functions in visual basic.

10.8.1 Data type

The characteristics of a variable that determines what kind of data it can hold. Data types include **Byte**, **Boolean**, **Integer**, **Long**, **Currency**, **Decimal**, **Single**, **Double**, **Date**, **String**, **Object**, **Variant** (default), and user-defined types, as well as specific types of objects. The user-defined types are further defined types using any number of the basic types listed above.

10.8.2 Data Type Summary

The following table shows the supported data types, including storage sizes and ranges.

Table 10-3 The List of Visual Basic Supported Data Types and Sizes

Data type	Storage size	Range
Byte	1 byte	0 to 255
Boolean	2 bytes	True or False
Char	2 bytes	0 to 65535 (unsigned)
Integer	4 bytes	-2,147,483,648 to 2,147,483,647
Long(long integer)	8 bytes	-9,223,372,036,854,775,808 to 9,223,372,036,854,775,807
Single (single-precision floating-point)	4 bytes	-3.402823E38 to -1.401298E-45 for negative values; 1.401298E-45 to 3.402823E38 for positive values
Double (double-precision floating-point)	8 bytes	-1.79769313486231E308 to -4.94065645841247E-324 for negative values; 4.94065645841247E-324 to 1.79769313486232E308 for positive values
Currency (scaled integer)	8 bytes	-922,337,203,685,477.5808 to 922,337,203,685,477.5807
Decimal	16 bytes	+/-79,228,162,514,264,337,593,543,950,335 with no decimal point; +/-7.9228162514264337593543950335 with 28 places to the right of the decimal; smallest non-zero number is +/-0.0000000000000000000000000001
Date	8 bytes	January 1, 100 to December 31, 9999
Object	4 bytes	Any Object reference
Short	2 bytes	-32,768 to 32,767
String (variable-length)	10 bytes + string length	0 to approximately 2 billion
String (fixed-length)	Length of string	1 to approximately 65,400
Variant (with numbers)	16 bytes	Any numeric value up to the range of a Double
Variant (with characters)	22 bytes + string length	Same range as for variable-length String
User-defined (using Type)	Number required by elements	The range of each element is the same as the range of its data type.

10.8.2 Constant

A **Constant** is a named item that retains a constant value throughout the execution of a program. A constant can be a string or a numeric literal, another constant, or any combination that includes arithmetic or logical operators except logarithms and exponentiation. Each host application can define its own set of constants. Additionally, in VB a constant can be defined by the user with the "**Const** " statement. You can use constants anywhere in your code in place of actual values.

Syntax for declaring a constant:

Const *nameofConstant* [***As*** *Typename*] = **Value**

Example: **Const** *curMinWageRate* **As** Currency = **5.75**
Or: **Const** *curMinWageRate* = **5.75**

Also an example of a String constant:

Const *strAuthorsName* = **"Bright Siaw Afriyie"**

The following are valid word separators for proper casing. They actually represent most important non-printable constants.

Table 10-4 List of Constants for non-printable characters

Description	Constants	VB Constants
Null	Chr$(0)	vbNull
horizontal tab	Chr$(9)	vbTab
linefeed	Chr$(10)	vbLf
vertical tab	Chr$(11)	vbVerticalTab
form feed	Chr$(12)	vbFormFeed
carriage return	Chr$(13)	vbCrLf or vbCr
space (**SBCS**)	Chr$(32)	System.Windows.Forms.Keys.Space

The actual value for a space varies by country for **DBCS** (double bytes character set). A double-byte character set (DBCS), also known as an "expanded 8-bit character set", is an extended single-byte character set (**SBCS**), implemented as a code page. DBCSs were originally developed to extend the SBCS design to handle languages such as Japanese and Chinese. Some characters in a DBCS, including the digits and letters used for writing English, have single-byte code values. Other characters, such as Chinese ideographs or Japanese kanji, have double-byte code values.

10.9 Arrays

An array is a set of sequentially indexed elements having the same intrinsic data type. Each element of an array has a unique identifying index number. Changes made to one element of an array don't affect the other elements.

Note: Arrays of any data type require **20 bytes** of memory plus **4 bytes** for each array dimension plus the number of bytes occupied by the data itself. The memory occupied by the data can be calculated by multiplying the number of data elements by the size of each element. For example, the data in a single-dimension array consisting of 4 **Integer** data elements of 2 bytes each occupies 8 bytes. The 8 bytes required for the data plus the 24 bytes of overhead brings the total memory requirement for the array to 32 bytes. A **Variant** containing an array requires 12 bytes more than the array alone.

10.9.1 How an array is defined in Visual Basic.Net

Note: An array can be defined in terms of a single or multi-dimensional. Below are to create single and multi-dimensional arrays in Visual Basic.Net

1. Syntax for creating a single dimension array:

Dim **ArrayName(**From *Lower Bound* To *Upper Bound***) As DataType**

Example:	`Dim ArrayNumbers(1 To 5) As Integer`
Or:	`Dim ArrayNumbers(0 To 4) As Integer`

The above statement will create a single dimension array "`ArrayNumbers`" that can store only 5 numeric elements of an integer type. Below is a visual representation of this array.

Figure 10-13. Visual representation of single-dimension array

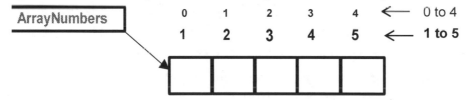

Note: Only values of integer type can be inserted into this array. To calculate the size of this array we will go through the following four steps:

Step 1: Describe the array as follows

- Dimension of the array   = **Single**
- Number of array elements = **5**
- Type of each array element = **Integer**

Step 2: Calculate The Overhead

ArrayNumber	= 20 bytes
Dimension Size	= 4 bytes

Step 3: Calculate Size of Elements

No. of Element   X Size Of (Type)

5 Elements   X Size Of (Integer)

5 X 2 bytes = 10 bytes

Step 4: Add Steps 1 through 3   = 34 bytes

Below is how a single dimensional array is implemented in a visual basic.net program. The iteration is from 0 to 1999 which is equivalent to 1 to 2000.

```
Imports System
Imports System.Collections
Public Class MainClass
    Shared Sub Main(ByVal args As String())
      ' Get the number of items.
      Dim num_items As Integer = 2000
      ' One-dimensional array.
      Dim array1(0 To num_items - 1) As Integer
      For i As Integer = 0 To num_items - 1
          array1(i) = i
      Next i
      ' Free the first array's memory.
      Erase array1
    End Sub
End Class
```

2. Syntax for multi-dimension array:

Dim ArrayName(*LBound* To *Ubound*,*LBound* To *Ubound*) As Type
Example: Dim ArrayNumbers(0 To 4,0 To 2) As Integer
Below is a visual representation of two dimension array.

Figure 10-14. Visual representation of multi-dimension array

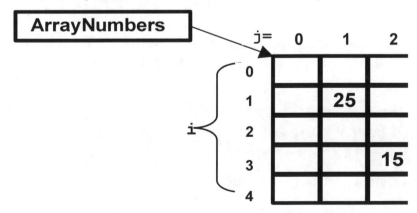

The array has two sets of index variables (`i,j`). Index i ranges from 0 to 4 while index j ranges from 0 to 2. Therefore a variable can be stored at any location indicated by `ArrayNumbers(i,j)`. For an example the positions for the values **25** and **15** are indicated as follows:

`ArrayNumbers(1,1)=25`   and   `ArrayNumbers(3,2)= 15`

10.9.2 Navigating Through Array Elements

This can be achieved through the use of *For* and *Loop* commands. Each iteration of such loops will represent the index corresponding to the position of an array element.

> **For . . . Next Statement**
> **Do . . . Loop Statement**

The **For** and **Do** loops repeat a block of statements while a condition is **True** or until a condition becomes **True**.

Syntax: For . . . Next Statement

`For [{I = LBound	Until` ` UBound}` *condition*`]` ` [`*statements*`]` ` [Exit For]` ` [`*statements*`]` ` Next I`	`Calculate squares of` `integers from 1 to 5` `For I = 0 To 4` `  ArrayNumbers(I)= (I+1)*(I+1)` `  If I < 0  Then` `    Exit For` `  End If` `Next I`

Figure 10-15. Memory content for a Single Dimension Array

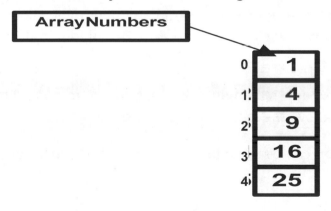

After the execution of the array program, the content of the array *ArrayNumbers* will look like the diagram shown above. The array contains the square values of integers from **1** to **5**: `1,4,9,16,and 25`

Do . . . Loop Statement

Do [{**While** | **Until**} *condition*]
   [*statements*]
  [**Exit Do**]
  [*statements*]
 	
Loop
	Do
	   [*statements*]
	  [**Exit Do**]
	  [*statements*]
	
	Loop [{**While** | **Until**} *condition*]

The **Do Loop** statement syntax has these two parts:

Part	Description
condition	Optional. Numeric expression or string expression is **True** or **False**. If condition is Null, condition is treated as False.
statements	One or more statements that are repeated while, or until, condition is True.

Any number of **Exit Do** statements may be placed anywhere in the **Do Loop** as an alternate way to exit a **Do Loop**. **Exit Do** is often used after evaluating some condition, for example, **If Then**, in which case the **Exit Do** statement transfers control to the statement immediately following the **Loop**.

When used within nested **Do Loop** statements, **Exit Do** transfers control to the loop that is one nested level above the loop where **Exit Do** occurs.

Similarly, the **Do…While/Loop** can be used to iterate the an Array just like the **For…Next loop.**

```
Do [{While | Until} condition]        'Calculate squares of
    [statements]                       integers from 1 to 5
[Exit Do]                              I = 0 'Initialize I to 0
    [statements]                       Do While I < 5
Loop                                   I = I + 1 'Increase I by 1
                                       ArrayNumbers(I) = I*I
                                       If I >= 5  Then
                                           Exit Do
                                           End If
                                       Loop
```

10.9.3 Navigating Through Multi-Dimension Array

The Loop syntax will be nested. This implies there will be loops inserted inside other loops. The depth of nested loop will correspond with the number of dimensions on the array. For example a single dimension array will require a single level of loop. A two-dimension array will require a two-depth level of nested loop. And three-dimension array will require a three-depth level of nested loop.

Figure 10-16 For Loop   **Figure 10-17 Do...While Loop**

		i = 0	*initialize i to 0*
For i = 1 to n	*start of i loop*	**Do**	*start of i loop*
For j=1 to m	*start of j loop*	j = 0	*initialize j to 0*
[Statement]		**Do**	*start of j loop*
Next j	*j increment by 1*	[Statement]	
Next i	*i increment by 1*	j = j +1	*j increment by 1*
		Loop While j < 3	*stop condition for j*
		i = i + 1	*i increment by 1*
		Loop While i < 5	*stop condition for i*

The total loops around the [Statement] in figure 10-16 **For-Loop** is (**n x m**) and also shows how the **For-Loop** can be used to navigate in 2-dimensional array.

This example in figure 10-17 shows how **Do...Loop** statements can be used. The inner **Do...Loop** statement loops 15 times (i.e. 3 x 5), sets the value of the flag to **False**, and exits prematurely using the **Exit Do** statement. The outer loop exits immediately upon checking the value of the flag.

```
Dim Check As Boolean
Dim Counter As Integer
Check = True
Counter = 0        'Initialize variables.
Do    ' Outer loop.
  Do While Counter < 20     'Inner loop.
     Counter = Counter + 1   'Increment Counter.
     If Counter = 10 Then     'If condition is True.
        Check = False  'Set value of flag to False.
        Exit Do          'Exit inner loop.
      End If
   Loop
Loop Until Check = False    'Exit outer loop immediately
```

10.10 Instantiating Classes

Instantiating a class is simply creating an object out of non-abstract class. We are going to use the VB.Net code in example **VB.Net Code 10-2,** but this time we are a going to rewrite the code in the class Person to include **constructors**

```
MustInherit Class Person            'Cannnot be instatiated
   Public Name As String
   Public Address As String
   Public City As String
   Public State As String
   Public ZIP As String

   MustOverride Sub PrintName()

   Sub Print()
     PrintName()
     Console.WriteLine(Address)
     Console.WriteLine(City & ", " & State & " " & ZIP)
   End Sub
End Class

Class Customer Inherits Person          'Inherit from the base class  instantiated
    Private mCustomerID As Integer

    ' Customer constructor
    Public Sub New(ByVal nameValue As String, _
      ByVal address As String, _
      ByVal cityValue As String, _
      ByVal stateValue As String, _
      ByVal zipValue As String, _
      ByVal customerIDValue As Integer)
       mCustomerID  = customerIDValue
End Sub
```

Defining Class Employee

```vb
Overrides Sub PrintName()
    Console.Write("Customer ")
    Console.WriteLine(Name)
  End Sub
End Class

Class Employee
  Inherits Person
      Private mEmployeeID As Integer
      Private mWage As Double
      Private mHours As Double
      Private mSalary As Double
      Private mName As String
      Private mAddress As String
      Private mCity As String
      Private mState As String
      Private mZip As String

  Public Sub New(ByVal nameValue As String, _
      ByVal employeeIDValue As Integer, _
      ByVal address As String,_
      ByVal cityValue As String, _
      ByVal stateValue As String, _
      ByVal zipValue As String, _
      yVal wageValue As Double, _
      ByVal hoursValue As Double, _
      ByVal salaryValue As Integer)

      mEmployeeID = employeeIDValue
      mName = nameValue
      mAddress = address
      mCity = cityValue
      mState = stateValue
      mZip = zipValue
      mWage = wageValue
      mHours = hoursValue
      mSalary= salaryValue

  Overrides Sub PrintName()
      Console.WriteLine(mEmployeeID & " " & mName & " " & _
        mAddress & " " & mCity & " " & mState & " " & mZip & _
            " " & mWage & " " & mHours & "   " & mSalary)
    End Sub
End Class
```

Instantiating Class Employee with keyword NEW to object EmployeeList

```
Public Class AllEmployee

  Shared Sub Main( )
     Dim Employeelist(4) As Employee

     Employeelist(0) = New Employee("0235", "Bright A. Siaw", _
                "1129 Beechwood ln", "Cedar Hill", "Texas", "75104", _
                25.75, 80.0, 2060.0)
     Employeelist(1) = New Employee("5865", "Lucy A. Siaw", _
                "1129 Beechwood ln", "Cedar Hill", "Texas", "75104", _
                18.5, 80, 1480.0)
     Employeelist(2) = New Employee("8905", "Samuel A. Siaw", _
                "1129 Beechwood ln", "Cedar Hill", "Texas", "75104", _
                12.75, 60, 765.0)
     Employeelist(3) = New Employee("8905", "Ernest K. Siaw", _
                "1129 Beechwood ln", "Cedar Hill", "Texas", "75104", _
                12.85, 75, 963.75)


        Dim i As Integer
        For i = 0 To 3
           Employeelist(i).PrintName( )
        Next i
     End Sub 'Main

  End Class
```

10.11 Storing Data in Text File

So far no data has been stored; all the processing took place in the memory of the computer. We have to write more instructions to commit the program to put data on the storage device. We now have to modify the above program to reflect what is given below. The changes are made by adding on the top of MustInherit Class (Person) the following class libraries the will permit the manipulation of text file:

```
Imports System.IO
Imports System.Text.RegularExpressions
Imports System.Threading.Thread
```

Also we will need to add another function that will return all the data elements of the Class Employee. This is the function **ToStandardString()**.

Now declare read and write file variable and create the file Employee.txt as follows:

```
Dim oWrite As System.IO.StreamWriter
Dim oRead As System.IO.StreamReader
oWrite = File.CreateText("Employee1.txt")
```

*Instantiating Class Employee and creating object **Employeelist***

```vbnet
Imports System.IO
Imports System.Text.RegularExpressions
Imports System.Threading.Thread

Public Function ToStandardString() As String
    Dim strdata = mEmployeeID & " " & mName & " " & mAddress & _
                " " & mCity & " " & mState & " " & mZip & _
                " " & mWage & " " & mHours & "   " & mSalary
    Return strdata
End Function

Public Class AllEmployee
    Dim oWrite As System.IO.StreamWriter
    Dim oRead As System.IO.StreamReader

 Shared Sub Main()
    Dim oWrite As System.IO.StreamWriter
    Dim oRead As System.IO.StreamReader
    oWrite = File.CreateText("Employee.txt")

    Dim Employeelist(4) As Employee   'Create array of 4 items

    Employeelist(0) = New Employee("0235", "Bright A. Siaw", _
        "1129 Beechwood ln", "Cedar Hill", "Texas", "75104", _
        25.75, 80.0, 2060.0)
    Employeelist(1) = New Employee("5865", "Lucy A. Siaw", _
        "1129 Beechwood ln", "Cedar Hill", "Texas", "75104", _
        18.5, 80, 1480.0)
    Employeelist(2) = New Employee("8905", "Samuel A. Siaw", _
        "1129 Beechwood ln", "Cedar Hill", "Texas", "75104", _
        12.75, 60, 765.0)
    Employeelist(3) = New Employee("8905", "Ernest K. Siaw", _
        "1129 Beechwood ln", "Cedar Hill", "Texas", "75104", _
        12.85, 75, 963.75)
    Dim i As Integer
    For i = 0 To 3
        Employeelist(i).PrintName()

        oWrite.WriteLine(Employeelist(i).ToStandardString)
    Next i
    oWrite.Close()
  End Sub 'Main

End Class 'AllEmployee
```

After running the program the program it will create a text file **Employee.txt.** Below is the content of **Employee.txt:**

Figure 10-17 the content of Employee.txt

0235 Bright A. Siaw 1129 Beechwood In Cedar Hill Texas 75104 25.75 80 2060

5865 Lucy   A. Siaw 1129 Beechwood In Cedar Hill Texas 75104 18.50 80 1480

8905 Samuel A. Siaw 1129 Beechwood In Cedar Hill Texas 75104 12.75 60 765

8905 Ernest K. Siaw 1129 Beechwood In Cedar Hill Texas 75104 12.85 75 964

10.12 User- Defined Types

The user-defined types are further defined types using any number of the basic types listed above. This is mostly needed when programmers are expected to customize the list of records in a database table. Actually discussion of user-defined types and data structures is beyond the scope of this book. The syntax and examples are shown below to will introduce a basic concept and common usage of user-defined data types.

Syntax:
Type *NameofDataStructure*
　　[*FieldName* **As** *TypeName*]
　　　　·
　　[*FieldName* **As** *TypeName*]
End Type

Assuming you wanted to create a data table that contains a list of employee wages as illustrated below:

Table 10-5. A List Of Employee Records.

No	EmployeeID	Name	Wage/US$	Hours	Salary/US$
1	0235	Bright A. Siaw	25.75	80	2,060.00
2	5865	Lucy A. Siaw	18.50	80	1,480.00
3	8905	Samuel A. Siaw	12.75	60	765.00
4	9085	Ernest K. Siaw	12.85	75	963.75
5	9095	Agnes A. Siaw	19.85	75	1,488.75

We will now call the data structure ***EmployeeRecord*** and list of records ***EmployeeList.*** We will also note that there are five different columns called **data-fields** with assigned names in the very top line of each column. The data field names include **No., EmployeeID, Name, Wage,** and **Hours.** The record number labeled **No.** will be omitted in this process for now. The corresponding user-defined data type will be as shown below:

```
Type EmployeeData
        EmployeeID As String *5
        Name As String * 30
        Wage As Currency
        Hours As Single
        Salary As Currency
End Type
```

Now, we also learned from the data table that there are four records. To accommodate all the four records we will create an ***array*** of our user-defined type. This array will match the list of records known as the **EmployeeList.**

      Dim EmployeeList(5) As EmployeeData

Or   Dim EmployeeList(0 To 4) As EmployeeData

The array elements for index '**0**' correspond to the elements in record number '**1**'. To obtain the elements in record no. 1, you will need to proceed as follows:

```
EmployeeList(0).EmployeeId returns '0235'
EmployeeList(0).Name returns 'Bright A Siaw'
EmployeeList(0).Wage returns 25.75
EmployeeList(0).Hours returns 80
EmployeeList(0).Hours returns 2,060.00
```

Similarly, any of the values in any part of the record list can be changed using the above syntax. For example, the name value "**Bright Siaw Afriyie**", can be changed to "**Eric Owusuh Siaw**", as follows:

```
EmployeeList(0).Name = 'Eric Owusuh Siaw'
```

Now what value would the following statement return?

```
(a)  EmployeeList(2).Name
(b)  EmployeeList(4).EmployeeId
(c)  EmployeeList(3).Name
(d)  EmployeeList(2).Wage
(e)  EmployeeList(0).Salary
```

The remaining records are left for the reader to figure them out.

What size of memory space in terms of bytes would be required to store the **EmployeeList** *array and all its elements?*

Solution

Note: *The sizes of the data-types used in this calculation make reference to Visual Basic*

To calculate the memory space requirement, the following steps will be used:
a. Calculate the size of **EmployeeData** record a user-defined type
b. The size of the initial array of EmployeeData which is **EmployeeList**
c. The total size of all elements in **EmployeeList** array of records

Step a: The size of a user-defined type is equal to the sum of the sizes of each individual type.

The size of EmployeeData

EmployeeId (*String of length* 5)	=	5 Bytes
Name (*String of length* 30)	=	30 Bytes
Wage (*Currency datatype*)	=	8 Bytes
Hours (*Single datatype*)	=	4 Bytes

Total Size of **EmployeeData**   = **47 Bytes**. . . . **(1)**

Step b: The size of the array:
      EmployeeList(0 To 4) As **EmployeeData**

Array Overhead	=	20 Bytes
Array Dimension (1)	=	4 Bytes

Total Overhead Size   = **24 Bytes** . . . .**(2)**

Step c: The total size of the 4 array elements.
          (each of **EmployeeData** data-type)

5 X Size of **EmployeeData**   = **235 Bytes** . . . **(3)**

The total memory space required to store the array **EmployeeList is:**
  ⇨   **EmployeeData + Overhead =   (2)+ (3)**
  ⇨   **Total Values   =   24 + 235 Bytes**
                  =   259 Bytes

10.12.1 Data Types Conversion

Also as an assignment the reader will have to calculate how much memory space is required to store the above data table.

Below are some useful conversion tools in visual basic programming language.

Table 8.5. Conversion Keyword Summary

Action	Keywords
ANSI value to string.	Chr
String to lowercase or uppercase.	Format, Lcase, UCase
Date to serial number.	DateSerial, DateValue
Decimal number to other bases.	Hex, Oct
Number to string.	Format, Str
One data type to another.	CBool, CByte, CCur, CDate, CDbl, CDec, CInt, CLng, CSng, CStr, CVar, CVErr, Fix, Int
Date to day, month, weekday, or year.	Day, Month, Weekday, Year
Time to hour, minute, or second.	Hour, Minute, Second
String to ASCII value.	Asc
String to number.	Val
Time to serial number.	TimeSerial, TimeValue

Note: Use the **StrConv** function to convert one type of string data to another.

10.12 Assignments and Exercises
Answer all questions.

1. List and describe the four major steps involved in software development using the Fahrenheit-to-Celsius conversion method.

2. Why is it important to perform analysis prior to actual programming in Software project?

3. What is a data type? Give two examples and describe their uses.

4. What is an array? Distinguish between a data type and an array. Which one of the two would be best suited for describing a record?

5. What Is an Object?

    a. Demonstrate by example how an object can be created from a class.

6. What is a Message?

7. What is a Class?

    a. Describe how to create a class in Visual Basic.Net

8. What is Abstract Class?

9. What is a Base Class?

10. What is a Sub Class?

11. What is a Super Class?

12. What Is Inheritance?

    a. Which class can be inherited but cannot be instantiated?

13. What Is Encapsulation?

14. What Is Instance?

15. What Is Extends?

16. What Is Method?

17. What Is Class Method?

18. What Is Instance Method?

19. What Is Class Variable?

20. What Is Instance Variable?

21. What Is Interface?

22. What Is Package?

23.
```
Dim Employeelist(4) As Employee
Employeelist(0) = New Employee("1119", Carlos"," "," ")
```

    a. Why is the code trying to do?

    b. Which is a class and which is an object?

    c. Which type of object is involved?

24. Given this expression: **Dim** *arraynames*(5**) As** String * 20.

    a. Briefly interpret the expression in your own words.

    b. Calculate the size of the *arraynames* with option base 1.

    c. Assuming the initial memory address for the *arraynames* was 7780, calculate the starting address of the third record or index no. 3

25. Refer to the table 10-5 above and answer the following questions:

    a. What is the size of each employee record?

    b. What is the size of array required to accommodate the *Employeelist* carrying 1000 employees?

    c. Calculate the memory address to locate the record bearing the name "Samuel" assuming the beginning address is 5820.

Project:

26. Design a program using visual basic.net as illustrated below in Figure 10-18

Figure 10-18 Employee Payroll Program

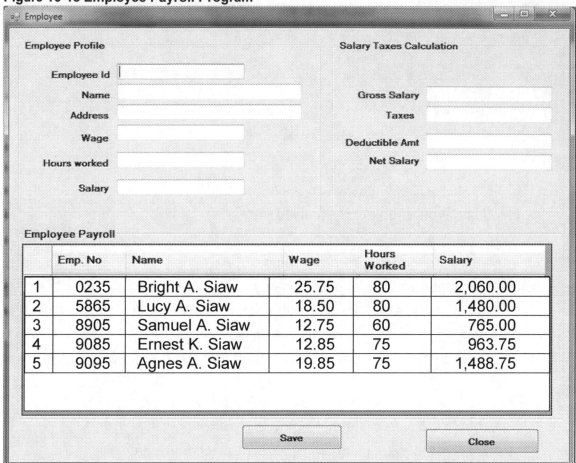

	Emp. No	Name	Wage	Hours Worked	Salary
1	0235	Bright A. Siaw	25.75	80	2,060.00
2	5865	Lucy A. Siaw	18.50	80	1,480.00
3	8905	Samuel A. Siaw	12.75	60	765.00
4	9085	Ernest K. Siaw	12.85	75	963.75
5	9095	Agnes A. Siaw	19.85	75	1,488.75

a. Perform the analysis, design and derive an algorithm for the program.

b. Design the windows form as shown above while noting that payroll list in a **DataGridView** control.

c. Write a function that reads the data file Employee.txt and loads the list of the five records of employee payroll into the form indicated in the figure 10-18 above.

d. Write a function that writes or append new records that are inserted in the Employee profile into the data file Employee.txt.

27. **Project two:** Design a program using visual basic.net as described below :
Fizzbuzz Plus is a game I learned long ago in the elementary school French class, as a way to practice counting in that language. Players take turns counting, starting with one and going up. The rules are simple: when your turn arrives, you should say the next number. However if that number is a **multiple of five**, you should say the word "**fizz**" instead. If the number is a **multiple of seven**, you should say "**buzz**". And if it is a **multiple of both**, you should say "**fizzbuzz**".
If you mess up you're out , and the game continues without you.

What to do ?:

1. You are required to write a stand-alone executable program in dotNet .

2. The program should be able to accommodate one game results which must include all the multiples of five and seven below 250.

3. The program should display the results in a 3-column table on the screen

4. Users should be able to input into the program the maximum count or limit of iteration for each game (Note: by default the maximum count is 250).

5. Documentation should include the following:

    a. Well documented source code on CD-Rom and a printed hardcopy.
    b. Proof of execution.
    c. User's Guide.
    d. Analysis including class diagram, flow chart and pseudo-code of the program. (Outline of analysis: definition of problem, proposed solution, pseudo-code.)

GLOSSARY

3-D reference	A pattern for referring to the workbook, worksheet, and cell from which a value should be read.
action button	Navigation buttons that can be added to slides.
action query	A type of query that updates or makes changes to multiple records in one operation.
active cell	The cell that is currently selected and open for editing.
active cell	A selected cell.
Active Directory	A network service that stores information about resources, such as computers and printers.
Active Server Pages (ASP)	Pages stored on a server that generate different views of the data in response to choices users make on a Web page.
Add-In	A supplemental program that can be used to extend Excel's functions.
add-ins	Supplemental programs that extend a program's capabilities.
adjustable objects	Objects with an adjustment handle (which looks like a small yellow diamond) that allows you to alter the appearance of the object without changing its size.
adjustment handle	A small yellow diamond that indicates a shape is adjustable. You can use this handle to alter the appearance of the shape without changing its size.
agenda slide	A slide used at the beginning of a presentation that outlines in bulleted points the presentation's material.
aggregate function	A function that groups and performs calculations on multiple fields.
alignment	The manner in which a cell's contents are arranged within that cell (for example, centered).
animated pictures	GIF (Graphics Interchange Format) or digital video files that you can insert into a slide presentation as a movie.
animation scheme	A set of professionally designed animations divided into three categories: Subtle, Moderate, and Exciting.
append query	A query that adds a group of records from one or more tables to the end of one or more tables.
arc	A curved line whose angle you can change by dragging an adjustment handle.
arguments	Specific data a function requires to calculate a value.
arithmetic operator	An operator that performs an arithmetic operation: + (addition), - (subtraction), * (multiplication), or / (division).

ASCII	Acronym for American Standard Code for Information Interchange, a coding scheme for text characters developed in 1968. ASCII files have the extension .asc.
ASP	See Active Server Pages.
aspect ratio	The relationship between a graphic's height and width.
attribute	A changeable characteristic of a shape—such as fill, line, and shadow—or of text—such as style, font, color, embossment, and shadow.
auditing	The process of examining a worksheet for errors.
AutoComplete	The ability to complete data entry for a cell based on similar values in other cells in the same column.
AutoContent Wizard	A wizard that takes you through a step-by-step process to create a presentation, prompting you for presentation information as you go.
AutoCorrect	A feature that corrects common capitalization and spelling errors (such as changing as teh to the) as you type them.
AutoFill	The ability to extend a series of values based on the contents of a single cell.
AutoFilter	A Microsoft Excel tool you can use to create filters.
AutoForm	A feature that efficiently creates forms using all the available fields and minimal formatting.
AutoFormats	Predefined formats that can be applied to a worksheet.
automatic layout behavior	A feature that recognizes when you insert an object onto a slide and changes the layout to fit the objects on the slide.
AutoRepublish	An Excel technology that maintains a link between a Web document and the worksheet on which the Web document is based and updates the Web document whenever the original worksheet is saved.
back-end database	The part of a split database that is stored on a server for security reasons, and which usually consists of the tables and other objects that you don't want people to be able to modify.
background	The underlying colors, shading, texture, and style of the color scheme.
binary file	A file coded so that its data can be read by a computer.
Boolean	A data type that can hold either of two mutually exclusive values, often expressed as yes/no, 1/10, on/off, or true/false.
Bound	Linked, as when a form used to view information in a table is linked to that table.

Briefcase	A replication folder that you use to keep files in sync when you work on different computers in different locations.
browser	A program that lets users view Web documents.
bullet points	A list of items in which each item is preceded by a symbol.
button	A graphical image or text box that executes a command. Buttons appear on toolbars, in dialog boxes, and in other display elements.
case	The capitalization (uppercase or lowercase) of a word or phrase. Title case has the first letter of all important words capitalized. Sentence case has only the first letter of the first word capitalized. ZIP is all uppercase and zip is all lowercase. Toggle case changes uppercase to lowercase and vice versa.
cell	The box at the intersection of a row and a column.
cell	The intersection of a row and a column.
cell range	A group of cells.
cell reference	The letter and number combination, such as C16, that identifies the row and column intersection of a cell.
change markers	Icons that indicate where reviewers have made a revision to a slide.
chart	A diagram made up of different elements that help display a datasheet's information.
charts	Visual summaries of worksheet data, also called graphs.
class module	One of two types of modules in Microsoft Visual Basic for Applications (VBA). A class module is associated with a specific form or report.
clip art	Professionally designed images that can be incorporated into PowerPoint presentations.
Code	VBA programs; also called procedures, referred to in Access as modules.
collate	To assemble or print in order.
color menu	The color palette associated with Drawing toolbar buttons, such as Fill Color, Line Color, or Font Color.
color scheme	A set of eight complementary colors available for designing your PowerPoint slides. A color scheme consists of a background color, a color for lines and text, and six additional colors balanced to provide a professional look to a presentation.

columns	Cells that are on the same vertical line in a worksheet.
combo box	A control in which you can either select from a drop- down list or type an option.
comma-delimited text file	A data file consisting of fields and records, stored as text, in which the fields are separated from each other by commas.
command button	A control shaped like a button to which you can attach code that runs when the button is clicked.
Comment	A note embedded in code that helps people reading the code understand its purpose.
comments	Notes that can be written and viewed by multiple reviewers, and hidden or displayed as needed.
comparison operator	An operator that compares values, such as < (less than), > (greater than), and = (equal to).
Component	A part of a database that is used to store and organize information. Also known as a database object.
compress	To reduce the file size of an image. Sometimes picture quality is compromised for smaller file size.
Compression	A means of compacting information for more efficient means of transportation.
conditional formats	Formats that are applied only when cell contents meet certain criteria.
conditional formula	A formula that calculates a value using one of two different expressions, depending on whether a third expression is true or false.
connection pointer	A small box pointer with which you drag a connection line between two connection points.
connection points	Small blue handles on each side of a shape that you use to add a connection line between two shapes.
Constant	A named item that retains a constant value throughout the execution of a program, as opposed to a variable, whose value can change during execution.
Control	An object such as a label, text box, option button, or check box in a form or report that allows you to view or manipulate information stored in tables or queries.
control boxes	The gray boxes at the beginning of a row or column in a datasheet that correspond to the different data series.
control property	A setting that determines the appearance of a control, what data it displays, and how that data looks. A control's properties can be viewed and changed in its Properties dialog box.

control source	The source of a control's data—the field, table or query whose data will be displayed in the control.
Criteria	The specifications you give to Access so that it can find matching fields and records. Criteria can be simple, such as all the records with a postal code of 98052, or complex, such as the phone numbers of all customers who have placed orders for over $500 worth of live plants within the last two weeks and who live in postal codes 98052, 98053, and 98054.
crop	To trim the edges of an image by hiding parts of it.
crosstab query	A query that calculates and restructures data for easier analysis.
data access page	A dynamic Web page that allows users to directly manipulate data in a database via the Internet.
data consolidation	Summarizing data from a set of similar cell ranges.
data list	One or more columns of data depicting multiple instances of a single thing (such as an order).
data map	A pattern of data represented in an XML file.
data marker	A graphical representation in a chart of each data point in a data series. The data is plotted against an x-axis, a y-axis, and—in three-dimensional charts—a z-axis.
data point	The value in a datasheet's cell that, together with other data points, comprise a data series.
data series	A group of related data points.
data series marker	A graphical representation of the information in a data series.
data source	A database or file to which a data access page is connected.
data type	The type of data that can be entered in a field: text, memo, number, date/time, currency, AutoNumber, Boolean (Yes/No), OLE object, and hyperlink. You set the data type by displaying the table in Design view.
data warehouse	A company that serves as a data repository for a variety of data and that may make use of replication to keep each database synchronized when more than one version of the database is updated in more than one remote location.
database application	A database that is refined and made simpler for the user by the sophisticated use of queries, forms, reports, a switchboard, and various other tools.

database program	A program that stores data. Programs range from those that can store one table per file (referred to as a flat database) to those that can store many related tables per file (referred to as a relational database).
database security	The protection of database information from accidental damage, destruction, or theft through the use of encryption, passwords, access permissions, replication, and other security measures.
database window	The window from which all database objects can be manipulated or accessed.
datasheet	A numerical representation of chart data in a grid of rows and columns.
Datasheet view	The view in which the information in a table or query can be viewed and manipulated.
Decrypting	"Unscrambling" a database that has been encrypted for security reasons.
delete query	A query that deletes a group of records from one or more tables.
delimited text file	A type of text file format in which each record and each field is separated from the next by a known character called a delimiter.
Delimiter	A character such as a comma (,), semicolon (;), or backslash (\), or pairs of characters such as quotation marks (" ") or braces ({}), that are used to separate records and fields in a delimited text file.
demote	To indent a title or bulleted item on a slide, moving it down in the outline to a lower-level item (a bullet item or sub-point).
dependents	The cells with formulas that use the value from a particular cell.
design grid	The name given to the structure used in Design view to manually construct and modify advanced filters and queries.
Design Master	In replication, the term for the version of the database from which replicas are made and where changes made to replicas are copied and synchronized.
design template	A presentation with a designed format and color scheme.
Design view	The view in which the structure of a table or query can be viewed and manipulated.
DHTML	Acronym for Dynamic Hypertext Markup Language.
digital signature	An electronic, secure stamp of authentication on a document.
docked toolbar	A toolbar that is attached to the edge of the PowerPoint window.

dotted selection box	The border of a selected object that indicates that you can manipulate the entire object.
driver	A program that controls access to a file or device.
duplicate query	A form of select query that locates records that have the same information in one or more fields that you specify.
Dynamic Hypertext Markup Language (DHTML)	A new version of the standard authoring language, HTML, that includes codes for dynamic Web page elements.
dynamic Web page	A page whose content is created in response to some action on the part of a user who is viewing the page over the Internet.
dynamic-link library	A file with programming code that can be called by a worksheet function.
embed	To save a file as part of another file, as opposed to linking one file to another.
embedded object	An object created with another program but stored in PowerPoint. You can update an embedded object in PowerPoint.
encrypted	Encoded for privacy protection.
Encrypting	"Scrambling" data for security reasons.
error code	A brief message that appears in a worksheet cell, describing a problem with a formula or a function.
Event	An action performed by a user or by Access, to which a programmed response can be attached. Common user events include Click, Double Click, Mouse Down, Mouse Move, and Mouse Up. You can use macros or VBA modules to determine how Access responds when one of these events occurs.
exclusive use	A setting used when you want to be the only person who currently has a database open. You must open a database for exclusive use when setting or removing a password that limits database access.
export	The process of converting and saving a file format to be used in another program.
Exporting	The process of creating a file containing the information in a database table in a format that can be used by other programs.

Expression	A combination of functions, field values, constants, and operators that yield a result. Expressions can be simple, such as >100, or complex, such as ((ProductPrice*Quantity)*.90)+(Shipping+Handling).
Expression Builder	A feature used to create formulas (expressions) used in query criteria, form and report properties, and table validation rules.
Extensible Markup Language (XML)	A content-marking system that lets you store data about the contents of a document in that document.
Extensible Markup Language (XML)	A refined language developed for Web documents that describes document structure rather than appearance.
field	A column in a data list.
Field	An individual item of the information that is the same type across all records. Represented in Access as a column in a database table.
File Transfer Protocol (FTP)	A communications method that you use to quickly transfer and save files over the Internet.
fill handle	The square at the lower right corner of a cell you drag to indicate other cells that should hold values in the series defined by the active cell.
Fill Series	The ability to extend a series of values based on the contents of two cells, where the first cell has the starting value for the series and the second cell shows the increment.
filter	A rule that Excel uses to determine which worksheet rows to display.
First Line Indent marker	The small upper triangle on the horizontal ruler that controls the first line of the paragraph.
fixed-width text file	A common text file format that is often used to transfer data from older applications. Each record is always the same number of characters long, and the same field within the records is always the same number of characters. In other words, the same field always starts the same number of characters from the beginning of each record, and any characters not occupied by real data are filled with zeros.
Flag	A marker that can be set to true or false to indicate the state of an object.
flat database	A simple database consisting of one table.
floating toolbar	A toolbar that is not attached to the edge of the PowerPoint window.

Form	A database object used to enter, edit, and manipulate information in a database table. A form gives you a simple view of some or all of the fields of one record at a time.
Form view	The view in which you can enter and modify the information in a record.
formats	Predefined sets of characteristics that can be applied to cell contents.
formula	An expression used to calculate a value.
freeze	To assign cells that will remain at the top of a worksheet regardless of how far down the worksheet a user scrolls.
front-end database	The part of a split database that is distributed to the people who analyze and enter data. The actual data tables are stored on a server for security reasons.
function	A predefined formula.
Function	A named procedure or routine in a program, often used for mathematical or financial calculations.
function procedure	In VBA, a procedure that is enclosed in Function and End Function statements and returns a value.
Goal Seek	An analysis tool that finds the value for a selected cell that would produce a given result from a calculation.
graphic	A picture or a drawing object.
graphs	Visual summaries of worksheet data, also called charts.
grayscale	A black and white image that displays shades of gray.
Group	One of four elements—the other three being object, permission, and user—on which the Access user-level security model is based.
grouping	An action that allows a set of shapes to be handled or changed as a single unit.
grouping level	The level by which records are grouped in a report. For example, records might be grouped by state (first level), then by city (second level), and then by postal code (third level).
Handout Master	The part of a template that controls the characteristics (background color, text color, font, and font size) of the handouts in a presentation. To make uniform changes to the handouts, you change the Handout Master.
hanging indent	Paragraph formatting adjusted by small triangles on the horizontal ruler where the first line of text is indented less than the subsequent lines.
Hanging Indent marker	The small lower triangle on the horizontal ruler that controls all lines in a paragraph except the first.

home page	The first page of a Web site or PowerPoint presentation.
hovering	Pausing the pointer over an object for a second or two to display more information, such as a submenu or ScreenTip.
HTML	Acronym for HyperText Markup Language.
HTML	See Hypertext Markup Language.
HTML tag	An HTML command that determines how the tagged information looks and acts.
HTTP	Acronym for HyperText Transfer Protocol.
hyperlink	A reference to a file on the World Wide Web.
hyperlink	A " hot spot" or "jump" to a location in the same file, another file, or an HTML page, represented by colored and underlined text or by a graphic.
Hypertext Markup Language (HTML)	A document-formatting system that tells a Web browser such as Internet Explorer how to display the contents of a file.
HyperText Transfer Protocol (HTTP)	The World Wide Web's formatting protocol that determines how commands are executed and how browsers interact.
import	The process of converting a file format created in another program.
Importing	The method whereby data is brought into an Access database from a different database or program.
indent marker	A marker on the horizontal ruler that controls the indent levels of a text object.
input mask	A field property that determines what data can be entered in the field, how the data looks, and the format in which it is stored.
insertion point	The blinking vertical line that appears in the presentation window, indicating where text or objects will appear when you type or insert an object.
Intranet	A secure, proprietary Web-based network used within a company or group and accessible only to its members.
Keyword	A word that is part of the VBA programming language.
label control	An area on a form that contains text that appears on the form in Form view.
LAN	Acronym for local area network.
landscape	Horizontal orientation (10 x 7.5 inches) of an image on the output media.
landscape mode	A display and printing mode whereby columns run parallel to the short edge of a sheet of paper.

Layout Preview	A view of a report that shows you how each element will look but without all the detail of Print Preview.
Left Indent marker	The small square on the horizontal ruler that controls how far the entire paragraph sits from the edge of the text object. The Left Indent marker moves the First Line Indent marker and the Hanging Indent marker, maintaining their relationship.
legend	A list that identifies each data series in the datasheet.
link	A formula that has a cell show the value from another cell.
linked object	An object created in another program that maintains a connection to its source. A linked object is stored in its source document, where it was created. You update a linked object within its source program.
Linking	The process of connecting to data in other applications.
lobby page	An information page that appears on the server before the broadcast starts.
local area network (LAN)	A computer network that connects computers, printers, and other hardware to a server or group of servers.
locked cells	Cells that cannot be modified if their worksheet is protected.
logical operator	One of the Boolean operators: AND, OR and NOT.
Lookup Wizard	The wizard in Access that simplifies the creation of a Lookup list.
macro	A series of recorded automated actions that can be replayed.
macro	A command or series of commands (keystrokes and instructions) that are treated as a single command and used to automate repetitive or complicated tasks.
Macro	A set of automated instructions that perform a sequence of simple tasks.
mailto	A special type of hyperlink that lets a user create an e-mail message to a particular e-mail address.
main form	One form that is linked to one or more tables.
main report	One report that displays records from one or more tables.
make-table query	A query that creates a new table from all or part of the data in one or more tables. Make-table queries are helpful for creating a table to export to other Microsoft Access databases.
many-to-many relationship	A relationship formed between two tables that each have a one-to-many relationship with a third table.
mapped network drive	A drive to which you have assigned a drive letter. Used for quickly accessing files stored in locations that are not likely to change.
margin markers	Small squares on the ruler that move both the upper and lower indent markers.

Mask	A field property that determines what data can be entered in a field, how the data looks, and the format in which it is stored.
master	A design pattern that is uniformly applied to slides, handouts, and speaker notes.
MDE	See Microsoft Database Executable.
menu	A list of commands or options available in a program.
Merge and Center	An operation, initiated by clicking the Merge and Center toolbar button, that combines a contiguous group of cells into a single cell. Selecting a merged cell and clicking the Merge and Center toolbar button splits the merged cells into the original group of separate cells.
metadata	Data that describes the contents of a file.
Microsoft Clip Organizer	A tool that enables you to collect and organize clip art images, pictures, sounds, and motion clips.
Microsoft Database Executable (MDE)	A compiled version of a database. Saving a database as an MDE file compiles all modules, removes all editable source code, and compacts the destination database.
Microsoft Visual Basic for Applications (VBA)	A programming language that uses a visual environment to simplify the development of programs, such as those that create user interfaces (the methods used to communicate with a computer). The VBA approach is now the standard in many programming languages.
Microsoft Visual Basic for Applications (VBA)	A high- level programming language developed for the purpose of creating Windows applications.
Module	A VBA program.
more colors	Additional colors that you can add to each color menu.
move handle	The four vertical dots at the left end of a toolbar by which you can move the toolbar around.
named range	A group of related cells defined by a single name.
named range	A group of cells in an Excel spreadsheet.
native format	The file format an application uses to produce its own files.
navigation button	One of the buttons found on a form or navigation bar that helps users display specific records.
navigation frame	A graphical panel used for navigating from slide to slide in a PowerPoint presentation on the Web.
network security	Technologies to protect your network connections to the Internet or other public networks.

network server	A central computer that stores files and programs and manages system functions for a network.
Normal view	A view that contains all three panes: Outline/Slides, Slide, and Notes.
Notes Page view	A view where you can add speaker notes and related graphics.
Notes Pages Master	The part of a template that controls the characteristics (background color, text color, font, and font size) of the speaker notes in a presentation. To make uniform changes to the speaker notes, you change the Notes Pages Master.
Notes pane	Area in Normal view where you can add speaker notes.
object	In PowerPoint, any element that you can manipulate.
Object	One of the components of an Access database, such as a table, form, or report.
Office Assistant	A help system that answers questions, offers tips, and provides help for Microsoft Office XP program features.
Office Clipboard	A storage area shared by all Office programs where multiple pieces of information from several different sources are stored.
Office Online	A clip art gallery that Microsoft maintains on its Web site. To access Office Online, you click the "Clip Art on Office Online" link at the bottom of the Clip Art task pane.
offset	The direction and distance in which a shadow falls from an object.
one-to-many relationship	A relationship formed between two tables in which each record in one table has more than one related record in the other table.
one-to-one relationship	A relationship formed between two tables in which each record in one table has only one related record in the other table.
Open DataBase Connectivity (ODBC)	A protocol that facilitates data transfer between databases and related programs.
Operator	See arithmetic operator; comparison operator; logical operator.
optimistic locking	Locking a record only for the brief time that Access is saving changes to it.
option button	A control on a form that allows users to select preferred settings.
Outline/Slides pane	Area in Normal view where you can organize and develop presentation content in text or slide miniature form.
Package for CD	A feature that helps you ensure that you have all the presentation components you need when you have to transport a PowerPoint presentation for use on a different computer.

Page	See data access page.
paragraph	Text that begins and end when you press Enter.
parameter query	A query that prompts for the information to be used in the query, such as a range of dates.
Parsing	In Access, the process of analyzing a document and identifying anything that looks like structured data.
password	A unique set of letters and characters used to allow access to documents or processes.
Password	A secret sequence of letters and other symbols needed to log on to a database as an authorized user.
Paste Options	A button, which appears after you paste an item from the Clipboard into your workbook, that lets you control how the item appears in the workbook.
Permission	An attribute that specifies how a user can access data or objects in a database.
pessimistic locking	Locking a record for the entire time it is being edited.
photo album	A personal collection of digital images to use in presentations.
Pick from List	The ability to enter a value into a cell by choosing the value from the set of values already entered into cells in the same column.
pivot	To reorganize the contents of a PivotTable.
PivotChart	A chart that is linked to a PivotTable and that can be reorganized dynamically to emphasize different aspects of the underlying data.
PivotChart	An interactive chart that is linked to a database.
PivotTable	A dynamic worksheet that can be reorganized by a user.
PivotTable	An interactive table that is linked to a database.
Places bar	A bar on the left side of the Save As and Open dialog boxes that provides quick access to commonly used locations in which to store and open files.
Populate	To fill a table or other object with data.
portrait	Vertical orientation (7.5 x 10 inches) of an image on the output media.
portrait mode	A display and printing mode whereby columns run parallel to the long edge of a sheet of paper.
PowerPoint Viewer	A program that allows you to show a slide show on a computer that does not have PowerPoint installed.
precedents	The cells that are used in a formula.

presentation window	The electronic canvas on which you type text, draw shapes, create graphs, add color, and insert objects.
primary key	A field or group of fields with values that distinguish a row in a data list from all other rows in the list.
primary key	One or more fields that determine the uniqueness of each record in a database.
Print Preview	A view of a report that allows users to see exactly how the report will look when printed.
Procedure	VBA code that performs a specific task or set of tasks.
program window	An area of the screen used to display the PowerPoint program and the presentation window.
promote	To remove an indent on a bulleted item or sub-point of a slide, moving it up in the outline to it a higher-level item (a bulleted item or title).
properties	Information about a PowerPoint presentation such as the subject, author, presentation title, and so on.
property	A file detail, such as an author name or project code, that helps identify the file.
Property	A setting that determines the content and appearance of the object to which it applies.
pure black and white	A black and white image that displays only black and white without any shades of gray.
query	A statement that locates records in a database.
Query	A database object that locates information so that the information can be viewed, changed, or analyzed in various ways. The results of a query can be used as the basis for forms, reports, and data access pages.
range	A group of related cells.
range	A block of cells in a worksheet or datasheet.
read-only	The designation of a file that can be viewed but not altered.
Record	All the items of information (fields) that pertain to one particular entity, such as a customer, employee, or project.
record selector	The gray bar along the left edge of a table or form.
record source	The place from which information derives between two bound objects, such as a field that pulls information from a table.
referential integrity	The system of rules Access uses to ensure that relationships between tables are valid and that data cannot be changed in one table without also being changed in all related tables.

refresh	To update the contents of one document when the contents of another document are changed.
relational database	A sophisticated type of database in which data is organized in multiple related tables. Data can be pulled from the tables just as if they were stored in a single table.
Relationship	An association between common fields in two tables.
relative reference	A cell reference in a formula, such as =B3, that refers to a cell that is a specific distance away from the cell that contains the formula. For example, if the formula =B3 were in cell C3, copying the formula to cell C4 would cause the formula to change to =B4.
Replica	A copy of the Design Master of a database.
Replicating	The process of creating a Design Master so that multiple copies of a database can be sent to multiple locations for editing. The copies can then be synchronized with the Design Master so that it reflects all the changes.
report	A special document with links to one or more worksheets from the same workbook.
Report	A database object used to display a table or tables in a formatted, easily accessible manner, either on the screen or on paper.
RGB (Red, Green, and Blue) values	The visible spectrum represented by mixing red, green, and blue colors.
rich media	The combined use of motion and sound in media.
Rich Text Format (RTF)	A common text format that many programs can open.
rotating handle	A small green handle around a shape used to adjust the angle of rotation of the shape.
row selector	The gray box at the left end of a row in a table that, when clicked, selects all the cells in the row.
rows	Cells that are on the same horizontal line in a worksheet.
running a query	The process of telling Access to search the specified table or tables for records that match the criteria you have specified in the query and to display the designated fields from those records in a datasheet (table).
Saving	The process of storing the current state of a database or database object for later retrieval. In Access, new records and changes to existing records are saved when you move to a different record; you don't have to do anything to save them. You do have to save new objects and changes to existing objects

scalable font	A font that can be represented in different sizes without distortion.
scaling	To size an entire object by a set percentage.
scenarios	Alternative data sets that let you view the impact of specific changes on your worksheet.
schema	A document that defines the structure of a set of XML files.
Schema	A description of the structure of XML data, as opposed to the content of the data. Applications that export to XML might combine the content and schema in one .xml file or might create an .xml file to hold the content and an .xsd file to hold the schema.
ScreenTip	Information displayed about a button, icon, or other item on the screen when you point to the item.
security level	A setting that determines whether presentations that contain macros can be opened on your computer.
select	To highlight an item in preparation for making some change to it.
select query	A query that retrieves data matching specified criteria from one or more tables and displays the results in a datasheet.
selection box	A gray slanted line or dotted outline around an object.
Selector	A small box attached to an object that you click to select the object.
shape	An object that can be drawn free-form or created using tools provided by PowerPoint. Shapes can be sized, moved, copied, and formatted in a variety of ways to suit your needs.
sharing	Making a workbook available for more than one user to open and modify simultaneously.
sharing a database	Providing access to a database so more that one person can access it to add or alter its information.
sheet tab	The indicator for selecting a worksheet, located in the lower left corner of the workbook window.
sizing handle	A white circle on each corner and side of a shape that you can drag to change the shape's size. To preserve the shape's proportions, you can hold down the Shift key while resizing a shape.
slanted-line selection box	The border of a selected object that indicates that you can edit the object's content.

Slide Master	The part of a template that controls the characteristics (background color, text color, font, and font size) of the slides in a presentation. To make uniform changes to the slides, you change the Slide Master.
Slide Master view	The view from which you make changes to slides, using the Slide Master View toolbar. You switch to Slide Master view by pointing first to Master and then to Slide Master on the View menu.
Slide pane	Area in Normal view where you can view a slide and add text, graphics, and other items to the slide.
Slide Show view	A view where you can preview slides as an electronic presentation.
Slide Sorter view	A view where you can see all slides in a presentation in miniature.
slide timing	The length of time that a slide appears on the screen.
slide transition	The visual effect when moving from slide to slide in presentation.
Smart Tag	A button that helps you control the result of certain actions, such as automatic text correction, automatic layout behavior, or copy and paste.
smart tags	A Microsoft Office technology that recognizes values in a spreadsheet and finds related information on the Web.
sort	To reorder the contents of a worksheet based on a criterion.
source document	The original document, created in the source program, to which an object is linked.
source program	The program that created the document that has been linked to a slide object.
splash screen	An introductory screen containing useful or entertaining information. Often used to divert the user's attention while data is loading.
split bar	A line that defines which cells have been frozen at the top of a worksheet.
SQL	See Structured Query Language.
SQL database	A database that supports SQL and that can be accessed simultaneously by several users on a LAN.
standard module	A VBA program that contains general procedures that are not associated with any object.
static HTML page	A Web page that provides a snapshot of some portion of the database contents at one point in time.

status bar	The bar at the bottom of the presentation window that displays messages about the current state of PowerPoint.
String	A series of characters enclosed in quotation marks.
Structured Query Language (SQL)	A database sublanguage used in querying, updating, and managing relational databases—the de facto standard for database products.
sub procedure	A series of VBA statements enclosed by Sub and End Sub statements.
Subdatasheet	A datasheet that is embedded in another datasheet.
subfolder	A folder within a folder.
Subform	A form inserted in a control that is embedded in another form.
subpoints	Indented items below a bulleted item.
Subreport	A report inserted in a control that is embedded in another report.
subtotals	Partial totals for related data in a worksheet.
summary slide	A slide that lists titles of slides in a presentation and which can be used as a home page or an agenda slide.
Switchboard	A form used to navigate among the objects of a database application so that users don't have to be familiar with the actual database.
Synchronizing	The process of comparing the information in a database replica with the database's Design Master and merging any changes.
Syntax	The format that expressions must conform to in order for Access to be able to process them.
Table	Information organized in columns (records) and rows (fields).
Table Wizard	The Access tool that helps users construct tables.
tables	Data lists in a database.
tags	Marks used to indicate display properties or to communicate data about the contents of a document.
	Codified characters that determine how text and graphics are displayed in a Web browser.
task pane	A pane that enables you to quickly access commands related to a specific task without having to use menus and toolbars.
	A pane that provides a quick and easy way of initiating common tasks.
template	A workbook used as a pattern for creating other workbooks.

Template	An applied pattern used in creating the slides, handouts, and speaker notes in a PowerPoint presentation. A template uses masters—sets of colors, text formats, and graphics to achieve different designs. You can use a template provided by PowerPoint or create your own.
	A ready-made database application that users can tailor to fit their needs.
text animation	An effect applied to text that makes it appear on a slide in increments: one letter, word, or section at a time.
text box control	A control on a form or report where data from a table can be entered or edited.
text label	A text object used primarily for short phrases or notes.
text object	A box that contains text in a slide and is handled as a unit.
text placeholder	A dotted-lined box that you can click to add text.
Thesaurus	A feature that looks up alternative words or synonyms for a word.
thumbnails	Miniature representations of graphics or slides.
tick-mark labels	The labels that identify the data plotted in a chart.
Title Master	The part of a template that controls the characteristics (background color, text color, font, and font size) of the title slides in a presentation. To make uniform changes to the title slides, you change the Title Master.
title slide	The first slide in a presentation.
title text	Tex t that identifies the name or purpose of a slide.
toggle	An on/off button or command that is activated when you click it and deactivated when you click it again.
toolbar	A graphical bar in the presentation window with buttons that perform some of the common commands in PowerPoint.
Toolbar Options button	The button at the right end of a toolbar that provides access to hidden buttons and other toolbar options.
transaction record	The written record of transactions.
transparency film	Clear sheets for use in overhead projectors that can be written or printed on like paper.
trend line	A projection of future data (such as sales) based on past performance.
Unbound	Not linked, as when a control is used to calculate values from two or more fields and is therefore not bound to any particular field.

UNC	See universal naming convention.
UNC Path	**Universal Naming Convention path.** A path format that includes the computer name, drive letter, and nested folder names.
ungrouping	An action that allows grouped shapes to be restored to individual shapes that can be handled independently.
unmatched query	A form of select query that locates records in one table that don't have related records in another table.
update query	A select query that changes the query's results in some way, such as by changing a field.
URL	Acronym for Uniform Resource Locator. An address on the World Wide Web.
User	A person authorized to access a database but who generally is not involved in establishing its structure.
validation rule	A test that data must pass to be entered into a cell without generating a warning message.
validation rule	A field property that tests entries to ensure that only the correct types of information become part of a table.
Variable	A name or symbol that stands for a value that can change.
VBA	See Microsoft Visual Basic for Applications
VBA	See Microsoft Visual Basic for Applications.
VBA procedure	A VBA program.
View	The display of information from a specific perspective.
Visual Basic Editor	The environment in which VBA programs are written and edited.
Visual Basic Editor	The environment in which VBA code is written.
Visual Basic IDE	See Visual Basic Editor. Integrated Development Environment
Web browser	An application, such as Microsoft Internet Explorer, used to find and display Web pages.
Web browser	An application used to view Web pages on the World Wide Web.
what-if analysis	Analysis of the contents of a worksheet to determine the impact that specific changes have on your calculations.
WIF	Acronym for workgroup information file.

wildcard character	A placeholder for an unknown character or characters in search criteria.
Wizard	A helpful tool that guides users through the steps for completing a specific task.
word processing box	A text object used primarily for longer text.
word wrap	A feature that automatically moves the insertion point to the next line within an object as you type.
WordArt	Stylized text for enhancing titles and headings in PowerPoint presentations.
workbook	The basic Excel document, consisting of one or more worksheets.
Workgroup	A group of users in a multi-user environment who share data and the same workgroup information file. When you install Access, the setup program creates a default workgroup and sets up two groups, Admins and Users, within that workgroup.
workgroup information file (WIF)	The file where information about the objects, permissions, users, and groups that comprise a specific workgroup is stored.
worksheet	A page in an Excel workbook.
Worksheet	A page in a Microsoft Excel spreadsheet.
workspace	An Excel file type (.xlw) that allows you to open several files at once.
World Wide Web (WWW)	A network of servers on the Internet that support HTML-formatted documents.
WWW	See World Wide Web
x-axis	The horizontal plane in a chart on which data is graphically represented. Also called the category axis.
XML	See Extensible Markup Language.
y-axis	The vertical plane in a chart on which data is graphically represented. Also called the value axis.

INDEX

.xls, 17, 18, 19, 28, 29, 33
.xlsm
.xlsx, 19, 28
.xlt
xls, xltx, 17, 19

3

3-D chart, 236, 237

A

absolute, 6, 15, 24, 125, 128, 130, 136, 137, 139, 151, 157
Absolute
Cell References, 2, 24, 135, 136, 139, 157
abstract, 350, 352, 353, 374
acceptance test, 345
Access database, 122, 395, 397
accessible, 15, 81, 138, 365, 395, 401
Accessories, 74
Accounting, 13, 14, 80, 83, 85, 102, 103, 104, 309
Action, 230, 268, 288, 326, 334, 381
Add-Ins tab, 17, 27
addresses, 11, 124, 135, 136, 141, 157, 356
adjacent, 15, 54, 56, 88, 90, 105, 127, 138, 165, 181, 220, 239, 241
algorithm, 339, 340, 341, 342, 343, 345, 347, 366, 384
Alignment
Paragraph, 20, 21, 53, 61
Alignment group, 20, 53, 61
alphabetical, 67, 218, 312
alphanumeric, 5
analogous, 11, 351
analysis, 8, 215, 326, 336, 339, 344, 345, 346, 347, 382, 384, 385, 390, 394, 406

Analysis, 147, 189, 199, 200, 201, 202, 203, 206, 207, 209, 211, 212, 339, 344, 347, 385, 406
animation, 253, 283, 284, 285, 287, 386, 404
Animation Pane, 285, 287
ANSI code, 96
Apple II
Computer, 5, 6
application
program, 2, 5, 6, 7, 9, 153, 188, 311, 316, 317, 318, 320, 341, 346, 358, 359, 364, 368, 390, 397, 403, 404, 406
area, 16, 39, 43, 50, 51, 121, 123, 171, 172, 179, 205, 229, 230, 237, 241, 243, 247, 361, 395, 396, 398, 399
Area charts, 235, 237
arithmetic
operations, 14, 15, 128, 137, 138, 347, 356, 368, 386, 398
ASCII or Unicode, 71, 72
Assignment s, 133
audience, 253, 254, 255, 276, 277, 286, 289, 293, 301
Auditing, 24, 101, 113, 138
AutoCalculate, 67
AutoComplete, 59, 387
AutoCorrect, 35, 44, 45, 387
AutoFill, 2, 31, 68, 195, 387
AutoLookup, 326, 334
Automatic recalculation, 10
automation, 120
autonumber, 325
AutoSum
Sum, 2, 35, 67, 158, 159
Average, 139, 146, 227
averages, 15, 138, 326

B

background, 32, 67, 88, 167, 212, 229, 250,
Background, 212, 259
bar, 16, 20, 38, 54, 67, 80, 116, 199, 200,
Bar charts, 235, 237
basic
concept, 9, 378
behavior, 122, 123, 221, 351, 387, 402
Between, 29, 31, 191, 192, 228
bijective, 10
binary, 19, 28, 124, 127, 128, 310, 347, 387
Black Box, 351
Bold, 36, 64, 71
Boolean
true or false, 13, 135, 317, 387, 390, 396
Bounce, 285
bubble chart, 239
build, 153, 225, 340, 363
bytes
bits, 309, 316, 318, 367, 368, 369, 370

C

Calc, 5, 8, 9, 17
calculators, 311
CALLERID, 325
CAPS LOCK, 170
Category, 58, 85, 103, 108, 110, 123, 130, 212
CAUSE, 185, 186
CEILING, 131, 132, 134
cell
Addressing, 5, 8, 1, 23,, 57, 192, 224, 230, 405
Cell Size, 53, 181, 182
cells, 2, 5, 6, 8, 9, 40, 43, 45, 150, 180, 181,
    236, 237,
Cells group, 20, 45, 46, 47, 53, 164, 173, 175,
    176, 177, 178, 181, 182
    Character Map, 72, 73, 74, 75, 76
    characteristics, 9, 10, 49, 357, 366, 404
    characters, 17, 18, 53, 59, 404, 406
    Charts, 10, 16, 22, 215, 254, 290, 293, 294,
    class, 309, 312, 355, 357, 363, 385, 388
    Class method, 351, 355
    classification, 312, 313
    Classifying, 311, 312

Clipboard
Group, 20, 37, 39, 40, 41, 69, 71, 89, 398
clips, 282, 397
Close, 16, 20, 48, 106, 158, 224, 238, 275
Clustered, 236, 237
coding, 339, 342, 345, 346, 349, 387
Coding, 311, 312, 344, 345, 349
collections, 27, 309
Colors
Theme, 71, 261, 263, 300
column
width, 2, 30, 33, 53, 94, 104, 107, 160, 163,
    171, 179, 181
Column charts, 235, 236
columns, 2, 5, 12, 15, , 47, 62, 163, 164,
    171 395, 404
combo, 67, 324, 389
comma-delimited
text, 17, 389
Comments, 25, 26, 37, 43, 60, 69, 306
communicate, 188, 253, 350, 397, 404
Communication, 311, 314, 333
Comparison, 307, 309, 312
compile errors, 346
component, 8, 12, 16
computer, 5, 6, 11, 12, 168, 231, 289, 405
CONCATENATE, 100, 101, 102, 113, 114,
    134
Concentric, 7
Concepts
of Spreadsheet, 5, 9, 310, 339, 350, 357
Concourse theme, 261

condition, 15, 95, 138, 213, 371, 372, 373
conditional
complex nested, 15, 32, 35, 96, 111, 125, 128,
    129, 130, 137, 213, 336, 389
configuration, 363
constants, 336, 356, 368, 392
constructors, 336, 353, 374
contextual
menu, 46, 47, 50, 51, 225, 257, 278
contiguous, 11, 30, 89, 225, 396
cells, 11, 30
convention, 10, 405

Conversion, 311, 312, 333, 381

Copy, 21, 35, 39, 42, 62, 86, 89, 91, 158, 177, 178, 179, 230, 294, 296, 297

CountIF, 189, 194, 195, 196

counts, 139, 194, 326

criteria, 60, 195, 210, 231, 243, 328, 389, 392

Crosstab, 326, 334

cross-tabulate, 8

CTRL, 36, 52, 67, 71, 103, 133, 165, 180
   Currency, 14, 87, 102, 131, 323, 366,

curriculum, 16

Custom, 27, 71, 106, 110, 123, 168, 228, 283

custom-build, 15, 137

Cut

copy text, 21, 39, 41, 179, 304

D

Dark, 224

Data Entry, 307, 309, 310, 320, 324, 330

Data Format, 10, 13

Data Organization, 307, 309, 316

Data Processing, 307, 309, 310, 311, 315, 329

data source, 87, 90, 122, 123, 124, 247, 292, 390

Data Systems, 7

Data tab, 17, 25, 124, 226, 227, 228, 229, 230, 231, 243

Data types, 366

databases, 8, 307, 309, 316, 396, 398, 403

datasheet, 234, 293, 294, 326, 334, 388, 389, 390, 391, 395, 400, 401, 403

Datum, 333

Dbase, 309

dBase III and IV, 17

DBCS, 368

   Debug, 154, 362, 363

   decimal notation, 10

   decimal points, 14, 84, 86, 94, 95, 103

   Delete, 38, 42, 46, 47, 51, 100, 164, 165, 176, 187, 211, 224, 245, 258, 268, 298, 326

   dependencies, 9

   derivation, 15, 136

Design, 78, 221, 264, 297, 298, 331, 390, 403

designing, 339, 388

desktop, 29, 265

development, 6, 153, 346, 350, 361, 382, 397

devices, 76, 314, 315, 316, 363

diacritical

character, 72, 75

diagram, 13, 26, 242, 372, 385, 388

Dialog, 23, 91, 110, 130, 211, 221, 273, 322

dimensional, 10, 291, 294, 369, 370, 373, 390

discrete, 339, 340, 341

disseminating, 309

dissolves, 284

Do, 220, 275, 280, 348, 371, 372, 373

Double, 38, 78, 176, 293, 303, 366, 367, 392

Doughnut charts, 235, 239

E

Editing group, 20, 21, 24, 48, 59, 182

electromechanical tools, 311

electronic spreadsheet, 5, 33

elements, 33, 114, 140, 157, 358, 368, 388

encapsulating, 350

Encapsulation, 351, 382

equation

formula, 33, 109, 128, 356

event, 32, 153, 347, 349, 363

Exciting., 283, 386

Exit, 16, 53, 275, 371, 372, 373

exponential

exponent, 53, 83, 96, 100

Extends, 351, 382

extension, 9, 19, 28, 262, 264, 321, 387

F

facts, 29, 254, 290, 307, 309, 310, 319

Fahrenheit, 343, 366, 382

fields, 222, 235, 320, 351, 379, 393, 400, file, 8, 17, 28, 77, 122, 150, 289, 290314, 316, 358, 362, 397, 406

File, 17, 59, 67, 129, 212, 253, 264, 288, 306, 318, 333, 393

Filename, 33

Fill pane, 301

Filter, 22, 225, 230, 243, 325, 327, 328, 329
fixed-point, 126
floating-point, 126, 127, 128, 367
FLOOR, 131, 132, 134
flow chart, 348, 385
font, 32, 36, 53, 69, 71, 96, 133, 167, 187, 262, 361, 387, 394, 401, 404
Font group, 20, 21, 71, 78, 166, 170
For, 362, 363, 369, 371, 372, 373, 379, 394
Form, 222, 242, 324, 330, 357, 360, 393,
Format Cells, 56, 89, 104, 108, 110, 212
Formatting
format, 2, 17, 21, 64, 81, 96, 161, 194, 210, 213, 290, 296
formula
formulas, 2, 14, 15, 24, 42, 82, 98, 115, 118, 135, 160, 181, 232, 389, 394, 400
FoxPro, 309
fraction
Values, 13, 30, 83, 108, 127, 131
Freeze, 26, 64, 163, 171, 172, 173
Freeze Panes, 26, 64, 172, 173
functions, 2, 6, 24, 56, 100, 130, 132, 135, 137, 159, 253, 311, , 336, 386, 392, 397
fundamental, 250, 336
Fundamentals, 215

G

Get External Data, 25, 124, 231
gigabytes
byted, 316
global, 11, 171, 261, 347, 363
Goal Seek, 189, 207, 208, 209, 211, 212, 394
GotFocus, 363
graphic, 12, 16, 41, 211, 212, 213, 214, 245, 246, 247, 291, 293, 294, 295, 296, 297, 298, 299, 300, 301, 305, 332, 387, 394
graphs, 12, 16, 388, 394, 399
grid
cells, 5, 9, 10, 391
Gridline, 166

H

handouts, 250, 254, 394, 396, 404

Handouts, 273, 274, 306
Header or Footer, 23
headers, 10, 101, 113, 168, 215, 216, 218, 242
Help, 16, 17, 27, 64, 91, 101, 113
hierarchy, 270, 296, 298, 307, 319, 351
histograms, 12, 16
Home menu, 17, 190
homogenous, 340
horizontal, 9, 77, 173, 185, 186, 236, 237, 238, 266, 368, 393, 394, 395, 401
hyperlink, 30, 250, 275, 276, 280, 281, 282, 306, 390, 394, 396

I

Ignore
Once, All, 44
images, 17, 250, 253, 254, 277, 278, 388, 397, 399
implementations, 11, 15, 137
implemented, 350, 368, 370
import data, 122, 231
Indent
Paragraph, 21
index, 310, 333, 368, 371, 379, 383
Info, 16, 17
InfoPath, 72
Inheritance, 351, 382
input – process – output, 341
instance, 30, 176, 178, 179, 180, 187, 320, 350, 351, 352, 355, 357
Instance, 351, 352, 355, 382, 383
instantiated, 350, 352, 382
Instantiating, 374, 376, 377
INT, 131, 132
Integer, 317, 323, 363, 365, 366, 367, 369, 370
Integration test, 345
Interface, 352, 383
intersections, 10
I-P-O, 315, 341
Italic, 71
iteration, 155, 370, 371, 385

J

joysticks, 315

K

keyboard, 9, 12, 72, 73, 81, 195, 199, 206, 299, 310, 341
KeyPress,, 363
keystrokes, 221, 266, 396
kilobytes
bytes, 316

L

label, 10, 11, 12, 13, 29, 30, 36, 65, 163, 195, 389, 395, 404
languages, 72, 107, 271, 342, 343, 344, 345, 351, 358, 363, 368, 397
Layout, 17, 23, 78, 166, 168, 169, 212, 240, 241, 257, 258, 262, 299, 304, 395
Life Cycle, 307, 309
ligature
character, 72
Light,, 224
Line charts, 235, 236
Links, 22, 43, 265, 270, 275, 280, 288
literal,, 367
Load, 363
logical
spread sheet, 254, 312, 316, 319, 345, 368, 396, 398
spreadsheet, 9
Long, 89, 366, 367
Long Date, 89
lookup, 324
Loops, 155, 339, 366
Lotus
Symphony, 9
Lotus 1-2-3, 5, 6, 7, 9, 121

M

Macintosh, 5, 17, 18, 115
Macintosh., 115
magnetic, 312, 314, 318, 319
Mail Merge, 124

Manipulation, 311, 312, 333
mantissa, 127
Manual, 23, 135, 152
Margins, 23
Match case, 49, 60
mathematical, 43, 108, 139, 343, 346, 394
maximum, 9, 11, 12, 30, 33, 119, 122, 124, 385
Medium, 224
megabytes
bytes, 316
memory, 8, 31, 309, 342, 356, 363, 369, 370, 376, 380, 381, 383
Messages, 350, 361, 382
metadata, 310, 333, 397
Method, 351, 352, 382, 383
methodologies, 339
methods, 18, 218, 221, 229, 336, 350, 351, 352, 353, 357, 397
microphones., 315
mimic, 69, 77
modems, 315
Moderate, 283, 386
Modern, 15, 137
Mouse, 23, 37, 40, 69, 288, 392
movies, 282
multimedia, 282, 302
Multimedia, 253, 282
multiplication, 13, 386
MustInherit, 352, 376

N

navigate, 221, 235, 250, 253, 266, 267, 277, 305, 373, 403
negative
or positive, 14, 30, 55, 77, 81, 111, 116, 127, 367
New, 279, 281, 306, 320, 331, 352, 355, 383
Next loop, 372
nonadjacent, 90, 91, 105, 165, 225
nonnumeric, 93
NUM LOCK, 72, 73, 96
Number group, 20, 58, , 102, 120, 130, 160

O

object, 275, 291, 303, 336, 351, 374, 383, 391, 392, 393, 399, 400, 401
Office Theme, 167
Open, 16, 28, 29, 62, 99, 100, 158, 178, 189, 246, 289, 306, 331, 398, 399
operators, 14, 24, 135, 222, 231, 368, 392, 396
Options, 16, 23, 42, 80, 115, 161, 179, 185, 211, 218, 235, 290, 398, 405
Oracle, 309
Organization chart, 295, 302
orientation
portrait, landscape, 68, 188, 240, 395, 399
Orientation, 23, 240
output, 12, 309, 315, 342, 346, 356, 361, 399

P

packages, 2, 5, 10, 153, 316, 352
Page Break, 23, 66, 67
Page Setup, 23, 67, 240, 241
Painter, 21, 35, 69, 71, 161, 284
palette, 276, 277, 388
parameter, 326, 398
parentheses, 24, 81, 94, 103, 104, 110, 139, 159
Paste, 21, 43, 69, 91, 161, 179, 212, 230, 398
pasting, 39, 40, 41, 43, 54, 63
percentage, 13, 96, 109, 133, 237, 301, 330, 401
peripheral, 76
Pie charts, 235, 236, 239
Pivot Table, 215, 231, 232, 233, 234, 243
placeholders, 94, 257
platforms, 5, 7
pointer, 26, 40, 78, 165, 180, 272, 301, 305, 389, 394
populated, 221, 244
Portable Document Format
PDF, 18
Post-It Notes, 50
PowerPoint, 41, 72, 167, 244, 255, 277, 295, 306, 399, 402, 406
precision, 82, 122, 127, 128, 129, 342, 367

Precision, 83, 124, 126, 128, 129, 130
presentations, 9, 253, 302, 388, 399, 401,
Preview, 66, 78, 192, 246, 271, 285, 399
Previewing, 2, 287
primary, 55, 237, 244, 330, 332, 334, 399
principle, 341
Print, 16, 23, 67, 166, 240, 271, 306, 354, 395,
Print Area, 23, 241
Printing, 2, 273
private, 363, 365
procedure
function, 91, 101, 109, 122, 154, 165, 363, 394, 403, 405
processing
data, 155, 309, 316, 329, 347, 376, 406
programming, 5, 9, 153, 155, 336, 345, 363, 392,
programs, 7, 9, 15, 41, 69, 71, 103, 121, 138, 271, 309, 336, 398, 401, 406
project, 27, 33, 62, 133, 157, 187, 210, 242, 301, 329, 347, 358, 364, 382, 400
Properties, 220, 221, 290, 323, 330, 357, 389
Property Explorer, 361
Pseudo-code, 342, 347, 348
public, 350, 363, 365, 397
publish, 248, 363
pv
nper, 198, 212

Q

Quattro Pro, 5, 9
Quick Access Tool, 20
quiz, 34, 63, 278, 280, 282

R

Radar charts, 235, 239
Random, 29, 31
Ranges, 5, 24, 135, 137, 139
rational
irrational numbers, 126, 127
raw, 8, 9, 307, 309, 315, 319
Real-time update, 10
Recent, 16, 265, 358

records, 217, 223, 230, 243, 307, 325, 378, 379, 391, 401, 405

Redo, 2, 267, 268

references, 6, 14, 33, 136, 147, 157, 180, 244, 366

Regression test, 345

rehearse, 255

Relative

Cell References, 2

release, 5, 6, 9, 23, 40, 163, 168, 177

Repeat, 2, 57, 94, 143, 184, 190, 223, 226, 267, 268

Reproduction., 311, 315

REPT

functions, 100, 101, 102

Restore, 185, 186

retrieval, 314, 401

retrieve, 12, 314, 326, 334

retrieving, 314, 326

Reusability, 351

Review tab, 17, 25, 26, 43, 50, 51, 52, 55

Ribbon, 17, 26, 39, 47, 80, 138, 152, 183, 218, 257, 258, 272

RIGHT, 100, 101, 102, 113, 114, 134

Right-click, 46, 51, 82, 105, 165, 176, 230, 299, 301

ROUND

function, 82, 128, 129, 131, 132, 134

ROUNDDOWN, 131, 132

rows

row, 2, 5, 10, 29, 43, 55, 67, 102, 138, 163, 216, 230, 237, 277, 291, 391, 401, 404

Rules Manager, 193, 213

Run, 154, 320, 362, 363

runtime errors, 346

S

Save

Save As, 16, 19, 105, 158, 168, 248, 264, 270, 321, 399

SBCS, 368

Scale, 23

scan, 125

scatter, 16, 235, 237, 238

scenario, 125, 200, 202, 203, 204, 206, 211, 214, 245

Scenario

Manager, 8, 200, 203, 204, 205, 206, 211, 214, 245

scheme, 258, 262, 263, 283, 386, 387, 388, 391

Scientific

format, 13, 14, 53, 81, 83, 85, 212

scientific notation, 83, 96, 122

scroll, 100, 171, 172, 173, 183, 184, 185, 186, 222, 224, 266

Section Break, 23

Select, 21, , 39, 40, 114, 116, 120, 130, 139, 246, 261, 281, 303, 324, 331, 332, 334

Send, 16, 306

Server, 309, 358, 386, 387

Shape, 297, 298, 299, 301

shapes, 237, 254, 389, 394, 399, 405

Sheets, 10, 11, 20, 57, 105, 165, 177, 178

Short Date, 89, 116

Show

or hide, 130, 181

Slicers, 234, 235

Slide, 253, 257, 258, 259, 261, 262, 266, 267, 279, 280, 281, 283, 292, 302, 303, 304, 397, 402

slide master, 250, 259, 261, 302

slider, 20, 301

SmartArt graphics, 167

Solid, 301

Solution, 347, 359, 361, 364, 380

SOLUTION, 185, 186

Sorting, 307, 309, 311, 312, 327, 329, 333

sounds, 282, 288, 289, 290, 397

Sparklines,, 22

Special, 13, 14, 37, 40, 42, 69, 83, 86, 88, 89, 91, 111, 112, 124, 145, 150, 161, 179, 212

Specify

colors, conditions, 95

spell checker

errors, 43

Spelling

Spell, 26, 37, 43, 44, 69

Spin, 285

split pointer, 173

spreadsheet, 2, 5, 6, 7, 8, 15, 33, 55, 67, 125, 157, 188, 194, 214, 231, 242, 296, 310, 397, 402

SQL, 307, 309, 327, 328, 329, 403

Standard, 71, 126, 171, 246, 247, 273, 293, 300, 304, 358, 364, 387

state, 2, 80, 230, 351, 355, 393, 394, 401, 403

statements, 155, 306, 351, 371, 372, 373, 394, 403

static, 363, 403

statistical, 15, 138, 231, 238

stock chart, 238

Storage, 311, 314, 316, 333, 367

storing data, 309, 314

streamline, 324

Stress test, 345

String, 317, 366, 367, 368, 370, 379, 380, 381, 383, 403

Style, 69, 70, 80, 109, 130, 224, 225, 296, 299

Styles group, 20, 69, 70, 96, 111, 218, 225, 296, 300

subordinates, 295, 296

subroutine, 15, 138, 363

Subroutines, 10

Subtle, 283, 386

subtypes, 236, 237

sum, 8, 15, 30, 34, 67, 82, 138, 139, 140, 159, 196, 197, 198, 236, 237, 244, 326, 347, 380

SumIF, 196, 197, 198

summations, 15, 138

sums, 30, 147, 326

surface chart, 238

symbol, 12, 14, 25, 30, 72, 74, 80, 83, 96, 102, 103, 104, 133, 143, 287, 388, 405

synonym, 310

syntax errors, 342, 346

System Tools, 74

T

table, 17, 32, 76, 102, 124, 133, 161, 164, 199, 229, 242, 276, 291, 309, 320, 332, 364, 378, 390, 401, 404, 405

Tables group, 215, 217, 242

tasks, 253, 265, 294, 311, 396, 399, 404

Team, 17, 27

Team tab, 17, 27

template, 17, 19, 100, 105, 106, 169, 174, 187, 240, 250, 261, 302, 350, 391, 397, 402, 404

terabytes

bytes, 316

Terminologies, 5

testing strategy, 345, 346

Theme effects, 264

Themes,, 23

thumbnails, 224, 404

timesaver, 284, 324

timetable, 15, 138

topographic, 238

Track Changes, 51, 52

Transforming, 311, 312

transition, 282, 284, 402

Transparency, 301

Transpose, 43

Trap, 44, 47, 49

trigonometric, 15, 138

TRUNC, 132

typewriters, 311

U

Underline, 71, 304

Undo,, 2, 267

unhide, 102, 113, 171, 174, 179, 181, 186, 187

Unit Test, 345

Unprotect

Sheet, 55

user-defined data, 378, 379

V

validate, 315, 345

Validation, 43

Values

numbers, text, dates, 9, 10, 12, 29, 31, 43, 60, 79, 89, 131, 189, 205, 214, 356, 380

Variable, 318, 319, 352, 365, 383, 405

Variant, 155, 366, 367, 369
VBA macros, 174
VBA projects, 18, 19
Verifying, 311, 312
vertical, 9, 77, 173, 236, 237, 238, 259,
266, 368, 388, 395, 397
vertically
Vertical, 10, 11, 83, 300
video, 254, 286, 386
View, 17, 20, 26, 29, 31, 50, 57, 66, 68,
78, 172, 180, 185, 240, 262, 270, 304,
402, 406
View tab, 17, 26, 29, 31, 57, 78, 172,
180, 185, 240
VisiCalc, 5, 6, 7
Visual Basic for Applications, 7, 15,
138, 153, 174, 388, 397, 405

W

watchdog, 324
watermark, 77
Web, 17, 41, 121, 231, 248, 306, 386,
390, 392, 398, 402, 403, 406
While/Loop, 372
Windows
Operating System, 5, 7, 9, 17, 18, 29, 57,
64, 73, 105, 122, 174, 178, 358, 359,
368, 397
Wizard, 29, 31, 66, 124, 246, 257, 332,
387, 396, 404, 406
Word, 26, 41, 69, 124, 153, 167, 255,
295, 306
WordPerfect, 9
workbook
worksheet, 2, 11, 17, 19, 33, 36, 65, 83,
99, 100, 101, 168, 171, 175, 183, 187,
212, 236, 241, 386, 398, 402, 404

X

XFD, 11, 12, 31
XML, 7, 8, 18, 19, 28, 248, 268, 390, 392,
393, 401

Y

Y2K, 120

Bibliography and References

Microsoft e-learning website

Microsoft dot Net Library

Excel VBA Programmer's Reference by John Green ISBN:1-861002-54-8

OOP With Microsoft Visual Basic.Net and C#.Net by Robin A. Reynolds-Haertle

http://www.homeandlearn.co.uk/excel2007/excel2007s8p4.html

http://office.microsoft.com/en-us/excel-help/CH010151261.aspx

http://www.dummies.com/how-to/content/

http://www.proprofs.com/quiz-school

Certificate in Computer Science: http://www.nos.org/srsec330/

Computer Organization and Design. The hardware/software Interface. *John L. Hennessy and David A. Patterson. Morgan Kaufmann Publishers, Inc, Sans Francisco, California*

ISBN 1]55860]281]X

Data Communications, Computer Networks and Open Systems Fourth Edition. *Fred Halsal. Addison Wesley Publishing Company. ISBN 0]201]42293]X*

Modern Electronic Communication, Fifth Edition. *Gary M. Miller] Prentice]Hall International Publishers.*

How to do everything with your PC. *Robert Cowart – Osborne/McGraw Hill ISBN 0072127767*

The do•]it•]yourself PC book: An illustrated guide to upgrading and repairing your computer. *MacRae Kyle] Berkeley California Osborne/McGraw Hil l] ISBN 0072133775*

Teach yourself PC's in 24 hours. *Greg Perry M – Sams Pub. Indianapolis Ind. ISBN 0672311631.*

The first week with my new PC: a very basic guide for mature adults and everyone else who wants to get connected. *Pamela R. Lessing*

ISBN 1892123223

http://blogs.technet.com/office2010/archive/

http://office2010.microsoft.com/en]us/

http://www.infoplease.com/ce6/sci/A0857507.html

http://www.buzzle.com/articles/advantages•]disadvantages]internet.html

http://www.apc.org/en/news/environment/world/e]stands]environment]ict]tools]empower] activists]s

http://en.wikipedia.org/wiki/Technology]Enhanced_Learning

S. G. Nash, A History of Scientific Computing (1990); D. I. A. Cohen, Introduction to Computer

Theory (2d ed. 1996); P. Norton, Peter Norton's Introduction to Computers (2d ed. 1996); A. W. Biermann, Great Ideas in Computer Science: A Gentle Introduction (2d ed.1997); R. L.

Oakman, The Computer Triangle: Hardware, Software, People (2d ed. 1997); R. Maran, Computers Simplified (4th ed. 1998); A. S. Tanenbaum and J. R. Goodman. Structured Computer Organization (4th ed. 1998).